Feminist Perspectives on Tort Law

Feminist Perspectives on Tort Law offers a distinctly feminist approach to key topics in tort law. Ten original essays written by feminist legal scholars from the UK, US, Canada and Australia encompass a range of ways of thinking about women, tort law and feminism. The collection provides a fresh and original analysis of issues of long-standing concern to feminists as well as nascent areas of concern. These include conceptions of harm, constructions of reasonableness, the duty of care, the public/private divide, sexual wrongdoing, privacy and environmental law.

Written with both scholars and students in mind, *Feminist Perspectives on Tort Law* is an important and timely addition to key debates in tort law.

Janice Richardson is a Senior Lecturer in the Faculty of Law, University of Monash. She is author of: *Selves, Persons, Individuals: Philosophical Perspectives on Women and Legal Obligations* (Aldershot: Ashgate, 2004) and *The Classic Social Contractarians: Critical Perspectives from Contemporary Feminist Philosophy and Law* (Aldershot: Ashgate, 2009) and is co-editor, with Ralph Sandland, of *Feminist Perspectives on Law and Theory* (London: Routledge-Cavendish, 2000).

Erika Rackley is a Senior Lecturer in the Law School, Durham University, UK. She is author of *Women, Judging and the Judiciary: From Difference to Diversity* (London: Routledge, 2012), co-author, with Kirsty Horsey, of *Tort Law* (Oxford: Oxford University Press, 2nd edn, 2011) and co-editor, with Rosemary Hunter and Clare McGlynn, of *Feminist Judgments: From Theory to Practice* (Oxford: Hart, 2010).

REFERENCE

Feminist Perspectives on Tort Law

Edited by
Janice Richardson
and Erika Rackley

Routledge
Taylor & Francis Group

LONDON AND NEW YORK

First published 2012
by Routledge
2 Park Square, Milton Park, Abingdon, Oxon, OX14 4RN

Simultaneously published in the USA and Canada
by Routledge
711 Third Avenue, New York, NY 10017

A GlassHouse Book

Routledge is an imprint of the Taylor & Francis Group, an informa business

First issued in paperback 2013

British Library Cataloguing in Publication Data
A catalogue record for this book is available from the British Library

Library of Congress Cataloging in Publication Data
Feminist perspectives on tort law / edited by Janice Richardson and
Erika Rackley.
    p. cm.
    Includes index.
  "Simultaneously published in the USA and Canada."
  1. Torts—England. 2. Women—Legal status, laws, etc.—England.
3. Torts—Wales. 4. Women—Legal status, laws, etc.—Wales. 5. Torts.
6. Feminist jurisprudence. I. Richardson, Janice, 1961– II. Rackley, Erika.
KD1949.F46 2012
346.4203—dc23   2011040914

ISBN 978–0–415–61920–2 (hbk)
ISBN 978–0–415–73189–8 (pbk)
ISBN 978–0–203–12282–2 (ebk)

Typeset in Baskerville
by Keystroke, Station Road, Codsall, Wolverhampton

Contents

Notes on Contributors

Elizabeth Adjin-Tettey is a Professor in the Faculty of Law, University of Victoria, Canada. She is co-author, with Jamie Cassels, of *Remedies: The Law of Damages* (Toronto: Irwin Law, 2nd edn, 2008) and has written widely on the marginalising effects of traditional tort principles, including the implications of the defence of constructive consent for marginalised women in claims of sexual battery.

Nikki Godden is a PhD candidate and part-time tutor in the Law School, Durham University, UK. Her thesis considers the limitations of the criminal justice system's response to rape and explores alternative or additional legal routes to justice for rape victims, such as through claims in tort and restorative justice.

Reg Graycar is a Professor in the Law School at the University of Sydney, Australia. She has written widely on tort law, feminism and equality. She is co-author, with Jenny Morgan, of *The Hidden Gender of Law* (Sydney: The Federation Press, 2nd edn, 2002). She is a member of a number of international advisory boards including for Social Science Research Network, Women, Gender and the Law, and Centre for Feminist Legal Studies, University of British Columbia. She is also a member of the editorial boards of the *Australian Feminist Law Journal*, the *Adelaide Law Review*, *Griffith Law Review*, the *Media and Arts Law Review* and *Australian Feminist Studies*.

Kirsty Horsey is a Lecturer in the Law School, University of Kent, UK. She is co-author, with Erika Rackley, of *Tort Law* (Oxford: Oxford University Press, 2nd edn, 2011) and on the editorial board of *Feminist Legal Studies*.

José Miola is a Senior Lecturer in the Law School, Leicester University, UK. He is author of *Medical Ethics and Medical Law: A Symbiotic Relationship* (Oxford: Hart Publishing, 2007) and is on the editorial board of *Clinical Ethics* and the *Medical Law Review*.

Patricia Peppin is a Professor in the Faculty of Law, Queen's University, Canada (cross appointed to medicine). She has written widely on tort law, health care and feminism and contributed an essay on tort to the first Feminist Perspectives collection ('A Feminist Challenge to Tort Law', in A. Bottomley (ed) *Feminist Perspectives on the Foundational Subjects of Law* (London: Cavendish Publishing, 1996)).

Nicky Priaulx is a Senior Lecturer in the Law School, Cardiff University, UK. She is author of *The Harm Paradox: Tort Law and the Unwanted Child in an Era of Choice* (Abingdon: Routledge-Cavendish, 2007) and co-editor, with Anthony Wrigley, of *Ethics, Law and Society* Volume V (Aldershot: Ashgate Publishing, 2012).

Erika Rackley is a Senior Lecturer in the Law School, Durham University, UK and co-convenor of the research group Gender and Law at Durham (GLAD). She is co-author, with Kirsty Horsey, of *Tort Law* (Oxford: Oxford University Press, 2nd edn, 2011) and co-editor, with Rosemary Hunter and Clare McGlynn, of *Feminist Judgments: From Theory to Practice* (Oxford: Hart, 2010).

Janice Richardson is a Senior Lecturer in the Law School at Monash University, Australia. She is author of: *Selves, Persons, Individuals: Philosophical Perspectives on Women and Legal Obligations* (Aldershot: Ashgate, 2004) and *The Classic Social Contractarians: Critical Perspectives from Contemporary Feminist Philosophy and Law* (Aldershot: Ashgate, 2009) and co-editor, with Ralph Sandland, of *Feminist Perspectives on Law and Theory* (London: Routledge-Cavendish, 2000). She has published extensively in journals, including: *Angelaki, Feminist Legal Studies, Law and Critique, Ratio Juris, Economy and Society, BJPIR, Minds and Machines* and *Women's Philosophy Review*.

Dayna Nadine Scott is an Associate Professor in Osgoode Hall Law School and the Faculty of Environmental Studies, York University. She has written widely on environmental risk and regulation, with a focus on legal remedies available for pollution-related harms. She is Director of the National Network on Environments and Women's Health.

Jenny Steele is a Professor in the Law School, University of York, UK. She has written widely on tort law and in particular on the relationship between law and risk. She is author of *Risks and Legal Theory* (Oxford: Hart Publishing, 2004) and *Tort Law: Text, Cases and Materials* (Oxford: Oxford University Press, 2nd edn, 2010) and co-editor, with T.T. Arvind, of *Tort Law and the Legislature: Common Law, Statute, and the Dynamics of Legal Change* (Oxford: Hart Publishing, forthcoming). She is a contributing editor of *Clerk and Lindsell on Torts* (Sweet & Maxwell, 20th edn, 2010).

Foreword

The law of tort is at the heart of a normative regime within which the obligations of individuals towards one another are socially and legally prescribed. It is no wonder then that it holds such fascination for feminist legal scholars. On the one hand, a historical repository of gendered legal norms which situated women almost exclusively in terms of their formal relation to men; on the other hand, a potential tool for redressing the kinds of 'gendered' harms which law has traditionally overlooked. This schizophrenic tendency is a theme which pervades the rich vein of feminist tort scholarship, coming from around the world but emanating in particular from common law jurisdictions such as Canada, Australia, the US and the UK. Over the last few decades feminists have been at the vanguard of boundary challenges to tort liability, particularly in relation to claims deriving from sexual, physical, technological or environmental harm. In this context, tort law has proved fertile ground for the feminist legal imagination, in which new remedies have been fashioned out of old and new meanings forged around existing concepts and doctrinal traditions. At the same time, feminists exhibit ambivalence about taking the logic and tenor of tort law to its limits. This is partly because it is has proven so difficult to unpick the gendered values and assumptions or dislodge the normative privileging which underpin key categories and concepts in tort (for example, categories of damage or conceptualisations of the duty of care); but it is also because the focus of tort on individual responsibility in the context of injury and harm sits somewhat at odds with more progressive articulations of social or collective responsibility for misfortune. The more feminists are drawn into language and logic of tort, the further they are removed from envisioning ways of responding to life's vicissitudes which are not premised on calling individuals to account. And while the latter may be a desirable, indeed a therapeutic, step to take, it does not necessarily get to the root of the problem, which may well be more readily ascribed to structural and/or societal factors. Moreover, such feminist engagements may be said to be overly dependent upon the articulation of injured subjectivities, producing a politics of injury which is, at one and the same time, both empowering and disabling.

While it is clear that tort law demands careful navigation, this has not deterred feminists from extensive exploration and engagement in the field. One of the simplest and most common of feminist approaches, evident in this collection and in many other instantiations of feminist tort scholarship, is a form of disparate impact analysis, whereby tort law and doctrine is evaluated in terms of the extent to which its application yields differential results for men and women claimants. However, while this kind of work is practical and often a necessary part of a broader feminist strategy to tackle particular social problems which disproportionately affect women, for example domestic violence or sexual abuse, it is not the limit of feminist achievement in the field. What is perhaps of far greater significance is the way in which feminist engagement has helped to disclose and dislodge a normative under-pinning to tort which is by no means self-evident. Feminist scholarship has also contributed to the development of new critical techniques for probing the bound-aries of legal categories and concepts, laying the ground for the development of new conceptual and analytical tools to deal with the challenges posed by social, political, technological and environmental change. Finally, feminist tort scholarship has disrobed the legal person at the heart of the tortious regime, revealing all too plainly his gendered character and composition, in turn yielding feminist efforts to conceive and articulate personhood in more inclusive ways.

Perhaps though, most important, is the way in which feminist tort scholarship (re)presents tort law as a living, organically evolving creation of legal discourse and practice. Feminist scholarship in this field is a particularly fine example of the fruitfulness of a critical approach to law, and in this context the current collection continues a rich and varied tradition of critical legal enquiry which takes the boundaries of our knowledge and understanding of tort law towards new and rarely travelled terrain.

Joanne Conaghan
Kent Law School
November 2011

Chapter 1

Introduction

Janice Richardson and Erika Rackley

A feminist perspective does more than merely offer a different viewpoint. It provides a critique of a status quo that purports to be gender neutral but in fact takes the male body and lifestyle as the norm to the detriment of women. For example, the way in which women in our culture, at this time, resolve disputes has only recently been analysed as anything other than an immature approach of the attitude taken by men. This is not to say that there is anything natural about such differences. We change as society changes and the optimistic view of feminism, which in many ways has been borne out, is that it is possible (though by no means inevitable) for societies to become more just. In this sense, feminists are more optimistic than the US judges who, as Reg Graycar notes in this collection, assess loss of future earnings claims by women (who have been negligently injured by another) based upon average female earnings rather than the (higher) average earnings. In doing so, they make a statement that they envisage a future in which women will continue to be discriminated against in the workplace, earning lower salaries than men. Feminist perspectives, in contrast, open up the possibility of a different future.

When applied to tort law, the law of civil wrongs which gives the individual the right to sue to protect her/his rights, feminist perspectives have the power to challenge the neutrality of existing arrangements that treat the harms that men suffer as more worthy of protection, for example. The relationship between tort law and feminism is long-standing (see, for example, Conaghan 2003; Chamallas and Kerber 1990; Bender 1988 though compare Schwartz 2001). Some claims for justice for women simply involve a claim for fairer treatment within the existing system. They bring with them the hope that legal rules will not be changed to the claimant's detriment simply because she is a woman, such as the reference to a different type of justice (distributive not calculative) in the UK wrongful birth cases (*McFarlane v Tayside Health Board* [2000]). Other claims for justice involve altering the system in different ways. Not all of these changes represent a zero sum game in which men lose if women gain. On the contrary, many contributors to this book raise concerns about, for example, the regulation of drug companies (Peppin) and issues of professional negligence, particularly involving the police and the medical profession (Horsey and Miola), which impact on (vulnerable) men as well as women. Nevertheless, whilst fulfilling the aims of redistribution and deterrence in tort law is of benefit to both men and women, these are rightly feminist concerns because, as the contributors illustrate, women suffer disproportionately from negligence in such areas. In particular, the view of men as neutral representatives of humanity is starkly problematic in the area of drug research where there is a knowledge deficit because of insufficient testing of drugs on women's bodies.

As well as assessing the aims of tort law and whether they are being fulfilled, the chapters in this book open up debates about how different aspects of the law of tort are conceptualised. For example, when the tort system focuses only upon individual harm, the possibility of social harm to a community (such as that which occurs when a company has negligently polluted their land thereby disrupting the sex ratio) is occluded (Scott). Similarly, the way in which damages for loss of the ability to do housework (awarded when a woman is negligently injured) was initially a feudal right paid to her husband and then characterised as a non-economic loss (akin to losing the ability to play golf) belittles the economic worth of housework (Graycar). The courts' role in expressing and shaping the values of society is relevant here because the meaning of tort judgments affects more than the individual claimant. When women's traditional role as carers is not valued, or is sentimentalised in a way that minimises the cost of care to the carer, or when a survivor of rape is given paltry damages, the courts make a public statement about the worth of women. This 'worth' is not their 'price' but the respect that should be accorded to them. When this is denied, the courts are helping to shape a society in a way that is to women's detriment as well as that of the individual claimant.

Whilst some chapters focus upon sexual harm and areas of law that are clearly of direct concern to women (see, for example, Godden and Adjin-Tettey), there are others that examine legal concepts such as duty of care in negligence and the general calculation of damages that do not initially appear to be gendered. To highlight the injustices in these areas involves exploring beneath the surface of tort law. Some problems discussed are old and the contributors ask 'where we are now?' after years of feminist critique – typically with mixed results. Other areas are new, arising as a result of new technology, for example, that can allow men to produce 'revenge porn' (sexual material taken during the relationship, sometimes surreptitiously, depicting a former lover that is publicised, usually on the internet (Richardson)). In the tradition of feminist critique, the contributors both reveal injustices to women in the way that tort law operates in UK, Australia, Canada and US and suggest solutions to this constantly developing area of law.

The chapters

In 'Duty of Care and Ethic of Care: Irreconcilable Difference?' Jenny Steele focuses on the question of how the courts decide whether a duty of care is owed, by the defendant, in negligence cases, a question that initially appears to be both abstract and gender neutral. She first considers Carol Gilligan's influential work in moral psychology, which Steele employs to examine legal rather than moral assumptions. Gilligan's empirical studies show that boys and girls (in the US in 1982) employed different approaches to justice. Steele is clear that these studies do not demonstrate an essential, fixed sexual difference that is attributable to 'human nature' but nevertheless finds the empirical results useful for the questions that they raise about law in our culture. In the study, boys are found to employ rules to settle any arguments that arise in a game, whereas girls would rather abandon the game than risk damaging their relationships. Gilligan famously describes this as an illustration of boys being governed by an 'ethic of justice' and girls employing 'an ethic of care'. Gilligan has shown that, in a move familiar to feminists, the male position was viewed as the norm within moral psychology. Girls and women were an afterthought, initially subsumed within a universal category of humanity, of which men were viewed as the best instantiation, seeing themselves as both 'male' and also 'gender neutral'. To the extent that women were perceived at all, they were simply viewed as not measuring up to male norms.

Steele applies Gilligan's conceptions of two different types of justice to law. She asks whether the 'legal sense' of justice, associated with the boys' (historically contingent) 'ethic of right' is any more definitive of what is involved in law than it was in moral development: does the ethic of right represent only one interpretation of the legal process? In other words, could the practice of law be viewed in broader terms? Armed with this question, she then turns to tort law and, in particular, the legal concept of duty of care, to highlight its individualism, its historical and possible future development. She analyses the rhetorical aspect of law, in particular highlighting the repeated judicial assertion that there are 'no touchstones', to guide the decision as to whether a duty of care exists in a particular case. Steele points out that this is unsurprising, given that the idea of a touchstone was that it should provide a way of distinguishing true from false gold. Given that judicial decisions regarding duty of care are taken pragmatically, there is no true or false gold to be found.

In the next chapter, 'Endgame: On Negligence and Reparation for Harm', Nicky Priaulx considers how harms that women suffer are marginalised by the way in which legal categories are drawn, in particular, the 'heads of damage' needed to prove a claim in negligence. For example, in the UK, in cases involving the reproductive torts, such as wrongful birth cases (in which a negligent sterilisation or advice result in an initially unwanted pregnancy), damages have been limited according to arguments that are at odds with the usual principles of tort law. Perhaps even more troubling are the (dissenting) arguments against the idea that women should be awarded damages for pain and suffering as a result of the birth *at all* because birth is 'natural' (see, for example, Lord Millett in *McFarlane v Tayside Health Board* [2000]). Priaulx argues that the distinction drawn between the categories of 'physical damage' and 'psycho-social damage' is difficult to maintain. It is predicated upon a mind/body split, which does not reflect human experience of harm. Someone with a personal injury will also experience psycho-social disruption and vice versa. In addition, there are a growing number of cases that challenge such a boundary directly, such as wrongful birth cases and the case of negligent destruction of the sperm preserved from a dead spouse. She detects a move towards a broader conception of harm 'that is *more* capable of accommodating critical aspects of our humanity'. These claims can include a hybrid approach of harm that is both physical and psycho-social.

This initial analysis prompts Priaulx to examine the extent to which tort law overall can ever prove just or whether a more radical change in the law is required. She points out that, whilst it may be fairer to extend damages in tort to avoid incoherent distinctions, this will only reach a small number of beneficiaries. In addition, an award of damages addresses the harm in a limited way by an award of money. She turns to the recent (controversial) empirical claims in 'hedonic' studies (ie studies of happiness) that we react to good or bad events in the short term but then return to a previous level of happiness. Such claims raise the argument that, in practice, people adapt to their disabilities, which do not therefore inherently limit their enjoyment of life – potentially suggesting support for those who wish to limit compensation, if it is to be based upon the fictional attempt to restore the status quo or solace. A further concern, derived from this research is that the legal process itself reinforces the idea of disability as tragedy. She then considers the question of whether compensation for injuries should be based upon their overall effects. An alternative to the legal fiction that the aim of tort compensation is to restore the claimant to her/his earlier position would be to consider the damages as a public statement that puts right a social wrong; that recognises the rights and moral worth of the claimant – an issue is raised in Elizabeth Adjin-Tettey's chapter on harm in relation to sexual wrongdoing, discussed below.

In 'Pollution and the Body Boundary: Exploring Scale, Gender and Remedy' Dayna Nadine Scott considers whether tort law can provide a remedy for the effects of 'endocrine disruption', caused by negligently produced pollution. Endocrine disruption occurs when particular types of synthetic chemical (which are similar in physical structure to sex hormones) trigger different biological processes in the bodies of humans (and animals) who are exposed to them. She focuses upon the plight of the Aamjiwnaang First Nation, a Canadian aboriginal community, where chronic chemical pollution has resulted in it having the lowest boy to girl birth ratio in the world. This raises a number of questions. Obviously, the scientific claim must be proved (something which, as Peppin discusses in the context of product liability, is often no mean feat). However, assuming that there is clear evidence, Scott shows that such a claim raises difficulties for the common law, or indeed any law, that compensates only for individual harm. It is not possible for an individual woman to demonstrate that she would have given birth to a boy but for the chemical pollution, despite the fact that the number of boys born is far fewer than prior to the pollution. Further, the birth of a girl does not constitute harm to her mother, as an individual, despite the views of misogynists. Scott's analysis goes beyond the usual questions of causation in negligence. She points out that the harm alters depending upon the scale employed to analyse it. It could be characterised as a harm to the community because the disruption in the sex balance threatens the possible collective future of the community as a body, as it results in young women leaving the community to find a partner, for example. As such it is a *social* fact

(Durkheim 2002). Feminists would not want to subsume their individual rights to the community, of course, as in the dreams of communitarians, but should this wrong by the polluters go without any recompense in the civil courts?

Just as Priaulx questions the supposedly natural divide between physical and psycho-social harm (that maps the Cartesian split between mind/body – the subject of much feminist critique) so Scott questions the assumptions about what is 'natural' or 'normal' by drawing upon contemporary feminist theories of the body. As she explains, this move 'challenges tort scholars to imagine law differently'. She echoes Priaulx's concern to move away from assessing damage only on the basis of 'factually observable' change in the physical structure of individuals. An alternative perception of scale involves viewing the harm as one that occurs at a molecular level within the body, extending our view of battery, for example. She shifts the perspective to 'a more contextual approach based upon social perceptions of change' and considers different torts that may be useful to address this harm, what they offer and how they frame how we think about both the injury and the body (individual or social) that has suffered the harm. On a practical level, she concludes that there is no one tort that can adequately address the harm to the community or the molecular change to the body but that it is possible to move in that direction. In addition, she opens up questions about the way the individual 'self' is envisaged within tort law; the way in which this harm raises questions about bodily boundaries. Also, by considering the argument that there is no natural category of sexual identity, defended in the work of theorists such as Judith Butler (1999), Scott then raises the more difficult question as to whether there is a 'natural' balance between two sexes, along with the question of intersexuality.

In 'Trust in the Police? Police Negligence, Invisible Immunity and Disadvantaged Claimants' Kirsty Horsey criticises (what amounts to) police immunity for negligent investigation in the UK. Despite ample opportunities to forge a new path, and the example of other common law countries, the UK courts continue to refuse to find that the police owe a duty of care to the victims of crime in situations when it is alleged that the criminals would not have been at large (and hence able to commit the crime) but for police incompetence – even in cases of clear and systematic negligence. This raises particular problems for women with regard to the investigation of rape and of domestic violence. These are areas in which women have historically been let down by the state, in part because of the liberal state's reluctance to intervene within the home (though it is worth noting that the leading case in the UK in this context (*Smith v Chief Constable of Sussex Police* [2008]) involved domestic violence in a homosexual relationship). Horsey argues that the use of public policy by the courts, shielding the police from the impact of their negligence, is potentially a violation of Article 6 of the European Convention on Human Rights, the right to a fair hearing. The UK Supreme Court has described their decisions in such cases as the result of a process of weighing up the public good against the rights of the individual claimant. In their view, individual rights must give way to the greater public good of allowing the police to continue their work unhindered; to avoid defensive practices and diversion of resources from the police. In contrast, Horsey points out that there is also a social good involved in holding police to account for their negligence. There is a *public interest*, as well as a social good for the most vulnerable members of society, in uncovering systematic failings within the police. Horsey's argument in relation to rights therefore mirrors those on human rights employed by Eady J when he points out that privacy rights should not be conceived in terms of balancing the rights of the individual against public interest in freedom of speech because there is also a *public interest* in the protection of privacy (see Richardson, this volume).

Patricia Peppin's chapter, 'Knowledge and Power: Drug Products Liability Actions and Women's Health', also considers an area in which both women and men have a common interest but which raises feminist concerns because women have suffered disproportionately. In this case, the common concern is in the safety of pharmaceuticals and medical interventions, along with provisions necessary to allow patients to make informed choices as to their medication, thereby increasing their autonomy. Her chapter illustrates a further common theme, as a result of which men usually do benefit at the expense of women: that harm to women has occurred as a result of their marginalisation. In this instance, she illustrates how the injury derives from two sources. First, women are harmed because of a 'knowledge deficit' about the safety and efficacy of drugs and medical interventions for women. Peppin details how this has occurred as a result of deficiencies in the clinical trial process simply because drug testing has mainly been conducted on men. Just as Steele discusses how men's approach to justice (in this culture) has been taken as the norm in a way that disadvantages women, Peppin gives an even starker example of the impact of men being viewed as the norm. She shows that medical research has also taken male bodies as the norm when testing drugs. In this context, the error of viewing men as the gender-neutral representative of all humanity has been physically dangerous for women. In addition, well-meaning legislative attempts to protect pregnant women have backfired because they have resulted in inadequate testing of drugs that are to be used by pregnant women themselves. Hence, the problem of lack of research on women resulted in steps being taken that inadvertently increased the problem. As she explains, this continues today:

> As the literature indicates, men were considered to be adequate substitutes for women and so all-male samples were thought to be scientifically appropriate (Rosser 1989; Scott 1993). At the same time, the differences in women's bodies arising from hormonal fluctuations made women less attractive for drug research since these variations confounded the data. Even today, laboratory research is conducted largely on male mice and rats, for the same reasons, even for conditions such as dementia and pain that occur predominantly in women (Pigg 2011).
>
> (Peppin, this volume)

In addition to this knowledge deficit, Peppin illustrates how women's health and autonomy is further undermined by the way that the marketing of drugs and medical interventions draws upon sexist stereotypes and medicalises health. Methodologically, Peppin draws together both a detailed historical analysis of the failures of drug companies, as illustrated by thalidomide, diethylstilbestrol (DES) and Dalkon Shield amongst other cases, with a discourse analysis of the medical advertising. She then turns to law to consider what has prevented products liability torts from regulating drug companies. In a wide-ranging analysis covering Canada, UK, Australia and the US she demonstrates how the drug companies and the law are failing girls and women.

She concludes by detailing how the law should be changed such that products liability tort law is able to achieve the aim of patient autonomy, or at least to do less harm to women. First, the focus of litigation should move to promoting more and better testing of drugs and medical devices: 'inclusive research, improved risk assessment, prior to approval, and long-term testing in the prior to market period'. Secondly, she argues that market excesses can be targeted by 'failure to warn actions' (based upon fraud, misrepresentation and breach of consumer statutes) that demonstrate that adverts can undermine product warnings. Such litigation is also useful in raising public awareness of the twin problems of knowledge deficit and impact of drug promotion.

Peppin's analysis of the failure of the law to regulate the drug companies is followed by José Miola's assessment of medical negligence in 'The Standard of Care in Medical Negligence – Still Reasonably Troublesome'. The concern, expressed by feminists and others, that the UK judiciary has been too deferential to the medical profession, is well known. As Miola demonstrates, this has a disproportionate impact upon women, who have borne the brunt of both medical paternalism and stereotyping by judges. In addition, women are subject to greater medical intervention through pregnancy and longer old age, for example. In common with Reg Graycar's chapter, which updates her work over a 25-year period, Miola's chapter is an assessment of 'where we are now'. He asks whether criticism by feminists (particularly Sally Sheldon's (1998) critique of *Bolam v Friern Hospital Management Committee* [1957] in this book series) has made a difference to the way that medical negligence law now operates. Since Sheldon's critique of the *Bolam* test in the UK, the cases of *Bolitho v City and Hackney Health Authority* [1997] and *Chester v Afshar* [2004] have been hailed as moving away from judicial deference to the medical profession. It is no longer the case that the courts must accept what a reputable body of medical opinion views as correct, irrespective of their own judgment. However, there are differences of academic opinion on whether '*Bolam* is dead'. As Miola points out, the law may now enable judges to rule that a medical body of opinion is unreasonable but that does not mean that they will do so. However, Miola cautiously welcomes development in the case law as a move in the right direction, whilst pointing to a number of remaining concerns. He views the decision in *Chester* as particularly positive in protecting patient autonomy. However, he worries about the stereotyping of women that still occurs within the case law and the male perspective lurking behind (male) judicial claims to be objective, a problem that can potentially be addressed with more women on the bench. In addition, he raises issues about the stereotyping of female doctors as well as female patients.

The next three chapters move from the medical context and the tort of negligence to the personal torts and different examples of sexual wrongs. Janice Richardson considers the developing tort that protects against invasions of privacy. She focuses upon a particular type of privacy case: the disclosure of private information that is sexual in nature. An examination of these cases undermines the cliché that heterosexual male sexuality is uncomplicated, given the complex motivations of men who disclose sexual material about ex-girlfriends. Some appear to be motivated by a desire for revenge. However, some motives are more complex. One Australian case, for example, discussed by Richardson, currently before the criminal courts but also potentially a tort, involved a man secretly broadcasting himself and his sexual partner whilst they were having sex, to friends in another room by employing Skype, for motives that appeared to be associated with male bonding in a military academy. In contrast, the cases in which women have disclosed sexual material about their male partners, along with the only homosexual disclosure case in the UK, appear to have been motivated mainly by financial profit.

Richardson argues that the meaning of 'privacy' itself is changing at this point in time, as a result of both changes in women's status in the West, and computer-medicated communication. Feminist criticism of the public/private divide is well known. By adhering to the idea that 'an Englishman's home is his castle' the courts have historically condoned violence and abuse of women within the home. The theoretical counterpart was to define women's subordinate status as natural, 'personal' and 'private' and hence not a fit area of analysis within political or legal philosophy. Women have challenged both these aspects of the public/private divide. Richardson considers the development of case law in both the UK and Australia, highlighting the judiciary's understanding of the harm that occurs in cases of invasion of privacy that involve the disclosure of sexual material. The majority of legal cases in the UK concern men who have engaged in extra-marital affairs. Whilst footballers, for example, are rich and now adept at using the law to obtain their controversial super-injunctions, better procedures are required for those who suffer as a result of the uploading of 'revenge porn', a problem that disproportionately affects young women. (It is no answer that they should check for cameras before having sex, given how easily these can be hidden.)

Richardson comments that the specialist UK judges reveal a more nuanced appreciation of the impact of the disclosure of private information than is evident in much legal theory. She critiques the approach of Charles Fried, who conceptualises private information as a sort of capital that we can spend upon those with whom we want to be intimate. She views this as an impoverished view of what it is to be a person based, as it is, on possessive individualism, the treatment of ourselves as property owners of human attributes. It would be ironic if the courts treated individuals as commodified in this way but refused to allow public recognition of sexual wrongs on the spurious basis that it would commodify (rather than publicly acknowledge) the wrong. Fortunately, this has not occurred in the area of privacy. In contrast, she welcomes the view of selfhood employed by the European Court of Human Rights in which privacy is not viewed in terms of the right to be isolated. Instead, invasions of privacy are characterised as threatening our relationships with others by virtue of the disclosure. This shifts from a view of the atomistic individual to see selfhood as something that emerges in relation to others. Such an approach envisages privacy rights as protecting relationships rather than a piece of property owned by an individual. In addition, the UK courts have stood up to an aggressive gutter press that is a 'repeat player' in the courts, defending its attempts to commodify women and sexual relations under the guise of free speech. However, women need a practical, fast and cheap way of dealing with this problem that may require a technological solution, especially if, unlike footballers, they may not feel able to access the courts.

In 'Tort Claims for Rape: More Trials, Fewer Tribulations' Nikki Godden considers the use of tort law to provide recognition and remedy in rape cases, mainly focusing on the UK. Despite significant legislative changes and political goodwill, the conviction rate in cases of rape remains unacceptably low. Given the apparent inability of the criminal justice system to adequately respond to the 'harm' of rape (though this is not to suggest that efforts ought not continue to be made to ensure that it does), Godden considers the potential role for the law of tort. Encouragingly, she analyses a number of civil claims for rape that have been successful in the courts. She assesses different elements of the tort, with mixed conclusions. One advantage is that, in a civil claim, the defence of consent is treated differently from the criminal courts. Tort law requires proof (on the balance of probability) that the claimant gave actual or 'apparent' consent (that is, that her actions or behaviour gave the objective appearance of consent). Consistent with the aims of tort, which are to safeguard the claimant's rights and liberties, it does not consider the defendant's belief per se. And, while there has been some attempt to increase the burden of proof, it is now clear that this is not appropriate in a civil claim. However, more negatively, defendants in the civil courts (as in the criminal courts) utilise so-called 'rape myths', for example, by referring to the claimant's sexual history, in order to try to humiliate and discredit her by invoking sexual double standards. Given the fact that the press is keen to publicise such details of a woman's sex life, the problem has much in common with 'revenge porn' discussed in Richardson's chapter. It is also evident in other areas of tort law, such as the attempts by drug companies to put off female claimants by attacking their sexual history in the Dalkon Shield litigation, described by Peppin.

Godden then turns to the issue of damages. As Adjin-Tettey, Priaulx and Graycar also demonstrate in this book, the level and categorisation of damages in tort cases have typically privileged men's interests over those of women. Godden illustrates this by considering how damages for rape in *W v Meah D v Meah* (set at £6,750 and £10,250) were derived. The judge considered rape as akin to personal injury thereby failing to capture the pain of sexual assaults. Godden agrees with Joanne Conaghan's argument that this is certainly an area that merits aggravated damages (Conaghan 1998: 146). In later cases, the gendered nature of the harm has been recognised and there is some progress as it ceases to be analysed merely in terms of personal injury. Godden raises the same concern as Priaulx that the litigation process may encourage a claimant to portray herself as a victim. However, she counterbalances this worry with the fact that without such cases these wrongs would go without legal recognition or reporting. She concludes that it is therefore significant that improvements have been made in this area of tort law.

The analysis of the potential use of tort law to deal with sexual wrongs continues in Elizabeth Adjin-Tettey's chapter: 'Sexual Wrongdoing: Do the Remedies Reflect the Wrong?'. In an analysis of the common law generally, and in Canada in particular, she asks whether improved access to the tort system has resulted in effective remedies for rape survivors. In common with the previous chapter, she considers the way in which harm is categorised in tort. This includes an enquiry into judicial attitudes to compensation for injuries. The harm produced by a sexual wrong is largely viewed as intangible, characterised in terms of distress and loss of enjoyment of life. As discussed in Priaulx's chapter and as Graycar also analyses (to be discussed below), intangible damages are viewed as being suspect and subject to exaggeration. This risks under compensating the victim of sexual wrongs and also reflects a problem highlighted elsewhere: that women's testimony has been treated as less credible than men's (Kennedy 2005).

Adjin-Tettey illustrates how different common law countries devalue intangible harm. In Canada, the aim of such damages is not to provide full compensation but to provide solace, an approach based upon the point that it is impossible to compensate claimants fully for non-economic harm. However, she argues, there is no logical reason why the inability of the courts to be able to compensate for a traumatic event should lead to low damages per se. She examines a number of different arguments that have been suggested in support of only paying minimal amounts of compensation for intangible harms, which is the way in which women's harms are often categorised, as in the case of rape. For example, it has been claimed that compensation for intangible harms should only be forward looking because money is of no use for the intangible harms already suffered. She points out that this would only encourage the defendant to delay proceedings.

In addition, the argument has been made that to award compensation for sexual wrongs against women would be to treat women's sex as if it were a commodity. Adjin-Tettey points out that this is a common argument used when the judiciary is uncomfortable in making awards for women. As discussed above and by Priaulx, it is an argument used in some of the wrongful birth cases to deny the women, who give birth as a result of negligent sterilisation, the usual remedy of damages. In the wrongful birth cases the commodification argument is used to deny the cost of care to the carer, despite the fact such care has been commodified by the courts in terms of 'loss of consortium cases', discussed below and in Graycar's chapter. As Adjin-Tettey argues, in cases of sexual wrongdoing, this misplaced worry about commodification would leave a woman who has suffered a serious wrong without a proper remedy. The defendant would win even if the sexual wrongdoing had been proved. As such, it would make a public statement about the relative moral worth of that woman and her abuser. An alternative way of viewing the case is to draw from Jean Hampton's (1993) reading of Kant to argue that there should be an award that acts as a public statement that the wrongdoer has held himself out as of higher status than the claimant, able to use her as a means to an end. The court's judgment should demonstrate publicly that this is not true; that she is a person worthy of respect. If they make paltry awards of damages in cases of sexual wrongdoing the courts fail in their duty to make this public statement of equality, thereby adding to the harm itself.

In the final chapter 'Damaging Stereotypes: The Return of "Hoovering as a Hobby"', Reg Graycar returns to detailed work that she commenced in 1985, investigating the systematically lower damages awarded to women in tort claims. She evaluates the extent to which there has been any progress towards greater equality as a result of feminist critique. This is an area of tort law that her work has helped to shape. The progressive Australian judgment in *Sullivan v Gordon* [1999], which allowed a woman to claim damages for loss of ability to care for others, cited her research in support. Her analysis covers three areas of compensation in tort law. They are not areas that initially appear to be gendered, such as damages for rape discussed above, and yet Graycar uncovers the judicial reasoning whereby women's damages in tort can be shown to be depressed as a result of gendered assumptions.

First, she considers cases in which women are negligently injured in accidents. She shows that their damages for loss of earning capacity are much lower than those of men because of sexist assumptions that women are not as attached to the labour market. Graycar illustrates how this view has prevailed even in cases when women have very highly paid jobs. It is assumed that they will give these up in favour of traditional child care responsibilities. Women's loss of earnings calculation therefore carries with it large reductions for 'vicissitudes of life' based upon the idea that their earnings would have diminished even without the accident. In addition, in the US, there has been controversy as the courts have used tables of average female earnings rather than average earnings to calculate compensation for future loss of earnings. Given that these are much lower than average earnings, the compensation is accordingly diminished.

Secondly, Graycar considers the head of damage for 'loss of consortium'. This is an area in which judges have been willing to put a price upon women's work within the home, as part of a claim for damages made by her husband, that derived from his feudal right to sex and the performance of housework. As Graycar illustrates, even when there has been some progress in that this loss of the ability to do housework is viewed as the woman's loss, it is treated as a loss of amenity, that is a non-economic loss. As mentioned above, this is a problematic category. In Australia such harms have been the target of legislatures for either reduction or abolition. The loss of the ability to do housework has been classified in this manner, despite the fact that housework does have a commercial value. As Graycar's evocative title suggests, this judicial classification of harm reflects a view that housework is akin to a hobby, the satisfaction of which has been lost, thereby belittling the economic worth of such labour.

Graycar's final area of analysis also occurs as a result of such judicial devaluing of housework. She traces how gendered assumptions affect the damages awarded for the cost of caring for accident victims, which is mainly performed by women. At least in this area, Australia has recognised the economic worth of such work, albeit that it is awarded to the accident victim and not the carer. However, since the lead case in 1977, damages have been diminished based upon the dated assumption that care work is part of 'ordinary currency of family life' and so it is excessive to pay for such services (*Kovac v Kovac* [1982]; Graycar 2002: 85–7). In addition, she details the assumptions that courts rely upon that turn out to be empirically false, such as the view that housework is shared equally. Finally, Graycar considers the possible improvements as a result of feminist work in highlighting these injustices. Whilst this has shown some progress, there are also more recent setbacks in this line of cases.

This characterises many of the conclusions in the book. There is some hope that tort law could develop to cover harms women suffer but also some frustration at the direction that tort has taken in other areas, after years of feminist critique. This is particularly the case regarding the way in which the essence of tort law – 'harm' – is classified. As well as old concerns, there are harms that are more recent, arising as a result of new technology that require better, practical ways of protecting privacy rights. Similarly, medical advances potentially extend our lives but also produce new problems that have been shown to affect women disproportionately. The tort system is not stable but is being transformed to deal with social and technological change. Together the essays in this collection offer not just feminist *perspectives* on tort law, but a feminist agenda for that change.

Cases

Bolam v Friern Hospital Management Committee [1957] 1 WLR 582
Bolitho v City and Hackney Health Authority [1997] 4 All ER 771
Chester v Afshar [2004] UKHL 1 AC 134
Kovac v Kovac [1982] 1 NSWLR 656
MacFarlane v Tayside Health Board [2000] 2 AC 59
Smith v Chief Constable of Sussex Police [2008] EWCA Civ 39
Sullivan v Gordon [1999] 47 NSWLR 319 (NSWCA).
W v Meah; D v Meah [1986] 1 All ER 935

Bibliography

Bender, L. (1988) 'A Lawyer's Primer on Feminist Theory and Tort', *Journal of Legal Education*, 38: 3–38.
Butler, J. (1999) *Gender Trouble*, London: Routledge.
Chamallas, M. and Kerber, L. (1990) 'Women, Mothers, and the Law of Fright: A History', *Michigan Law Review*, 88: 814.
Conaghan, J. (1998) 'Tort Litigation in the Context of Intra-familial Abuse', *Modern Law Review*, 61(2): 132–61.

—— (2003) 'Tort Law and Feminist Critique', *Current Legal Problems*, 56: 175.

Durkheim, E. (2002) *Suicide: A Study in Sociology*, London: Routledge.

Graycar, R. (2002) 'Sex, Golf and Stereotypes: Measuring, Valuing and Imagining the Body in Court', *Torts Law Journal*, 10: 205.

Hampton, J. (1993) 'Feminist Contractarianism' in L. Anthony and C. Witt (eds) *A Mind of One's Own*, Boulder, Colorado: Westview Press.

Kennedy, H. (2005) *Eve was Framed: Women and British Justice*, London: Vintage.

Schwartz, G. (2001) 'Feminist Approaches to Tort Law', *Theoretical Enquiries in Law* 2: 175.

Sheldon, S. (1998) 'Rethinking the *Bolam* Test' in S. Sheldon and M. Thomson (eds) *Feminist Perspectives on Health Care Law*, London: Cavendish, 15–32.

Chapter 2

Duty of Care and Ethic of Care: Irreconcilable Difference?

*Jenny Steele**

Introduction: feminist perspectives and the duty of care

The particular focus of this chapter is the legal category labelled 'duty of care'. One might have expected the duty of care to have been the subject of some close feminist critique in its own right, given its centrality and its core features (including abstraction, boundary-drawing, an emphasis on rights and duties imbued with moral rhetoric, and a conflation of 'care' with being reasonably careful). [1] To the extent that such critique has been lacking, [2] it may be partly because feminist scholars, like others, are at risk of being attracted by the surface morality of the duty of care. Where the concern of feminist tort scholars has been to show the failure to recognise particular harms the prescription, without an accompanying critique of duty of care, is at least implicitly to extend the reach of duty. There is a risk that feminism, alone among critical approaches, will regard the duty of care in terms of 'promise unfulfilled', [3] rather than as more deeply suspect. It might be argued that feminist scholarship is legitimately uninterested in artificial classifi-cations such as 'tort' or 'negligence' in any event, preferring to look across various dimensions of legal systems to expose law's gendered practices as a whole.[4] And yet, if key legal categories thereby remain unexplored, some of the broader potential of feminist legal theory will remain unrealised.

It has been suggested that to adopt a feminist perspective is 'first and foremost, to bring a gendered perception of legal and social arrangements to bear upon a largely gender-neutral understanding of them' (Conaghan 2000: 359, drawing upon Lacey 1998). This embraces gendered analyses of legal arrangements generally, rather than confining feminist critique to analysis of 'gender issues'. Importantly, it also refers to a 'largely gender-neutral *understanding*' of social and legal arrange-ments. It is essential to be aware that the mainstream (ostensibly gender-neutral) understanding of legal arrangements is to be found not only in legal institutions, but also in the academy. Indeed, I find it strongly arguable that in recent years the academy has been narrower and more 'mainstream' in its understanding of the law of tort in particular – and especially the duty of care – than have legal institu-tions. The fact that the exercise in restriction of duty has come from the courts does not alter this, to the extent it is accompanied by greater complexity and a recognised need to look to more detailed relationship factors. Indeed greater restrictions upon the duty of care have been accompanied by a greater attention to the context of particular categories of case, and by a recognition that tort law does not provide the only, or necessarily the most appropriate, way of analysing relationships. The exercise in attention to categories of case inevitably incorporates a substantial degree of abstraction (the creation of categories), but it also allows a much greater role for contextual and outcome-based analysis than the universalising abstraction of a relationship *consisting of* the doing of harm by one party to another.[5] Ultimately, perhaps this is not surprising. Academic law tends to prioritise the ordering of material and the discernment of general principles for the purpose initially of exposition, and I would argue increasingly with exclusionary intent,[6] while legal institutions (courts, legislatures, legal advisors, and so on) have to grapple with the diversity of legal relationships – even if their rhetoric is sometimes designed to achieve the appearance of certainty (for a variety of reasons) rather than to acknowledge these tensions.[7]

Further, and returning to the broad encapsulation of a feminist perspective above, to the extent that any feminist perspective takes gender as the key to its reading of social and legal arrangements (and to its perception of what is missing in other presentations of them), a feminist perspective will be a *distinctive* form of critical perspective. The problem of course is in identifying what a 'gendered' perspective might legitimately and productively consist of, in the light of more recent waves of anti-essentialist feminist thinking.[8]

The next section of the chapter turns for inspiration to feminist contract scholarship. Some important features of feminist analysis of contract are identified, and the question is raised of whether these same features can be brought to bear on the law of negligence. In particular, feminist contract scholarship has drawn upon cultural feminism to intensify the impact of relational analysis of contracting. Using these insights, and moving to the next section, I reflect on the neglected role of the 'legal' in one of the key sources of cultural feminist legal theory, namely Carol Gilligan's *In a Different Voice* (1982). In both these sections, I draw on the work of Mary Joe Frug, who applied her distinctive post-modern feminism to the law of contract and its elucidation in academic debate and student texts. More generally, Frug's analysis of Gilligan's work suggests a route to questioning not only the 'ethic of care', but also the 'ethic of right', without losing the potential of both. There is space for a potential relational perspective which does not fall into what Frug referred to as 'crude Gilliganism' (which might also be called crude essentialism) (1992: 38).

Finally, and armed with this, I turn to the duty of care itself. Clearly the duty of care purports to deal with interactions between parties, but is it 'relational' in any meaningful sense? Here I seek to place the resurgent rhetoric of individualism within a broader context. It is suggested that the position of the abstract and universal duty of care as a hallmark of the most mature legal thinking, as liberal theorists have tended to present it,[9] is no more justified than the position of the 'ethic of justice' or 'ethic of right' as a hallmark of the most mature moral thinking, as the giants of developmental psychology appear to have thought it was. In fact, courts on the whole realise that responsibility is not the same as duty, and that responsibility in tort is not the full extent of responsibility in law or anywhere else. The difficulty arises with the persistent attraction of individualist rhetoric which appears to use the idea of rights and duties as definitive of responsibilities. Both the idea of maturity, and the idea of the respective roles of responsibilities and rights, are core to Gilligan's work and would in my view be appropriately highlighted by a 'progressive' reading of Gilligan.[10] Indeed, in the last chapter of her book, Gilligan argued that 'To understand how the tension between responsibilities and rights sustains the dialectic of human development is to see the integrity of two disparate modes of experience that are in the end connected' (1982: 174). There is a *dialogue* between 'fairness' (the abstract standard, giving rise to rights and duties) and 'care' (the connected standard, giving rise to more far-reaching responsibilities).[11]

Learning from feminist contract scholarship

What are the key features of feminist contract scholarship which will assist the enquiry in this chapter?[12] One such feature is that much of it draws inspiration from other critical literature on contract and therefore takes an identifiable place in the critical legal family.[13] As Lacey has argued, other critical theories too are concerned to dig beneath the surface of social and legal arrangements to illuminate their deeper logics.[14] In contract theory, there is a general identification of surface rhetoric with the classical model of contracting, in which the will of the parties is key. Although it has been understood for many years that a shift to more 'objective' standards had the effect of injecting a considerable degree of fiction into the law of contract (suggesting that the courts were seeking the will of the parties when in fact they were imposing their own standards of reasonableness), the 'freedom of contract' model still provides much of the language of contract law.[15] The objective 'reasonableness' standard in contract has much in common with tort's objective standards and employs much of the same language. Although it was initially much clearer that the tort approach involved a standard imposed by the court, significant complexity is added through concepts such as 'assumption of responsibility' and, more generally, proximity in the law of tort. These tend to be attacked by mainstream tort scholars, missing their point I think, as lacking in clear content and predictability. These ideas are really just a way of structuring the idea of 'reasonableness' with a bit more specificity, pointing to relationship factors, which is to say to features of the relationship between parties other than the doing and suffering of harm.[16] Equally important is a debate about the *function* of the law of contract, where a dichotomy is recognised between theorists who consider the role of the law of contract to be the facilitation, regulation, and good ordering of contract and exchange;[17] and those who consider the point of the law of contract to be the correction of wrongs, particularly breaches of contract, for moral reasons.[18] To the extent that the second approach has tended to involve a search for morality inherent to the idea of a contract, similar to the idea of an inner morality to tort law structured around the doing and suffering of harm, the first of these has amounted to a more contextual reading. 'Relational' contract theory is connected to this 'contextual' side of the divide.

Relational contract theory has proved attractive to feminist contract scholars (and vice versa) for a number of reasons.[19] One of these is undoubtedly that its prescriptions are light on abstraction compared to standard models, descending to the level of particular parties and their relationships. It is also premised on the need for cooperation in achieving the parties' goals; puts legal concepts in their place by suggesting that they may be more or less (ir)relevant to the parties' practice; and emphasises the significance of a long-term relationship between parties in many contexts. This, of course, raises its own issues about power and vulnerability within the context of extended relationships of different sorts. In fact, tort claims may themselves arise in the interstices of such relationships. But, in short, relational contracting raises to the surface the relationships between actual parties, and their attempts to achieve their goals, rather than placing legal standards and remedies at the core, with a consequent focus on the morality of rule-breaking and the legal response to such breaches.

A much closer connection with the idea of 'the legal sense' as envisaged by developmental psychology could be attempted here, particularly the way in which the developmental psychology addressed by Gilligan had associated 'legal' sensibility with the rules applied to games typically played by boys, in which the rules are seen as ways of continuing the game provided they are applied in an even-handed and impersonal way. Adjusting the rules to suit particular parties would undermine their even-handed nature. In the games played by girls, rules were more often adapted or set aside, and in the event of conflict a game may simply be abandoned – relationships were more important, but also harder to escape (1982: 9).[20] If empirical work on contracting is correct (Beale and Dugdale 1975),[21] it seems that the issues emphasised by cultural feminists while not at the forefront of legal doctrine are much more in evidence in the social (economic) sphere that private law seeks to regulate. In particular, in the changed conditions of today, we might question the broad generalisation that Gilligan draws, that the 'male' standard observed 'fits the requirement for modern corporate success' (1982: 10). One lesson is that law needs to be responsive to the complexity of relationships; another is that the status of law (including legal rules and principles) in the practice of contracting may have been overestimated. Parties to contracting might take a much more pragmatic approach to legal rules and might prioritise the continuation of the relationship over the application of the rules; and indeed it is possible that law should and can develop to respond to this rather muted status for its principles. These insights do not of course provide the answer to all problems, and as Mulcahy and Brown have both argued they raise a whole host of new challenges for feminist analysis. The point is, however, that these challenges are inherently related to some of the core insights of feminism in respect of law and its intervention in human relationships. Feminist analysis thus becomes a potential source of constructive theory in respect of contracts, and a healthy exchange between feminist and other contextual approaches becomes possible.

Relational contract theory remains vibrant, but it is by no means new. Indeed, it is about as old as the 'old big three' feminist legal theories,[22] and contributed one of its texts to an exercise in textual analysis by Frug (see also Brown 1996). Frug's analysis as a whole is well worth revisiting not only because of its analysis of contract literature, but because of its application of the same method to a reading of Gilligan's work on difference. Here I want to point out some of the nuances of this method. Post-modern feminism is listed by Dixon as one of the 'new three' feminisms, and has the potential to evade crude essentialism ('crude Gilliganism'), whilst maintaining a gendered reading of a wide variety of narratives – an acceptance, so to speak, that 'complex Gilliganism' might illustrate some important *human* truths.[23] I would also point out that Frug's analysis is as occupied with academic interpretation and exposition of contract law as with the law itself, and is interested in the rhetoric both of the law and its surrounding literature as well as (or as a route to finding clues as to) its deeper nature. 'Feminine' qualities in published work pressing a relational analysis of contracting were contrasted by Frug with classically 'masculine' language and qualities in an economic analysis – both, as it happened, written by men (Frug 1992: chapter 7, discussing Posner and Rosenfield 1977 and Hillman 1983).

Neither this, nor the measured critique of Gilligan explored in the next section, means that women disappear from Frug's post-modern analysis of law and its literature. But some of the uses to which she puts the presence of women in a contract case book are both illuminating and important. At one point, having noted the lack of cases involving women for the most part (consistent with an 'authoritarian neutrality' of tone), Frug argued that the selection of four out of five cases with women claimants in the section of the case book dealing with standard term contracts, raising issues of their enforceability, led to a particular sense that standard term contracts are *generally* acceptable, and that the qualifications to their enforceability are something to do with an exceptional category of case, namely those where gender is in issue (Frug 1992: 98–9).[24] To similar effect is the prevalence of cases involving women in the section on equitable remedies, particularly given the authors' clear view that the expectation measure of damages provides the dominant remedy. Frug's reading of the place of women in the contract case book therefore suggested that women were associated with exceptions to general rules, those general rules being particularly associated with freedom of contract and the will of the parties. Where there were women there was legally relevant 'context', but this was the exception not the rule. And while this might (or might not) show us something about the way in which the law approaches women, it does show us something about the way that the case book writers approached the law. General lessons about the prioritising of one side of a potential dichotomy can be drawn from the representation of cases involving women. And here is the most general point: feminist readings can indicate that vibrant ideas within the law and legal discourse are relegated to the status of 'exceptions', because of the adoption of a standpoint from which one particular approach is regarded as the general rule. This is reflected in the progressive reading of Gilligan's work.

I would agree with Frug that a reading of the rhetoric of the law can show us much about the underlying thought processes of the law. For example, there are numerous cases in the law of tort where judges have declared that some principle or other is not a 'touchstone' of liability (and no cases, to my knowledge, where any concept or principle has been described as *being* a touchstone of liability). This could be seen as a sort of nervous habit, using a metaphor because the precise language for translating reasons into legal principles are lacking,[25] and because of a reluctance (though a patchy one) to appeal directly to the alternative, which is a response to all the features of the particular relationship.

Arguably, the most overtly post-modern of authorities on the duty of care is *Caparo Industries plc v Dickman* [1990], given its frank admission that terms such as 'foreseeability' and 'proximity', previously thought to be determinative of the existence of a duty, were merely 'labels' used to present or explain the courts' pragmatic judgments. *Caparo* has been quite badly reviewed in mainstream legal analyses, and rejected by the Australian courts (*Sullivan v Moody* [2001])[26], on the basis that it does not perform the role of a precise legal test. Nor, in fact, does it purport to do so, preferring to offer some structure to a multi-faceted exploration of the relationship between the parties.[27] It also, like quite a few negligence cases, involved a corporate claimant who tried to get cover from another commercial party for free, though this was dealt with more politely, less visibly, and much less rhetorically than the case of an injured *individual* trying to pass responsibility to others in cases such as *Tomlinson v Congleton Borough Council* [2003]. The parallels between these cases are not generally mentioned for they are thought to fall into different 'categories': personal injury, which the law is thought to prioritise (another academic exercise in prioritisation), and economic losses, which the law of tort is conventionally thought not to prioritise.[28] Indeed, the perception that economic losses are marginal may explain the greater freedom to use pragmatic, rather than moralistic, terminology: the boundary-drawing exercise is thought to require less justification. In *Caparo*, Lord Bridge actually declared that duties of care were arrived at 'pragmatically' and that all of the concepts applied in determining duty questions were really 'convenient labels' to apply to pragmatic decisions. The point is that there *is* no 'touchstone' of liability, because the point of a touchstone is to tell the difference between true or false gold. Since duty propositions are not true or false but subject to pragmatic determination by the court, there is no job for a touchstone to perform, and it is not surprising that all the judicial references are to ideas which are *not* touchstones. Analysis of the rhetorical strategies – direct, evasive; cautious, certain; abstract, situated – deployed in judgments can reveal underlying tensions and lead to consideration of their causes.

The 'legal sense' of *In a Different Voice*

In a Different Voice was not, of course, a work of legal theory, but was concerned to challenge the treatment (or absence) of the female voice in developmental psychology. Gilligan's identification of the feminine – and of women – with an 'ethic of care' has captured the imagination and been subject to critique in equal measure. Gilligan did not invent difference nor was she the first psychologist to attempt a positive rendition of what had been seen to be the failure of women to reach the male norm of adulthood. She was also by no means the first to associate the dominant norm of moral development with the sense of 'justice' or, more directly 'the legal sense'. This latter term Gilligan ascribes to Piaget (1932), explaining that Piaget identified 'the legal sense' ('essential to moral development') with the application of rules and development of fair procedures for adjudicating conflicts, particularly through the development of games. Girls, Gilligan reports, were regarded by Piaget as much more 'pragmatic' when it came to rules, and much more willing to make exceptions to them. This, he thought, meant that the 'legal sense' – and thus moral sense – was less developed in girls than in boys (Gilligan, 1982: 10). Gilligan challenged the idea that the legal sense, read in this way, was central to moral development, by positing a different, and equally sophisticated, moral sense associated with the feminine. The universalisation of this 'different voice' has been widely debated. But neither she, nor (more importantly) those who have commented on her work, seem to have wondered directly whether the legal sense, described in this way, is any more definitive of what is involved in the law, than of what is involved in moral development. Does Piaget's 'legal sense', identified with the ethic of right, represent only one interpretation of the legal – based, moreover, on a sense that the role of the legal is analogous to the resolution of conflicts between opponents in a game, rather than between parties in a wide range of different relationships (some of cooperation, some of dependency, and so on)? A richer sense of the legal is a corollary to a richer sense of relationship.

I argue that the 'ethic of right' is as questionable as a statement of law's development as it is of moral development. Frug's progressive reading of Gilligan is helpful, just as her reading of the contract case book was helpful, and (importantly) for much the same reasons. Her suggestion is that we 'ground the sex differences Gilligan identifies in the context of the moral development theory she sought to change, overlooking the many instances where Gilligan seems to speak of sex differences as if they are universal' (Frug 1992: 40). Similarly, I suggest we ground the 'ethic of rights' in certain theories or representations of law, rather than treating it as universal for law. The position of the ethic of rights can be challenged in the same way for law as for moral development. To the extent that the abstract duty of care shows all the hallmarks of the ethic of rights, it too can be challenged. This would swim against the tide of academic opinion, which has tended to praise the abstract duty of care, and decry pragmatic attempts to reduce it to the level of more specific relationships (which is to say, relationships not defined solely in terms of the harm done by one of the parties to the other, nor according to broad brush categories).

One important contribution of the recent 'feminist judgments project' (Hunter, McGlynn and Rackley 2010) is that it demonstrates that legal judgment, like moral judgment, can be ordered so that underlying contextual features of the parties' lives are recognised. Equally to the point, in ordering social relationships, the law in Piaget's sense does not always take a central role. For example, Gilligan attributes to Lever (1976) a finding that girls, in particular, were inclined to abandon a game in the face of conflict, rather than to devise a series of rules for resolving disputes: 'girls subordinated the continuation of the game to the continuation of relationship' (Gilligan, 1982: 10). It is therefore not only Gilligan's 'ethic of care' which strikes a chord with relational theory. It is also present in the work she set out to criticise and to supplement,[29] so that her chief contribution lies in challenging the received hierarchy, and revealing neglected narratives.[30] The same exercise can be applied to the nature of law as to moral development, or indeed to the law of contract or tort.

Duty of care through a relational perspective: antithesis or not?

A more difficult question is whether relational theory can be applied successfully to the duty of care at all. There are two sides to this question. One is that the duty of care might be taken to be 'relational' enough as it stands. This, I will suggest, is not true, and certainly not true of the received understanding of Lord Atkin's version. The other is to question whether the duty of care can be anything other than the law of duties between strangers – the antithesis of relational responsibility in the feminist sense. Once again there is much of interest in Gilligan's review of her predecessors' work. Drawing on the work of Janet Lever (1976), Gilligan reports a contrast in what boys and girls learn from their play:

> . . . boys learn both the independence and the organizational skills necessary for coordinating the activities of large and diverse groups of people. By participating in controlled and socially approved competitive situations, they learn to deal with competition in a relatively forthright manner – to play with their enemies and to compete with their friends – all in accordance with the rules of the game. In contrast, girls' play tends to occur in smaller, more intimate groups, often the best-friend dyad, and in private places. This play replicates the social pattern of primary human relationships in that its organization is more cooperative. Thus it points less, in Mead's terms, toward learning to take the role of 'the generalized other', less toward the abstraction of human relationships. But it fosters the development and sensitivity necessary for taking the role of the 'particular other' and points more toward knowing the other as different from the self.
>
> (Gilligan 1982: 10–11)

Taking the first side of our question, has the duty of care been largely exempted from direct feminist critique because it already seems to be a counter to the rigidity of established legal rules (specifically, privity of contract), thus increasing the responsibility of perpetrators of harm through malleable conceptual categories such as foreseeability and proximity? This may have been its initial effect although, arguably, Lord Macmillan's acknowledgement of the potential for overlapping analyses – narratives? – of the same situation was the more 'relational' approach. It says something about the mainstream liking for abstract general rules (or in this case principles) that the Atkinian version was taken as the beacon for the unified tort of negligence (and the most abstract aspects of his judgment have been elevated).[31] Taking Lord Macmillan's judgment as pre-eminent might have given the very different impression that all relationships can be approached in more than one way – and would not have encouraged thinking about negligence to drift so far from its origins in contractual relationships. But thinking again about the surface rhetoric of Lord Atkin's judgment, it could be said to show multiple hallmarks of gendered jurisprudence. It proceeds using abstract categories; is clearly oriented to relationships between strangers (the subject of the Good Samaritan parable); and is overtly moralistic but deliberately limits the need for altruism in law. 'Duty', it might be said, is premised on the morality of strangers, and could not be more clearly distinct from 'responsibility' as a feminist relational theory might see it.[32] Duty of care is as much about the entitlements of potential injurers as of claimants, and can be seen as a legal branch of the rules of interaction, strongly reminiscent of the idea of rule-application in boys' games summarised above. The rhetoric involved is abstract, universal, definitive, moralistic and rights-based.

The duty of care is also predominantly a line-drawing exercise, so the idea of injury free from responsibility to compensate is as inherent to it as the idea of duties to take care (and to compensate for harm). Though not necessarily in accord with what Lord Atkin had in mind, the duty of care is also much more cautiously applied to cases of omission, and here feminist analysis has sometimes picked it up. But more generally, the neighbour principle is inherently about the delineation of categories of people to whom there is (and is not) responsibility if one fails to take care. Care here is about 'being careful', and is only 'other regarding' in the sense that I need to be careful of certain interests of certain people. I do not have to have anyone else's interests at heart, though the later idea of assumption of responsibility may begin to introduce such a positive need to care. Although ostensibly focused on relationships, the *Donoghue* instantiation of the neighbour principle is not relational in a contextual sense, but seeks to be definitive of rights and duties arising between parties conceived of essentially as strangers, setting out the rules of interaction. Those rules in place, competition which accords with the rules is fair and healthy and injuries, though of course regrettable, are not the concern of those who inflict them. This addresses the second side of our question.

Here is part of the problem for torts scholarship. Approached from a relational perspective, contracting has clear potential as a human activity, and what is in issue is the desirable role of law in relation to this activity. But from the same relational perspective, what is tort law actually about? It appears to be about 'correcting' harms, which is to say largely through awards of monetary damages. This is not inherently a particularly cooperative enterprise. Where a harm caused by a breach of duty is established, money is moved from the one side to the other, matching the harm.[33] Even if we try to extend the range of harms recognised by the law of negligence (and perhaps of tort more generally), we cannot get around the fact that success in an action does not lead to any enhanced cooperation, unless perhaps we are willing to think about torts as one part of a much bigger picture where things tick along in distributive or enterprise liability terms – an enormous yet single-minded undertaking which does not fit well with the idea of particularity in relationship. For those who are interested in using feminist legal methods for constructive development of the law beyond reform of particular legal rules, tort does not provide a particularly appealing model. Oddly (or perhaps not?) the duty concept is at its more appealing when applied to those losses around the edges of contract, at the margins of tort according to the abstract model (more particularly since they tend to respond to economic losses), and not generally at the heart of legal gender studies either. Here the law of negligence has been more cautious, more contextual and more responsive to the nature of the parties involved, acting as a supplement to contractual duties. Arguably, this is where *Donoghue* also should be situated, were it not for the temptation of abstract generalisation.

The disintegration of duty and the misleading rhetoric of individualism

The direction of change in the duty of care in English law could be seen as indicating that the problem of the *point* of tort law has been noticed by the courts themselves, most particularly at the highest level. Core to this recognition is the damages remedy, and its impact. There is no evidence that this was a primary concern of Lord Atkin's in *Donoghue*, but subsequent developments have magnified the economic impact of his exercise in generalisation. Road traffic claims were in their infancy in 1932, and the influence of these claims (and attendant compulsory insurance) has been highly significant, arguably contributing to the growth of damages awards in general and certainly influencing the reform of contributory negligence (Steele 2012). Injuries at work were largely dealt with outside the tort system in 1932, but the abolition of Workmen's Compensation and of the remnants of common employment in 1948 brought these claims firmly into the common law fold. Statutory duties accompanied by civil liability have since grown exponentially under the influence of European law, the measure of liability being premised on the tort measure. State liability was opened up by the Crown Proceedings Act 1947, leading, ultimately, to some of the most complex jurisprudence in all of negligence law; and there has been an exponential growth in the welfare state, in regulation and in public law generally. Where relationships are in issue, where do negligence liabilities fit in relation to these other developments?

The response of the courts has been to shift away from broad abstract principles concerned with foreseeability and proximity. For example, courts now seek out assumptions of responsibility, placing the emphasis on special relationships (the particular other, rather than the general other, we could say), and raising pertinent questions about the relationship between 'responsibility' and 'duty'. Of course, those assumptions are a matter for the court to try to discern, not for the parties to choose. But that too is no particular problem from a relational perspective. We have multi-factoral approaches to duty, particularly concerned with vulnerability (in Australia) and pragmatic approaches dependent on all facets of particular relationships (in the UK). But most dramatically, we have restriction in the categories of duty, leaving many foreseeable harms outside the reach of the tort of negligence at all.[34] New variants of legal theory may bubble up to justify 'principled exclusions' from the duty of care, but the truth is more pragmatic than that. Relational legal theory can help to explain why criticism of such restrictions as either 'policy-driven' or unpredictable miss the mark. Particularity is not the same as 'policy' (the forbidden opposite to principle in some core variations of liberal legal theory), but about sensitivity, and the reverse of abstraction.

That being the case, feminist theory also has the resources to contribute to a critique of the new individualist rhetoric with which some of the current restrictions to duty of care have been laced. This is a form of appeal to the rules of the game, or perhaps just a playing to the public gallery. Its proponents could equally well think tort law's remedies, in particular, have minimal potential for positive reconciliation. The route taken is to revert to the archetypal 'ethic of rights': to address the duty concept in a manner which reinforces its exclusionary elements and its moral overtones, its individualism and its abstraction – also its appeal to fair play. In other words, all the elements which both difference feminism, and in a more measured sense post-modern feminism with its eye on rhetoric, would count as 'male'.

But current restrictions on the duty of care also need to be addressed in terms of the pragmatic concerns which lie beneath, and in terms of the search for alternative remedies, which are common at the present time to other cases at the limit of the duty of care. 'No duty' cases are currently definitive of the very priority of 'duty'. 'Duty' and 'right' contrast with 'responsibility' and 'care' in that they are abstract and clear cut in their limits. They have to have these limits partly because they are so bound up with economic consequences, itself a consequence of the damages remedy. This is partly why the courts are currently engaged in differentiating between the rights of private law, and the rights of the European Convention and the Human Rights Act 1998: there is no wish to attach an economic imperative to the idea of rights in this context. This economic connection, and the effect of it on legal development, has not yet been fully analysed by feminist tort theory.[35]

There is a more pernicious effect of all of this, however, which is that the rhetoric has power of persuasion over the user. The habit of limitation in duties of care, combined with individualist rhetoric, shows signs of infecting areas other than negligence. There are areas where liability has a stronger or more particular purpose connected with the nature of the relationship between the parties, and these are increasingly infected with a sense that it is not 'fair' to impose stricter liability. Here I take a brief look at individualist rhetoric and of less easily recognised counter-currents. First, and most noticeable, are cases where individual responsibility of injured parties is emphasised while defendants are declared to be free from duties. Secondly are cases where tort claims give way to alternative logics (including cases where there is an alternative remedy). These cases raise issues around the relationship between torts and welfare provision, particularly in a context in which the Human Rights Act 1998 is having a considerable impact. Thirdly, and least satisfactory, are those cases where the habitual rhetoric of bounded responsibility and fairness to defendants has begun to affect the law of employer and employee, particularly in cases where women are strongly represented among the claimants.

The most renowned exercise in individualist rhetoric asserting the absence of duty was the decision of the House of Lords in *Tomlinson* [2003]. Here a young adult who suffered severe paralysis after diving into shallow water in a disused quarry was found not to have been owed a duty by the occupier of the premises, a local authority. The rhetoric of the decision, particularly emphasising that the danger was obvious (the claimant should have avoided it himself), drew attention not only to the absence of duty, but also (as part and parcel of this) to the claimant's need to take responsibility for himself. There is a section of the judgment headed 'Free Will' (*Tomlinson* [2003]: [44]), and a suggestion that 'there is an important question of freedom at stake' – the freedom 'of responsible parents and children with buckets and spades' seeking 'harmless recreation' on the beaches, which would be disrupted should there be liability to an 'irresponsible' visitor in these circumstances (*Tomlinson* [2003]: [46]).[36] The House of Lords even named others whose claims had already been rejected in lower courts, pointing out that these individuals were actually more irresponsible (even stupid) than the claimant in the present case.

> It is a terrible tragedy to suffer such dreadful injury in consequence of a relatively minor act of carelessness. It came nowhere near the stupidity of Luke Ratcliff, a student who climbed a fence at 2.30 am on a December morning to take a running dive into the shallow end of a swimming pool (see *Ratcliff v McConnell* [1999] 1 WLR 670, or John Donoghue, who dived into Folkestone Harbour from a slipway at midnight on 27 December after an evening in the pub: *Donoghue v Folkestone Properties Ltd* [2003] QB 1008. John Tomlinson's mind must often recur to that hot day which irretrievably changed his life. He may feel, not unreasonably, that fate has dealt with him unfairly. And so in these proceedings he seeks financial compensation: for the loss of his earning capacity, for the expense of the care he will need, for the loss of the ability to lead an ordinary life. But the law does not provide such compensation simply on the basis that the injury was disproportionately severe in relation to one's own fault or even not one's own fault at all. Perhaps it should, but society might not be able to afford to compensate everyone on that principle, certainly at the level at which such compensation is now paid. The law provides compensation only when the injury was someone else's fault. In order to succeed in his claim, that is what Mr Tomlinson has to prove.
>
> (Lord Hoffmann, *Tomlinson* [2003]: [4])

One purpose of this blunt pronouncement was undoubtedly to draw a line for future cases of obvious danger, and to remove such cases from litigation. But through the rhetoric of the judgment, something more than certainty was secured: responsibility was moralised and the general message conveyed was one of 'tough luck', and of 'tough but fair', clear rules, illustrating the rhetorical force that can be attached to the idea of 'no duty'.[37]

Arguably, the strength and unapologetic clarity of the line-drawing in this case – which even named and humanised the victims while denying a duty – also reflect the strength of the perceived need to justify a denial of duty to a seriously injured claimant. Taking out the individualist aspects of the rhetoric, however, we see other features even of this particular case. The comments of Lord Hoffmann could also be read as containing a *refusal* to allow tort damages to offer the last word on social responsibility. Citizens are cared for (to one level or another) through state welfare and the voluntary actions of others.[38] Duties to take care, and to compensate in the event of harm, are a more limited category, and not to be confused with the care that is shown for vulnerable members of society generally. This aspect of the rhetoric tries to disentangle negligence and its remedies from the sense of solidarity between citizens, so that shortcomings in solidarity are not to be made up by courts deciding negligence cases generously. The explicit reference to the generous nature of damages awards might be underlined. But the distinction between solidarity and negligence duties is overshadowed by the emphasis on free will and responsibility of the claimant.[39]

Subsequent cases have of course followed the *Tomlinson* lead and exonerated occupiers, even in cases involving child claimants. In the latter cases, though, courts tend to underline the adverse effects on other members of the public of having to take precautions to avoid liability, rather than the fecklessness of the claimants (see, for example, *Baldacchino v West Wittering* [2008] (involving a beach) and *Keown v Coventry Healthcare Trust* [2006] (hospital grounds where members of the public could take recreation)). However, there are also stronger counter-currents at the rhetorical level. So, for example, parents whose toddler drowned at a holiday park were not to conclude that they themselves were in any sense being held to blame when a court decided that no duty had been owed to warn them of a danger: the determination of legal duties and no duties should *not* always be taken to set out a moral conclusion about the parties (*Bourne Leisure Ltd v Marsden* [2009]).[40] In another 'no liability' case where the rhetoric was restrained and decidedly sympathetic to all parties, parents who hired a bouncy castle on which another couple's child suffered catastrophic injuries were not to be expected to be as aware of significant risks based on official documentation as would a commercial operator or employer (*Perry v Harris* [2008]).[41] Here the lesson is not the opposition of legal and moral expectations, but their connection: the legal standard to be applied in this context is that of the reasonable parent, and no more. These last two cases concern those who are *expected* to care, namely parents. There is a difference in the rhetoric compared to that applied to adventurous young risk-takers, as in *Tomlinson*. This rhetoric can be treated as gendered. Since all the cases involve the perils of leisure activities, it might well be asked what 'game' the law is here regulating, and whether its rhetoric changes with the characters involved.[42]

Another source of insight into the role of individualism at the margins of the duty of care is in those cases where tort comes up against alternative legal frameworks applicable to the situation. As already explained, the availability of overlapping *legal* (as well as other) narratives is familiar from *Donoghue v Stevenson* itself, but the complexity and innate uncertainty of an approach in which the duty of care coexists with other potential routes to legal responsibility has not made this a popular understanding. The key case, analogous to *Tomlinson* and from the same era in the House of Lords, is *Gorringe v Calderdale Metropolitan Borough Council* [2004], which blocked any derivation of duties of care from broad public law duties. In another exercise in line-drawing, clearly intended to preclude a wide range of cases from being argued, the attempt by the claimant to shift blame onto a local authority was again inherently disparaged by the terms of the decision.[43]

Like *Tomlinson*, *Gorringe* has achieved its intended effect. Numerous restrictive decisions concerning tort in the context of positive duties of the state and regulatory agencies to benefit claimants have followed, and the introduction to the scene of a new legal status for Convention rights has only intensified the effect. This has happened in part because the new and more limited remedies available under the Human Rights Act 1998 are thought more appropriate than tort's full compensatory remedies where complaints essentially turn on violations of rights by public authorities. The impact on tort needs some interpretation but may turn out to be profound, positively encouraging the question referred to in *Tomlinson*, of whether tort's damages are really an appropriate response to a wide range of harms. Examples of this can be found in *Marcic v Thames Water Utilities Ltd* [2003], *Home Office v Mohammed and Others* [2011] and *Murdoch v Department for Work and Pensions* [2010] (where the alternative remedy was a civil debt for recovery of sums owed, the allowable claim being for non-payment). The rhetoric of *Home Office v Mohammed* is particularly significant because it was far from protective of the state and yet tort's role in protecting rights was subordinated even to that of the Parliamentary Ombudsman. This illustrates that the rise of a public law frame for considering the claims of individuals to be cared for (benefited or protected), has had a significant impact on the perceived importance of tort. Where once the existence of such duties was thought to justify a *progressive* expansion in the duties owed to individuals by the state, growing scepticism about the relevance of a damages remedy has led to the restriction of tort in favour of a multitude of other responses.

In both these sets of cases, the rhetoric of individual responsibility and rights has proved to be rather superficial, despite its strategic success in helping to secure a more restrictive direction in the development of the law. It would be best to summarise these cases as limiting the range of relationships in which courts consider the duty of care – and, importantly, its associated liabilities – to offer an appropriate narrative, and a recognition that it does not provide the only narrative.[44] The limitations of the duty of care itself explain its limited utility in capturing a range of responsibilities. Unfortunately, the surface rhetoric of individualism tends to work against this interpretation. The mainstream presentation of negligence as correcting harm done by one party to another in the context of no particular preceding relationship has ultimately, some decades later, made it inherently unattractive as an encapsulation of relationships. While in *Donoghue* the 'duty of care' narrative was powerful enough (with the help of Lord Atkin's rhetoric) to be dominant, courts have increasingly seen it as overly simplified or plainly inappropriate.

This is not to say that an emphasis on relationships would perceive all consequent limitations in tort duties to be an appropriate response. In particular, negligence thinking exerts a considerable influence in areas where the nature of the relationship may give positive reasons for taking care beyond those applicable to strangers. Perhaps the clearest recent example is the narrow majority decision of the Supreme Court in *Baker v Quantum Clothing Group Ltd* [2011]. Overturning a decision of the Court of Appeal, Lord Mance for the majority argued that the duty in section 29 of the Factories Act 1961 should be read as analogous to a negligence duty – what could the employer reasonably have thought and done? Any more would impose an unfair burden, and an applicable industry Code of Practice in respect of protection at *higher* levels was read as providing protection to employers who did not protect employees at lower levels: it set out the rules of the game. Lord Kerr in dissent, like the Court of Appeal in this and a number of other industrial injury cases in recent years, emphasised instead the positive duty of employers not only to keep their employees safe from foreseeable dangers, but also to give positive thought to the risks associated with their employment.[45] The decision in *Baker* encroaches into the territory of this positive duty to consider risks to employees and to 'give thought' to the harms which may affect them. Employment cases involving physical injury (rather than psychiatric harm) have not been an obvious focus for feminist analysis, but it is noticeable that in the three most significant recent cases in which the House of Lords and then Supreme Court have either rejected liability, or shown little enthusiasm for the principles applied, the claimants have been female employees.[46] Women are disproportionately represented in the groups where injury was less readily foreseeable, because they were apparently in the 'softer', less risky jobs. Gender roles were relevant to the very features of their claims which caused them to fail, or to encounter greater difficulties, where analysis is premised on the norms of negligence.

Conclusion

The allure of the duty of care is that it appears to liberalise legal remedies and to supplement the existing contractual rules with more flexible principles capable of responding to parties' relationships. But a critical relational perspective will show that this attraction is largely misplaced. Indeed, the allure of duty and its rhetoric partly explains the way that tort scholarship lags behind contract scholarship in its appreciation even of the pragmatic and limited nature of its subject. Feminist method can in my view help to reveal some of the tensions in duty of care, without collapsing into essentialism, because it can reveal the complexity of relational narratives and the shortcomings of abstract duty.

There is also, however, a question of history and of legal development, suggested by Gilligan's analysis but oddly neglected to date. Legal sensibilities are surely not fixed in time.[47] The vibrancy of relational contract theory and its connection with the most commercial of spheres suggests that relational analysis, which pre-dates Gilligan's work, could be freed from the limitation of 'care' and might capture a great deal about the needs faced by legal systems in today's societies and economies. Armed with a progressive reading of Gilligan, and with an emphasis on maturity and her questioning of hierarchies rather than on 'difference', we may wonder whether the generalised duty of care itself was just a phase we were going through.

Notes

*   Thanks are due to Janice Richardson and T.T. Arvind for their very pertinent comments on an earlier version. Remaining defects are of course my responsibility.

1   See further 'duty of care through a relational perspective: antithesis or not?', below. In terms of centrality, there is jurisdictional variation in the common law. The 'duty of care' has been important in the UK, Canada, and Australia, amongst other jurisdictions, but (controversially, from some liberal points of view) it has not had the same significance in US law (Goldberg and Zipursky 2001).

2   This is of course a matter of degree. In particular, Bender (1989–90) has sought to rework negligence so that 'care' means 'responsibility'. The outlandishness of the result and its distance from the law of tort as we know it makes the point very effectively. On the whole, however, the critique of objectivity has been deployed against the standard of reasonable care (eg Conaghan 1996), while arguments have been put forward for the expansion of categories of harm (to include gendered harms), and for reform of damages.

3   See, for example, Peppin (1996), beginning with the promise of negligence in responding to the 'relatedness' of people (a promise which she finds not to be fulfilled). I will take a more sceptical approach to the promise of the 'duty concept' itself. Note also Conaghan (2003), drawing attention to the conception of social relations viewed primarily in terms of isolated acts of individuals, which encapsulates some features of the 'abstract' (Atkinian) duty of care.

4   This is the model of Graycar and Morgan (2002), and is argued for specifically in Graycar and Morgan (1996).

5   This is the model expressly adopted by Weinrib (1995) as characteristic of private law. This has been immensely influential in academic private law but strikes me as the very opposite of the contextual understanding of relationships which ought to be central to feminist analysis. Notice, for example, the deliberate strategy of using the parties' names in the various 'feminist judgments' in Hunter, McGlynn and Rackley (2010), and the multiplication of relevant factors drawn from the parties' lives. This lies in contrast to lawyers' learned skills of abstraction in order to universalise, but notably *can* be successfully incorporated into legal judgment.

6   The meaning of 'principle' has changed over the years, maybe as a consequence of Dworkinian theory and its popularity. In the first edition of his *Introduction to Contract*, Atiyah was able to juxtapose a claim to have taken a principled (as opposed to rules-based) analysis of the law with a claim that he took functions and effects as seriously as legal doctrine (Atiyah 1961: v). Principled analysis in this sense – drawing out key themes – had the potential for a critical edge, which has been lost as principles are defined by opposition not only to rules, but also to 'policies' or 'pragmatism' (the very things that

Atiyah thought were illuminated by his variety of analysis, generalising from individual instances to the larger picture).

7   For an account of the tensions between these threads in legal reasoning in private law (specifically the law of contract), also criticising the dominance of the principled rather than the pragmatic account in liberal jurisprudence, see Waddams (2011).

8   How to face this problem was the key theme of Conaghan (2000), quoted above. The problem has not become any easier over the intervening decade or so. See the very useful overviews by Dixon (2008) and Chamallas (2010–11). The key problem is how to identify 'gender', given the influence of (for example) Butler (1990).

9   Dworkin has argued that the law 'works itself pure' as it generalises its principles more and more (Dworkin 1986). Beever (2007) has argued that tort law should revert to the principled state of negligence under *Donoghue* [1932] (as he perceives it to have been), cleansed of policy considerations. A contextual relational approach, considering the nature of particular relationships as germane to the rights and responsibilities arising, is at odds with both of these.

10   As to which, see further 'The legal sense of *In a Different Voice*', below.

11   This note, on which Gilligan's book ends, clearly works against an entirely deterministic reading of her work.

12   Given the volume and diversity of feminist legal theory, I have drawn highly selectively from the available sources.

13   A comparison can be drawn perhaps with the work of Jennifer Nedelsky, which draws freely on non-feminist critiques of rights as well as on feminist sources in elaborating a relational view of rights: see for example, Nedelsky (1993; 1999).

14   Lacey (1998: 13) referring to Marxist theory, critical legal theory, critical race theory and queer theory. But legal realism more generally might be thought to fit this description.

15   A point emphasised by Atiyah (1961: 'Introduction').

16   This draws attention to the fact that many or indeed most negligence cases outside road traffic accidents do not arise between strangers and/or involve alternative sources of potential responsibility (including public law or statutory responsibilities).

17   It is important to point out that 'regulation' and 'good ordering' are intended to be malleable terms which can be understood to raise more or less procedural or substantive issues of (for example) fairness, thereby potentially justifying limitations to freedom of contracting.

18   Smith (2006) suggests a mixed approach. This is very different from Atiyah's original Introduction.

19   Particularly useful exemplars are Mulcahy (2005); Mulcahy and Andrews (2010); Brown (1996); Wightman (2000) and Frug (1992). The links between feminism and other contextual (relational) approaches are further explored by Campbell (2005).

20   Early research in the role of rules had simply not included girls at all.

21   This is debated: see for example the exchange between Bernstein (1999) and Macaulay (2000).

22   Chamallas (2010–11) lists the big three 'older' feminisms, drawing on Dixon (2008), as liberal, dominance and cultural or relational feminism. The newer three are listed as partial agency or sex-positive feminism; intersectional or anti-essentialist feminism (exploring other dimensions of identity such as race and sexual orientation); and postmodern feminism.

23   I would relate this insight to the ambitions (and achievements) of the Feminist Judgments project (Hunter, McGlynn and Rackley 2010), since judgments to be successful must carry authority for all those subject to them. Therefore, the feminist reading must seek a better reading generally, not only for women, than the ostensibly mainstream version. This is one of the ways in which a feminist approach can be argued to offer more than simply a 'perspective'.

24 Frug proposes that a feminist reading might lead to the conclusion that standardised contracts can be unfair for men as well as for women (1992: 99)

25 One of the cases where this happened is replete with other metaphors. The difficulty here was that the Court of Appeal found it difficult to fit its preferred answer within the proliferation of 'no duty' mandates in the area where tort duties overlap with statutory powers and duties (*Connor v Surrey County Council* [2010]).

26 Ironically perhaps the High Court in this case adopted an even more open-ended 'multi-factoral' approach.

27 While this does have something in common with the approach in *Sullivan v Moody*, and may well lead to some similar conclusions in novel cases, it focuses more expressly on features of the relationship between the parties rather than, for example, desirable or undesirable policy outcomes. This is not to say that the *Caparo* approach excludes policy considerations, but it tends to mediate its approach to policy through the relationship of the parties.

28 I don't believe this to be true, and would find it very surprising if it were. I think it is rather that the boundaries of behaviour are set differently where economic losses are concerned, because they can be caused in so many ways. Actually the remedies of tort law are focused on the economic impact of harms (Bender 1989–90; Steele 2011; Stanton 2012).

29 There is a risk, pointed out by Frug, that the darker side of relationships (their propensity to form a web which is not only connecting, but also has the 'sticky, trapping character of a spider's web', and their own potential for hierarchy), will be glossed over in Gilligan's work given the nature of her undertaking (to disrupt the identification of maturity with the ethic of right), (Frug 1992: 45).

30 For debate around this strategy and exploration of the deeper roots of the received approach contested by Gilligan, see Richardson (2007).

31 Lord Atkin did of course add the idea of 'proximity of relationship' to his neighbour principle, and the abstract refrain of some parts of his judgment have arguably been disproportionately sampled in ensuing debate.

32 A point effectively made by Biggs and MacKenzie (2000), though introducing a collection without an essay about tort.

33 The tort of negligence typically concerns itself with actual rather than threatened harms, so the question of injunctive relief for negligence has tended to arise as a matter of theory rather than practice.

34 To the extent that this is premised on differentiation between types of harm, the difficulties of drawing the lines between recoverable and irrecoverable harm in any meaningful way is discussed by Priaulx, this volume.

35 Bender (1989–90 and, at more length 1990), discusses the economic form of damages in order to propose that something less easily internalised by business should be chosen – such as a literal duty to care. I have argued that there is an interesting relationship between theories which try to secure more money (compensation is not good enough) and emerging ideas that money is inappropriate (compensation would sully the idea of rights) (Steele 2011).

36 The risk-taking activities of young adults is emphasised, but this is particularly aimed at the case of young men: see Lord Scott's rather hesitant syntax when he asked 'why should the council be discouraged by the law of tort from providing facilities for young men and young women to enjoy themselves in this way?' (*Tomlinson* [2003]: [94]). More directly, Lord Hoffmann referred to the incidence of serious diving injuries almost exclusively among young adult men, and particularly to the expert evidence of Dr Penny which used the expression 'macho male diving syndrome' (*Tomlinson* [2003]: [49]). Were macho rules thought appropriate for macho games? See the earlier discussion of games and the 'legal sense' in work referred to by Carol Gilligan.

37 Contrast the remarks of Sedley LJ in the court below, concurring with Ward LJ: 'negligence is fact-specific, and we are able neither to determine what the occupiers' duties are in other places nor to predicate our decision on what its effect on those occupiers might be' (*Tomlinson* [2002]: [42]). The language used by the Court of Appeal was generally muted and lawyerly, in contrast to the vivid expression in the House of Lords. Its judgment was reversed.

38 Lord Hoffmann does not here mention the voluntary actions of others, and scholars have rightly explained that voluntary carers are not often made visible in the law. See for example Herring (2007).

39 I emphasise 'solidarity' rather than care because the case can be seen as part of a continuing relationship between private law and regulatory responses: see further Lee (2012), Campbell (2010).

40 Moses LJ pertinently stressed that 'sometimes these cases are bedevilled with the quest to attach blame either to the parent or the occupier'. This would be 'absurd and offensive' (*Bourne Leisure* [2009]: [16], [17]). But notice the felt need to emphasise this.

41 All of these cases are of the type that tend to be discussed in tabloid newspapers in connection with 'blame culture' or 'compensation culture', and the courts may be seen to be struggling to express a decision about legal duties and liabilities in a context where the public may think of them in different terms, about responsibility and blame.

42 See the discussion in the previous section.

43 'On the face of it, the accident was her own fault. . . . But she claims in these proceedings that it was the fault of the local authority . . .' (Lord Hoffmann *Gorringe* [2004]: [8]).

44 Even in a rare recent case where the Court of Appeal found a route to a negligence duty in the context of statutory powers and duties of a public nature (*Connor* [2010]), Sedley LJ pointed out that all employers, not just local authorities, owe duties not only to their employees but also to shareholders, regulators and the like, which may pull in different directions ([119]). Complexity and competition in legal narrative is not confined to the public sphere, and indeed public law (regulation) has a far broader influence than this.

45 The significance of risk assessment was likewise identified as a key trend in employers' liability over the last 20 years by Smith LJ in *Threlfall v Kingston-upon-Hull City Council* [2010], and summarised in terms of a need to 'take positive thought for the risks arising from . . . operations' ([35]).

46 *Baker v Quantum Clothing* [2011] was a case of occupational deafness in the knitting industry among employees exposed to a level of noise below that prioritised in the applicable Code of Practice, which was based on the available research. None had been conducted on this level of exposure. *Sienkiewicz v Grief* [2011] was an application of *Fairchild v Glenhaven Funeral Services* [2002] to an office worker, whose employment did not follow the same pattern as the employees in *Fairchild* [2002] and *Barker v Corus UK Ltd* [2006] in that there was only one employer. Levels of exposure were lower and the first instance judge was persuaded that occupational exposure did not double the background risk of living in Ellesmere Port. The Supreme Court seemed to distance itself from the fairness of *Fairchild*, despite applying it. Problems have also been encountered by family members suffering secondary exposure to dust, suggesting a presumed lack of imagination in reasonable foreseeability. *Smith v Northants* [2009] concerned a care worker whose work involved collecting people with disabilities from their homes. The employer was exonerated from absolute liability under the Provision and Use of Work Equipment Regulations 1992 because it did not 'control' the equipment (a ramp) which gave way: it was not 'work equipment'. Baroness Hale, dissenting, stressed the possibility of other narratives which would produce a different sense of the fairness of attaching responsibility to the employer: 'My Lords, perhaps it all depends upon how you tell the story' (*Smith v Northants*: [32]).

47 A general point about the ahistorical nature of much 'difference' feminism is made by Conaghan (1996: 167), who also raises the dangers of applying the 'ethic of care' to tort. See also Kerber (1986).

Cases

Baker v Quantum Clothing Group Ltd [2011] UKSC 17
Baldacchino v West Wittering [2008] EWHC 3386
Barker v Corus UK Ltd [2006] UKHL 20
Bourne Leisure Ltd v Marsden [2009] EWCA Civ 671
Caparo Industries Plc v Dickman [1990] 2 AC 605
Connor v Surrey County Council [2010] EWCA Civ 286
Donoghue v Stevenson [1932] AC 562
Fairchild v Glenhaven Funeral Services [2002] UKHL 22
Gorringe v Calderdale Metropolitan Borough Council [2004] UKHL 15
Home Office v Mohammed and Others [2011] EWCA Civ 351
Keown v Coventry Healthcare Trust [2006] 1 WLR 953
Marcic v Thames Water Utilities Ltd [2003] UKHL 66
Murdoch v Department for Work and Pensions [2010] EWHC 1988
Perry v Harris [2008] EWCA Civ 907
Sienkiewicz v Grief [2011] UKSC 10
Smith v Northants [2009] UKHL 27
Sullivan v Moody [2001] 207 CLR 562
Threlfall v Kingston-upon-Hull City Council [2010] EWCA Civ 1147
Tomlinson v Congleton Borough Council [2002] EWCA Civ 309.
Tomlinson v Congleton Borough Council [2003] UKHL 47

Bibliography

Atiyah, P. (1961) *Introduction to the Law of Contract*, Oxford: Clarendon Press
Beale, H. and Dugdale, T. (1975) 'Contracts Between Businessmen', *British Journal of Law and Society*, 45
Beever, A. (2007) *Rediscovering the Law of Negligence*, Oxford: Hart Publishing
Bender, L. (1989–90) 'Changing the Values in Tort Law', *Tulsa Law Journal*, 25: 759–73
—— (1990) 'Feminist (Re)Torts: Thoughts on the Liability Crisis, Mass Torts, Power, and Responsibilities', *Duke Law Journal*, 848–912
Bernstein, L. (1999) 'The Questionable Empirical Basis of Article 2's Incorporation Strategy: A Preliminary Study', *University of Chicago Law Review*, 66: 710
Biggs, H. and MacKenzie, R. (2000) 'Gendered Readings of Obligations: Social Lore or Strict Legal Forms?', *Feminist Legal Studies*, 8: 1–4
Brown, B. (1996) 'Contracting Out/Contracting In: Some Feminist Considerations', in A. Bottomley (ed) *Feminist Perspectives on the Foundational Subjects in Law*, London: Cavendish
Butler, J. (1990) *Gender Trouble: Feminism and the Subversion of Identity*, London: Routledge
Campbell, D. (2005) 'Afterword: Feminism, Liberalism and Utopianism in the Analysis of Contracting', in L. Mulcahy and S. Wheeler (eds) *Feminist Perspectives on Contract Law*, London: Glasshouse
—— (2010) 'Gathering the Water: Abuse of Rights After the Recognition of Government Failure', *J. Juris* 487
Chamallas, M. (2010–11) 'Past as Prologue: Old and New Feminisms', *Michigan Journal of Gender and Law* 17: 157–74
Conaghan, J. (1996) 'Tort Law and the Feminist Critique of Reason', in A. Bottomley (ed) *Feminist Perspectives on the Foundational Subjects in Law*, London: Cavendish

—— (2000) 'Reassessing the Feminist Theoretical Project in Law', *Journal of Law and Society*, 27: 351–85

—— (2003) 'Tort Law and Feminist Critique', in M.D.A. Freeman (ed) *Current Legal Problems*, Oxford: Oxford University Press, 175–209

Dixon, R. (2008) 'Feminist Disagreement (Comparatively) Recast', *Harvard Journal of Law and Gender*, 31: 277–321

Dworkin, R. (1986) *Law's Empire*, London: Fontana

Finley, L. (1989) 'A Break in the Silence: Including Women's Issues in a Torts Course', *Yale Journal of Law and Feminism*, 1: 41–73

Frug, M.J. (1992) *Postmodern Legal Feminism*, London: Routledge

Gilligan, C. (1982) *In a Different Voice*, Cambridge: Harvard University Press

Goldberg, J. and Zipursky, B (2001) 'The Restatement (Third) and the Place of Duty in Negligence Law', *Vanderbilt Law Review*, 54: 167

Graycar, R. and Morgan, J. (1996) 'Legal Categories, Women's Lives and the Law Curriculum OR Making Gender Examinable', *Sydney Law Review*, 16: 431

—— (2002) *The Hidden Gender of Law*, 2nd edn, Sydney: The Federation Press

Herring, J. (2007) 'Where are the Carers in Healthcare Law and Ethics?', *Legal Studies*, 27: 51–73

Hillman, R.A. (1983) 'An Analysis of the Cessation of Contractual Relations', *Cornell Law Review*, 68: 617

Hunter, R., McGlynn, C. and Rackley, E. (2010) *Feminist Judgments: From Theory to Practice*, Oxford: Hart Publishing

Kerber, L. (1986) 'Some Cautionary Words for Historians', *Signs*, 11: 304–10

Lacey, N. (1998) *Unspeakable Subjects: Feminist Essays in Legal and Social Theory*, Oxford: Hart Publishing

Lee, M. (2012) 'Occupying the Field: Tort and the Pre-emptive Statute', in T.T. Arvind and J. Steele (eds) *Tort Law and the Legislature: Common Law, Statute, and the Dynamics of Legal Change*, Oxford: Hart Publishing

Lever, J. (1976) 'Sex Differences in the Games Children Play', *Social Problems*, 23: 478–7

Macaulay, S. (2000) 'Relational Contracts Floating on a Sea of Custom? Thoughts About the Ideas of Ian Macneil and Lisa Bernstein', *North Western University Law Review*, 94: 775

Mulcahy, L. (2005) 'The Limitations of Love and Altruism – Feminist Perspectives on Contract Law', in L. Mulcahy and S. Wheeler (eds) *Feminist Perspectives on Contract Law*, London: Glasshouse

Mulcahy, L. and Andrews, C. (2010) *Baird Textile Holdings v Marks and Spencer Plc*, in R. Hunter, C. McGlynn and E. Rackley (eds) *Feminist Judgments: From Theory to Practice*, Oxford: Hart Publishing

Nedelsky, J. (1993) 'Reconceiving Rights as Relationship', *Review of Constitutional Studies*, 1: 1–26

—— (1999) 'Reconceiving Autonomy: Sources, Thoughts and Possibilities', *Yale Journal of Law and Feminism*, 1: 7–36

Peppin, P. (1996) 'A Feminist Challenge to Tort Law', in A. Bottomley (ed) *Feminist Perspectives on the Foundational Subjects in Law*, London: Cavendish

Piaget, J. (1932) *The Moral Judgment of the Child*, New York: The Free Press

Posner, R. and Rosenfield, A. (1977) 'Impossibility and Related Doctrine in Contract Law: An Economic Analysis', *Journal of Legal Studies*, 6: 83

Richardson, J. (2007) 'The Law and the Sublime; Rethinking the Self and Its Boundaries', *Law and Critique*, 18: 229–52

Smith, S. (2006) *Atiyah's Introduction to the Law of Contract*, 6th edn, Oxford: Clarendon

Stanton, K. (2012) 'Legislating for Economic Loss', in T.T. Arvind and J. Steele (eds) *Tort Law and the Legislature: Common Law, Statute, and the Dynamics of Legal Change*, Oxford: Hart Publishing

Steele, J. (2011) 'Satisfying Claims? Money, Tort, and Damages in Consumer Societies', in *Social and Legal Studies* (forthcoming)

—— (2012) 'The Law Reform (Contributory Negligence) Act 1945: Dynamics of Legal Changes', in T.T. Arvind and J. Steele (eds) *Tort Law and the Legislature: Common Law, Statute, and the Dynamics of Legal Change*, Oxford: Hart Publishing

Waddams, S. (2011) *Principle and Policy in Contract Law: Competing or Complementary Concepts?*, Cambridge: Cambridge University Press

Weinrib, E. (1995) *The Idea of Private Law*, Harvard: Harvard University Press

Wightman, J. (2000) 'Intimate Relationships, Relational Contract Theory, and the Reach of Contract' *Feminist Legal Studies*, 8: 93–131

Chapter 3

Endgame: On Negligence and Reparation for Harm

Nicky Priaulx

Introduction

The central query of this chapter is the extent to which the law of negligence *should* expand to better accommodate our human experience of personal harm and injury. It is well recognised that the law of negligence falls far short of offering universal coverage in responding to harm. As Conaghan and Mansell note, 'While some kinds of harms are easily assimilated within the traditional corpus of law, others do not lend themselves so easily to tortuous characterization' (1999: 161). In social life, while it may seem obvious that a serious harm has been sustained, in negligence some claims quickly fall between the floorboards. This may be owing to the absence of fault, or the inability to show a causal link, however, of interest here are those kinds of harms which negligence struggles to admit, and those which it treats as thoroughly unproblematic.

As the following discussion explores in the context of human harms, negligence illustrates a continued preference for physical bodily harm in determinations of actionability. Only on rare occasions does the damage concept acknowledge harms which flow from anything other than a physical bodily injury. While many of us might think of a physical injury such as a fractured skull as evidently harmful, where the *preference* for physical bodily harms in negligence operates perniciously is by virtue of what is generally excluded: harms, which though often just as serious and potentially corrosive of life, fail to manifest themselves principally through the physical body, but rather admit of a psycho-social nature.

That the damage concept operates so exclusively has attracted an extensive critical commentary. For many, negligence is open to criticism for being unprincipled, inegalitarian and capricious, as well as embracing archaic views of humanity which smack of unreality. Undeniably this raises the global concern of the operation of torts and its societal efficacy. In so far as that preoccupies most mainstream tort theorists, as all the contributions to this collection emphasise, it is *also* critical to centralise a feminist perspective which looks at the *particular* operation of torts. In so far as negligence has operated to *generally* exclude harms of a psycho-social character (which in theory applies to all), once we scratch below the formal surface of that policy, we find a less than universal impact or distribution. An analysis of the damage concept illustrates a long-standing neglect of harms which women suffer, as women. Tort law, as Conaghan argues, 'while quick to defend and protect interests traditionally valued by men, is slow to respond to concerns which typically involve women, for example, sexual harassment or sexual abuse' (Conaghan 1996: 48). In this respect then, if the aim is for a fairer system, any reform agenda will need to pay close attention to the general and the particular operation of legal policy.

How negligence should develop to address these weighty concerns presents an enormous jurisprudential challenge. Negligence cannot accommodate all 'harms' so a choice must be made as to which are accommodated. In the face of an emerging set of claims which present hair-splitting scenarios, in having the look and feel of a conventional personal injury case but lacking the physical bodily damage strictly demanded, this chapter argues that what is becoming increasingly apparent is the absence of a robust normative justification to guide the courts as to where those lines should be drawn. Commentators are also divided on the question and generally fall into two broad camps: those who advocate that negligence *extends* to accommodate broader harms, these being every bit as real and harmful as physical ones; and those who determine that the boundaries of negligence should be preserved by *restricting* its remit to address only the repercussions of physical bodily harms. Irrespective of whether that produces arbitrary and unfair results, negligence must have limits. These two positions leave us with quite a stark choice – between incrementally bolting on new forms of harm to existing kinds of damage recognised, or restricting it to a narrow range of harms which fail to speak to the experiences and life dialogues of many which tort ought to speak to.

As the chapter notes, neither position presents a genuine solution once we consider the broader operation of negligence law. What both positions overlook are quite foundational questions concerning how negligence operates in practice, and the thorny question as to what we hope to achieve through providing reparation for harm via negligence. This is the 'endgame' question which the chapter urges that we now need to address: why do we provide redress at all? It is now critical that reformers, and indeed those seeking to advance women's interests, return to ask really foundational questions of torts and to more closely scrutinise taken-for-granted ideas which have shaped not only the damage concept, but the reparative ideal itself.

To illustrate the kind of foundational thinking the author has in mind, the chapter focuses on the most taken-for-granted kind of harm: physical bodily harm. The issue here is *not* the priority afforded to by contrast with psycho-social harms, but rather the 'common sense' notion that physical bodily harm is experienced as universally and especially harmful and causative of serious loss. Insights from behavioural science and litigation practice not only raise serious questions which go to the core of what negligence *is*, but ultimately raises doubts as to the potential of negligence to *ever* operate as an egalitarian system.

Challenging the preference for corporeal harm

In the law of negligence, 'damage' holds a central role and is said to form the 'gist of the action' (Stapleton 1988: 213). Therefore, a claimant will not only need to establish a duty of care, a breach of that duty, and that the breach has caused the damage complained of – she must also show that the type of harm she has suffered is one that is accepted by the law as 'actionable'. Though the concept of 'damage' is poorly defined in negligence, the suffering of a 'plain and obvious physical injury' presents no problem (Atiyah 1997: 94). Therefore, gastroenteritis suffered through swallowing parts of a snail in a bottle of ginger beer, cancer or lung diseases suffered through exposure to asbestos in the workplace, will most certainly constitute physical harms for the purposes of negligence (Witting 2002). Beyond these so-called 'obvious' injuries things become more complex. Defined under section 38(1) of the Limitation Act 1980, 'personal injury' 'includes any disease and any impairment of a person's physical or mental condition'. Yet while that definition of personal injury seems to allow for a more expansive reading in also addressing mental harms, in terms of what kind of injury may trigger an actionable claim in negligence, it is well known that emotional harm, which falls short of psychiatric illness (such as mere anxiety, inconvenience or discomfort), is never actionable, while a medically verified psychiatric illness is only actionable under limited circumstances.[1] As such, the concept of damage as it relates to human harm constitutes a remarkably narrow category; as Lord Hoffmann noted in *Rothwell v Chemical and Insulating Co Ltd* [2007]:

> Damage in this sense is an abstract concept of *being worse off*, physically or economically, so that compensation is an appropriate remedy. It does not mean simply a change in physical condition, which is consistent with making one better, as in the case of a successful operation, or with being neutral, having no perceptible effect upon one's health or capacity.
>
> (*Rothwell v Chemical and Insulating Co Ltd* [2007]: [7]; my emphasis)

No reference is made to emotional harm as a form of damage; such harm is treated as a category of consequential loss for which one must first establish prior physical damage. Other than the narrowly circumscribed situations where claimants can demonstrate that a duty of care exists to protect them from purely psychological harm, anything short of that, claimants must demonstrate the prior existence of a physical injury 'hook' for emotional harms to be recoverable (Stapleton 1988).

It is at this point, the boundary between actionability and non-actionability, that the operation of the damage concept becomes objectionable. It is an exclusive category that acts as the gatekeeper for financial reparation. As such, while there is no problem in saying that generally a duty of care will be owed for a more than negligible physical injury which results from a positive act of a defendant, in relation to psycho-social harms the same cannot be said. The kind of harm matters, and in so far as the law has general anxieties about the character of psycho-social harms and holding defendants liable for these, no matter how serious or disabling the harm that results and how careless the defendant, claimants will struggle to gain reparation for their loss. While there are established instances where psychological harm is treated as damage,[2] the courts restrict the liability situations via the concept of duty. As such, if psychological harm is a kind of damage, it is tenaciously guarded and ring-fenced. Though conceptually capable of embracing a broader understanding of what 'damage' means, far beyond physical bodily trauma, the law of negligence eyes with suspicion harms which manifest themselves not as bodily abnormalities, but as psycho-social tragedies.

That the damage concept works to offer minimal recognition of harms of a purely psycho-social nature has been the subject matter of a lengthy and voluminous critique. The modern day consensus tends to point to the absence of justification for drawing distinctions between physical harm and psycho-social harm. The thrust of commentary suggests that if one searches for a robust justification as to *why* or *how* lines can be drawn between such harms, one will struggle to find it. As Conaghan and Mansell (1999: 35) comment, 'physical injury is often accompanied by emotional distress while psychiatric harm is regularly exhibited through an array of physical symptoms (such as vomiting, insomnia, weight loss and other 'stress-related' illnesses)'. While medicine and science illustrate the 'close and symbiotic relationship between mental and physical health', the distinction between these categories nevertheless remains 'deeply embedded in the doctrinal substance of negligence law' (Conaghan and Mansell 1999: 35). Much of what can be said to be deleterious about a physical state, *is* psychological and subjective. Pain, for example, while having physiological dimensions has psycho-somatic ones too; it is also a 'social and cultural phenomenon' (Winance 2006: 1110).

The arbitrariness inherent in such line drawing becomes more evident once we contemplate our own subjective experience. In view of how *we* feel, the assumption that physical harm makes us especially 'worse off' or provides an objective means of assessing when serious harm has occurred, rather crumbles. If we consider the impact of different events that we experienced, from a physical ail such as a broken leg, to events which are not strictly speaking, *physical*, such as the loss of a loved one, to caring for a sick and elderly parent – all of these events are mediated through persons possessing bodies with remarkably similar effects. Whilst they endure they can prove to be psychologically and socially corrosive in their impact. They relate to our emotional being in the world, and our connections with, and responsibilities to, others. They possess physical and emotional dimensions in so far as they can result in declines in physical and mental health, but often imperceptibly and gradually; they often entail hard work, both physically and emotionally, in supporting others. Many of these can be regarded as chosen situations, but structurally they will feel unavoidable. These kinds of experiences may be part of the package of life, but for as long as they endure they keep us standing in the same spot. They can disable us. It is in this important sense that these experiences fail to differ from the experience of injuring oneself skiing in terms of the meaning of our lives and interference with the things we most value. If one considers the effects of dealing with that broken leg is that one suffers pain, has to reorganise how to get around, cannot play football for the time being and must endure the hassle of frequent hospital visits, we start to see how the assumption that physical harms are different in nature from other kinds of harms, looks rather artificial indeed. On this analysis at least, if we think about the precise way that any of these events might interfere with our lives, our hopes and aspirations, when destabilising events are the product of negligence, there seems to be no sound theoretical basis for calling one set of experiences 'life' and another 'injury'.

For some, however, the events which harm them may quickly be deemed 'life' by virtue of the line drawn between physical and psycho-social harms. For example, too often the harms that women sustain as women, have fallen into the 'vicissitudes' or 'life' category as is demonstrated by the slow recognition of mental disturbance as a legally cognisable harm, or through the scaling back of meaningful compensation for parents of unwanted children born as a result of negligence in family planning procedures (see *McFarlane v Tayside Health Board* [2000]; Priaulx 2007). That tort fails to 'see' many of the injuries that women sustain as women – of reproductivity, pregnancy, childbirth and the emotional and life capital lost through caring for a child that one had planned not to have – is deeply embedded within the analytical categories that control liability and remedies. These categories are not objective but require 'substantive choices to be made about which claimed injuries it will remedy' (Lieberman 1977: 63). Because categories such as damage reflect a choice as to which aspects of human social life should be treated as injurious, we need to be watchful as to which, and more particularly, whose social experiences it picks up. As Conaghan comments:

> [I]njury has a social as well as an individual dimension: people suffer harm not just because they are individuals but also because they are part of a particular class, group, race or gender. Moreover, their membership of that particular class, group, race or gender can significantly shape the nature and degree of the harm they sustain. The problem with law then is its failure to recognize that social dimension. Consequently, and in the context of gendered harms, it fails to offer proper redress.
>
> (Conaghan 1996: 408)

In all of these respects then the preference for physical harm over harms of a psycho-social nature not only serves to draw lines between kinds of harm, but entire categories of victim whose biographies express harm in ways that fail to fit the dominant dialogue of negligence law. Under such circumstances, tort will behave as if the experiences which harm and injure us are simply part of the normal (rather than injured) life course. For example, it is only since the late 1970s that sexual harassment has been transformed from behaviour widely regarded as a 'harmless' part of normal human engagement to behaviour constituting sex discrimination, deserving of a legal response (Conaghan 2002). And it is important here to recognise how these analytical categories can march on for decades whilst failing to speak to the innumerate experiences of classes and populations of people to whom it officially purports to apply to. In the context of emotional harms, as Martha Chamallas and Jennifer Wriggins argue, while the traditional justification was that the law was directed at protecting material interests and physical harm, leaving emotions and relationships beyond legal protection, this 'basic demarcation line had important gender implications for compensation':

> [L]osses typically suffered by men were often associated with the more highly-valued physical realm, whilst losses typically suffered by women were relegated to the lower-valued realm of the emotional or relational.
>
> (Chamallas and Wriggins 2010: 37–8)

And that privileging of physical harm over emotional harm 'persists to this day' (Chamallas and Wriggins 2010: 38). As a vast body of feminist literature powerfully illustrates in making visible the manner by which law has excluded those experiences and risks which either exclusively, or more frequently pertain to the biographical experience of being a woman (see Conaghan 1996; Graycar and Morgan 2002; West 1997) the concern for negligence law to reflect psycho-social harms is more than a wish for inclusive symbolism. The question of the kinds of harms picked up has serious repercussions in relation to which injuries, and indeed very often, *whose* injuries are addressed by tort.

The litany of problems attending the preference for physical bodily harm in negligence is not, of course, *news*. What is perhaps most surprising is that negligence *continues* to operate in this way despite long-standing and wide-spread cognisance of the serious problems attending the kinds of harms that negligence addresses and those that it does not. Judges have long recognised that harms of a psycho-social nature 'may be far more debilitating than physical harm' (Lord Steyn in *White v Chief Constable of South Yorkshire Police* [1999]: 492), yet remain prepared to continue restricting recovery for purely psychological harm. However, an emerging genus of case, the 'damage hybrid', seems set to pose the most serious challenge to established boundaries of the damage concept. Such cases make even more transparent the serious shortcomings of the operation of the damage concept, and in the wake of such claims, it will be correspondingly even more difficult for the judiciary to restrict recovery in a principled way.

Arguably, claims for purely psychological damage via 'nervous shock' constituted the first serious assault on the damage concept in easing negligence towards admitting harms of a purely psycho-social nature. These cases demanded explicit consideration as to the limits of negligence and its receptiveness to different kinds of harms. While these cases now receive some level of recognition and have required the courts to address the assumptions underpinning the dichotomy between physical injury and harms of a psycho-social nature, these claims continue to be treated restrictively. However, what could be termed 'damage hybrid' cases or what Horsey and Rackley refer to as claims for 'messed up lives' (2011: 160), might well constitute the second assault. Holding strong psycho-social and practical dimensions, these hybrid claims sit somewhere in between two recognised forms of damage in negligence law: first, the conventional personal injury case which involves an unproblematic form of physical bodily injury, and secondly, that of the purely psychological damage via 'nervous shock' situation, in particular where a primary victim sustains psychiatric trauma as a result of narrowly escaping physical injury (see, for example, *Page v Smith* [1996]). As the next section explores, though meeting with varying levels of success, the 'hybrid damage' cases have very ably revealed the arbitrariness and lack of principle attending the damage concept because these cases look *so much* like the conventional personal injury case in all but the specific kind of damage sustained. Moreover, and quite critically, what is particularly striking is that the courts have shown an increased willingness to depart from the idea that strictly bodily physical harm is necessary to satisfy damage. Whilst greater acceptance of such claims will be welcomed by some in starting to address the weighty criticism attending the narrow interpretation of the damage concept, for others, this will be one incremental step too far.

On the limits of legal incrementalism

Incrementalism, where categories like damage grow in order to encompass a broader range of situations and harms which had not previously been actionable, is part and parcel of the legal enterprise. With a few peaks and troughs en route, the tort of negligence itself has emerged literally out of a case involving alleged snail remains in a bottle of ginger beer (*Donoghue v Stevenson* [1932]) into the 'super-size' tort that it is today to cover a broad range of liability situations which a century ago would have been unthinkable.[3] For some palates, its super-size nature is too much to stomach. Patrick Atiyah, for example, complained that concepts of fault, causation and harm, the 'very concept of negligence', have been stretched out of all recognition in the 'favour of injured accident victims' (Atiyah 1997: 32) with the effect that 'the whole system is shot through with absurdity and unreality' (1997: 94). Central to Atiyah's concern was the increased recognition of harms within negligence, lamenting that, 'at one time damages for injury, especially personal injury, were almost entirely confined to cases where the victim suffered a plain and obvious physical injury' (Atiyah 1997: 52). Also concerned with such expansionist tendencies is Tony Weir, who comments that, 'it is undeniable that the progressive socialization of harm diminishes the responsibility, indeed the autonomy, of the individual' (Weir 2001). For those on the other side of the fence, this talk of stretching is problematic for defending the status quo, which amounts to being content with a system of redress that treats like harms *un*alike and operates to systematically disadvantage individuals whose experience of harm fail to fit under-socialized legal categories. As Conaghan comments:

> from a feminist perspective it is difficult to see how the autonomy of women is diminished by developments which facilitate legal redress in the contexts of acts of sexual violence and abuse, raising a question as to *whose* autonomy Weir perceives to be threatened.
>
> (Conaghan 2003: 186)

Crudely speaking, these two sides of the debate pretty much typify the arguments around the kinds of harms that the concept of damage in negligence should accommodate and the direction that law should take. As the historical development of negligence shows in relation to the poor recognition of non-physical harms, the law would appear to reflect a strong conservative pull, but challenging times lie ahead. While the damage concept has been typified as the subject matter of 'academic neglect' (Nolan 2007: 60), as an analytical category, far greater interest can now be discerned in the question as to the boundaries of this concept by both academics and, *critically*, lawyers. The incremental urge to expand categories of negligence in the name of equality and fairness, or indeed to line the pockets of lawyers, seems sensationally attractive.

The 'damage hybrid' looms hard here. Suits for wrongful conception (see *McFarlane v Tayside Health Board* [2000], *Rees v Darlington Memorial Hospital NHS Trust* [2003]), to claims for the careless destruction of sperm samples (*Yearworth and others v North Bristol NHS Trust* [2009]) are certainly recent and controversial illustrations of legal inventiveness where the factual variants had failed to squarely fit 'orthodox conceptions' of personal injury and damage. The success of the educational neglect claims alleging damage in the context of the failure to ameliorate dyslexia, though initially baffling the courts as to whether the damage should be typified as a mental injury sufficient to constitute a personal injury or a form of economic loss (*Phelps v London Borough of Hillingdon* [2001]), were later accepted as claims for personal injury 'in a post-Cartesian World' (Lord Hoffmann *Adams v Bracknell* [2004]: [10]). Even judges themselves can be artful at unwittingly pushing at the boundaries of damage. Though failing to fit what the damage concept in negligence requires, notably physical bodily harm, by a majority the House of Lords in *Rees* created a 'Conventional Award' of £15,000 that would apply to all cases of wrongful conception to reflect the loss of autonomy experienced as a result of unsolicited parenthood. In so far as the present author saw this more as a consolation prize in the face of denying a proper remedy (Priaulx 2007), others see the award as representing 'a significant departure from previous categories of recognised harm' (Nolan 2007: 71) towards a more 'rights-based' conception of damage. While Nolan's reflection on such cases prompts him to suggest that the expansion of the categories of actionable damage 'should be welcomed as evidence' that courts are not privileging interests capable of precision in monetary terms over those which are not, like the intangible harms (2007: 87), that kind of conclusion seems slightly overcooked. Nevertheless, undeniably these developments constitute a quite significant shift away from a strict conception of damage as physical bodily harm, and towards a broader conception of harm that is *more* capable of accommodating critical aspects of our humanity.

For the doom-monger, this will surely be the opening of Pandora's Box, for in the wake of that shift, heavy intellectual challenges potentially lie before the court where lawyers will seek to capitalise upon the shifting boundaries of damage. Hybrid claims deeply challenge these demarcation lines because unlike the, say, bystander claims involving purely psychological injury, these cases look very similar to the contexts in which conventional personal injury claims arise. Where the circumstances look so hair-splittingly similar, courts keen to restrict negligence will be left having to draw flawed distinctions between physical harm and psycho-social harm – a distinction which, as we have noted, seems impossible to do. This will be a major challenge for English law. Cases faring less well in the past for failing to demonstrate an obvious physical injury or satisfy the requirements of primary victim status may be repackaged for success. For example, while the action of claimants suffering distress after being trapped in a lift failed on the grounds of there being no actionable damage in *Reilly v Merseyside Regional Health Authority* (1995), cases involving negligent imprisonment might more convincingly run in serious instances where claimants have been deprived of their liberty, given the importance of 'freedom of movement as an interest in its own right' (Nolan 2007: 63). For some, the educational neglect claims, whilst only intended to apply to cases involving an undiagnosed and untreated learning disorder, constitute the starting point for a range of broader challenges (Harris 2000); on compelling facts, the right to education might seem sensibly embraced within the damage concept and only a small incremental step away from *Phelps*. From these kinds of cases, to the reproductive torts, it is not difficult to imagine factual variants. While the Court of Appeal in *Yearworth* found that the destruction of cancer survivors' stored sperm admitted an actionable claim, the principle seems barely stretched by extending this to permit claims for the wrong embryo being implanted, and indeed to all the claimants thereby affected. It is just one small step. These and even further reaching claims, such as sex ratio skewing of an entire community as a result of environmental pollution (Scott 2010) suggest that a broader conception of damage at least sends out a wider invitation to 'have a go'. Meantime, the pressure for negligence law to adopt a more generous approach to the highly restricted purely psychological damage-via-shock cases, continues unabated (Teff 2009). The point, however, is this: the greater recognition of the hybrid claim and shift away from an admittedly capricious notion of damage changes the legal landscape.

What has been claimed to constitute a second assault on the damage principle, via these hybrid injuries, may turn out to be the most serious. It is questionable whether the courts have sufficient conceptual resources to cope with such cases. Their resemblance to the conventional personal injury case creates such a strong moral case for extending damage to embrace these in revealing the arbitrariness of the lines currently drawn between physical and psycho-social harms. There is, arguably, no real difference that can be discerned as to the circumstances of the case, other than the nature of the damage sustained. Yet to suggest that these individuals are *not* harmed, or that their suffering is less than that which would be sustained by virtue of a physical bodily injury, seems absurd. The moment that the courts discern a greater inquisitiveness into the psycho-social aspects of these cases, the line between deserving and undeserving cases will fall away. So much of what it means to be injured and harmed is located at psycho-social level. As such, some well-meaning commentators might argue, the appropriate response to this incoherence and unfairness would be for the law to expand so as to encompass them.

At the same time, we should be reflective about the nature of the hybrid claim, about expansionism generally, and what this heralds for the law. Given the variety of situations that have arisen thus far, from frustrated reproductive plans, to deprivations of liberty, it is difficult to conceptualise a sensible 'endgame' position here, for two reasons. First, while the courts are open to criticism for their heavily reliance upon the floodgates argument in the context of purely psychological damage – which appears speculative in the absence of evidence or a comparative analysis of jurisdictions who seem far less troubled by the prospect of broader liability in the context of occasional but avoidable catastrophe as to discount it (Diaz 2010) – the hybrid claims nevertheless *do* seem to raise different considerations. The circumstances which shape them are amorphous, unlimited and could arise in virtually any sphere of normal daily life. For those that would point to the capability of other essential ingredients of negligence concepts to fend off the floodgates to manage a more fluid damage concept, this appears fairly myopic given the extent to which all the concepts of negligence are conceptually linked and quite critically informed by the damage sustained. As such a loosening of the damage concept beyond physical harms alone may achieve little, or too much, as to constitute a significant if not irreparable breach in the sea-wall. Arguably, *arbitrariness* in determining which kinds of damage should be the subject matter of redress may be the thing that sustains the negligence tort itself.

The second consideration as to 'endgame' is by far the most important, for what is questionable is what might be gained by extending negligence to accommodate broader harms in the sense of what precisely that can do *for humanity*. A striking feature of the debates highlighted here is how disconnected these are from what constitute pretty fundamental weaknesses attending the torts system. Though there are compelling moral and legal grounds for extending negligence, many of the 'advances' we perceive ourselves as making within the law start to look somewhat partial when situated in their broader social context. Take, for example, the efforts of scholars to extend the law of tort to recognise traditionally excluded forms of injuries in the name of 'equality'[4] – this really boils down to 'equality' *within* tort. Tort law abiding by the principle of equality in the sense of drawing no formal distinctions between individuals on the pure grounds of gender, race or ability, must surely be viewed as significant – at least gains for those that come before the law. Beyond aspirations for equality *within* negligence, the overall social accomplishment will be a great deal harder to make out. If one takes into account the fact that tort reaches a rather small (and privileged) community of injured beneficiaries, that many injuries are sustained without fault and in ways that tort simply does not capture, that many claims are settled and never reach court, and that our response to injury is financial compensation, equality gains start to look far less impressive *outside* of tort. And whatever benefits torts can deliver decline further once we heap on the other known limitations of torts which Patrick Atiyah and others have so ably alerted us to through engagements with how the system works in *practice* (see, for example, Lewis 2006).

The point is this: we have been so concerned with making gains *within* the law that we have neglected to *address* the system as a whole. The gains made within the system may serve largely rhetorical ends because of the way that negligence really works. For the feminist legal project this poses a sizeable dilemma. Extending the damage principle to humanise tort and embrace the kinds of experiences which profoundly harm us may be a laudable aim in theory, but in practice we are only reaching a limited and privileged range of beneficiaries, in a highly limited way – with money (see further, Priaulx, forthcoming). Hybrid claims, I think, strongly compel some reflection as to how we respond to harm, and the limits of our current approach. Though the arguments that financial compensation is not commensurable with harms of an intangible nature and cannot 'restore' tend to be commercially motivated and consciously designed to encourage policy-makers to cap or abolish such awards (Janutis 2006), there is nevertheless something in the claims. There is no doubt that the hybrid cases looked at here can resonate in economic loss, however, like physical harms, most will also possess a significant intangible component too. We would do well to consider whether financial compensation might be a rather lazy and impoverished means of providing account to victims for the non-economic consequences of injury whether stemming from physical injury or, indeed, 'messed up lives'. Either way, it looks like something less than a genuine account for the losses victims do sustain.

None of this is to say that no advances have been achieved through, for example, feminist legal activism in extending torts to embrace broader harms, but simply that our efforts may achieve diminishing returns *within* tort. We might have become a little too addicted to 'bolting on' new forms of harm because this seems like the right thing to do, but possibly to the neglect of other tasks which will be every bit as important for achieving equality for all: notably checking to see whether the foundations upon which we build are solid. This should of course compel an analysis of the broader problems ailing the negligence system, but here I wish to concentrate on one specific issue which strikes me as critical in assessing both the boundaries of the damage concept and the efficacy of negligence as a system of redress for human harm and injury: the foundational assumptions attending physical harm. In so far as a concern has been raised here as to what we are 'building' upon, the taken-for-granted nature of physical injuries as being *especially* harmful, is one that tends to get overlooked.

Physical harms and serious effects

Debate around the question of whether psycho-social harms should be recognised as a form of damage has been typically polarised. If one gets drawn into this debate (which is easy to do), the decision is between these positions, or marginal variants lying in between. However, the moment that one endeavours to stand outside of them, one starts to see that the difficulty with the arguments on *both* sides is that they end up reaffirming what negligence is *already* doing. If we consider what is unquestioned throughout, physical harm stands as the assumed common denominator: one restricts damage to that, or *adds* to it. For those seeking to *extend* damage to accommodate psycho-social harm, the argument is typically grounded by showing how *similar* psycho-social injuries are in their effects to physical ones – and that those effects are *just as serious*. It is a perfect analogical argument which makes incremental shifts difficult to resist: if 'B' looks like 'A', and 'A' is well-accepted and established, the law should treat like cases alike by allowing 'B' also.

For the time being we will focus on well-established 'A' rather than getting bogged down in the question of whether the law should expand to accommodate type 'B'. The idea that negligence ought to prioritise injuries which result in the *most serious* consequences goes to the heart of all the issues explored thus far. From the perspective of justice to tortfeasors and indeed, claimants, it offers the strongest philosophical and conceptual basis for establishing which negligently caused injuries the law recognises (those which go beyond what everyone is expected to tolerate in daily life), and those it does not. Both Abraham Maslow (1971) and Joel Feinberg (1987), for example, offered lengthy analyses vindicating the notion that physical harms were ones which were the most invasive of our human needs and as such one might surmise that they are deserving of the most vigorous legal protection. This would, to a large degree, appear to be in line with the law. While the conceptual basis for why the damage concept privileges physical bodily harms is unclear, one may infer that this is based on assumptions that, either these are the *most serious*, and/or objectively safe determinants of serious effects. We should start reviewing some of these assumptions.

Physical harm and hedonic adaptation

Though not focused on law, the assumed relationship between injuries and their effects has been the subject of analysis in hedonic psychology, or what to us lawyers might best be labelled 'happiness studies' in so far as the dominant measure used in a controversial theory called 'hedonic adaption' or, more recently, 'adaptive preferences', is happiness. In the original theory, Brickman and Campbell (1971) proposed that while people react to good and bad events, in a short time they return to a position of neutrality. The authors found that because people are goal-seeking in nature and constantly strive to be happy, happiness and unhappiness merely constituted temporary and short-lived reactions to such events. In what became a classic piece of research, Brickman and his colleagues sought to provide empirical backing to the theory and from this concluded that lottery winners were not happier than non-winners, and that people with paraplegia were not substantially less happy than those who can walk. As Diener et al comment, the appeal of the study lay in it not only offering an explanation 'for the observation that people appear to be relatively stable in happiness despite changes in fortune' but also in explaining why 'people with substantial resources are sometimes no happier than those with few resources and that people with severe problems are sometimes quite happy' (Diener, Lucas and Schollon, 2006: 306).

At intuitive level, the theory has appeal. If we consider all the good and bad events that have occurred in our lives, our joy at getting a new job, our heartache at the loss of a loved one, we will note that the impact of emotions felt at that time, later wore off. For many of us, we do indeed get used to things, and they (hopefully) become the background in the context of the events that lie ahead. But to what extent can this observation be useful to law? Of interest here, Bagenstos and Schlanger (2006) sought to apply this theory directly to the law of damages. What they claimed was that hedonic damages in the United States should not be awarded based on disability. This head of damages broadly corresponds with aspects of intangible damages in the UK[5] in so far as it compensates for the limitations on 'the injured person's ability to participate in and derive pleasure from the normal activities of daily life, or for the individual's inability to pursue his talents, recreational interests, hobbies or vocations' (Bagenstos and Schlanger 2006: 3). In something of a double-pronged attack on the practice of awarding hedonic damages, the authors placed strong reliance upon hedonic psychology noting that 'disability does not inherently limit enjoyment of life to the degree that these courts suggest. Rather, people who experience disabling injuries tend to adapt to their disabilities' (Bagenstos and Schlanger 2006: 4). Arguing that such damages and the processes of litigation might also be viewed as discriminatory, the authors claim that the legal process serves to reinforce stigma around disability in presenting disability as 'a tragedy' (Bagenstos and Schlanger 2006: 27).

Of interest here is the promise and the limits of using insights from hedonic psychology to inform our analysis about the link between physical damage, effects and compensability. An important starting point is to note that the body of research around hedonic adaptation is very much work-in-progress and has produced contradictory results. Diametrically opposing findings as to the extent of adaptation can be found elsewhere (see, for example, Sharanjit 2006; Fuhrer 1992). Easterlin notes that 'there is a demonstrable tendency in the psychological literature to overstate the extent of adaptation to life events', and that the extent of adaptation to a disabling condition may 'vary depending on the personality or other characteristics of the individual affected' (Easterlin 2003: 11177) while Diener et al have cautioned against putting adaptation theory into practice given the many questions that necessitate researchers' attention (Diener, Lucas and Schollon 2006: 312). For these main reasons, hedonic adaptation theory does not support the kinds of policy action that Bagenstos and Schlanger have reached.[6] In particular, the finding which seems to be repeated throughout the literature subsequent to Brickman's study, is that the central assumption of the hedonic treadmill theory, notably that adaption to circumstances occurs in similar ways for all individuals, is false. As Diener et al found in their longitudinal studies, 'the size and even the direction of the chance in life satisfaction varied considerably across individuals' (Diener, Lucas and Schollon 2006: 310).

There is, I think, good reason to be open to some of the (provisional) insights that hedonic psychology can offer, although a more measured analysis of the theory underpinning Bagenstos and Schlanger's proposals actually supports quite a different conclusion to the one they arrived at. Rather than limiting one's attention to damages, they compel a far more extensive review of the assumptions underpinning *damage*. Even if there is no evidence that all people adapt to the experience of disability, there is evidence that some do, and that the extent of adaptation will be variable, depending on a potentially wide range of factors relating to an individual's social, psychological and economic situation. Moreover, given that we should be alert to what assumptions are being made about disability, for these appear troublingly to equate disability with the living of a tragic life – an image of impairment which disability rights activists have fought so hard to combat – so too should we be alert to the assumptions which are being made by the law. Combined, the analysis highlights some really fundamental questions: the extent to which the damage concept in negligence accepts physical injury as a universally and especially harmful event causative of serious loss, and quite critically, what it is about the human experience of injury that compels redress.

The seriousness dilemma

Our analysis so far has been premised on the basis of what look like serious physical injuries. Yet to what extent does this parody the kinds of injuries that negligence addresses? In so far as the hedonic adaptation literature typically relates to serious injuries that would amount to a disability, our concerns around the assumptions attending physical harm are amplified further when we consider that very often the kinds of injuries compensated for in negligence fall far short of that. As Bell (2006) notes, whiplash injuries constitute a major source of claim, generating around 200,000 claims for compensation per annum, and costing insurers over £750 million per year. This is not to diminish the harmful impact of whiplash, but to note that not only do the majority of sufferers make very speedy recoveries, but it is 'rare for claimants to develop chronic symptoms or disability' (Bell 2006: 350). As a general matter, 'the condition is one of temporary discomfort and the award is for the "pain and suffering" of the claimant' (Bell 2006: 350). Such factors, which point to a significant disparity between the 'theory' of torts and what actually occurs in practice, also drives a cutting critique by Lewis where he notes:

> [T]he main function of the tort system is not to provide for the future loss of income and care needs of those seriously disabled by accident or disease. Such especially needy claimants are relatively rare. Instead the system overwhelm-ingly deals with small claims . . . In these cases claimants suffer very little, if any, financial loss. They make a full recovery from their bodily injury and have no continuing ill effects. They make no claim for any social security benefit as a result of their accident. . . . [I]n a few cases the damages claim, in effect, is being made only for the non-pecuniary loss. In settlements in general the largest component by far is the payment for pain and suffering. The stereo-typical injury is the minor whiplash which follows a low speed car 'shunt'. It is these types of cases which account for the extraordinarily high costs of the system compared to the damages it pays out.
>
> (Lewis 2001: 103)

From the perspective of 'seriousness' then, while some have suggested that 'much distress is the psychiatric equivalent of a cold or flu' and 'even when severe, much distress reflects threatening or discouraging circumstances that most individuals can resolve' (Mirowsky and Ross 2003: 29), so too, it might seem, can the same kind of considerations apply to physical harm. While negligence affords priority to physical harm, which holds an unproblematic status in law, we find the same inherent variability with physical harms as has been argued as constituting a problem with psycho-social ones. Some physical harms as they are suffered do not look terribly serious, and we also find that something of a practice is developing so that these less deleterious effects are being taken seriously. This is *not* to say that negligence does not deal with serious injuries, but rather that the 'fairy tale' version of negligence (or at least one that would provide some justification *for* negligence) is that this is what happens all the time. And in line with the thesis running here, that variability in the experience of harm is precisely what we would expect to find. Whether we are addressing a physical injury or not, it is the psycho-social *effects* that harm us.

An alternative basis for determining actionability has been suggested by Teff (2009) in his analysis of liability for negligently caused psychiatric and emotional harms. Amongst his suggestions of how to address the problem of where 'the law places its marker as representing damage deserving of compensation' he proposes that there should be a 'uniform monetary threshold that excludes minor, transient harm, whether physical, psychiatric or emotional' (Teff 2009: 183–4). Noting that such a monetary threshold would 'admittedly introduce a new element of arbitrariness into the existing legal framework for mental harm', he comments that it would mean that the law could 'relinquish the many other arbitrary elements which have made that framework so unsatisfactory' (Teff 2009: 184). While his proposals merit lengthier analysis than can be provided here, in so far as they appear to offer a fairer basis for compensating victims in relating to injurious effects rather than distinguishing between different kinds of damage, the key issue for our focus is on how precisely we evaluate seriousness.

If the assumption underlying the priority afforded to physical injuries is based on the notion that this constitutes the most objective evaluation of the kinds of injuries that are likely to result in serious effects, our analysis casts quite some doubt upon this. But what it also casts doubt upon is the process of evaluating seriousness too: who decides, and from whose perspective? If *fairness* is at issue, evaluations of seriousness cannot be made at objective level, though arguably this is what the 'damage' concept was geared up to do. This is still what would be required under Teff's proposals, for one still has to draw lines between compensable and non-compensable kinds of harm. Despite his remark that 'there will always be hard cases at the margins' (Teff 2009: 184), one has to suspect that enterprising lawyers will press hard against those margins. Moreover, we could expect to see a fresh form of arbitrariness emerging under such proposals. Two individuals can suffer the same event, yet manage the consequences in dramatically different ways. Beyond the trite remark that our personalities and managing capabilities are different, much of this will depend upon the social contexts in which we are embedded; a person of reasonable means with a supportive web of relations is probably better situated to cope with the effects of injury. In this sense, while the fairest means of establishing the effects of injury and its consequential psycho-social effects will be from the subjective perspective of the victim, and as such will be variable, this creates an enormous challenge for the law, jurisprudentially and practically.

Assessing which injuries should be compensated based on the effects, removes a significant control mechanism of negligence where liability depends on the nature of the harm wrongfully caused. In its absence, however, because of the variability that would be inherent in determining actionable claims it is not so clear that the law would be well equipped to maintain the boundaries of negligence, or indeed which essential ingredients become key indicators of how we 'treat like cases alike'.

Conclusion

For the time being then, we have quite a sizeable dilemma. An analysis of psycho-social harm suggests that there is no good reason for distinguishing between physical bodily injuries and other kinds of harm, at least if the seriousness of damage (which must surely lie in its effects) is at issue.[7] If seriousness is not at issue, this does not dispose of our critique, for then negligence is left without any justification for determining what is recognised as damage and what is not (and arguably, this might be *the* problem). All that remains is the argument that we need to maintain limits – yet that is a justification which fails for failing to be a justification. Yet an analysis of the same factors, and practical issues of how tort works, suggests that the current preference for physical harms in negligence is every bit as variable and unstable as harms of an intangible nature. What this tells us is that the *kind* of injury is an incredibly poor indicator for determinations of loss. Because loss is essentially felt at psycho-social level and this is highly variable, there will be no means of objectively determining seriousness. The manner and extent to which events prove harmful to us depend upon the biographical detail of our individual lives. So what this leaves us with is a choice: putting up with capricious lines which make fallacious assumptions about seriousness, harm and harming conditions, or of drawing no lines at all.

And it is a pretty stark choice. When we enquire about the extent to which negligence should reflect our human experience of injury we end up in what appears to be a no-win situation in attempting to establish a fair and inclusive means of providing redress for harm. The damage concept operates so as to be unfair, incoherent and serves to systematically exclude a range of claims that are every bit as deserving (often more so) as the majority of situations to which negligence affords priority, but here lies the rub: even if we make the damage concept *more* accommodating, these problems of unfairness, incoherence and systematic exclusion simply do *not* go away. Not only would a failure to draw lines between different kinds of harm (as well as stipulating the other circumstances by which tortious liability will occur) result in there being 'no realistic limit on the amount of liability that injurers would face' (Abraham 2001: 1209), but more broadly, negligence would not then be negligence. Any system which falls short of universal application, in so far as it distributes in an exclusive way, will and *must draw lines*. As such this inevitably involves making arbitrary choices between cases where it would be splitting hairs to determine the difference.

What this analysis supports then, is the need to think about negligence in a far more foundational way given that the problems attending the reparation of human harm seem inescapable. Our critique of the very psycho-social and practical factors that suggest intangible harms are just as harmful as physical ails ironically seems to squarely apply to *physical ails* despite it being taken-for-granted as an inevitably loss-generating category of harm. As such, a psycho-social critique serves to cast some measure of doubt on the availability of justifications for redress for *any* kind of injury. Indeed, what we find is that irrespective of the nature of the harm involved, negligence suffers from a striking absence of a clear and conceptually convincing basis for what harms we do include, why we include them and what we hope to do by responding to harm. But what is clear is that if the aim is *fairness*, and we wish to locate an equitable way of distributing the effects of harm and loss, negligence will not and *cannot* provide it.

Notes

1   Providing damage has been established (notably, of the physical sort), negligence has no problem in addressing intangible harms, such as psychological or emotional harms, as items of *consequential loss* for the purposes of damages. The distinction, though muddy at times, is that 'damage' concerns liability and is a crucial factor for an actionable claim, whereas items of consequential loss are only relevant for the assessment of damages, once liability has been established. With one exception in the field of human harms, notably the restrictive category of purely psychological damage cases which are only cognisable (and for which a duty is owed only) under highly circumscribed conditions, consequential loss cannot frame the damage itself.

2   See, for example, the purely psychological damage claims FKA 'nervous shock', ranging from the recognition of primary victims in cases such as *Page v Smith* (1996), through to the more restrictive category of secondary victims as demonstrated in *Alcock v Chief Constable of South Yorkshire Police* [1992]. See further, Horsey and Rackley (2011) and Teff (2009).

3   For engaging accounts of the development of negligence, see further Horsey and Rackley (2011), Weir (2000) and Ibbetson (1999).

4   See, for example, Chamallas and Wriggins (2010) in which the authors explore the doctrinal, practical and structural obstacles to gender and race equality, and advocate reforms that will extend tort law's protection to disadvantaged categories of person.

5   Note, however, that this is only a broad correspondence, and in particular with lost amenity. The basis for awarding damages for pain, suffering and loss of amenity (PSLA) has been identified as conceptually questionable (Ogus 1972) and continues to be so. Nevertheless, while there is no explicit reference to 'happiness' in PSLA awards, the motivation for awarding such damages appears fairly similar if seeking to restore the intangible effects of injury.

6   Problematically, the authors (who are lawyers, not psychologists) not only prove to be highly selective in the studies they include (those highlighting a high level of adaptation)

but overlook all of the serious concerns attending hedonic psychology (from hedonic psychologists). See Bagenstos and Schlanger (2006: 2).
7   In relation to asymptomatic pleural plaques, discussions around the damage concept very clearly intimate that seriousness (at least for Lord Hope in that particular case) is at issue: 'an injury which is without any symptoms at all because it cannot be seen or felt and which will not lead to some other event that is harmful has no consequences that will attract an award of damage. Damages are given for injuries that cause harm, not for injuries that are harmless' (Lord Hope in *Rothwell* [2007]: [47]).

Cases

Adams v Bracknell [2004] UKHL 29
Alcock v Chief Constable of South Yorkshire Police [1992] 1 AC 310
Donoghue v Stevenson [1932] AC 562
McFarlane v Tayside Health Board [2000] 2 AC 59
Page v Smith [1996] AC 155
Phelps v London Borough of Hillingdon [2001] 2 AC 619
Rees v Darlington Memorial Hospital NHS Trust [2003] UKHL 52
Reilly v Merseyside Regional Health Authority (1995) 6 Med LR 246
Rothwell v Chemical and Insulating Co Ltd and another [2007] UKHL 39
White v Chief Constable of South Yorkshire Police [1999] 2 AC 455
Yearworth and others v North Bristol NHS Trust [2009] EWCA Civ 37

Bibliography

Abraham, K.S. (2001) 'The Trouble With Negligence', *Vanderbilt Law Review*, 54: 1187–223
Atiyah, P.S. (1997) *The Damages Lottery*, Oxford: Hart Publishing
Bagenstos, S. and Schlanger, M. (2006) 'Hedonic Damages, Hedonic Adaptation and Disability', *Washington University in St Louis Faculty Working Paper Series* No 06-09-01
Bell, P. (2006) 'The Social Construction of Bodily Injury', *The Geneva Papers*, 31: 340–56
Brickman, P. and Campbell, D. (1971) 'Hedonic Relativism and Planning the Good Society', in M.H. Apley (ed) *Adaptation Level Theory: A Symposium*, New York: Academic Press
Chamallas, M. and Wriggins, J.B. (2010) *The Measure of Injury: Race, Gender and Tort Law*, New York: New York University Press
Conaghan, J. (1996) 'Gendered Harms and the Law of Tort: Remedying (Sexual) Harassment', *Oxford Journal of Legal Studies*, 16: 407–31
—— (2002) 'Law, Harm and Redress: A Feminist Perspective', *Legal Studies*, 22: 319–39
—— (2003) 'Tort Law and Feminist Critique', *Current Legal Problems*, 56: 175–209
Conaghan, J. and Mansell, W. (1999) *The Wrongs of Tort*, London: Pluto Press
Diaz, J.A. (2010) *Non-Physical Damage: A Comparative Perspective*, Canterbury, the University of Canterbury, New Zealand: Unpublished
Diener, E., Lucas, R. and Schollon, C. (2006) 'Beyond the Hedonic Treadmill: Revising the Adaptation Theory of Well-Being', *American Psychologist*, 61: 305–14
Easterlin, R. (2003) 'Explaining Happiness', *Proceedings of the National Academy of Sciences of the USA*, 100: 11176–83
Feinberg, J. (1987) *Harm to Others*, Oxford: Oxford University Press
Fuhrer, M. (1992) 'Relationship of Life Satisfaction to Impairment, Disability and Handicap

Among Persons with Spinal Cord Injury Living in the Community', *Archives of Physical Medicine and Rehabilitation*, 73: 552–7

Graycar, R. and Morgan, J. (2002) *The Hidden Gender of Law*, Sydney: Federation Press

Harris, N. (2000) 'Liability Under Education Law in the UK – How Much Further Can It Go?', *European Journal for Education Law and Policy*, 4: 131–40

Horsey, K. and Rackley, E. (2011) *Tort Law*, 2nd edn, Oxford: Oxford University Press

Ibbetson, D. (1999) *A Historical Introduction to the Law of Obligations*, Oxford: Oxford University Press

Janutis, R.M. (2006) 'Struggle over Tort Reform and the Overlooked Legacy of the Progressives', *Akron Law Review*, 39: 943–73

Lewis, R. (2001) 'Increasing the Price of Pain: Damages, The Law Commission and *Heil v Rankin*', *Modern Law Review*, 64(1): 100–11

—— (2006) 'The Politics and Economics of Tort Law: Judicially Imposed Periodical Payments of Damages', *Modern Law Review*, 69(3): 418–42

Lieberman, J.K. (1977) 'The Relativity of Injury', *Philosophy and Public Affairs*, 7(1): 60–73

Maslow, A. (1971) *The Farther Reaches of Human Nature*, New York: Penguin Books

Mirowsky, J. and Ross, C.E. (2003) *Social Causes of Psychological Distress*, Piscataway, New Jersey: Transaction Publishers

Nolan, D. (2007) 'New Forms of Damage in Negligence', *Modern Law Review*, 70(1): 59–88

Ogus, A. (1972) 'Damages for Lost Amenities: Damages for a Foot, a Feeling or a Function?', *Modern Law Review*, 35(1): 1–16

Priaulx, N. (2007) *The Harm Paradox: Tort Law and the Unwanted Child in an Era of Choice*, Aldershot: Routledge-Cavendish

—— (Forthcoming) 'On Law's Promise: Rethinking How We Think About Law's Limits', *Studies in Law, Politics and Society*

Scott, D. (2010) 'Injuries Without Remedies: Body Polluted: Questions of Scale, Gender and Remedy', *Loyola of Los Angeles Law Review*, 44: 121–56

Sharanjit, U. (2006) 'Impact of the Timing, Type and Severity of Disability on the Subjective Well-Being of Individuals with Disabilities', *Social Science & Medicine*, 63: 525–39

Stapleton, J. (1988) 'The Gist of Negligence', *The Law Quarterly Review*, 104: 213–38

Teff, H. (2009) *Causing Psychiatric and Emotional Harm: Reshaping the Boundaries of Legal Liability*, Oxford: Hart Publishing

Weir, T. (2000) *Tort Law*, London: Sweet & Maxwell

West, R. (1997) *Caring for Justice*, New York: New York University Press

Winance, M. (2006) 'Pain, Disability and Rehabilitation Practices: A Phenomenological Perspective', *Disability and Rehabilitation*, 28: 1109–18

Witting, C. (2002) 'Physical Damage in Negligence', *Cambridge Law Journal*, 61(1): 189–208

Chapter 4

Pollution and the Body Boundary: Exploring Scale, Gender and Remedy

Dayna Nadine Scott*

This chapter explores whether tort law can provide a remedy for the injury of 'endocrine disruption', at an individual or a collective level.[1] Endocrine disruption occurs when synthetic chemicals with structural similarities to common sex hormones 'trick' the body into triggering various biological processes and reactions. Many activists in the environmental justice movement want to be able to say unequivocally that the 'gender-bending' of endocrine disruption is a new, dramatic and horrifying harm. But taking the example of the declining sex ratio of the Aamjiwnaang First Nation, a Canadian aboriginal community experiencing chronic chemical pollution, demonstrates that finding a 'harm' or 'injury' in law is fraught with difficulties. On an individual level, an altered sex ratio (the number of boy babies born relative to the number of girls) cannot constitute a harm. No one mother could ever prove that she specifically was harmed; that she specifically should have conceived a boy. But her chances of welcoming a son seem to be less than they should be.[2] The concern, from the perspective of the First Nation, is essentially one of cultural survival. It is the collective loss of a viable future. Thus the notion of a collective harm highlights the fact that this problem is situated in the context of an aboriginal community already struggling, as many are, with stemming the loss of culture and tradition amongst their people. Further, because emerging environmental health harms are often localised and concentrated around the worst pollution sources, and because they tend to be distributed along race and class differentials, endocrine disruption is a central concern of the environmental justice movement.

Understanding the nature of contemporary pollution harms or 'injuries' is essential to the crafting of effective remedies. In particular, the chapter seeks to destabilise the tendency in the environmental justice movement to conceptualise harms on the basis of unquestioned assumptions about what is 'natural' and what is 'normal' through the application of contemporary feminist theory of the body. It also seeks to challenge tort scholars to imagine law differently. Legal scholars have begun exploring the idea that tort law is 'too corporeal' – that it is tethered too tightly to proof of physical damages – and should move towards the recognition of interests-based damage assessments in specific contexts. But even where recent scholarship in tort has included some calls for expansion of what should count as harm or physical damage, the scale at which we look to find such damage remains primarily at the level of the individual, the single unitary legal subject. Perhaps, as has been suggested, we should move away from assessing physical damage only on the basis of a 'factually observable' change in the physical structure of persons, and adopt a more contextual approach based on social perceptions of damage. The way that pollution manifests, and the blameworthiness of its perpetuation in certain communities, demands that tort law evolve, and that we, as legal scholars, work creatively to devise new legal remedies for emerging injuries.

This chapter offers a critique of tort remedies grounded in feminist theory of the body. It exposes how tort law is invested in a notion of an individuated legal subject, which in this case fails to capture the critical interconnectedness of bodies in a community inseparable from the social, political, historical and colonial context. The analysis considers various torts on a conceptual level, and what they might offer the Aamjiwnaang First Nation in the way of remedies. In each case, what the tort can do depends on how the injury, and the scale at which the entity taken to have suffered the injury, is conceived.

The chapter concludes that none of these remedies are adequately able to account for the way the pollution has saturated the community, been soaked up in bodies and altered social and cultural relations. But brainstorming around tort law's potential remedies, at various scales, allows for the body to be opened up – for the gender-bending synthetic chemicals flowing through bodies to become visible, for their free movement between individuals and their worlds to be exposed – to the point that our insistence on a fixed bodily boundary, and a centrally controlled self, begins to break down. Further, the analysis demonstrates that the scale at which we conceive of an 'injury' shapes the determination of whether the injury is seen as 'remediable', and on what terms. These conceptions and determinations then, in turn, shape ideas about the allocation of blame for the harm. Essentially, the argument is that our constructions of 'injury' – where and how we choose to find it – carry consequences for communities affected by contemporary pollution harms.

The chapter proceeds through three parts. I begin by reviewing the contamination of the Aamjiwnaang First Nation, and describe how the struggle of this small reserve community, and its members' campaign against endocrine disruption, has garnered the attention of environmental justice activists worldwide. Next, I explain how tort law might conceive of the harm or the 'injury' that is visited on the Aamjiwnaang community, including what the gender dimension of that harm might be. Finally, I begin to brainstorm around the way that various torts might operate at different scales of injury to provide a remedy for the Aamjiwnaang people.

The contamination of Aamjiwnaang First Nation[3]

The Aanishinaabek people of Aamjiwnaang First Nation live on a reserve located immediately adjacent to Sarnia's notorious petrochemical corridor. The area hosts one of Canada's largest concentrations of industry, and has the air pollution to prove it. Sarnia sits in southwestern Ontario, at the southern tip of Lake Huron, bordering Michigan, USA. The north end of town, with its executive estates and golf courses, gradually gives way to a working-class core, and a string of large petrochemical, polymer and chemical industrial plants, as well as coal-fired utilities along both sides of the St Clair river.

For the community of Aamjiwnaang, living in the shadow of Canada's 'Chemical Valley', a recent epidemiological study confirmed what many had suspected for years – that the community's 'sex ratio' (the number of boy babies born relative to the number of girls) was declining at an alarming rate. It was widely speculated that chronic exposure to toxic chemical pollution, specifically a group of endocrine disrupting chemicals provocatively nicknamed the 'gender-benders', was responsible. Residents that had wondered about why they needed two softball teams to accommodate the girls on reserve, when they could barely field one team of boys had their answer. A research partnership was launched and the team had soon documented a marked decrease in the number of males born into the community. The study appeared in a prestigious journal and the Aamjiwnaang First Nation was left to deal with the unwelcome distinction of the world's lowest documented birth ratio (Mackenzie et al 2005).

It is widely speculated that the noted decline in sex ratio could be correlated with the community members' exposures to industrial pollutants. In fact, it fits perfectly into a scientific picture that is being pieced together throughout the Great Lakes region. Other studies conducted on wildlife populations in this region have found changes in the sex ratios and reproductive ability of fish, bird and turtle populations, which are thought to be due to exposures to endocrine disrupting chemicals (Gilbertson 2002). Endocrine disruptors are said to have a 'hormone-mimicking' effect. They may induce long-term effects upon low-dose exposures in susceptible developmental phases. There are a number of competing hypotheses for how, specifically, these environmental contaminants disrupt the human endocrine system, and how they might be influencing sex ratio. According to the hypothesis with the most traction, interference with a mother's hormonal milieu at key developmental stages very early in a pregnancy can induce sex-specific mortality in miscarriage. Essentially, the hypothesis is that embryos that would become boy babies are disproportionately lost in early miscarriages, usually occurring before the prospective mother even becomes aware that she may have been pregnant.

Activists living in pollution hotspots are increasingly identifying with and being inspired by the environmental justice movement. They see 'connections between social welfare and the environment, pollution and the home, and pollution and discrimination, that have gone unnoticed (or conveniently ignored) by mainstream environmentalists' (Verchick 1996: 46). A central focus is the notion of 'disproportionate burdens' – the claim that while pollution is everywhere, it is most easily found in a few choice places, particularly those inhabited by the poor, the racialized, and the marginalized (Luke 2000). The aim of organizing is to expose the fundamental power differential that exists between the polluters and 'the polluted'. As a result, many activists in the environmental justice movement want to be able to say unequivocally that the 'gender-bending' of endocrine disruption is a new, dramatic and horrifying harm.

The mantra of the environmental justice movement – that some of us live more downstream than others – is a stark and obvious truth in Sarnia's Chemical Valley (Scott 2008). Talfourd Creek gathers its waters in an industrial corridor home to 40 per cent of Canada's chemical production before it meanders through the Aamjiwnaang reserve and empties into the St Clair River (MacDonald and Rang 2007: 5). There are 62 large emitting industrial facilities within 25 kilometers of the reserve (MacDonald and Rang 2007: 5). In 2005 there were 5.7 million kilograms of toxic air pollutants released from the facilities on the Canadian side of the border alone (MacDonald and Rang 2007: 5). The Aamjiwnaang First Nation has been confined to a small portion of its traditional territory by colonialist law, has been steadily surrounded by oppressive industry, and many residents now feel that it is being slowly choked out by the legacy of a century of petrochemical production.

While the skewed sex ratio garners media attention, and is undoubtedly a potent symbol of the complexity of contemporary pollution harms, it is by no means the only manifestation of the pervasive body-altering pollution that the residents report. They experience elevated rates of cancer and diabetes, developmental and attention-deficit disorders, asthma and other respiratory ailments (Scott 2008). In recent years, community members have expressed a building anger as residents learn of the extent of their health problems and the mounting evidence linking those problems to the actions of their industrial neighbours. They are a deeply injured community (Scott 2008).

Identifying the injury

Communities struggling with contamination face significant challenges in seeking to achieve 'environmental justice' through tort litigation (Collins and McLeod-Kilmurray 2011; Toffolon-Weiss and Roberts 2004: 261). These 'toxic torts' are, in fact, notoriously difficult to win, and prohibitively expensive to mount. In my analysis, the 'injury' suffered by the Aamjiwnaang First Nation is a classic example of how contemporary pollution harms are currently beyond the reach of effective resolution through tort law.

To find an injury in law we need to identify a cause-and-effect relationship that culminates in a tangible harm. Not only is the causality contested in this case, but *a tangible harm* is elusive. Thinking specifically of the issue of the declining sex ratio, how should we characterise what has been lost in the Aamjiwnaang situation? Only chances – chances to welcome sons. No one mother could ever prove that she specifically was harmed; that she specifically should have conceived a boy. No actual child has been harmed. But it is difficult to fathom that there is no harm being done. It is clear that there is wounding to be accounted for.

Cultural anthropologist Sarah Lochlann Jain employs the term 'wound' to capture the sense that harms exist out there in the world that are not contained in the legal notion of 'injury' (2006: 6). And, as she reminds us, 'wellness and wounding will always be at play within various cross-cutting hierarchies' pre-existing in our society (2006: 5). '[W]ounding itself', Jain states, 'brings a mode of attention to objects into being . . . objects only emerge as separate from the [agent] when something goes wrong' (2006: 5). It is as if the chronic chemical pollution in the streams, rivers, air and soil of the Aamjiwnaang reserve is suddenly rendered visible by the duly documented epidemiological study of the plummeting sex ratio.

How should we understand the harm or the injury that the Aamjiwnaang community has suffered, and continues to suffer? Or, as a colleague (half-jokingly) put it to me, 'What's the harm in a few less men?' Why does this sex ratio dynamic, a declining proportion of boys born into a community, present a challenge to tort law? Jain observes that tort law's prerequisite is that the (injured) 'physical body . . . come[s] to the table as a preceding artifact being reclaimed after having been unjustly altered' (2006: 6). It is offered up as collateral for the 'justness' of a legal logic through which certain practices, like the discharge of endocrine disrupting chemicals into the environment, in theory, become morally reprehensible or unacceptable. But, on top of the inability of the Aamjiwnaang community to produce a single or distinct injured body, 'unjustly altered', the chronic low-dose exposures to pollution that are suspected to be responsible for the 'injury' are (for the most part, at least) legally sanctioned and permitted. The actions of the corporate polluters, instead of being seen as morally reprehensible, are in fact state-sanctioned acts of productive economic activity.

It is in this respect that I have argued that the law appears ambivalent to the endocrine disrupting pollution (Scott 2008). The basis upon which the prevailing regulatory approach rests is that pollution is permitted according to certain specified limits set down in a regulation and adopted in a 'Certificate of Approval' granted to each facility.[4] The system is built on the assumption that cases where this legally sanctioned pollution results in proven harm will be rare, and that the state can rely, in these situations, on tort law to step in and provide compensation.

The ambivalence of our law, then, derives from the continued prominence of the understanding of environmental health harms as incidental, and not central, to industrial production. Any harm caused by legally sanctioned, permitted pollution (as most of it is in Sarnia's chemical corridor) is treated as a by-product or an accidental side-effect of the economic activity. It is construed as unintentional. And yet, pollution is a 'fixed feature' of modern economies (Luke 2000: 248). As Richard Lazarus has noted, 'pollution in our regulatory environment finds the pathway of least resistance. It finds those places where the laws are least enforced and least understood' (1997: 714). The production of chemicals, the refining of oil and the generation of electricity in the Sarnia corridor has harm and wounding embedded in it. It is equally the *production* of pollution.

'Wounding'

'Wounds adhere differently to different people' (Jain 2006: 58). And the act of wounding, as Jain shows, focuses attention on things which were previously not clearly in view. But the fact that the chronic contamination of the Aamjiwnaang territory was only rendered visible by the sudden notoriety of having the world's lowest birth ratio, is also largely due to the nature of toxic chemical pollution. It is invisible. The 'risks' associated with it are virtually undetectable without scientific investigation. They manifest as 'harms caused by molecules' (Cranor 2006: 12).

To understand the mechanics of endocrine disruption, for example, the way that certain chemicals mimic hormones in the body by binding with available receptors and influencing gene expression, we are forced to rely on biomedical ways of knowing. The consequences of exposure tend to eventually manifest themselves in ways that start from within the body and work their way out (Erikson 1991). Further, the latency period associated with many contemporary environmental health risks underscores their psychological impact in that it renders the experience of risk unbounded: 'an "all clear" is never sounded' (Erikson 1991: 21). Bodies contain chemicals banned years before the individual's birth; contamination can be extremely long-lasting, and can be passed down from generation to generation. For example, in part because it is widely accepted among epidemiologists that exposures to toxic chemicals in one generation may produce effects in the next, no one can tell the Aamjiwnaang community whether they face a present danger, or are experiencing the latent manifestation of exposures long past: as one Band member states, 'was it me, was it my dad, my mom? ... we don't know who's been exposed'.[5]

The gendering effect of endocrine disruption

The mechanics of endocrine disruption are often described in the following way. Certain synthetic chemicals share structural features with common sex hormones; these chemicals, or 'xenoestrogens', mimic hormone action in the body by binding with, and activating, available hormone receptors.[6] The endocrine systems of the body are understood as responsible for regulating complex and interconnected physiological processes, and thus synthetic chemicals that interfere with these systems are thought to have profound and wide-ranging effects on health.[7] As hormones travel in the blood in very small concentrations, even very low levels of xenoestrogens can disrupt the flow of internal communications, triggering biological responses and functions in the processes of growth and embryonic development. Accordingly, susceptibility to xenoestrogens is thought to depend highly on sex and on the timing of exposures.

We rarely hear about the phenomenon of endocrine disruption without reference to the controversial theory of 'feminisation' (Mittelsteadt 2008: F4). This posits that we are experiencing, not just in humans but also in wildlife, a feminisation trend that is observable across a variety of markers including decreased sperm counts, increasing testicular cancers, declining levels of testosterone and high incidence of undescended testes (Solomon and Schettler 2000: 1472; Langston 2008: 41).[8] 'These things theoretically have a common etiology', according to Devra Davis (Mittelsteadt 2008). It is hypothesised that a declining sex ratio may be just one of a number of manifestations of a feminisation trend that is tied to endocrine disruption as very broadly experienced across the industrialised world (Solomon and Schettler 2000: 1472–3; Mittelstaedt 2008).

The gender dimension of the 'harm' experienced by the Aamjiwnaang community is as difficult to demonstrate as it is to dismiss. The impact of pollution seems not only to be gendered, but *gendering*. By this I mean that the endocrine disruptors do not just dole out their environmental health horrors disproportionately as between men and women, or girls and boys, they actually seem to be driving whether we get girls or boys. The pollution is feared to be actively 'producing' sex, and to the extent that it is related, gender.

The Aamjiwnaang experience is marked by the individual trauma of repeated miscarriage and the collective loss of a viable future. The skewed sex ratio, conceptualised as a 'harm', is one that is both visited specifically on women, and felt by the community as a whole. As Joanne Conaghan has argued and the previous part has made clear, harm is an 'unstable, slippery concept, highly dependent on context and very much the subject of interpretation' (2002: 320). But at the same time, as Robin West has argued, the question of what constitutes a 'harm' is central to legal theory (1997: 94). Further, the question is a critical one for feminists: as Martha Chamallas and Linda Kerber have shown, tort law traditionally falters when it is faced with claims based on harms for which there is no 'precise masculine analog' (1990: 814).

According to Robin West's 'connection thesis', women's material connection to future human life necessarily produces a gendered notion of harm (1988). The prospect of pregnancy, of contributing to a future generation, marks the key difference between women and men. Underlying all branches of feminist theory, West says, is the notion that 'women's existential state . . . is grounded in women's unique potential for physical, "material connection" to human life' (West 1988: 14). This is the one place where even feminism's divisions dissolve: we all come together, she says, on the 'discovery or rediscovery of the importance of women's fundamental material difference from men':

> . . . Women are actually or potentially materially connected to other human life. Men aren't. This material fact has existential consequences ... [it] defines women's subjective, phenomenological and existential state, just as surely as the inevitability of material separation from the other defines men's existential state.[9]
>
> (West 1988: 14)

In the context of suspected reproductive harms, it is obvious how deeply West's notion is internalised. Aamjiwnaang mothers and potential mothers, even if they are not uniquely 'harmed', are usually identified as the medium through which the poisoning occurs: they are seen as sites of contamination. The notion of the mothers as mediums for the pollution is reinforced by various strategies of resistance that have been employed by residents of the Aamjiwnaang community themselves, including 'body burden' testing and 'body mapping' exercises, and even self-help strategies such as leaving the reserve when trying to become or once becoming pregnant.[10] This is true even as the epidemiological evidence remains contested as to the significance of the maternal influence. In fact, the scientific literature that links endocrine disruptors with skewed sex ratios focuses on male *and* female reproduction, with researchers often unwilling to make a call at this point as to which is the more likely mode of action (Scott 2009: 247-248).

Sex is typically understood as a stable and pre-cultural biological reality that may be verified through a visual assessment (Bloom 2010) while gender is often understood to be socially constructed – a product of our socialisation. But it is not just gender that is constructed, of course, it is sex as well. In the present example, focusing our gaze on the declining sex ratio and the mechanics of endocrine disruption brings the body into focus and exposes the active construction and categorisation of bodies into discrete sexes.

Conventional wisdom holds that sexual identity occurs 'naturally' as a binary category, which consists of two 'opposite' sexes: male and female. That there are only two mutually exclusive categories is not questioned in the environmental health movement. But as the growing literature on intersexuality makes clear, many bodies, even in 'nature', do not conform to the rigid boundaries of a male/female classification (Bloom 2010). Conservative estimates put the incidence of intersexuality at around 1 in 2,000 births, with as many as 1 in 100 of us born with bodies 'differing' from the standard traits of male or female.

Where we draw the line between 'male' and 'female' is now recognised as arbitrary, and sex is better understood as occupying a continuum (Nye 1998: 229). But, many will protest, surely genetics settles the matter conclusively: it is the presence or absence of the Y chromosome that creates a binary. Students of introductory biology courses may recall a standard narrative something along these lines: *A person's sex is predetermined in the sperm gamete. The cells of the egg gamete all possess the XX sex chromosomes. Around half of the sperm gametes contain the X chromosome and others possess the Y chromosome. In light of this, there are two possibilities that can occur during fertilisation between male and female gametes, XX and XY. Since sperm are the variable factor, they are responsible for determining sex* . . .

In life, it turns out, it is more complicated. In some cases, babies are born with an extra X or an extra Y, and some babies are born with only one X. In many more cases, babies are born with, or individuals develop later in their life, physical traits that do not comport with the category designated to them. For example, some XX individuals have both ovaries and the reproductive equipment we might typically associate with a male. And in many more cases still, individuals exhibit personality traits, or gender identities, that puts them on a collision course with prevailing cultural expectations about the characteristics that are typically associated with the two categories of sex identity. If this all seems new, it is because, as Anne Bloom demonstrates beautifully, several authoritative discourses and institutions (law and medicine chief among them) have 'collaborated' so as 'to make binary sexual difference appear more "natural" than it is' (2010: 403).

Hormones, of course, are implicated as well. According to the standard line, sex is determined by genetic factors, and sexual differentiation is driven by hormones. As Nelly Oudshoorn's (1994) work exposes, the 'discovery' of hormones early in the twentieth century became celebrated as providing the 'missing link' between genetic and physiological models of sex determination. It quickly became accepted that the 'intentions of genes must always be carried through by appropriate hormones' (Oudshoorn 1994: 20). Accordingly, hormones assumed the role of the 'chemical messengers' of masculinity and femininity.

If there is no 'natural' categorization of sexual identity as a binary, perhaps there is no 'normal' balance between *two* discrete sexes.[11] Without these critical assumptions in place, it is difficult to characterise the declining sex ratio of the Aamjiwnaang First Nation, even at a collective level, as a harm. If not through recourse to what is 'natural', on what basis can we determine that endocrine disruption, or pollution, is ever harmful? Can we say that uninvited changes to bodies are unwelcome? That just as 'risks', however rational to incur at a societal level, are unacceptable if they are imposed involuntarily or if they result in the unfair sharing of benefits and burdens, so the uninvited interference with bodies, with reproduction, in this case, is unacceptable?

One answer is that we validate the harms of the pollution that are tied to illness and suffering and not those that signify *difference*. Those harmed by the pollution are the people living in Aamjiwnaang – they are the women, men and children, mostly girls, but nevertheless the children of the Band. They are the:

> young aboriginal mothers, they are parents who routinely receive 'emergency alerts' over the radio indicating that they should 'Shelter in Place' as a result of an incident or a 'fugitive release' from neighboring industry, they are day-care workers responding to the sirens by shuffling toddlers inside and closing the vents, they are health clinic staff staring down bewildering statistics, they are teenagers struggling with asthma, developmental and attention-deficit disorders, and they are young children prevented from swimming in the contaminated creek that passes through their traditional powwow grounds.
> (Scott 2008: 311)

These are the people living with the effects of the chronic exposures to pollution that emanate from Sarnia's Chemical Valley. The community has more than its fair share of illness and suffering: 17 per cent of adults and 22 per cent of children surveyed have asthma; about 25 per cent of adults experience high blood pressure and/or chronic headaches; about 25 per cent of children suffer from learning disabilities and behavioural problems; and about 40 per cent of women have experienced miscarriage or stillbirth.[12]

Another answer is that we adopt an 'embodied' approach that validates the real and material consequences that the pollution is having *within* bodies. Instead of insisting on some 'unified and singular bodily form of the male and the female' this approach would place attention on the universal human condition of being 'in' our bodies (Mellor 1997: 9). Human embodiment spans all sorts of biological imperatives: from hunger and excretion to ageing and dying. It also includes change through various life stages driven by hormonal cycles. These cycles create 'windows of vulnerability' that have a distinct biological and thus gendered nature (Krupp 2000). It is here that estrogens take on a pivotal role, and the role of xenoestrogens, in particular, becomes salient. When synthetic chemicals, uninvited, take over for hormones, binding with available receptors and orchestrating physiological processes, it has real, tangible, material consequences for bodies. When this happens in the context of reproduction, it has *gendering* consequences.

Here, in the context of endocrine disruption on an aboriginal reserve surrounded by petrochemical production, these answers are attractive because they seem to offer the potential to underscore the blameworthiness of the ongoing pollution. But it is clear, the harm to the community's sex ratio is a harm in the abstract.

Why should the declining sex ratio garner so much attention when the actual suffering and poor health of living beings – women, men and children – attracts only indifference and dismissal? This brings us back to the glaring unfairness of the pollution's disproportionate impact on the native community in the context of their colonial history. In fact, understanding why the effects of chronic pollution might be manifest first on the Aamjiwnaang reserve and not in 'white' Sarnia goes a long way to re-centring the role of land, capital, race and colonisation. The Aanishinaabek people have occupied their lands at the southernmost tip of Lake Huron for hundreds of years. As Band member Ron Plain will tell you, on the Aamjiwnaang burial grounds, you will find the remains of four generations of his ancestors, all in one place, literally on the fenceline of a large refinery: 'we all lived *here* – all our lives'.[13] The permanence of both the pollution and of the Aamjiwnaang First Nation on the landscape, offers a possible explanation for why we might see a disproportionate effect of chronic pollution on this community: they are grounded both spatially and historically. If the mechanism behind the decline in sex ratio has a generational component, it makes sense that it would emerge in the First Nation community first. In south Sarnia, for example, which might experience comparable exposures to airborne pollutants, you are likely to find people who were born all over the country, if not the world. On the Aamjiwnaang reserve, you will not. It is a stark reminder of how contemporary pollution exists in social contexts that can exacerbate its effects.

Collective harm

The impact of the pollution on the Aamjiwnaang people is imposed not only on individual bodies, of course, but on the community as a whole. Through the work of feminist legal scholars to expose the nature of 'gendered harm', we have come to clearly understand that 'injury has a social as well as an individual dimension' (Conaghan 1996: 408; Howe 1991; Conaghan 2002; Conaghan and Mansell 1993; Bender 1990). As Joanne Conaghan states, a person's membership in a 'particular class, group, race or gender can significantly shape the nature and degree of harm they sustain' (1996: 408). It is in this vein that I turn next to the notion of a 'collective harm' with the hope that it can better capture the wounds flowing from the sex ratio skewing on the Aamjiwnaang reserve.

The concern has been stated in the language of cultural survival. It is a concern for the collective loss of a viable future. As one Band member has stated: 'our daughters will have to go outside our community for their partners'.[14] Thus the prospect of a collective harm highlights the fact that this problem is situated in the context of an aboriginal community already struggling, as many are, with stemming the loss of culture and tradition amongst their people.

'Injury', as David Engels argues, 'opens a window onto identity' (2000: 3). This is because '[w]hen we say that an individual has suffered an injury, we implicitly refer to a self that is constituted in a particular way and is therefore vulnerable to particular kinds of harm' (Engels 2000: 3). As I have argued in the past (Scott 2008; 2009), it is the specific history of the Aamjiwnaang First Nation which makes the community, as a whole, particularly vulnerable to pollution harm. Robert Verchick hammers the point:

> localized environmental hazards do not simply harm individuals, they erode family ties and community relationships . . . [they] create community-wide stress that will debilitate the neighborhood in emotional, sociological, and economic ways. To ignore this communal harm is to underestimate severely the true risk involved.
>
> (Verchick 1996: 84)

Further, because emerging environmental health harms are often localised and concentrated, and because they tend to be distributed along race and class differentials, the *wound* to the affected community, often takes on, as Verchick notes, a 'profound moral character' (1996: 84). Just as Native Americans have characterised the US military's poisoning of Indian land as genocide, so the charge of cultural extermination has been levelled by residents in the case of Aamjiwnaang with respect to the slow poisoning of their people and their traditional territory. In this way, the theory of endocrine disruption in the context of a First Nation encounters a history that has refused, at various times, racialised groups the capacity for children. Class bias and racism, as Angela Davis has aptly demonstrated, has always contributed to how we, collectively, figure out who may legitimately contribute to the next generation, to the 'future' (Davis 2008: 86).

As profound a wound as it is, it is clear that locating the injury of endocrine disruption in individuals is not easy. Even locating the harm at a collective level is fraught: conceptualising the wound suffered by the Aamjiwnaang people as a harm (at least in terms of the declining sex ratio) demands allegiance to notions of what is 'natural' and what is 'normal' that defy developments in feminist theory of the body. Contemporary pollution harms are diffuse, body-altering, cumulative and probably generational in character. There is wounding to be accounted for, but conceiving it as a harm is a task that pushes the limits of our current legal imaginary.

Imagining a remedy

A tort is a legal construct: it only exists in cases where there is a 'wrong' for which the law provides a remedy (Klar 2008: 1). In general, tort law provides that compensation, usually in the form of money damages, be paid for an injury suffered as a result of the wrongful conduct of others (Klar 2008: 1). Can tort law provide a remedy for the injury suffered by the Aamjiwnaang First Nation? In the first part of what follows, I offer a critique, grounded in feminist theory of the body, of tort damages as based on the idea of a liberal, individual legal subject. In the second part, I engage in a somewhat creative, or perhaps playful, take on torts in which I consider various torts on a conceptual level, and what they might offer the Aamjiwnaang First Nation in the way of remedies. In each case, what the tort can do depends on how the injury, and the scale at which the entity taken to have suffered the injury, is conceived.

Beyond individual legal subjects

The central difficulty for tort law in providing an effective remedy to the Aamjiwnaang community derives from its underlying assumption that 'society is composed of free, separate, autonomous individuals, competing with each other in pursuit of their own self-interest' (Conaghan 1996: 408). The *definition* of tort law is that it is the law governing the obligations that *persons* are deemed to owe each other (Ballentine, 1969). This is where a feminist critique gains traction. Where 'tort law, as traditionally presented, presupposes the essential separateness of individuals from each other, feminist perspectives recognise, from the very outset, our necessary interconnectedness' (Conaghan 1996b: 47).

Robin West, as noted above, challenges the notion of 'separateness' for women based on her connection thesis: 'women are *not* essentially, necessarily, inevitably, invariably, always and forever separate from other human beings' (1988: 2). Her thesis is strengthened by emerging work from scholars of fetal microchimerism, such as Aryn Martin (2010), who demonstrates that, not only is women's 'separateness' challenged by the *possibility* of reproduction, but the maternal body is irretrievably transformed by the experience of pregnancy. As these scholars have demonstrated, the boundaries of human individuality are permanently blurred by the fluid movement and exchange of cells that occurs between a mother and her fetus. Children of all genders will forever harbor cells belonging to their mothers within their own bodies. And so we can take the challenge to the separation thesis much deeper: not only can women not be conceived of as 'separate' from other life, but men cannot either. All living things are embedded and interwoven into larger webs of being.

The idea of humans as organisms embedded in dynamic systems invites a Deleuzian conception of the body, which does not rely on an individuated subject (Bottomley 2002: 140). In this conception, as Bottomley notes, the body becomes 'a site of patterns, flows and intensities in which the emphasis is continually on movement' (2002: 140). This leads to an understanding of the body 'not as an organism or entity in itself, but as a system, or a series of open-ended systems, functioning within other huge systems it cannot control . . .' (Grosz 2004: 3). Applying this perspective places the Aamjiwnaang people as subjects immersed in a social, ecological, political and historical context that accentuates their vul-nerabilities to the pollution – to the intensities and flows operating at a molecular level, to the energies and connections between synthetic hormones and avail-able receptors within bodies.[15] In emphasising the capacity of bodies to affect and be affected by other bodies, this conception, therefore, 'undermines a notion of a fixed boundary between subject and object and between the self and its other' (Richardson 2004: 27). It represents a shift away from the notion of the self as primarily subject to central control (Richardson 2004: 27–8). As Richardson (2004: 27) argues, however, this is not necessarily as conceptually debilitating as one might assume: 'A distinct self does emerge, but through patterns of relationality rather than in opposition from its other'.[16]

The challenge to these generally accepted boundaries of the person raises obvious questions of human agency (Richardson 2004: 31). We are all organisms 'assimilating, seeking, manipulating [our] worlds, even as [we] accommodate and respond to them' (Oyama 2000: 95). In other words, we are neither completely free and autonomous, nor passive. The image of endocrine disruption constructed by scientists in fact reinforces the idea that matter is inherently interactive, not inert. The metaphor is one of hormones as *messengers* – moving through the body, picking up 'packages' from the 'outside', delivering them to receptive agents, igniting and transforming productive processes – and it reinforces the understanding that bodies are dynamic systems, constantly in flux.[17]

As Richardson (2004: 31) argues, a 'refusal to delineate fixed boundaries between the self and its supposed "outside" offers a new approach to the law of obligations'. The focus on individuals as the point of departure in tort law is clearly bereft, inadequate. But that the fundamental entity of social existence must be the individual is central to liberal thought: 'we *are* individuals, because we are separate from one another' (Decoste 1993: 243). And this is not just in a physical sense, 'what is important for the liberal is that our individuation is normative' (Decoste 1993: 243). We are individuals because we choose. Individualism is the foundation for the sacred liberal values of choice, autonomy and self-determination (Decoste 1993: 243).

Janice Richardson's sustained critique of the centrality of the individual to tort law has been instrumental in our articulation of its implications:

> One of the basic assumptions in tort law is that we are envisaged as individuals who are owners of our own abilities, such as our ability to work and our bodies. If anyone negligently injures us or prevent us from being able to earn a living we can claim damages because we own parts of our bodies and life changes in a way that is analogous to the way in which we own property.
>
> (Richardson 2004: 77)

The declining sex ratio emerges as an eruption of unpredictability in a material world that is otherwise tightly structured by forces external to the Band. Where the subjects of pollution are not easily conceptualised as individual, liberal, monadic entities, but are instead understood as a community embedded in cultural histories, tied to the land, and inseparable from local intensities and flows, emitted particles, energies and connections operating on a molecular level, we need a broader conception of the legal subject to adequately understand the harm.

Why is 'the individual person' the appropriate unit or level of analysis for assessing damages in tort law? Why not assess it at the level of communities? Or conversely, at the molecular level?[18] At the level of cells? Legal scholars have begun exploring the idea that tort law is too corporeal – that it is tethered too tightly to proof of physical damages – and should move towards the recognition of 'interests-based' damages in certain contexts (Witting 2002, 2008; Nolan 2007). But even where recent scholarship in tort has included some calls for expansion of what should count as harm or 'physical damage' (Witting 2002, 2008; Nolan 2007; Priaulx 2004), the *scale* at which we look to find such damage remains locked at the level of the individual, the single unitary legal subject.

Witting (2002: 190) argues we should move away from assessing physical damage only on the basis of a 'factually observable' change in the physical structure of persons, and advocates for a more contextual approach based on social perceptions of damage. As Nolan (2007: 61) says, 'the boundaries of the concept of physical damage are not always clear' and could be expanded. This goes some way towards opening up the question of what constitutes physical damage, but leaves unexplored, for now, the matter of the appropriate scale on which we should measure it. In what follows, I begin to brainstorm the way that various torts might operate at different scales of injury to provide a remedy for the Aamjiwnaang people.

. . . If we take the injury to have occurred *inside bodies*, then perhaps we would turn to the tort of battery . . .

Offensive contact with the body/battery

Is there a right to physical integrity or bodily inviolability? Control over our bodies represents a key feminist objective. The notion that we are individual autonomous bodies would seem to demand that we are all able to 'resist the intrusions of others' (Hyde 1997: 97). Presumably this includes the ability to say 'yes' or 'no' to bodily penetration by synthetic chemicals capable of causing material changes to key metabolic processes within ourselves? *So what* if individual women in Aamjiwnaang can't demonstrate a factually observable change; a visible and tangible harm? Isn't *any* interference with our bodies that we have not consented to capable of constituting a harm?

Consider the tort of battery. It is said to protect a person's right to be free from offensive physical contacts. It guards the security of the person. The tort of battery 'does not require that the contact be physically harmful to its recipient, or cause any physical injury' (Klar 1988: 46). Apparently, any offensive contact qualifies, 'however trivial it may seem', if it has the potential to affect dignity and self-respect (Linden 1997: 43). It is the 'right to autonomy over one's own body which is protected' (Klar 2008: 46).

But to be actionable, the offensive contact must be either 'intentional' or 'negligent'[19] (Linden 1997: 43). The contact does not need to be 'person-to-person' but it must be 'physical' (Linden 1997: 50). In our example, what would constitute the offensive contact? Is it the synthetic estrogens entering the body? Is it when they bind to and activate receptors in cells? How can we attach *intention* to these contacts?

We could point to offensive *conduct*, such as the release of chemicals into the air or water, which we may be able to argue is intentional or negligent. An advantage of the tort of battery, over the tort of negligence for example, is that the burden of disproving intention or negligence falls on the defendant, once the elements of the tort are proven (Linden 1997: 51). Negligent battery is the unreasonable disregard of a 'foreseeable' risk of contact, even if the contact is not desired or substantially certain to occur (Klar 1988: 56). The polluters would bear the burden of providing emission data, dispersion models and epidemiological evidence; the polluters would have to argue that the 'contact' between *their* synthetic estrogens released freely into the air, and *our* estrogen receptors, hiding deep in our own bodies, was not foreseeable, predictable or inevitable.

Unfortunately, with the tort of battery, there is also a defence of legal authority. As mentioned, most of the pollution in Sarnia's Chemical Valley is legally authorised. The polluters have been issued permits to emit. These certificates of approval constitute a legally binding licence that sets out the conditions under which a facility can operate. So, as long as the facility stays within the maximum permissible contaminant emission levels as detailed in their permit, the defence of legal authority seems likely to preclude any finding of liability.

. . . If we take the injury to have occurred to *individuals*, we would look to the tort of negligence, and specifically, we might employ the 'lost chance' doctrine . . .

Lost chances/negligence

Where a plaintiff cannot establish that a defendant's negligence 'caused' her injury on a balance of probabilities, her claim in negligence will fail. This is true even where the defendant's negligent conduct increased the possibility of her injury, but did not 'probably' cause it. In the case of Aamjiwnaang mothers (or fathers), if the 'injury' was endocrine disruption, it seems likely that causation would prove difficult to make out. The imagined narrative would have to go something like this: '*the synthetic estrogen released by this polluter entered my body and activated estrogen receptors at a key moment in the embryo's early development thus "causing" me to conceive an embryo that would become a girl, instead of a boy* . . . But what if we redefine the very nature of the injury itself? What if the 'lost chances' to bear sons is the harm? The effect of the synthetic chemicals in the body produced – caused – an increased *chance* of conceiving an embryo that would become a girl (given there was already, surely, an almost even chance of that outcome). According to this narrative, the negligent actions of the polluters, which increased the possibility of endocrine disruption, effectively deprived the families on the reserve of chances to welcome boys. It would go like this: *the synthetic estrogen released by this polluter entered my body and increased the chances that I would conceive an embryo that would become a girl, instead of a boy* . . .". The lost chances themselves constitute the injury and the families are owed compensation.

Used more commonly in contract cases and increasingly in medical malpractice litigation, the 'lost chance' doctrine can compensate individuals for lost opportunities, based on probabilistic estimates of what would have been expected in the absence of negligence – of what 'could have been' (Pryor 2007: 561–563). So, if an agency improperly disqualifies a lottery ticket resulting in diminished chances of winning, for example, or if a doctor makes mistakes in the course of a person's cancer treatment and, as a result the patient has a diminished chance of survival, there is the possibility of recovery, in some jurisdictions, for 'lost chance'.[20]

For personal injury lawyers and litigators, the lost chance doctrine offers several advantages. Most importantly, injury and compensation are understood in terms of 'lost opportunity' or heightened risk, rather than resting on an ultimate injury, concrete and visible in the body. Thus, the doctrine potentially provides a way around the difficult questions of causation and harm that plague most toxic tort cases.

Usually in these cases, however, it is unproblematically stated that the plaintiff has lost her chance to avoid a preferred outcome – a more *favourable* result. For example, a leading proponent of the doctrine in the US, Professor Joseph King, states that the loss of chance is the loss of 'achieving a favourable outcome or of avoiding an adverse consequence' (King 1981: 1354). It rests on the idea that 'depriving a person of the chance of good results is in fact harmful to that person' (Klar 2008: 61). Chance has value. But does applying the doctrine to the declining sex ratio imply that boy babies are preferred to girls? That a boy would constitute a more favourable result? That a boy child is more valuable to families, to communities, than a girl child? How can we call a failure to produce 'boys' a harm without de-valuing girls?

We might turn to the 'wrongful birth' cases for insight in this regard (Klar 2008: 419). In these cases, parents make claims in negligence for faulty sterilisation procedures or incorrect contraception advice that result in the birth of an unwanted child (Richardson 2004: 75). Where a doctor's negligence results in the birth of a healthy child, a difficult issue arises with respect to the assessment of damages

(Richardson 2004: 420). The Alberta Court of Queens' bench have made surprising findings in this regard, stating categorically in one case that 'the benefits a child brings to a family outweigh the costs of that child to a family' (see, for example, *MY v Boutros* [2002]: [158]). Apparently, even where the child was unwanted, the parents took specific steps to avoid its birth and it would not have been born but for the negligence of a professional with a specific duty to prevent its birth, a healthy child can still categorically be considered a blessing (Richardson 2004; Priaulx 2004).[21] In other cases, however, there is a different formulation of the harm. It is not that the child, *herself*, is to be considered a harm, but that the negligent interference with autonomy, with reproductive choice and control, is a harm that should be compensated for (*Kealey v Berezowski* [1996]: [70–1] (Canada); see also *Darlington Memorial Hospital NHS Trust v Rees* [2003] (UK)).[22] What becomes very clear in thinking through these questions is the difficulty with objective determinations of harm. A healthy child, to some, is a blessing; to others, is a burden.

Perhaps the image that best exemplifies the nagging inadequacy of how we find a harm in the Aamjiwnaang situation, is not the classic 'lost chance' lottery ticket analogy (because money is universally accepted as a desired outcome in the context of lotteries!) – but a midway game at a fair. Suppose that all of the prizes available for winners in the game are, objectively speaking, 'equal' in value. You win the game and spin the wheel to determine your prize. But suppose the wheel is improperly weighted so that it is much less likely to stop on the prize that *you* want. Someone has interfered with your autonomy. Never mind that it is with respect to an outcome that you do not have full control over. There is an element of chance. This is true with respect to reproduction, as it is true with respect to cancer and lotteries and midway games.

. . . What about a class action in lost chance? At the *community* level, for the denial of the chance of continuing? Of reproducing and existing . . .

As explored earlier, the harm suffered by the members of the Aamjiwnaang First Nation is rendered visible through the 'statistical vision' of epidemiology (Jasanoff 2002: 64). At an individual level it cannot be seen, yet in the aggregate, it is obvious. There is perhaps a parallel here to the issue of pay equity.[23] Just as individual Aamjiwnaang mothers, encountering doctors' offices and public health units with complaints of 'so many girls' being born are easily dismissed, so individual women encountering lawyers and bosses with complaints of 'so little pay' are also routinely dismissed. But at the level of the population the claims come into sharp relief, and the imbalance, the unfairness, is exposed.

Once aggregated, they graduate from subjective claims into statistical correlations. The focus is no longer on individual harm, but on probabilistic harm across disembodied populations. But in exchange for the shift in focus that allows recognition of the aggregate harm, we forfeit detail at the level of individual lives. In revealing the pattern, individual stories get lost. And here – for both the depressed sex ratio and the depressed wages of women – the shift has the potential to overcome the tendency to dismiss each individual woman's complaint as a result of 'chance' and to bring back into play the social origins of the problem and the blameworthiness of those who perpetuate it.

Reparation/retribution

In each and every one of these imagined tort claims, it will always come down to a question of remedy. The primary remedy in tort is money damages (Conaghan and Mansell 1993: 56). In general, the aim is to translate the lost intangibles into money terms, which involves not only tricky exercises in valuation, but also a good deal of 'fortune telling' in that it demands the prediction of future events (Conaghan and Mansell 1993: 58). There is no question that the tort system at present reflects and reinforces the view that money can substitute for health (Conaghan and Mansell 1993: 61; Gibson 1993: 189).[24] Jain (2006: 12) calls this the 'trope of compensation'. Based on the idea of reparable harm, the legal logic demands that the injury be made calculable in market terms, so that the injury can be 'undone' through the monetary award of damages, and the injured can 'buy back' what was lost (Jain 2006: 12).

Can we 'buy back' what's been taken from the Aamjiwnaang community? This must be where the parallel with pay equity breaks down. Pay equity can be addressed in money terms – the claims are actually *about* money. A depressed sex ratio is not about money; and it is only tangentially about health. 'Recovery', in law, is meant to restore, repair or compensate a victim as a matter of justice (Klar 2008: 11, 13). It aims to return the injured person to the condition she would have been in had the injury not occurred. The prospect of recovery for the Aamjiwnaang community is what makes it very clear that the wound, in this case, is much deeper than the injury – the wound will never be closed by an award of damages (even if any were forthcoming).

Can this 'injury' be reversed? Can a community 'recover' from endocrine disruption? There is some ecological evidence that suggests it is likely that, at the population level at least, once the key exposures stop, the effects of endocrine disruption will begin to reverse (Kidd et al 2007). If this is the community's goal, then the remedy best suited is not damages – but injunction.

. . . Still conceiving of the injury to have occurred at the scale of *the community*, then, we might also consider the tort of nuisance.

Bad neighbours/nuisance

> Nuisance is attractive, at least conceptually, because the remedies available include both damages and injunction.
>
> (Klar 2008: 715)

The tort of nuisance deals with relations between neighbours (Conaghan and Mansell 1993: 107). Often, we think of neighbors in a physical sense, as groups or individuals occupying adjacent pieces of land or at least being in a permanent state of close proximity to each other, and generally, we acknowledge that neighbours do not 'choose' each other. It seems likely that the Aamjiwnaang First Nation and the Chemical Valley industry would meet this definition.[25]

There are two classes of claims in nuisance. The first, private nuisance, specifically addresses unlawful interference with the use or enjoyment of land (Collins 2008: 70–1). What is 'unlawful'? It is 'substantial and unreasonable' interference (*Tock v St John's Metropolitan Area Board* [1989]: [1192]). The second, public nuisance, applies when environmental harm generally affects a large class of people at the same time (Collins 2008: 71). For public nuisance, a plaintiff can only succeed if she suffers 'special injury' in the nature of personal injury or property damage (Collins 2008: 71). The First Nation interest in land on reserve is considered only 'possessory' – but that has been found to be sufficient to ground a claim for nuisance (Collins 2008: 74).

On the surface, it seems that there are good arguments for the Aamjiwnaang under both branches of nuisance law. Under private nuisance, however, the Band would have to overcome the hurdle of 'lawfulness' or 'legal authority', as discussed earlier. Under public nuisance, the Band would be returned to the problem of proving a personal injury. For these reasons, nuisance law has proven relatively impotent in fights between communities and industry (Conaghan and Mansell 1993: 107). Further, the 'wrong' would essentially lie in the violation of property rights, not interference with bodily integrity. As a result, even without assessing the loss in terms of money damages, it remains a commodification of the body, and of community, because it relegates those interests to the property interest.

This discussion has skimmed over the question of whether compensation is the only legitimate goal of tort law (Feldthusen 1993: 407–9). What about justice, deterrence, education, punishment of carelessness, retribution? In fact, in early conceptions of tort law, it was the victim's vengeance that was said to have been 'purchased' by the offer of compensation (Léger 1993: 165). Money flowed from the aggressor to the victim, essentially in exchange for community peace (Léger 1993). On reflection, it seems that, of all of these potential aims of tort law, compensation is the only one that really turns on the relationship between individuals – the others are more open to alternative conceptions of harm, and alternative scales at which to find injury, such as at the level of cells, or at the level of the community (Weinrib 1989: 501).

Conclusions

Contemporary pollution harms are pervasive, diffuse, body-altering, cumulative and generational in character. The links between those harms and the suspected chemical culprits are tenuous and contested. Further, the harms are not randomly distributed, or uniformly experienced. Tort law in its current form falls short of capturing the essence of this pollution because, in transforming it into a form cognisable by law, we are forced to locate the harm in separate, autonomous individuals. As Alan Hyde notes:

> law's discourse of the body constructs the body as a thing, separate from the person, but the bearer of that person . . . The legal subject is an individual, and so is that subject's body. Each body is an individuated entity with distinct boundaries, an outside and an inside.
>
> (Hyde 1997: 258)

Tort law, conventionally conceived, is an expression of the 'liberal preference for non-intervention by the state into social arrangements' (Conaghan 1996: 408). It offers a private law solution, between individuals; it is utterly unable to account for the way pollution has saturated the community, been soaked up in bodies, and dissolved boundaries between selves and others. But brainstorming around tort law's potential remedies, at various scales, allows for the body to be opened up – the gender-bending synthetic chemicals flowing through bodies become visible, and the way they freely move between individuals and their worlds is exposed to the point that our insistence on a fixed bodily boundary, and a centrally controlled self, begins to break down.

In fact, as the analysis above demonstrates, moving from harm at the cellular level, through to the community level, the scale at which we conceive of an 'injury' shapes the determination of whether the injury is seen as 'remediable', and on what terms. Further, as Felstiner, Abel and Sarat (1980–81: 635) demonstrated over 30 years ago, these conceptions and determinations are implicit in the process of 'naming', which shapes ideas about the allocation of blame for the harm. Accordingly, just as Alan Hyde (1997: viii–ix) shows how various constructions of the body in jurisprudence carry consequences for actual persons,[26] here we see that our own constructions of 'injury' – where and how we choose to find it – carry consequences for communities affected by contemporary pollution harms. In fact, in all likelihood, they carry consequences for the just resolution of many other 'injuries' for which we currently do not recognise a remedy.

As Lucie White shows, whether or not an 'injury' will indelibly mark its subject is indeterminable.[27] To say that the harm itself is *collective* is to open it up to a trajectory that depends on actors outside of the subject. Further, as Galanter (2010: 3) argues, there is a mutually constitutive relationship between injuries and remedies, such that the remedy itself, or the process of seeking the remedy, or of negotiating a path forward without a remedy, all may institute a process of healing, at various scales, that transforms the injury.

Alan Hyde argues that we should strive for a law and politics of embodied subjects (Hyde 1997: 262). As legal speakers, we choose when and how to 'configure the body in relationship to others' (Hyde 1997: 9). In our tort jurisprudence, in our determinations of what may count as 'harm', we need a jurisprudence that is truer to human experience. The task, as Leslie Bender frames it, is only to imagine creative new remedies that can work to restore dignity and social equality, and remedies that acknowledge collective harms based on the interconnectedness of life (Bender 1990: 901–9).

Notes

* The author would like to thank the organisers and participants of the 'Injuries Without Remedies' Symposium at Loyola Law School, 26 March 2010, especially Anne Bloom, without whose good energy, enthusiasm and encouragement this work would not have been completed. My research partners at the Health and Environment Committee of the Aamjiwnaang First Nation have been instrumental, over the past four years, in shaping my thinking and I continue to be inspired by their activism.

1 This chapter draws largely on work that has been published elsewhere: D.N. Scott (2010) 'Body Polluted: Questions of Scale, Gender and Remedy', *Loyola of Los Angeles Law Review*, 44: 121–56 and D.N. Scott (2009) '"Gender-benders": Sex and Law in the Constitution of Polluted Bodies', *Feminist Legal Studies*, 17: 241–65

2 This is not to suggest that 'welcoming a boy' should in any way bring a mother more joy or satisfaction or security than welcoming a girl. The issue is tackled head-on later in this chapter. It starkly lays bare the tightly interwoven nature of the biological and the cultural in the production of sex ratios across the globe. While sex ratios are depressed in some pollution hotspots, and some post-disaster zones, where they are suspected to be linked to unintentional endocrine disrupting chemical contamination of bodies and landscapes producing an abundance of girls, sex ratios are also sharply inflated in parts of the world where intentional sex selection made possible through the use of pre-natal diagnostic technologies has exploded – producing, of course, an abundance of boys (see, eg, Nolan 2011).

3 The case study draws largely on work that is previously published: D.N. Scott (2008), 'Confronting Chronic Pollution: A Socio-Legal Analysis of Risk and Precaution', *Osgoode Hall Law Journal* 46(2): 293–346

4 In Ontario, the regulation is O.Reg.419/05, Air Pollution.

5 Ron Plain, 'Exposing Canada's toxic shame' event, lecture delivered at the Faculty of Environmental Studies, York University, 12 March 2008: notes on file with author.

6 The term 'hormone-mimics' was made popular through the very influential 1997 book by Theo Colborne et al, *Our Stolen Future* (1996), which is said to have done for endocrine disruption what Rachel Carson's *Silent Spring* (1962) did for pesticides, in terms of inspiring an environmental movement.

7 For a description of the mechanics of endocrine disruption from the perspective of contemporary science, see Solomon and Schettler (2000). For a compelling account of how hormones emerged out of the historically and socially specific conditions of endocrine research environments in the early twentieth century, see Oudshoorn (1994). I am grateful to Mariana Valverde for putting me onto the critical work of Nelly Oudshorrn.

8 Nancy Langston (2008) also attributes rising 'rates of intersexuality' to endocrine disruption.

9 I return to, and further complicate, West's argument later in the chapter.

10 These strategies were shared with me by members of the Aamjiwnaang First Nation at the Aamjiwnaang Environmental Health Symposium, Sarnia, 26 March 2008: notes on file with author.

11 As Anne Bottomley has noted, these assumptions have been fundamental: 'knowledge of ourselves and of our world, has been predicated upon binary constructs of . . . male/female . . .' (2002: 127).

12 These data were presented by Sharilyn Johnston (Aamjiwnaang Environment Officer) and Ron Plain (Health and Environment Committee Member) at the Aamjiwnaang Environmental Health Symposium, Sarnia, Ontario, 27 March 2008: notes on file with author.

13 Ron Plain, 'Exposing Canada's toxic shame' event, lecture delivered at the Faculty of Environmental Studies, York University, 12 March 2008: notes on file with author.

14 Ron Plain, 'Exposing Canada's toxic shame' event, lecture delivered at the Faculty of Environmental Studies, York University, 12 March 2008: notes on file with author.

15 Michelle Murphy might call it a 'complex of molecular relations that extend outward in place and into the past, as well as forward to uncertain futures' (2008: 696).

16 Janice Richardson, as well as Battersby and Nedelsky, have written extensively on the relevance of metaphysical models of the 'body boundary' to legal theory. In this body of theory, the conventional model of body boundary as a 'container' for the self is critiqued. Richardson, in particular, urges a re-imagining of the self 'in a manner more subtle than that of a pre-formed entity trying to defend its own boundaries' (2007: 252).

17 Richardson employs Battersby's metaphor of water running through a sieve, always flowing but maintaining a steady level of water, to explain the idea of a self that is dynamic but maintaining a degree of stability. She states that is 'an image of a self that is carved out over time, neither passive nor completely autonomous' (2007: 242).

18 In Nicolas Rose's (2007) notion of the 'molecularization of life', the molecular realm is 'newly legible and politicizable' (Murphy 2008: 696). As life becomes populated by 'molecular-scale entities, processes and relationships' (Murphy 2008: 696) why not molecular-level harms recognised by law?

19 In the UK (unlike Australia and Canada) battery and trespass to the person more generally can only be committed intentionally. The case of *Letang v Cooper* [1965] established a cause of action in negligent trespass is not available, and this was recently confirmed by the UK Court of Appeal in the case of *Iqbal v Prison Officers Association* [2009]: [71].

20 The House of Lords in the UK rejected a claim in loss of chance related to a misdiagnosis of cancer in 2005 (*Gregg v Scott* [2005]).

21 For sharp commentary, see Richardson (2004).

22 In *Darlington*, Lord Bingham of Cornhill found that the 'real loss suffered in a situation of this kind' is that a parent, a mother, 'has been denied, through the negligence of another, the opportunity to live her life in the way that she wished and planned' ([2003]: [1097]).

23 Pay equity is a compensation practice aimed at addressing the gender wage gap by basing pay decisions on the value of work performed (Hartmann and Aaronson 1994: [71]). Sex-based wage discrimination, even though the wage gap hovers around 30 per cent, had to be proven to be believed; the same was true for the sex ratio disparity at Aamjiwnaang. See Hunter (1993) examining the history of gender-based wage discrimination and undervaluation of women's work.

24 See also Gibson (2003). This further reinforces the way that tort law is invested in the individuated legal subject: as Alan Hyde states, '[b]ehind of the entire practice of monetary compensation for bodily injury must lie a hazy notion of the body as "property" "lost" to its owner' (1997: 63).

25 Although, on certain environmental justice or historical accounts, this may be open to debate. Did the chemical industry 'choose' the Aamiwnaang First Nation as their neighbours?

26 Hyde's analysis uncovers the 'multiple competing constructions of the body [that] are available to legal and other speakers', and show that these constructions are 'neither natural, nor limited by biology' (viii–ix). As he demonstrates, actors choose amongst these competing constructions for instrumental purposes: he takes the project of 'denaturalisation' to be an aim of critical legal scholarship.

27 I attribute this idea to Lucie White's presentation at the symposium 'Injuries Without Remedies', 26 March 2010, Loyola of Los Angeles Law School.

Cases

Darlington Memorial Hospital NHS Trust v Rees [2003] UKHL 52
Gregg v Scott [2005] UKHL 2
Iqbal v Prison Officers Association [2009] EWCA Civ 1312
Kealey v Berezowski [1996] 30 OR 3d 37
Letang v Cooper [1965] 1 QB 232, Court of Appeal
MY v Boutros [2002] ABQB 362
Tock v St John's Metropolitan Area Board [1989] 2 SCR 1181

Bibliography

Ballentine, J. (1969) *Ballentine's Law Dictionary*, 3rd Edition. Rochester, NY: Lawyers Co-operative Pub. Co

Bender, L. (1990) 'Feminist (Re)torts: Thoughts on the Liability Crisis, Mass Torts, Power and Responsibilities', *Duke Law Journal*, 37: 848

Bloom, A. (2010) 'To Be Real', *North Carolina Law Review*, 88: 357

Bottomley, A. (2002) 'The Many Appearances of the Body in Feminist Scholarship', in A. Bainham, S.D. Sclater and M. Richards (eds) *Body Lore and Laws*, Oxford: Hart Publishing, 127–48

Carson, R. (1962) *Silent Spring*, Boston: Houghton Mifflin Co

Chamallas, M. and Kerber, L.K. (1990) 'Women, mothers and the law of fright: A history', *Michigan Law Review* 88: 814–864.

Colborne, T. et al (1996) *Our Stolen Future*, New York: Dutton

Collins, L. (2008) 'Protecting Aboriginal Environments: A Tort Law Approach', in S. Rogers et al (eds) *Critical Torts*, Toronto: Lexis, 2008, 61–80

Collins, L. and McLeod-Kilmurray, H. (2011) 'Material Contribution to Justice? Toxic Causation after Hanke v Resurfice', *Osgoode Hall Law Journal* 48: 411

—— (2002) 'Law, harm and redress: A feminist perspective', *Legal Studies*, 22: 319–339

Conaghan J. (1996) 'Gendered Harms and the Law of Tort: Remedying (Sexual) Harassment', *Oxford Journal of Legal Studies*, 16(3): 407

—— (1996b) 'Tort Law and the Feminist Critique of Reason', in A. Bottomley (ed) *Feminist Perspectives on the Foundational Subjects of Law*, London: Routledge, 47–85

—— (2002) 'Law, harm and redress: a feminist perspective', *Legal Studies*, 22: 319–339

Conaghan, J. and Mansell, W. (1993) *The Wrongs of Tort*, 2nd edn, London: Pluto Press

Cranor, Carl (2006) *Toxic Torts: Science, Law and the Possibility of Justice*, New York: Cambridge University Press

Davis, A. (2008) 'Racism, Birth Control and Reproductive Rights', in N. Ehrenreich (ed) *The Reproductive Rights Reader: Law, Medicine, and the Construction of Motherhood*, New York: NYU Press, 86–93

Decoste, T. (1993) 'Taking Torts Progressively', in K. Cooper-Stevenson and E. Gibson (eds) *Tort Theory*, North York: Captus University Press

Engels, D. (2000) 'Injury and Identity: the damaged self in three cultures', in L.C. Bower, D.T. Goldberg and M. Mushero (eds), *Between Law and Culture: Re-locating legal studies*, Minneapolis, MN: University of Minnesota Press, 3–21

Erikson, K. (1991) 'A new species of trouble', in S.R. Couch and J.S. Kroll Smith (eds) *Communities at risk: Collective responses to technological hazards*, New York: Peter Lang, 11–30

Feldthusen, B. (1993) 'If This is Torts, Negligence Must be Dead', in K. Cooper-Stevenson and E. Gibson (eds) *Tort Theory*, North York: Captus University Press

Felstiner, W.L.F., Abel, R.L. and Sarat, A. (1980–81) 'The Emergence and Transformation of Disputes: Naming, Blaming, Claiming . . .', *Law & Society Review*, 15: 631

Galanter, M. (autumn 2010) 'The Dialectic of Injury and Remedy', *Loyola of Los Angeles Law Review*, 44: 1

Gibson, E. (1993) 'The Gendered Wage Dilemma in Personal Injury Law', in K. Cooper-Stevenson and E. Gibson (eds) *Tort Theory*, North York: Captus University Press, 185–211

Gilbertson, M. (2002) 'Early Warnings of Chemical Contamination in the Great Lakes', in P. Harremoes et al (eds) *The Precautionary Principle in the 20th Century: Late Lessons from Early Warnings*, London: Earthscan Publications, 138–47

Grosz, E. (2004) *The Nick of Time: Politics, Evolution and the Untimely*, Durham, N.C.: Duke University Press

Hartmann, H.I. and Aaronson, S. (1994) 'Pay Equity and Women's Wage Increases: Success in the States, A Model for the Nation', *Duke Journal of Gender and Law Policy*, 1: 69.

Howe, A. (1991) 'The problem of priratized injuries: feminist strategies for litigation', in M. Albertson Fineman and N. Sweet Thomadsen (eds) *At the boundaries of law: feminism and legal theory*, New York: Routledge, 148–169

Hunter, R. (1993) 'Afterword: A Feminist Response to the Gender Gap in Compensation Symposium', *Georgetown Law Journal*, 82: 147

Hyde, A. (1997) *Bodies of Law*, Princeton, NJ: Princeton University Press

Jain, S.S.L. (2006) *The Politics of Product Design and Safety Law in the United States*, Princeton, N.J.: Princeton University Press

Jasanoff, S. (2002) 'Science and the Statistical Victim: Modernizing Knowledge in Breast Implant Litigation', *Social Studies of Science*, 32: 37

Kidd, K. et al (2007) 'Collapse of a Fish Population After Exposure to a Synthetic Estrogen', *Proceedings of the National Academy of Sciences (U.S.)*, 104: 8897

King, J.H. (1981) 'Causation, Valuation, and Chance in Personal Injury Torts Involving Preexisting Conditions and Future Consequences', *Yale Law Journal*, 90: 1353

Klar, L.N. (2008) *Tort Law*, 4th edn, Toronto: Carswell

Krupp, S.J. (2000) 'Environmental hazards: Assessing the risk to women', *Fordham Environmental Law Journal* 12: 111–138.

Lazarus, Richard J. (1997) 'Fairness in Environmental Law', *Environmental Law*, 27: 705–39

Langston, N. (2008) 'The Retreat From Precaution: Regulating Diethylstilbestrol (DES), Endocrine Disruptors, and Environmental Health', *Environmental History*, 13(1): 41

Léger, L. (1993) 'The Culture of the Common Law in the 21st Century: Tort Law's Response to the Needs of a Pluralist Society', in K. Cooper-Stevenson and E. Gibson (eds) *Tort Theory*, North York: Captus University Press, 162–77

Linden, A.M. (1997) *Canadian Tort Law*, 6th edn, Toronto: Butterworths

Luke, T. (2000) 'Rethinking Technoscience in Risk Society: Toxicity as Textuality', in R. Hofrichter (ed) *Reclaiming the Environmental Debate: The Politics of Health in a Toxic Culture*, Cambridge, MA: MIT Press, 239–54

MacDonald, E. and Rang, S. (2007) Exposing Canada's Chemical Valley: An Investigation of Cumulative Air Pollution Emissions in the Sarnia, Ontario Area (Toronto: Eco Justice)

Mackenzie, C., Lockridge, A. and Keith, M. (2005) 'Declining Sex Ratio in a First Nation Community', *Environmental Health Perspectives*, 113: 1295

Martin, A. (2010) '"Your Mother's Always With You": Material Feminism and Fetomaternal Microchimerism', *Resources for Feminist Research*, 33: 31–46

Mellor, M. (1997) *Feminism & ecology*. New York: NYU Press

Mittelstaedt, M. (2008) 'Humanity at Risk: Are the Males Going First', *Globe and Mail*, September 20: F4.

Murphy, M. (2008) 'Chemical Regimes of Living', *Environmental History*, 13: 695–703

Nolan, C. (2007) 'New Forms of Damage in Negligence', *Modern Law Review*, 70(1): 59.

Nolan, S. (2011) 'Rate of Aborted Female Fetuses Increases in India', *Globe & Mail*, 24 May 2011

Nye, J.L. (1998) 'The gender box', *Berkley Women's Law Journal* 13: 226–256

Oudshoorn, N. (1994) *Beyond the natural body: An archeology of sex hormones*. New York: Routledge

Oyama, S. (2000) *Evolution's Eye: A Systems View of the Biology-Culture Divide*, Durham, NC: Duke University Press

Prilaux, N. (2004) 'That's One Heck of an "Unruly Horse"! Riding Roughshod Over Autonomy in Wrongful Conception', *Feminist Legal Studies*, 12: 317

Pryor, J. (2007) 'Lost Profit or Lost Chance: Reconsidering the Measure of Recovery for Lost Profits in Breach of Contract Actions', *Regent University Law Review*, 19: 561

Richardson, J. (2004) *Selves, Persons, Individuals. Philosophical Perspectives on Women and Legal Obligations*, Aldershot: Ashgate

—— (2007) 'The Law and the Sublime: Rethinking the Self and Its Boundaries', *Law & Critique* 18: 229–52

Rose, N. (2009) *The politics of life itself: biomedicine, power, and subjectivity in the twenty-first century*, Princeton, NJ: Princeton University Press

Scott, D.S. (2008) 'Confronting Chronic Pollution: A Socio-Legal Analysis of Risk and Precaution', *Osgoode Hall Law Journal*, 46(2): 293

—— (2009) '"Gender-Benders": Sex and Law in the Constitution of Polluted Bodies', *Feminist Legal Studies*, 17: 241

—— (autumn 2010) 'Body Polluted: Questions of Scale, Gender and Remedy', *Loyola of Los Angeles Law Review*, 44: 121

Solomon, G.M. and Schettler, T. (2000) 'Environment and Health: Endocrine Disruption and Potential Human Health Implications', *Canadian Medical Association Journal*, 163: 1471

Toffolon-Weiss, M. and Roberts, T. (2004) 'Toxic Torts, Public Interest Law, and Environmental Justice: Evidence from Louisiana', *Law and Policy*, 26: 259

Verchick, R. (1996) 'In a Greener Voice: Feminist Theory and Environmental Justice' *Harv Women's L.J.* 19: 23

Weinrib, J. (1989) 'Understanding Tort Law', *Valparaiso University Law Review*, 23: 485

West, R. (1988) 'Jurisprudence and Gender', *University of Chicago Law Review*, 55: 1

—— (1997) *Caring for Justice*, New York: NYU Press

Witting, C. (2002) 'Physical Damage in Negligence', *Cambridge Law Journal*, 61(1): 189

—— (2008) 'The House that Dr Beever Built: Corrective Justice, Principle and the Law of Negligence', *Modern Law Review*, 71(4): 621

Chapter 5

Trust in the Police? Police Negligence, Invisible Immunity and Disadvantaged Claimants

Kirsty Horsey

Introduction

> The public policy consideration which has first claim on the loyalty of the law
> is that wrongs should be remedied and . . . very potent counter-considerations
> are required to override that policy.
>
> (Lord Browne-Wilkinson in *X (Minors) v*
> *Bedfordshire County Council* [1995]: [749])

It is ordinarily – and often rightly – difficult to establish a duty of care in negligence
between a public body and a private citizen. However, the chequered history of
cases where the police have been negligent in the conduct of their investigations
and similar activities – particularly when harm results from an omission and/or
the related actions of a third party – shows that the police's protection by the courts
in this respect amounts to a *de facto* immunity from suit. Though such immunity
would seem to be contrary to common law principles and perhaps even in violation
of a claimant's Article 6 of the European Convention on Human Rights right to
a fair hearing, the broad and unquestioned application of public policy reasons
used to justify judicial denials of duty of care show that it clearly exists in practice.
Despite doubts about the continued validity of this reasoning expressed by some
senior judges, the UK judiciary has been complicit in protecting the police and
consequently in failing to protect vulnerable groups within society.

In relation to 'operational' matters, similarly to other public bodies and private
individuals, negligent actions by the police result relatively easily in private law
duties.[1] Duty may also arise where it can be said that despite the harm being caused
by omission and/or the act of a third party there has been some responsibility
assumed on the part of the police towards the eventual claimant.[2] However,
instances of often heinous negligence or incompetence in the police's primary
function of investigating and suppressing crime typically leave claimants with no
avenue for tortious redress: the police owe them no duty of care. Faced with largely
unsubstantiated public policy arguments, claimants (who often have been subjected
to the gravest of harms) and their needs are deemed inferior to the perceived
'greater good' for society as a whole – that is, letting the police continue their work
unhindered (Lord Hope in *Smith v Chief Constable of Sussex Police* [2008]: [78]). These

policy reasons derive from *Hill v Chief Constable of West Yorkshire* [1989], the (in)-famous case which, according to Lord Steyn in *Brooks v Commissioner of Police for the Metropolis* [2005], established the so-called 'core principle' in this area of negligence (*Brooks v Commissioner of Police for the Metropolis* [2005]: [30]). In *Hill*, Lord Keith relied, *inter alia*, on the twin pillars of defensive practice and resource diversion to find that the police owe no duty of care to individuals in relation to ongoing criminal investigations or their wider public duty of crime suppression. He found that:

> [t]he general sense of public duty which motivates police forces is unlikely to be appreciably reinforced by the imposition of such liability so far as concerns their function in the investigation and suppression of crime . . . In some instances the imposition of liability may lead to the exercise of a function being carried on in a detrimentally defensive frame of mind ... A great deal of police time, trouble and expense might be expected to have to be put into the preparation of the defence to the action and the attendance of witnesses at the trial. The result would be a significant diversion of police manpower and attention from their most important function, that of the suppression of crime.
>
> (Lord Keith in *Hill* [1989]: [63])

It might be said that private law is not the place for such matters and that the behaviour of public bodies, including the police, is better controlled using public-functioning bodies such as ombudsmen, or independent investigations, such as those conducted by the Independent Police Complaints Commission (IPCC), or even by internal complaints and discipline procedures (Lord Hoffmann 1999: 162). While this argument may persuade in relation to what may be called 'day-to-day' negligence, it is wholly unpersuasive in relation to the systemic negligence that gives rise to the exceptional cases in this area. Indeed, one reason that claimants in the most notorious police negligence cases bring civil claims in the first place is perhaps because of their dissatisfaction with other avenues, coupled with the desire for the type of justice that private law supposedly brings. In *Hill*, for example, the claimant acknowledged that her motivation for bringing a civil action was not the possibility of gaining compensation (she had in fact pledged to give any compensation to charity). Instead, her desire was to instigate an enquiry into the conduct of the police force during the investigation with the dual aims of finding out why the investigation had failed her daughter and to prevent similar occurrences in the future (see Lord Templeman in *Hill* [1989]: [64]; Burton 2009: 294).

This chapter seeks to add to the growing critique of the judicially-created public policy justifications used to deny police duties of care to individuals harmed by their negligence (see, for example, Burton 2009; McIvor 2010; Wilberg 2010), by countering those arguments with other 'societal' public policy considerations. It will argue that the wholesale application of unsubstantiated public policy reasons to questions of duty does more than simply fail individual claimants – it has negative practical implications on society as a whole as well as for already vulnerable or disadvantaged individuals or groups.[3] Joanne Conaghan mooted a similar point in her discussion of *Waters v Metropolitan Police Commissioner* [2000], where she identified how a 'woman-centred' (rather than defendant-centred) approach may have led rather more quickly to a finding of duty (2002: 335). In Lord Hutton's opinion in *Waters* we can identify elements of wider competing policy arguments beginning to be considered (such as the 'serious state of affairs in the Metropolitan police' that would be revealed and the 'public interest' in ensuring this did not continue (*Waters* [2000]: [1619]). However, as Conaghan asked: what about policy arguments relating specifically to vulnerable groups such as rape victims (2002: 333 and 337), or even female police officers in a predominantly male environment 'where bullying is rampant, management is ineffectual and sexism is entrenched' (2002: 337)? This chapter develops Conaghan's insights. Using case examples from England and Wales, Canada and Australia, it considers the extent to which to the ubiquitous *Hill* policy justifications can be countered by reference to their regressive effect on vulnerable individuals or groups within society. While policy considerations *are* important, these should be closely scrutinised from both sides and none should be automatically presumed to outweigh others. Should judges be doing more to highlight counter-policy concerns? And, if they do not, is justice in these cases really being done?

Why should we trust in the police?

There have been numerous recent highly publicised stories of serious police failures and incompetence in the UK, bringing police negligence squarely into the public consciousness. This inevitably has a bearing on public perceptions of and confidence in the police. In 2010–11, the Independent Police Complaints Commission (IPCC), a body established in 2002 to maintain public confidence in policing and to independently investigate complaints, released several reports into serious police failings. Among these are its reports of the investigations conducted into Operations Danzey, Anflora and Minstead (relating to the criminal investigations undertaken by the Metropolitan Police Service (MPS) into John Worboys, Kirk Reid and Delroy Grant, respectively) (IPCC 2010c; 2011a; 2011b). All three IPCC enquiries highlighted egregious 'failings by the Metropolitan Police Service regarding sexual offences investigation' (IPCC 2010c: 22), including mistakes, miscommunications and gaps in information sharing. More recently, the IPCC was called to investigate an incident in which a mother and her two-year-old daughter were shot dead, following concerns expressed by the woman's neighbours and others that the police could and should have prevented the murders, having been aware of the ongoing problems faced by the woman for at least two years (BBC News 2011a).

IPCC press releases and subsequent news reports tell us of the eventual convictions of criminals who, due to police incompetence, were able to continue committing offences. Worboys (the so-called 'Black Cab Rapist') drugged, sexually assaulted and/or raped women in his taxi. Following a public appeal conducted after his arrest, over 80 of his victims contacted the police. He was eventually convicted in March 2009 on 19 charges, including one of rape. It subsequently transpired that Worboys had previously been arrested for the same crimes and released without charge. Disturbingly, the MPS's own findings showed 'poor compliance with the Standard Operating Procedures for investigation of rape and serious sexual assaults by front line officers and their supervisors' (IPCC 2010a: 5). The investigation focused mainly on complaints against the police from two of Worboys' victims. The first concerned insensitive treatment by police officers. The woman had been falsely informed that a file had been passed to the Crown Prosecution Service, that there was no trace of drugs in her system after her attack and that the suspect did not live near her. While her complaints were not substantiated (though the IPCC report noted that it was disturbing that the woman concerned should have *perceived* she was treated badly; 2010a: 8–10), others relating to the way the investigation into her assault was conducted, including a complaint relating to the police officers' favouring of the suspect's over the victim's evidence, *were* upheld. Regarding the latter, the report says:

> A Detective Constable became the officer in charge of this case on 29 July 2007. His first entry on the crime report made on 30 July 2007 includes the following statement: 'The victim cannot remember anything past getting in the cab, it would seem unlikely that a cab driver would have alcohol in his vehicle let alone drug substances'. This appears to be indicative of a mindset that had already been formed – that a black cab driver would not commit such an offence. This mindset would have meant that the cab driver, rather than the victim, had been believed, and would inevitably have damaged the victim's confidence in the police handling of her allegation.
>
> (IPCC 2010a: 10)

A second woman alleged that '[t]he Detective Constable who was the investigating officer in the case failed to investigate her allegation appropriately, coached her not to show emotion ahead of her interview, did not believe her and lost the case papers' (IPCC 2010a: 12).

All of this is truly disturbing. In its final report, the IPCC concluded that the 'overwhelming themes in these cases are of an actual or perceived sceptical or insensitive police response to victims of sexual violence, investigations that lack rigour and during which the victims feel they are not being kept informed' (2010a: 15) and that despite some internal improvement being made by the MPS, 'more needs to be done if public confidence in the police's response to reports of rape and sexual offences is to improve', acknowledging that this is 'widely regarded' as 'a long neglected area of policing' (IPCC 2010b). However, its formal recommendations were only that leaflets should be provided, outlining the kind of treatment victims of sexual offences should expect from the police, alongside a statement that 'the Met needs to work more closely with the voluntary sector, who have a crucial role working with victims to promote public confidence in the police' (IPCC 2010b).

In a similar case, Grant (known as 'the Night Stalker') was a serial sex attacker who preyed, primarily, on old women living alone in London, for almost 20 years.

His eventual conviction was followed by an apology from the MPS about mistakes made during the investigation, which led to a 10-year delay in his arrest, and therefore a number of attacks that could have been prevented. Similar failings surfaced in relation to the negligent handling of the prolonged investigation into the crimes of Reid, another serial sex attacker, first identified as a potential suspect in 2004 but only asked to give a DNA sample (which linked him to three earlier assaults) in 2008 when another police unit took over the investigation (IPCC 2011a). In a statement, the IPCC Commissioner for London, Deborah Glass, said:

> The fact that Reid was identified as a suspect in 2004 and yet went on to sexually assault more women before he was eventually arrested in 2008 is a real cause for concern. The public will understandably ask if some of these attacks could have been prevented and indeed, if the police took the victims as seriously as they should.
>
> (IPCC 2011a)

Taken together, these cases (and there are more) highlight systematic failures among police to carry out their investigative functions – particularly into sex crimes – diligently and with care. In relation to Worboys, the five officers concerned were internally disciplined (one Detective Constable and one Detective Inspector received written warnings, and the others received 'formal words of advice' (IPCC 2011b)). In the Grant and Reid investigations, the IPCC found that three officers and one Superintendent and two Detective Inspectors (respectively) had a case to answer as a result of their incompetence during the investigation. Additionally, in the Reid investigation, a Chief Superintendent and a Detective Sergeant received formal words of advice.

While this evidences that something does happen when complaints are made, it does not have the same effect as a judicial finding that police owe duties of care in their investigations would have, particularly in any deterrent sense. In the Minstead Report the IPCC states that one of its reasons for conducting the investigation was to enable it to report on any 'organisational learning for the police service, including whether any change in police policy or practice would help to prevent a recurrence of the incident investigated' (IPCC 2010c: 4). However, the threat of civil liability may be more of a deterrent and have more impact on changing police practice and challenging their perceptions and assumptions in future cases. Thus it may be suggested that in terms of both redress for victims and in encouraging changed practices, tort law would better fill the void. IPCC findings could be used as indicators of potential liability, rather than an end in themselves.[4]

Further exploring the numerous IPCC reports there are seemingly endless and less well-known cases where police indifference to victims' calls for help have contributed to the subsequent serious bodily harm or the death of that individual.[5] In many of the cases the IPCC's conclusion is that the police simply could have done their job better and that there was an obvious failure to protect. This means, then, that the IPCC is highlighting – at an alarmingly frequent rate – that there are serious problems in the execution of police duties. This in turn suggests that the courts are being irresponsible (to disadvantaged groups in particular) in ignoring this reality and hiding behind unproven policy justifications. In short, they are letting the police 'get away with negligence'.

A 2011 Home Office report shows that 'only half of the [UK] public trust our criminal justice system to protect them from criminals' and a widespread belief that the police have 'become disconnected from the public they serve' (Home Office 2011: 3). Blaming this on rises in bureaucracy and 'red tape', the report suggests that greater collaboration between the police and the public must be developed in order to generate co-operation (Home Office 2011: 5, 7). The report is introduced on the Home Office website as being designed to give '[t]he police and their partners . . . far greater freedom to do their jobs and use their discretion' and the public 'more power to hold the police and community safety partnerships to account and feel empowered to reclaim their communities'. Home Secretary Teresa May, in her introduction to the report, calls this 'giving power to the people' (Home Office 2011: 1). The report does not, however, address the police's lack of *legal* accountability (even in a section on 'prevention as well as cure', though it is acknowledged that misconduct cases can be referred to the IPCC). More importantly, it fails to recognise the effects this may have on public perception and confidence, particularly among already vulnerable or disadvantaged societal groups. In the light of the immunity already afforded to the police in negligence, the report's proposed removal of 'red tape' which purportedly hinders and 'obstructs' police work, alongside an increase in police discretion (Home Office 2011: 3) is distressing, as the expansion of their already wide powers is clearly not being met by equally stringent measures to ensure that these powers are reasonably deployed. Additionally, nowhere is there any consideration of the fact that despite the perceived (yet not proven) advantages to society in terms of costs and efficiency of policing that these proposals are supposed to bring about, that disadvantaged groups may be more diversely and disproportionately affected by 'red tape' removal and increased police discretion.[6]

Police negligence and duties of care

The undesirable effects of immunity

Writing extra-judicially after his retirement, Lord Bingham described the primary function of the law of tort as 'securing compensation', with a secondary role of discouraging negligent behaviour (2010: 3–4). This ought to mean that a 'broad brush' approach (McIvor 2010: 134) to a denial of duty in the context of crime investigation and suppression is untenable – yet this is exactly what happens, as seen in *Smith*, the most recent decision in the chain of police negligence cases extending over 20 years back to *Hill*. In *Smith*, four of the UK's most senior judges can be seen clinging inexorably to *Hill*'s core principle, which they see as stretching almost unquestionably through preceding cases and into the one before them. The facts of *Smith* are stark. Smith, a gay man, was attacked by his ex-partner Gareth Jeffrey with a claw hammer, suffering serious and permanent injuries. The police were aware of a previous assault on Smith by Jeffrey two years earlier and in fact had detained Jeffrey overnight on that occasion. For some time before the eventual attack in March 2003:

> Jeffrey sent Mr Smith a stream of violent, abusive and threatening telephone, text and internet messages, including death threats. There were sometimes ten to fifteen text messages in a single day. During February 2003 alone there were some 130 text messages. Some of these messages were very explicit: 'U are dead'; 'look out for yourself psycho is coming'; 'I am looking to kill you and no compromises'; 'I was in the Bulldog last night with a carving knife. It's a shame I missed you'.
>
> (Lord Bingham in *Smith* [2008]: [23])

Smith reported these threats and more to the police, giving details of the history of violence and providing Jeffrey's home address. However, '[t]he officers declined to look at the messages . . . made no entry in their notebooks, took no statement from Mr Smith and completed no crime form' (*Smith* [2008]: [24]). This first contact with the police was not the only time he was ignored or passed on.[7] Despite this, the lower court and the majority of the Law Lords hearing the case agreed that Smith's claims against the police in negligence should be struck out on the grounds that he had no prospect of succeeding, as the police owed him no duty of care in relation to the conduct of their investigation. Lord Bingham, in his words, 'had the misfortune to disagree with the other four members of the appellate committee' (2010: 4). He agreed with the Court of Appeal, which had unanimously found a duty of care on the facts assumed. He wrote: 'I considered, and continue to consider, that on the majority ruling the law of tort or delict in this area failed to perform the basic function for which it exists' (2010: 4).

As has been identified elsewhere (see, for example, McIvor 2008; 2010), *Hill*'s core principle is being stretched to do more than it was ever intended to do, and to cover factual scenarios to which it neither directly applies nor should even have been considered (see, for example, *Brooks v Commissioner of Police for the Metropolis* [2005]). Even in a relevant *type* of case, such as *Smith*, it is so heavily and unquestioningly relied on that it amounts to a kind of judicial crutch – or a get-out clause. What *should* be happening in these cases, bearing in mind both the fundamental principles that underpin tort law and the negative social effects that the application of blanket policy reasoning to vulnerable people or groups may produce,[8] is a balanced consideration of the reasons (public policy or otherwise) that exist in favour of *both* denial of duty and of finding duty (see Conaghan 2002: 338). This approach has been judicially indicated in many public body liability cases *not* involving the police (eg *X v Bedfordshire* [1995]), as well as by the European Court of Human Rights (ECtHR) (*Z v UK* [2001]) *and* in the seminal House of Lords' decision (notably handed down on the same day and by the same court as *Brooks*) of *D v East Berkshire Community NHS Trust* [2005]. It even featured in a major similar case (*Home Office v Dorset Yacht Co Ltd* [1970]), long before *Hill* was decided.[9]

That this feature of private law reasoning is being ignored is concerning – particularly as some of the claimants in police negligence cases can be identified as coming from groups already at some kind of legal or social disadvantage, and who might be using private law – and tort law in particular – as a vehicle to factors other than financial recompense, such as (as for the claimant in *Hill*) answers, deterrence, the raising of public awareness about certain vulnerable groups and/or of police incompetence, or even apology. Denying duties of care by relying solely on the *Hill* principle fails to do justice for these claimants – and the societal groups they belong to. This is particularly true when considering the 21st-century police force and its too frequent failings.[10] Wider ramifications of such heavy reliance on *Hill* can be identified in relation to vulnerable claimants, such as (but not limited to) rape victims, via continued poor rape reporting and conviction rates, as well as the maintenance of a 'traditional gender bias' in the criminal justice system in relation to rape (Larcombe 2011: 28).[11] Similarly, we could include police attitudes to victims of domestic violence,[12] race relations between police and citizens[13] and diversity within the police force itself.[14]

There should be proper judicial consideration of the policy reasons why wholesale denial of a duty of care from police to individuals may not be desirable. Most importantly, attention should be paid to ideas relating to public confidence in policing (especially for women, in conjunction with rape, domestic violence etc) and community trust in the police as fulfilling their *public* functions. It is terrible to state that individuals cannot be owed a duty of care *because* the primary function/ duty of the police is a public one, which involves detailed consideration of the effects on this function (and therefore the wider public) of *potentially* imposing liability, while at the same time failing to acknowledge – or even consider – that a finding of no duty possibly helps to result in exactly the kind of police behaviour and attitude that leaves the public with little faith in them.[15]

When are the vulnerable owed a duty?

It is not impossible for the police to owe a duty of care in negligence, even in matters that might be considered to exist outside or on the borderline of the 'operational' sphere. Case law shows that a clear duty (though narrowly defined) is owed to those in police custody where there is any knowledge or suspicion of mental vulnerability to take reasonable measures to ensure that prisoners can bring no harm to them-selves (*Reeves v Commissioner of Police for the Metropolis* [2000]; *Orange v Chief Constable of West Yorkshire Police* [2001]). This is predicated on the notion – one which weaves through all problematic duty areas in negligence – of there being an assumption of responsibility towards the party concerned, coupled with the foreseeability of harm. It has also been acknowledged that one officer owes another a duty to intervene to protect them from harm when circumstances are such as to render this reasonable. In *Costello*, finding this duty in the context of a female police officer being attacked in a custody cell while a male officer stood by and watched, the Court of Appeal considered the 'public interest' in establishing a duty of care in the circumstances. May LJ believed that 'the public would be greatly disturbed if the law held that there was no duty of care in this case', adding: 'The particular circumstances of this case should not be left solely to internal police discipline' (*Costello v Chief Constable of Northumbria Police* [1999]: [564]). It is to be hoped that what was being considered here, at least in part, was the effect that *not* finding a duty would have on the recruitment and retention of female officers and on women's perception of the police, particularly their response to women in situations of danger.

It is also clearly not impossible to ask courts to consider countervailing policy arguments even in cases related to the police's public duty of investigation and suppression of crime. Perhaps the closest example of this is found in *Swinney*. Here it was highlighted that in order to *help* the police perform this most primary of public functions, a duty should be owed to police informants in relation to the protection of their identity, precisely *because* of their vulnerability: the fact that they are *likely* to suffer harm should their identity become known to those they have given information about, if those who assume the responsibility to protect them from such harm should fail.[16] Hirst LJ stated that:

> other considerations of public policy . . . also have weight, namely the need to preserve the springs of information, to protect informers, and to encourage them to come forward without an undue fear of the risk that their identity will subsequently become known to the suspect or to his associates . . . [P]ublic policy in this field must be assessed in the round, which in this case means assessing the applicable considerations advanced in *Hill*'s case . . . together with the considerations just mentioned in relation to informers, in order to reach a fair and just decision on public policy.
>
> (Hirst LJ in *Swinney v Chief Constable of Northumbria Police* [1997]: [464]))

The underlying policy consideration was that the *public* must feel safe in the knowledge that, should they do their civic duty in this way, the police will protect them. If this was not the case, the court surmised, fewer people would give information to the police, resulting in an overall negative effect for society.

Similarly, in *Waters*, a duty was – eventually – found to be owed to a trainee female police officer who reported that she had been vaginally and anally raped by a fellow trainee officer in police quarters. Her complaint in negligence related not to the rape itself, but to the conduct of her colleagues after the rape (for which the Police Commissioner would be vicariously liable) and also to the way her superiors handled the bullying and victimisation she faced having reported it (in this respect she alleged the Commissioner was personally liable). Her claims were struck out by both the High Court and the almost derisive Court of Appeal (Conaghan describes parts of the leading judgment as 'cursory' and states that Swinton-Thomas LJ's judgment in particular 'drips with disdain' (2002: 327–8)). The Court of Appeal relied partly on *Hill*, alongside other policy justifications derived from *Calveley v Chief Constable of Merseyside Police* [1989], where it was found that the fact that police internal investigations, including disciplinary proceedings, were closely regulated by statute militated against a duty of care, even where they were negligently conducted.

By the time *Waters* reached the House of Lords, only the personal liability claim survived. And it was only here (and therefore thanks largely to her own perseverance in the face of considerable adversity – though timing may also have a lot to do with it)[17] that a duty of care was found. This was partly *because* of the message a finding of no duty would send to other rape victims (and women more generally). Lord Hutton recognised that:

> If the facts alleged by the plaintiff in her Statement of Claim are true they disclose a situation of gravity which should give rise to serious concern that a young policewoman should be treated in the way she alleges and that no adequate steps were taken by senior officers to protect her against victimisation and harassment.
>
> (Lord Hutton in *Waters* [2000]: [1615])

The policy justifications used to deny a duty in both *Hill* and *Calveley* were distinguished. Eileen Waters *was* owed a duty of care. In Lord Slynn's view, behind the heart of Eileen Waters' claim, lay 'the belief that the other officers reviled her and failed to take care of her because she had broken the team rules by complaining of sexual acts by a fellow police officer' which 'went beyond' either of those two cases and included a 'systematic failure to protect' her (*Waters* [2000]: [1610]). The claim did not relate 'only to negligence by the police in the investigation of an offence' (Lord Hutton in *Waters* [2000]: [1618]; also see Lord Slynn in *Waters* [2000]: [1613]) and was therefore not a case which 'plainly and obviously must fail' (Lord Slynn in *Waters* [2000]: [1614]). Lord Hutton considered it important that 'where the police claim immunity against an action for negligence public policy must be assessed in the round, which means assessing the considerations referred to in *Hill* together with other considerations bearing on the public interest in order to reach a fair and just decision' (*Waters* [2000]: [1618]). Dismissing the striking out application, he found that:

> If the present case goes to trial the preparation of the defence will take up much time and effort on the part of police officers, but this is a consequence faced by defendants in many actions and I do not consider that it is a consideration of sufficient potency to counterbalance the plaintiff's claim that she is entitled to have a remedy for a serious wrong. Moreover if the plaintiff succeeds at the trial in proving in whole or in substantial part the truth of her allegation that she was subjected to serious and prolonged victimisation and harassment which caused her psychiatric harm because she had made an allegation of a serious offence against a fellow officer and that the Commissioner through his senior officers was guilty of negligence in failing to take adequate steps to

protect her against such treatment, such proof would reveal a serious state of affairs in the Metropolitan Police. If such a state of affairs exists I consider that it is in the public interest that it should be brought to light so that steps can be taken to seek to ensure that it does not continue, because if officers (and particularly women officers who complain of a sexual offence committed against them by a male colleague) are treated as the plaintiff alleges, citizens will be discouraged from joining the police, or from continuing to serve in the police after they have joined, with consequent harm to the interests of the community. In my opinion this is a consideration which carries significant weight when placed in the scales against the argument that the continuance of the action will place unreasonable and disproportionate burdens on the police and distract them from their primary task of combating crime.

(Lord Hutton in *Waters* [2000]: [1619]–[1620])

In her close contextual feminist analysis of *Waters*, Conaghan (2002) highlights the narrowness of the typical judicial approach and the potential of this short-sightedness to close down avenues of redress that are socially, politically and legally desirable. The small glimmer of hope was that the Law Lords recognised[18] that the facts Eileen Waters alleged would, if true (as taken to be the case for the purposes of the hearings in negligence), raise serious concerns about the treatment of a young female police officer by her peers and superiors alike. The effect of this, on both serving and future female police officers, was considered, by Lord Hutton at least, to *outweigh* the policy argument that defending such claims – and investigating them properly in the first place – would require time and effort on the part of numerous officers, perhaps detracting their attention from other duties. The implications that judicial 'tolerance' of such a working environment would have on the recruitment and retention of female officers (and other minority groups),[19] as well as on the opinion of the police force in the eyes of the general public, particularly among women, ethnic minorities[20] and vulnerable others, must surely be the most important policy considerations. As Conaghan contends, *Waters* is a case that identifies and exemplifies many of the reasons why 'many people – but particularly women who are raped – continue to distrust the police' (2002: 333–4). She adds:

after all, [the police] are supposed to fight crime, investigate rape, interview rape victims and compile evidence for the prosecution. How could we not be concerned by an allegation that they not only ignore rape victims, but punish them for the temerity of complaining?

(Conaghan 2002: 332–3)

Do we need Hill? Looking to other jurisdictions

It is clear that these cases illustrate that a duty of care can and should be owed by the police in relation to officers' conduct even in the broad context of investigation and suppression of crime. It is also clear that these cases exemplify the fact that counter-policy arguments can and should be taken into account when assessing whether a duty arises. What is unfortunate is that such considerations have not become automatic, or even commonplace, in *all* police negligence claims, *despite* the overt recognition of the importance of such arguments in *Waters* or *Costello*, for example. However, other jurisdictions have proved to be more progressive in this respect.

In Canada, the courts have rejected *Hill*'s core principle in cases where there are stronger countervailing social/public policy arguments. These arguments include those relating to public confidence in the police and are particularly telling in relation to police attitudes towards rape victims. A good example is found in *Doe v Metropolitan Toronto (Municipality) Commissioners of Police* (1998). Here, the claimant sued the Toronto Metropolitan Police after being raped in her home by a serial rapist who was known by the police to be targeting women in a defined geographical area of the city and within a distinct group (single women living in first or second floor apartments with balconies). Thus, though the attack could have been on one of a considerable number of women, the case was distinguishable from *Hill* on proximity grounds. While the court recognised that at the time of the attacks the police were occupied with other important cases and therefore their resources and manpower were necessarily stretched – and that the police's ability to make discretionary decisions about how investigations were conducted was both desirable and necessary – these reasons were not enough to deny a finding of a duty of care owed by the police to the victim. MacFarland J held that the police owed the claimant (and presumably the rapist's other potential victims) a duty of care – but defined this narrowly as a duty to properly warn them that they were susceptible to an attack, *not* as a duty to prevent the crime happening at all, as this would have imposed an impossible burden on the police. Had Jane Doe been so warned, the judge concluded, she would have been able to take precautions to avoid being attacked – and such a warning would have been cheap and easy for the police to have issued. Perhaps the (female) judge's findings on the *reasons* why the officers concerned had chosen not to warn potential victims (their belief in rape myths and their thought that the women, if warned, would become 'hysterical' and so hinder the investigation (*Doe* 1998: 103)) helped her to see the wider social implications entailed in a finding of no duty (Moroz 1995; Hoyano 1999).[21] Interestingly (and perhaps tellingly), since *Doe*, there has not been a flood of claims – unmeritorious or otherwise – against the police in Canada and nor has the community suffered from the defensive police practices that have elsewhere too readily been assumed by judges to be a direct consequence of imposing duties of care on the police (Hoyano 1999: 930).

More recently, in *Hill v Hamilton-Wentworth Regional Police Services Board* [2007], the Supreme Court of Canada (SCC) recognised by a 6:3 majority the duty owed by the police to suspects of ongoing investigations. This was partly in recognition of the public's interest in responding to 'failures of the justice system, such as wrongful convictions or institutional racism' (*Hamilton-Wentworth* [2007]: [36]). Again, the policy reason *for* finding a duty outweighed the policy reasons from *Hill against* one (Chamberlain 2008: 1090).[22] Essentially, the SCC utilised a modified version of the two-stage *Anns*[23] test – first looking at the degree of foreseeability and proximity to determine that a *prima facie* duty should exist, and only *then* beginning to consider whether there are policy considerations that should negate it – and the court found there were not. In its summary of the judgment, the SCC says that:

> No compelling policy reasons negate the duty of care. Investigating suspects does not require police officers to make quasi-judicial decisions as to legal guilt or innocence or to evaluate evidence according to legal standards. The discretion inherent in police work is not relevant to whether a duty of care arises, although it is relevant to the standard of care owed to a suspect. Police officers are not unlike other professionals who exercise levels of discretion in their work but who are subject to a duty of care . . . The record does not establish that recognizing the tort will change the behaviour of the police, cause officers to become unduly defensive or lead to a flood of litigation. The burden of proof on a plaintiff and a defendant's right of appeal provide safeguards against any risk that a plaintiff acquitted of a crime, but in fact guilty of the crime, may recover against an officer for negligent investigation.
>
> (*Hamilton-Wentworth* [2007], judgment summary).[24]

Put simply, the SCC was not persuaded by fears of floodgates, or of limiting police discretion, and claimed that the 'defensive practices' argument was too vague to warrant serious consideration (Chamberlain 2008: 1090). Moreover, given the lack of sound empirical evidence to support such claims, the court was unwilling to accept them as true. Of course the existence of a duty of care does not ensure success – as *Hamilton-Wentworth* itself attests. In Canada the key hurdle is the standard of care that investigators should adhere to. Despite the fact that the investigation fell short of good practice, the officers concerned met the standard expected of reasonable officers at the time. Indeed, the SCC stressed the flexibility of the breach standard and the way it would be affected by 'the discretion inherent in police investigation' and the working practices of the relevant force at the time (*Hamilton-Wentworth* (1997): [68]–[73]).

The High Court of Australia has not yet been called to rule on a police negligence claim of the type we are discussing here. However, *Hill*-style reasoning seems to have found support in its other judgments on public body liability (for example, *Sullivan v Moody* [2001]; see Shircore 2006: 48). *Sullivan* raised a conflict of duty between doctors and social workers (negligently) investigating child abuse where the claimant was the father, therefore a finding of no duty was supported.[25] Arguably, similarities with cases involving suspects and/or victims of crime exist.[26] In *Tame v New South Wales* [2002], judicial denials of a duty of care owed by police were based on arguments almost identical to *Hill* (Gummow and Kirby JJ in *Tame v New South Wales* [2002]: [231]; Hayne J in *Tame v New South Wales* [2002]: [292]), though seemingly based more concretely on the idea of conflicting duties (broadly, public v private), thus following the broader principles applied to public body liability following *Sullivan*. As Shircore explains, a number of Australian state courts 'have held that inconsistent obligations owed to the person under investigation and potential victims operate to deny a duty of care owed by the investigating body to the person under investigation' (2006: 50; also see list: 51–3). This hints that a duty *could* be owed to potential victims (and see, in particular, *Batchelor v The State of Tasmania* [2005]), though if the *Hill* arguments find support in one instance it might be expected they would extend. Shircore contends that given both the Australian High Court and state courts' treatment of third party liability cases, finding a duty 'will not be an easy task', though higher degrees of foreseeability, coupled with claimant vulnerability and/or assumption of responsibility may be enough (2006: 50–1). She adds that 'the courts' differing methodologies [state and federal] demonstrate that, in Australia, the approach . . . is far from clear and consistent' (Shircore 2006: 51).

However, in a more recent state case, *Hill* was *not* followed and in fact a far narrower interpretation of its reach was indicated (*State of New South Wales v Tyszyk* [2008]). The facts are barely comparable to the type of cases we have so far been concerned with and in fact come closer to 'operational' negligence, though the defence contended that the principles from *Hill* should be applied as the police were investigating a crime at the time. Nevertheless, Campbell JA was at pains to stress that the defendants could not be protected from liability by *Hill* which, in his view, applied *only* to cases where a criminal at large poses a potential threat to any of a large group of people. In the end, no duty was found in any case because there was no proximate relationship justifying the imposition of a duty in respect of the omission that occurred. So liability was avoided 'on alternative grounds which were not only simpler but entirely more convincing' (McIvor 2010: 143).

The effect of reliance on **Hill**

These cases are important because they show that a different approach is possible. In the examples cited from both the UK and other jurisdictions, countervailing public policy claims prevailed and a duty was imposed on the police, even in relation to their so-called public functions and wider social duty in relation to the investigation and suppression of crime. We also see acknowledgements that the standard of care concept (and in some cases the 'ordinary' principles of duty of care) is flexible enough to restrict liability. Moreover, there is a realisation of the wider and potentially harmful effects of a no-duty finding on certain sections of society (for example, women, minority officers or rape victims) or indeed on the wider public perception of the police as a whole.

However, despite such recognition, along with more specific judicial acknowledgements of potential 'cracks' in the *Hill* principle – most obviously in *Smith* where Lord Hope acknowledges that the public policy grounds of *Hill* 'do not all stand up to critical examination today' (*Smith* [2008]: [73]),[27] it appears that as yet the UK courts are not prepared to make such considerations a common – let alone essential – feature of their deliberations. Moreover, though various inquiries and reports and an almost continuous proliferation of police blunders in the news challenge our trust in the police, our judges still do not step back and consider the potentially wider social implications of such heavy reliance on *Hill*.

In *Smith*, for example, the majority continued to rely on *Hill*, despite acknowledging doubts about the soundness of aspects of the core principle and a strong and clear dissenting opinion from Lord Bingham providing – albeit not flawlessly – another way to view potential liability in this context, essentially creating a standard of care-based test. In his view, a 'liability principle' (*Smith* [2008]: [44]) would not 'distract the police from their primary function of suppressing crime and apprehending criminals but calls for reasonable performance of that function' (*Smith* [2008]: [52]). So why were the rest of the Law Lords so resistant? Claire McIvor describes the majority's 'tone' as 'distinctly defensive' (2010: 134). They focused on the difficulty of assessing the credibility of the evidence given to the police and 'refused to engage in any kind of critical evaluation of the [core] principle, choosing instead to bluntly uphold its validity' (2010: 134). Lord Bingham had no such difficulty:

> [t]he answer is that given in any case where it is said that a professional should have been alerted to and should have responded to a risk. In the first instance the judgment is made by the professional in question. If that judgment is challenged, a judge must decide.
>
> (Lord Bingham in *Smith* [2008]: [59])

The majority opinions are illustrative of a myopic adherence to 20-year old principles and a distinct unwillingness to consider either that some of the assumptions the principle is based upon are wrong or that there might be alternative ways of viewing the public policy considerations for the benefit of society as a whole. Lord Hope, though viewing the police's failure in the case as 'highly regrettable' (*Smith* [2008]: [72]), went on to find that '[w]e must be careful not to allow ourselves to be persuaded by the shortcomings of the police in individual cases to undermine [the core principle from *Hill*]' (*Smith* [2008]: [75]). He then seemed to treat the facts of the case – which are disturbing at best, not only in the level of violence that one person can threaten and do to another but also in terms of the sheer complacency of the police in dealing with credible threats – as insignificant, thereby falling into the same trap as the police had done in considering the issue as a mere domestic incident:

> It is an unfortunate feature of the human experience that the breakdown of a close relationship leads to bitterness, and that this in its turn may lead to threats and acts of violence. So-called domestic cases that are brought to the attention of the police all too frequently are a product of that phenomenon . . . Not every complaint of this kind is genuine . . . Police work elsewhere may be impeded if the police were required to treat every report from a member of the public that he or she is being threatened with violence as giving rise to a duty of care to take reasonable steps to prevent the alleged threat from being executed.
>
> (Lord Hope in *Smith* [2008]: [76])

It is not acceptable for the police to write off domestic complaints in this way and this certainly should not be condoned by judges. Moreover, the effect of this reliance on *Hill* has a disproportionate effect on those that are already vulnerable. Domestic violence must be taken seriously by the police. A 2010 House of Commons Report showed that 1.2 million adults in the UK experienced domestic abuse from a partner or ex-partner in 2009, and that one in five adults have suffered such abuse (Thompson 2010). Another study showed that over 55,000 men and almost 4,000 women were convicted of domestic violence related offences in 2010 (BBC News 2011c). Stonewall claims that domestic violence is equally prevalent in same-sex relationships, stating that 'at least one in four LGBT people have experienced domestic violence in their relationships and from members of their families'.[28] The Commons report also acknowledged the potential *under*estimations inherent within such statistics:

> Domestic violence is a very private crime. Victims of domestic violence are less likely than victims of other forms of violence to report their experiences to the authorities because of beliefs that their abuse is not a matter for police involvement, their experiences too trivial, or from fear of reprisal.
>
> (Thompson 2010: 3)

It may well be then that the available statistics represent the 'tip of the iceberg'. This ought to mean that when such violence is imminent, likely and preceded by numerous specific threats, the police have an unquestionable obligation to do their very best to protect the potential victim. Yet we know that 'the police have a notable dislike for domestic violence calls' (Burton 2009: 291). As Mandy Burton also identifies, it is unlikely that the police would *better* protect against domestic violence if they themselves are protected from liability – the larger the ambit of their discretion the more room there is for negligence. Astoundingly, nowhere in *Smith* – where the facts exemplify exactly this problem in day-to-day police practice – is there acknowledgement that *not* imposing a duty on the police would increase negative perceptions of the police held by victims of domestic violence, same-sex or otherwise. Nor is there any recognition of the fact that this leads to strong countervailing policy reasons *against* the core *Hill* principle in the same way as for others (for example, police informants (*Swinney*), female officers (*Costello*) or victims of rape or harassment (*Waters*)). Some vulnerable claimants are more protected than others, it seems, and some not at all.

Policy: testing the *Waters*

The *Hill* principles arose in the context of late 1980s' policing. In *Hill*, Lord Keith found that while the police may make mistakes, 'it is not to be doubted that they apply their best endeavours to [their] performance' (*Hill* [1989]: [63]). Since that case, as indicated above, there have been, in judicial and other contexts, acknow-ledgements that such a 'rose-tinted' view of the police (McIvor 2010) is no longer sustainable, if it ever was. Elsewhere, McIvor has argued that the proximity component of the duty test is a sufficient restriction on liability (2008) thus rendering policy reasoning redundant. However, even this would leave many of the victims considered here without redress. In fact, policy considerations *are* important, *provided these are being looked at closely from both sides* and that none (such as those from *Hill*) are automatically relied on or presumed to outweigh more legitimate and empirically sound concerns. This is what the ECtHR interpretation of *Osman* (in *Z v UK* [2001]) tells us must happen, and indeed this does appear to take place in other contexts of public body liability – so why not in police cases?[29] As Burton states, '*Smith* confirms that *Osman* has not driven a fundamental reconsideration of the law of negligence in relation to police liability for inaction' (2009: 292). Yet in *Waters*, it was recognised that in some contexts (in that case, rape and intimidatory bullying of female police officers who report it) the wider public policy or 'societal' concerns may outweigh those identified in *Hill*. This has been recognised explicitly in Canada. However, given that *Waters* precedes *Smith* it is evident that such factors have not become part of judicial reasoning when our courts consider police negligence.

What makes this worse is that no evidence has ever been produced by either the judiciary or others who rely on judicial reasoning to support Lord Keith's claims in *Hill* – these claims are simply very persuasive. In fact, the exact opposite may be true – that is, we may be able to assume that imposing a duty on police would make them take *more* care. We (and the courts) should at least be more concerned about how the day-to-day job is done with regard to not only the public as a whole, but also individual citizens and, in particular, already vulnerable or under-represented groups towards whom (at least) the police should be more responsible. A notion of assumed responsibility is the thread that runs through duty not only in public body liability cases more generally but also those specific police cases where duties were found (for example, *Swinney*, *Costello*, *Reeves* and even *Waters*). So it is interesting also that the argument used to deny liability in *Smith* is that there was no assumption of responsibility – when the failure of the officers to assume any kind of responsibility was the very essence of the negligence alleged. It cannot be jus-tifiable, even in terms of public policy, that if the police do nothing (despite being presented with apparently credible evidence giving rise to a high degree of fore-seeability of harm),[30] there is literally no assumption of responsibility and therefore no duty *when it is their very failure to assume responsibility to do anything that is the foundation of the allegation of negligence*. That is a completely circular proposition and absolutely suggests *de facto* immunity against liability for inaction. Not only was *Smith* 'a failure to provide redress for one victim' but sadly it is also 'a licence for the police to continue to fail victims of crime generally and victims of domestic violence in particular' (Burton 2009: 293).

Moreover, while it is generally true that resources allocated to policing are better used on policing than on defending negligence claims, this too is an argument that has decreased in impact (McIvor 2010), and is rarely used in relation to other types of public body in which lives and bodily integrity are at stake, again with child welfare services providing the main example. Additionally, there is the counter argument that short-term losses to the public purse could equal longer-term gains (for example the short, sharp shock of liability and/or, for example, allocating funds to training and other prevention schemes to change the habits and perceptions of police may lead to fewer negligence claims to deal with in the long run).

Conclusion

In considering the potential liability of the police, regard must be had to the disparate (and sometimes seemingly conflicting) aims of tort. Not only are the foundations of tort to be found in corrective justice – that is, in terms of compensating those wronged by another – but a further primary aim or function is to discourage undesirable behaviour, that is to change things for the better. The essential challenge of the tort of negligence is to identify 'those kinds of undesirable behaviour which should give a right to compensation to those who suffer as a result' or 'put negatively, when, in cases of significant injury caused by undesirable behaviour, should a right be denied?' (Bingham 2010: 4).

It is the social 'undesirability' of certain behaviours of the police – both as individual officers and as a force – that has been scrutinised in this chapter. Certainly there is force to the argument that it is undesirable to maintain a wholesale protection or immunity of the police when their conduct can be so egregiously negligent as it was in *Smith*, or *Waters*, particularly when it might be said that their behaviour had been affected by assumptions held about certain groups or types of crime. The message such protection sends is also both undesirable and regressive – not only in relation to women but to other groups already vulnerable or disadvantaged in society, in particular in relation to their treatment by the police.

It *is* possible to owe a duty to the general public and a duty to an individual at the same time, with these not being in conflict, as both would achieve the same policy aims of upholding the police's public function of preventing and suppressing crime for the good of society. Where the task of preventing crime (a recognised duty to the public at large) includes known and specific potential crimes against an individual (in legal language a high degree of proximity and foreseeability based on real and credible evidence) then a second, narrower, duty should be created towards that individual (Bingham 2010: 13–14).

The difference between the approaches of courts in different jurisdictions, as has been shown, lies in the application of – and adherence to – policy reasoning and, in particular, the assumptions that underpin the policy arguments that have been so heavily relied on. In the UK, claimants face a steep uphill struggle – the onus is on them to prove that there are competing (or in fact radically outweighing) policy claims in the particular instance that justify the imposition of a duty of care upon negligent police. In Canada, in comparison, the onus is on *defendants* to show that there are sufficient and compelling reasons that justify negating the duty, though the breach in question must be sufficiently serious. In Australia, the reach of the *Hill* principle has been curtailed and limited *only* to those cases (like *Hill*) featuring a criminal at large, and a large and indiscriminate portion of the population who might be targeted. Interestingly, the 'liability principle' propounded by Lord Bingham in *Smith* more closely matches the Canadian approach and offers what seems to be a reasonable and measured approach to police liability, with an emphasis on foreseeability and proximity. In *Smith* this approach was felt to be 'difficult to operate in practice', 'too imprecise' and 'incapable of logical restriction' (Burton 2009: 290). So, perhaps unsurprisingly, the UK courts have chosen to reject it, instead remaining loyal to the equally imprecise policy reasons from *Hill*.

The purpose of holding the police accountable in negligence is not to punish either individual officers or the force more generally, but to redress a wrong. At present, victims are being failed twice: first by incompetent or ambivalent policing and secondly by the courts who fail to stand up to the police and hold them accountable when they fall well below a reasonable standard of care. The UK Law Commission recognised this in its 2008 consultation on public body liability. It suggested a new test for public bodies in recognition of their status and privileged position within society based on a concept of 'serious fault' that would allow the court to examine the 'conferral of benefit' in order to determine whether the claimant deserved protection from the harm suffered (Law Commission 2008: 54). However, as the Commission itself later acknowledged (Law Commission 2010), the proposals met with heavy criticism and were not further pursued. The then Labour government had remained adamant that public bodies should not be treated differently from private bodies and individuals, that all claims should be dealt with using the usual 'fair just and reasonable' test and denied that there were problems in the current system at all (2010: 24–5). Yet, the Law Commission insists that the result of this is that the police are afforded more protection than other defendants (2010: 25).

The role of the police within society is undeniably important. It is widely recognised that the police occupy a special role and need to be afforded certain powers and protections in order to do their job properly. But that is not to say they do not make mistakes. And, when they do, that they should not be held accountable, particularly when their negligence is the result of entrenched behaviours or assumptions held about certain types of victim or crime. Victims of police negligence of the seriousness of which we have discussed here should not be denied the opportunity to gain redress simply because the individuals at least partly responsible for their harm are police officers. The current practice of indiscreetly invoking policy reasons to deny that the police owe a duty of care to individuals is outdated and based on weak assumptions. Workable examples from other jurisdictions show that the imposition of such a duty on police officers is both possible and satisfying, and does not lead to increased levels of claims being made against the police. The mounting examples of what can be described at best as 'misguided' police investigations make it clear that it is simply not acceptable for our courts to continue to provide the police with blanket protection and that an approach where duty is based on foreseeability of harm, coupled with a standard of care test that encompasses the idea that the police must have certain discretions would be both more appropriate and beneficial to the public, particularly those already at an imbalance in terms of their relative power against that of the police.

Notes

1 Usually in respect to direct physical damage to person or property: see eg *Rigby v Chief Constable of Northamptonshire* [1985]; *Knightley v Johns* [1982].
2 For example the duty owed to those in police custody (*Reeves v Commissioner of Police for the Metropolis* [2000]) or to police informants (*Swinney v Chief Constable of Northumbria Police* [1997]).
3 It may also be that imposing liability could lead to longer-term gains, such as enhanced training or other prevention schemes to change the perceptions and practices of police officers, particularly in relation to disadvantaged groups or communities, perhaps leading eventually to fewer negligence claims to defend.
4 Note also that the IPCC's Chief Executive, Jane Furniss, recently acknowledged that the Commission 'is not fulfilling its remit' and that the system 'was incompatible with twenty-first century expectations' (Police Oracle 2010).
5 See the IPCC Annual Report and Statement of Accounts 2009–10, which includes reference to the Worboys and other investigations mentioned above, as well as investigations into various instances of police misconduct in the handling of the G20 protests. In the document the then IPCC chair, Nick Hardwick, said that in relation to 'failing to protect' there is 'a disturbing pattern of avoidable mistakes being repeated and the public not receiving the protection to which they are rightly entitled' (8). Specific comments were made in relation to 'gender abuse' and failure to protect (13 and 23–5). 'Key themes' of investigation by the IPCC were identified as 'Violence and Vulnerability' and 'Failure to Protect' (23). See also, in the context of IPCC investigations into police handling of reports of escalating domestic violence, Burton (2009: 293–4).
6 The most hopeful part of the report is the statement that '[w]e will learn from behavioural science to work with business, local authorities and others to ensure that products are manufactured in a way that reduces the opportunities for crime, the places where we live and work are designed to make it harder to commit crime, and people are better able to protect themselves from crime. We will establish a new Forum for Innovation in Crime Prevention to bring together experts from science, academia and business and stimulate new innovations to help cut crime' (Home Office 2011: 7).
7 A full account of the facts is provided in Lord Bingham's opinion (*Smith* [2008]: [21]–[27]). After the attack Jeffrey was convicted and sentenced to 10 years' imprisonment for making threats to kill and causing grievous bodily harm with intent.
8 In *Smith* this could be categorised as any/all of the following: victims of domestic violence, same-sex victims of (domestic) violence, victims of intimidation or victims of violence perpetrated by a partner or ex-partner (which has already in the context of sexual assault been shown to be an indicator of lower investigation and conviction rates: Larcombe 2011: 36–7).
9 In fact, in *Dorset Yacht*, while rejecting the 'defensive practices' public policy argument when asked to deny a duty of care owed by the prison officers to those harmed by the boys in their care, Lord Reid said that he believed 'that Her Majesty's servants are made of sterner stuff' ([1970]: [1033]), thus the policy considerations so raised did not preclude liability.
10 Examples include the eventual convictions of Worboys, Grant and Reid, discussed above, and the IPCC considerations of the police's handling of these investigations. See also the 'unlawful killing' verdict of the inquest into the death of Ian Tomlinson at the G20 protests in 2009, the subsequent cover-up of information given to the inquest by Met officers, the IPCC finding of the 'recklessness' of a senior Met officer in giving false

evidence to the inquest and the subsequent decision made apparently 'in the public interest' to prosecute the officer concerned for manslaughter (Lewis 2011).

11   Larcombe contends that increasing rape conviction rates alone is not a valid (feminist) objective of law reform and states that 'criminal justice systems are (still) unable to respond effectively to forms of violence disproportionately experienced by women and children' (2011: 30).

12   Where *Smith* is itself an exemplar of bad practice and/or in relation to same-sex violence. Also see 'Braintree murders' case (BBC News 2011a).

13   See *Brooks*, Clancy et al (2001) and also BBC News (2011b); IPCC (2011d). There is also substantial evidence of the over-representation of ethnic minorities in stop-and-search statistics and on the National DNA Database (see Human Genetics Commission 2009: 51–7). Further, the recent IPCC Report 'Confidence in the Police Complaints System 2011' highlights that ethnic minorities' 'top worries' in terms of going to the police were 'not knowing how to complain (45 per cent) and not being taken seriously (43 per cent), but close behind them, with 40 per cent of respondents agreeing, were fears about police harassment and of the complaint taking up too much of their time' (2011c: 4).

14   See eg *Waters* and *Costello v Chief Constable of Northumbria Police* [1999] in relation to female officers. Additionally, there is a wealth of literature on the (under)representation of ethnic minorities in British police forces, highlighted in the MacPherson Report (1999) and also see, eg, Cashmore (2001).

15   An example here can be identified in relation to the Irish Garda, members of which were recorded, while discussing the arrest of a female protestor demonstrating about the Corrib Gas Pipe, joking about raping her as a means of quelling her protest. As Vicky Conway points out (2011) 'Police officers deal with rape victims on a regular basis. They see the pain, trauma, anguish suffered by these people, women predominantly. For them to make a joke of that is an insult. They still don't see rape victims enough, in the sense that rape is a massively underreported crime. A lot of women and men fear coming forward and this "story" will not improve that situation. Rape is an exceptionally serious crime and for police officers to joke about that, to use it as part of their banter, is entirely unacceptable and could have dreadful consequences. And imagine the impact for the woman concerned, to hear men make such comments about you, simply because you exercise your right to protest'.

16   Though cf *Chief Constable of the Hertfordshire Police v Van Colle* [2008], heard in the House of Lords alongside *Smith v Chief Constable of Sussex Police* [2008]. In this case, Giles van Colle, a witness for the prosecution in a theft case, who had reported threats against him to the police, was murdered before he could give evidence. In a claim brought under the Human Rights Act 1998 the House of Lords found that the threats against him were not 'real and immediate' enough to amount to a violation of his Article 2 right. However, the officer concerned (and to whom the intimidating threats were reported) was disciplined for 'failing to perform his duties conscientiously and diligently', being fined five days' pay ([18]). As Mandy Burton points out, '[t]he implication of the House of Lords decision in *Van Colle* is that a witness in a criminal trial has no right to better protection from the police than any other member of the public' (2009: 288).

17   Given the (at the time fairly recent – and heavily impacting) ECtHR decision in *Osman v UK* [1999] and the passage of the Human Rights Act 1998.

18   Perhaps with the exception of Lord Jauncey who, despite allowing the appeal, described the rape alleged – and therefore the state of affairs in the police in relation to this – as 'relevant only as narrative' (*Waters* [2000]: [1614]).

19   Particularly in the wake of the MacPherson Report (1999) commissioned in the wake of the racist murder and subsequent poor police investigation (also suspected to have been tainted by racism) of black teenager Stephen Lawrence in South-East London in 1993. It found that the Metropolitan Police was 'institutionally racist' (see also *Brooks*).

Note that both the MacPherson Report and *Waters* relate to the Metropolitan Police Service, which proclaims itself as 'famed around the world and [having] a unique place in the history of policing' (http://www.met.police.uk/about/). Maintaining good public perceptions *of this particular force* should, therefore, have been high on the list of judicial policy concerns. Though there is no mention at all of the MacPherson Report in *Waters*, it is possible that, given the timing, this was in the Law Lords' minds.

20 The MacPherson Report made 70 recommendations 'aimed at the elimination of racist prejudice and disadvantage' within the force (ibid). See also the House of Commons Home Affairs Committee Twelfth Report: *The Macpherson Report – Ten Years On* (14 July 2009) in which, despite some improvements having been made, it is noted that 'there are a number of areas in which the police service continues to fail ethnic minorities' ([6]) and that young black and Asian people (particularly males) continue to disproportionately be stopped and searched and entered into the National DNA Database ([6]–[7]).

21 It is interesting, however, to compare this reasoning to feminist arguments which *criticise* the police telling women to be careful, evident to some extent in the recent phenomenon of 'SlutWalks', which started in Toronto and has spread to cities around the world. These protests were sparked by Constable Michael Sanguinetti, a Toronto Police officer, who suggested that 'women should avoid dressing like sluts' in order to be safe (see http://www.slutwalktoronto.com/about/why) – suggesting that 'reform' of officers in the Toronto force has not occurred since *Jane Doe*. SlutWalks have 'divided feminists' (see Gold 2011). See also Elizabeth Sheehy's guest editorial in (2010) 22(2) *Canadian Journal of Women and the Law*, a special edition on 'The State of Rape: Ten Years After *Jane Doe*', which tells us that 'police in Canada continue to unfound rape at a shocking rate' (2010: xxi) and, also, articles by Katherine Mazurok (2010), Melanie Randall (2010), and Shannon Sampert (2010), in the same journal.

22 In fact, the majority confirmed that a specific 'tort of negligent investigation' exists in Canada. Interestingly, the three dissenting judges thought that no such tort should be recognised in Canadian law for exactly the kinds of policy reasons given in *Hill* (*Hamilton-Wentworth* [2007]: [112]–[113]).

23 From *Anns v Merton London Borough Council* [1978], which was later rejected in *Caparo Industries plc v Dickman* [1990] as the delineator of duty of care in the UK.

24 Also see [50]–[51], [53], [55] and [61]–[65].

25 Therefore perhaps more comparable to the UK case *D v East Berkshire Community NHS Trust* [2005].

26 It may also be argued that a conflict of duty arose between the father and public interest in preventing child abuse more generally, so analogies can be drawn.

27 See also *Brooks*, where the assumption, originating from *Hill*, that no incentive to raise police standards was necessary was unanimously questioned (eg Lord Bingham: [3], Lord Nicholls: [6] and Lord Steyn: [28]. Lord Rodger and Lord Brown agreed with Lord Steyn).

28 *Stonewall*, 'Hate crimes: domestic violence' at http://www.stonewall.org.uk/beyond_barriers/information/hate_crimes/domestic_violence/default.asp [accessed 30 August 2011]. See also McCarry et al (2008).

29 See, in particular, claims made against child care authorities in which competing policy considerations have tended to be more explicitly weighed against each other: *D v East Berkshire Community NHS Trust* [2005] remains one of the best examples. This is also a sector where public expectations are high and yet here the policy arguments (which were once very similar – see *X (Minors) v Bedfordshire County Council* [1995]) have migrated – post *Z v UK* [2001] and the passage of the Human Rights Act 1998 – towards a finding of duty *because* of expectations regarding the care of vulnerable children and the authorities' assumed responsibility towards them.

30 See comments of the Law Lords, especially Lord Carswell, about inexplicable inaction and 'inertia' of the police (*Smith* [2008]: [107]).

Cases

Anns v Merton London Borough Council [1978] AC 728
Batchelor v The State of Tasmania [2005] TASSC 11
Brooks v Commissioner of Police for the Metropolis [2005] UKHL 24
Calveley v Chief Constable of Merseyside Police [1989] AC 1228
Caparo Industries plc v Dickman [1990] 2 AC 605
Chief Constable of the Hertfordshire Police v Van Colle [2008] UKHL 50
Costello v Chief Constable of Northumbria Police [1999] 1 All ER 550
D v East Berkshire Community NHS Trust [2005] UKHL 23
Doe v Metropolitan Toronto (Municipality) Commissioners of Police (1998) 160 DLR (4th) 289
     (Supreme Court (Can))
Hill v Chief Constable of West Yorkshire [1989] AC 53
Hill v Hamilton-Wentworth Regional Police Services Board [2007] SCC 41
Home Office v Dorset Yacht Co Ltd [1970] AC 1004
Knightley v Johns [1982] 1 WLR 349
Orange v Chief Constable of West Yorkshire Police [2001] EWCA Civ 611
Osman v UK [1999] 1 FLR 193
Reeves v Commissioner of Police for the Metropolis [2000] 1 AC 360
Rigby v Chief Constable of Northamptonshire [1985] 1 WLR 1242
Smith v Chief Constable of Sussex Police [2008] UKHL 50
State of New South Wales v Tyszyk [2008] NSWCA 107
Sullivan v Moody [2001] 207 CLR 562
Swinney v Chief Constable of Northumbria Police [1997] 3 All ER 449
Tame v New South Wales [2002] 211 CLR 540
Waters v Metropolitan Police Commissioner [2000] 1 WLR 1607
X (Minors) v Bedfordshire County Council [1995] 2 AC 633
Z v UK (29392/95) [2001] 2 FLR 612

Bibliography

BBC News (2011a) 'Braintree Murders: Christine Chambers Had Called Police Before',
     6 June 2011
—— (2011b) 'Brixton Riots 30 years On: What Has Changed?', 10 April 2011
—— (2011c) 'Women's Convictions For Domestic Violence "Double"', 6 June 2011
Bingham, Lord (2010) 'The Uses of Tort', *Journal of European Tort Law*, 1: 3
Burton, M. (2009) 'Failing to Protect: Victim's Rights and Police Liability', *Modern Law
     Review*, 72(2): 283
Cashmore, E. (2001) 'The Experiences of Ethnic Minority Police Officers in Britain: Under-
     recruitment and Racial Profiling in a Performance Culture', *Ethnic and Racial Studies*, 24(4):
     642
Chamberlain, E. (2008) 'Negligent Investigation: A New Remedy for the Wrongly Accused:
     Hill v Hamilton-Wentworth Regional Police Services Board, *Alberta Law Review*, 45(4): 1089
Clancy, A., Hough M., Aust R. and Kershaw C. (2001) 'Crime, Policing and Justice: The
     Experience of Ethnic Minorities. Findings from the 2000 British Crime Survey', London:
     Home Office
Conaghan, J. (2002) 'Law, Harm and Redress: A Feminist Perspective', *Legal Studies*, 22:
     319

Conway, V. (2011) 'The Policing of Corrib Exposed', *Human Rights in Ireland*, 5 April 2011 (blog post)

Gold, T. (2011) 'Marching with the SlutWalkers', *The Guardian*, 7 June 2011

Hoffmann, Lord (1999) 'Human Rights and the House of Lords' *Modern Law Review*, 62: 159

Home Office (2011) 'A New Approach to Fighting Crime' 2 March 2011

House of Commons Home Affairs Committee Twelfth Report: *The Macpherson Report – Ten Years On* (14 July 2009)

Hoyano, L. (1999) 'Policing Flawed Police Investigations: Unravelling the Blanket', *Modern Law Review*, 62: 917

Human Genetics Commission (2009) *Nothing to Hide, Nothing To Fear? Balancing Individual Rights and the Public Interest in the Governance and Use of the National DNA Database*, London: Department of Health

Independent Police Complaints Commission (IPCC) (2010a) 'Commissioner's Report: IPCC Independent Investigation Into the Metropolitan Police Service's Inquiry Into Allegations Against John Worboys', January 2010

—— (2010b) 'Findings of Investigation Into Met Handling of Worboys Case', January 2010

—— (2010c) 'Operation Minstead: Final Report', July 2010

—— (2011a) 'IPCC to Investigate Police Investigation of Kirk Reid', 28 February 2011

—— (2011b) 'IPCC Publishes Findings From Investigation Into MPS Response to Burglary Linked to Operation Minstead', 24 March 2011

—— (2011c) 'Confidence in the Police Complaints System: a Survey of the General Population in 2011', *IPCC Research and Statistics Series: Paper 20*

—— (2011d) 'IPCC Investigation Substantiates Race Complaint Against North Wales Police', 28 February 2011

Larcombe, W. (2011) 'Falling Rape Conviction Rates: (Some) Feminist Aims and Measures for Rape Law', *Feminist Legal Studies*, 19(1): 27

Law Commission (2008) Administrative Redress: Public Bodies and the Citizen: A Consultation Paper, Consultation Paper No 187

—— (2010) Administrative Redress: Public Bodies and The Citizen, Law Com No 322

Lewis, P. (2011) 'Tomlinson Police Officer to Face Manslaughter Trial', *The Guardian*, 24 May 2011

MacPherson, W. (1999) *The Stephen Lawrence Inquiry: Report of an Inquiry by Sir William MacPherson of Cluny* (Cm 4262-I), February 1999

Mazurok, K. (2010) 'Universally Particular: The Garneau Sisterhood's Challenge to the Rape Script', *Canadian Journal of Women and the Law*, 22(2): 463

McCarry, M., Hester M. and Donovan C. (2008) 'Researching Same Sex Domestic Violence: Constructing a Survey Methodology', *Sociological Research Online* 13(1): 8

McIvor, C. (2008) 'The Positive Duty of the Police to Protect Life', *Professional Negligence*, 24(1): 27

—— (2010) 'Getting Defensive About Police Negligence: The Hill Principle, the Human Rights Act 1998 and the House of Lords', *Cambridge Law Journal*, 69(1): 133

Moroz, C. (1995) 'Jane Doe and Police Liability for Failure to Apprehend: The Role of the *Anns* Public Policy Principle in Canada and England', *Advocates' Quarterly*, 17(3): 261

Police Oracle (2010) 'Police Complaints System "Not Meeting Today's Needs"', 22 March 2010

Randall, M. (2010) 'Sexual Assault Law, Credibility, and Ideal Victims: Consent, Resistance, and Victim Blaming', *Canadian Journal of Women and the Law*, 22(2): 397

Sampert, S. (2010) 'Let Me Tell You a Story: English-Canadian Newspapers and Sexual Assault Myths', *Canadian Journal of Women and the Law*, 22(2): 301

Sheehy, E. (2010) 'Editorial', *Canadian Journal of Women and the Law*, 22(2): i.

Shircore, M. (2006) 'Police Liability for Negligent Investigations: When Will a Duty of Care Arise?', *Deakin Law Review*, 11: 36.

Thompson, G. (2010) 'Domestic Violence Statistics: Standard Note: SN/SG/950', House of Commons Library, 10 March 2010

Wilberg, H. (2010) 'Defensive Practice or Conflict of Duties? Policy Concerns in Public Authority Negligence Claims', *Law Quarterly Review*, 126: 420

Chapter 6

Knowledge and Power: Drug Products Liability Actions and Women's Health

*Patricia Peppin**

While products liability law has provided a strong basis for consumer claims, its impact on women's lives and interests has been less clearly beneficial. Beginning in 1932 with the House of Lords' decision in *Donoghue v Stevenson* ([1932]: [599]), a duty of care has been owed by product manufacturers to the 'ultimate consumer' to take reasonable care in the 'preparation or putting up' of a product to avoid causing foreseeable injury. The principled basis of the decision was set out most broadly in Lord Atkins' familiar neighbour principle.

Further protection is offered to consumers through the duty on product manufacturers to warn of product risks, to an extent commensurate with the product's danger. The duty to warn is assessed on the basis of what manufacturers know or ought to know about the risks inherent in the product. These dual duties, in the areas of manufacturing and information disclosure, set standards for manufacturers. The purpose of these actions, like other tort actions, is compensation for harm and deterrence of wrongdoing. In addition to compensation and harm avoidance, the products liability action has two additional purposes: autonomy and product honesty. Autonomy is supported through the duty to disclose the information essential to choice while product honesty is to be advanced through requiring the information representing the product's risks. Knowledge that is full and accurate is essential to empowering patient choice.

Does the products liability action succeed in meeting these purposes for women? I will argue that the action's considerable potential to meet these goals has not been realised and that women and girls are adversely affected by its shortcomings. I will focus on the area of prescription drugs and devices to assess this question. The chapter begins with an examination of product liability actions for manufacturing failures and breach of the duty to disclose, through analysis of *Donoghue v Stevenson* and its descendants in Canada, the UK and Australia. The next section is an examination of the impact of this action on women, beginning with consideration of the mass tort claims brought through the latter half of the twentieth century for thalidomide, DES, the Dalkon Shield and breast implants. US actions will be examined in this section. Following the historical analysis, this section examines the nature of drug testing and the resulting knowledge deficit that has existed in relation to drug products used by women. The following section consists of an analysis of the duty to disclose action and learned intermediary rule that considers its application in actions related to birth control, breast implants and Vioxx. Following this analysis, the chapter examines how information is structured through promotion and considers its impact on understanding. The chapter concludes with an assessment of the success of disclosure actions in achieving compensation, avoiding harm, promoting autonomy and ensuring product honesty, and how products liability actions might become more successful actions for women.

Products liability law: claims for manufacturing breaches

Products liability actions in the UK, Canada and Australia are based on the House of Lords' decision in *Donoghue v Stevenson* [1932]. The action proceeded to the House of Lords from Scotland on the issue of whether a duty of care existed where a drink bottling company allegedly allowed a snail into its ginger beer bottle, resulting in the consumer suffering severe gastroenteritis and nervous shock after she consumed a ginger beer float. Lord Atkin formulated the duty of care in the 'neighbour principle', duty's most succinct and comprehensive statement:

> You must take reasonable care to avoid acts or omissions which you can reasonably foresee would be likely to injure your neighbour. Who, then, in law is my neighbour? The answer seems to be – persons who are so closely and directly affected by my act that I ought reasonably to have them in contemplation as being so affected when I am directing my mind to the acts or omissions which are called in question.
>
> (Lord Atkin in *Donoghue* [1932]: [580])

Lord Atkin further set out the 'manufacturer's principle' (Heuston 1957), stating the duty of care principle in the narrower context of the products liability action within which it arose:

> . . . a manufacturer of products, which he sells in such a form as to show that he intends them to reach the ultimate consumer in the form in which they left him with no reasonable possibility of intermediate examination, and with the knowledge that the absence of reasonable care in the preparation or putting up of the products will result in an injury to the consumer's life or property, owes a duty to the consumer to take that reasonable care.
>
> (Lord Atkin, *Donoghue* [1932]: [599])

The decision to recognise a duty of care in this circumstance, based on the broad statements of principle underlying it, was groundbreaking, and eventually led to the vast expansion of negligence law of the latter half of the 20th century. In significant departures from contemporary currents of products liability, these claims could be brought by the 'ultimate consumer', who needed no contractual relationship with the manufacturer, against the manufacturer of products, without being confined to particular kinds of defects, for foreseeable injuries caused to the consumer, without reference to any related intentional tort (Heuston 1957). The process was accelerated when Lord Wilberforce set out a framework for duty analysis in the two-stage test in *Anns v Merton London Borough Council* [1977]: [498]. First, a prima facie duty of care was established if there existed 'a sufficient relationship of proximity or neighbourhood' that harm was reasonably foreseeable. Once reasonable foreseeability was established, the onus shifted to the defendant to negative the duty or its scope, on the basis of policy considerations. The *Anns* case provided a framework through which the *Donoghue v Stevenson* principles were analysed and an explicit statement as to the role of the policy dimension established in that case.

In *Sutherland Shire Council v Heyman* [1985], the Australian High Court adopted a more restrictive test for duty, one that emphasised proximity as a distinct test separate from reasonable foreseeability instead of subsumed within it [446]–[447]. The House of Lords similarly reigned in the duty of care, first through overruling *Anns* on the basis of its unpredictability, unworkability and lack of a principled foundation in *Murphy v Brentwood District Council* [1991] and subsequently by creating the separate test of proximity to add to the reasonable foreseeability test, making it a three-stage test with the requirement that it be 'fair, just and reasonable' to impose a duty of this scope, in the leading case of *Caparo Industries plc v Dickman* [1990]. In *Sullivan v Moody* [2001], the High Court of Australia rejected such a three-stage analysis of foreseeability, proximity and policy, instead engaging in analysis of relevant connecting factors between plaintiff and defendant to determine duty.

The Supreme Court of Canada absorbed the *Anns* test into law in *Kamloops (City of) v Neilson* [1984] and the *Anns/Kamloops* test acted as the framework for duty analysis in Canada until 2001. At that time, the Supreme Court of Canada took steps similar to those taken earlier in Australia and the UK. In *Cooper v Hobart* [2001], the Court adopted a revised test for duty of care, to be applied if precedent does not already exist for this category of duty. The test, as clarified in *Childs v Desormeaux* [2006], includes proximity as a separate element from foreseeability in establishing duty, along with policy analysis of factors with respect to the relationship, such as 'expectations, representations, reliance, and the property or other interests involved' to be applied before proceeding to the defendant's attempt to negative duty on the basis of broader policy considerations affecting the overall system ([15]).

Applying the principles to drug products liability

The manufacturer's principle requires care in the design and production of the product so as to avoid foreseeable harm to the ultimate consumer. Companies create products, which reflect the state of knowledge. As well as requiring care to avoid adulteration of products by snails or flies (the lowest common denominator), the duty requires that products be designed safely. As a result, enough knowledge about the product's impact needs to be available to guide the manufacturer to avoid it. The reasonable foreseeability of the harm test requires such knowledge. The manufacturer's responsibility to avoid such product harm carries with it the responsibility to study the product's impact and be aware of its potential risks to persons who will use it. The standard of care is commonly analysed according to the *Bolton v Stone* [1951] test of probability of harm and gravity of the consequences. The cost of remedial measures and the social utility of the product are factors as well. For manufacturers, the custom of the industry and government standards would be relevant, although not determinative. Products that are ingested and used in intimate ways, such as food, drugs and implantable medical devices, are held to a very high standard of care (*Hollis v Dow Corning Corp* [1995]: [23]). An example of this type of knowledge is found in the McDonald's coffee case (*Liebeck v McDonald's Restaurants, PTS Inc* [1994]). The jury imposed liability on McDonald's and compensated Stella Liebeck for her severe burns after proof that its coffee was super-heated to 180 degrees Fahrenheit, a temperature so high that it would produce third-degree burns in 12 to 15 seconds. The company condoned this high risk in order to improve the coffee's flavour (Gerlin 1994: A1; Haltom and McCann 2004: 185–95).

Plaintiffs must prove that the breach of the duty of care has caused their harm. Causation in drug cases requires proof of the general scientific link: the evidence must demonstrate on the balance of probabilities that the drug causes that harm, such as the stroke in the oral contraceptive case *Buchan v Ortho Pharmaceuticals (Canada) Ltd* [1986]. Such proof may be very difficult for a plaintiff, as we saw in the breast implant litigation, where the lack of long-term studies made proof of an alleged causal link to auto-immune disorders virtually impossible. Writing after the issue had been studied more extensively; Marcia Angell commented that if there was 'any link to various autoimmune diseases, it was so small that it could not be detected'. After '15 reasonably good studies', 'no solid scientific evidence' existed for the link (Angell 1997: 216). In contrast, ruptures and capsular contracture (the creation of skin-covered nuggets of silicone) were demonstrably caused by the implants. In addition, the plaintiff must prove that the drug caused their particular harm in a scientific sense. The type of injury must have been reasonably foreseeable to the defendant and the harm must be of a type compensable by law.

Products liability claims may range from relatively small claims to mass tort actions. In each case, though, the plaintiff must litigate against a corporation and this fact imposes constraints on the ability to bring actions. The deep pockets of a corporate defendant may make it an appealing target, but those same resources can be effectively – and sometimes ruthlessly – deployed against plaintiffs. Those with fewer resources to mount such litigation are less likely to sue, or be able to sustain actions against delaying tactics and personal attacks that are sometimes used to cut off litigation. The expense of litigation acts as a considerable deterrent to plaintiffs in pursuing remedies through the courts, and legal aid is usually unavailable for personal injury claims of this sort.

The impact of drug development and manufacturing breach actions on women

Drugs have a differential impact on women. Women seek help from doctors and other parts of the health care system more often than men. Women take more drugs than men. Because of women's reproductive systems, along with the western cultural norm that women bear primary responsibility for birth control, women take oral contraceptives and emergency contraception. The social determinants of health include gender and such factors as poverty which increase the likelihood of illness and therefore of treatment with drugs. The social circumstances of women are more likely to include poverty and experiences of violence and abuse, and these may lead to greater need for health care. Women still act disproportionately as the caregivers for the health needs of others, including children and elderly relatives. Elderly women outlive men and have more complex health needs, often experiencing 'poly-pharmacy', the taking of multiple drugs, as a result. Persons with disabilities – elderly women among them – are more likely to be abused. On top of this, the drug development process has meant that less is known about the impact of drugs on women. This effect is magnified for pregnant women and elderly women. The disparity in scientific knowledge about the adverse effects of drugs means that women are less knowledgeable and more at risk of harm from the drugs.

Lessons from mass tort litigation

Thalidomide

Three instances of drug-induced injury are emblematic of corporate irresponsibility towards women and the mass harm produced by it. Thalidomide was introduced by the German company Chemie Grünenthal in 1957 as a sedative and was used as a sleeping pill and for morning sickness. It was widely marketed internationally under a variety of trade names, and this fact, combined with lack of testing, made identification of the problem more difficult (Law 1997: 360). Evidence of peripheral neuritis, a rare form of nerve damage, soon emerged, with the British Medical Journal publishing the first report in December 1960 (Silverman 2002: 405; Florence 1960: 1954) and its potent teratogenic effects became evident as babies were born with significant limb impairments involving foreshortened limbs, called phocomelia, cleft palates, internal organ defects and visual impairments. The *Sunday Times* investigation revealed that thalidomide caused deaths in the womb of up to 100,000 fetuses, while 10,000 babies were born alive (Sunday Times Insight Team 1979). The Sunday Times Insight Team demonstrated that Grünenthal and the UK manufacturer Distillers 'had not met the basic testing requirements of the time' (Flintoff 2008). No testing on fetal impact was carried out although the drug was heavily promoted in both countries as 'the best drug for pregnant and nursing mothers' (Silverman 2002: 405). Richardson-Merrell, the US licence-holder, was aware that a drug could cross the placenta to affect a fetus since their drug MER-29 had been shown to have such an effect, and the scientific literature provided such evidence for more than 200 drugs on various species. The company conducted no animal studies or clinical trials during pregnancy to determine whether thalidomide was actually safe. Instead, in the period prior to its application for approval, the company simply distributed thalidomide to doctors for use on more than 20,000 patients, including pregnant women, without adequate consent, oversight or reporting of consequences (Sunday Times Insight Team 1979: 68–72).

The product was removed from the market in 1961. In the US, where the product had not been approved, Congressional hearings were already taking place on drug regulation, and their response to the thalidomide damage led to the legislative requirement that manufacturers demonstrate the product's efficacy in relation to its intended use, to accompany the existing safety requirement already necessary to secure US Food and Drug Administration (FDA) approval for marketing (*US Food Drug and Cosmetic Act* [2010]; Waxman 2003; Law 1997: 361). Canada followed suit. Canada had remarkably left thalidomide on the market for three months after evidence of its damage had emerged internationally, claiming later, in response to tort claims by victims against the government, that they lacked the regulatory authority to require the company to remove the product from the market. They provided limited compensation in response (War Amputations of Canada 1989: 122–4, 539).

The thalidomide disaster epitomises the human cost of inadequate testing and heavy promotion accompanied by cavalier unconcern for the health of pregnant women. While the legislative regimes in place at the time were inadequate to prevent the mass harm, the tort system was also ineffective as a deterrent. The jurisdictional issue was resolved in favour of the plaintiff in Australia where the product had been sold without any warning, in *Distillers Co (Bio-Chemicals) Ltd v Thompson* [1971]. Tort actions on behalf of the thalidomide-injured children were typically settled, with gag orders imposed in some jurisdictions precluding other plaintiffs from benefiting from the information. Merrell's settlements with American and Canadian victims reportedly ranged from $100,000 to just under $1 million (Sanders 1992: 315), very small amounts for the lifelong impairments. Grünenthal settled for US$31 million and the German government for US$13.5 to 27 million with the German victims (War Amputations of Canada 1989: 7–8).

Diethylstilbestrol (DES)

The synthetic estrogen diethylstilbestrol (DES) was prescribed from 1947 to 1971 for prenatal use to prevent miscarriage even though evidence of the potential carcinogenic effect of natural and synthetic estrogens had been apparent in animal studies as early as the 1930s (Dutton 1988: 34, 37). Reliable studies demonstrated by the 1950s that DES was not effective for this purpose (Dutton 1988: 48–51, 54–7; Finley 1996: 66–7; National Film Board of Canada 1985). Diana Dutton noted that the FDA approved:

> what amounted to mass experimentation on pregnant women – the sanctioned use of a drug with known risks whose effectiveness had not yet been fully

proven. Yet only a short time later . . . the FDA would do nothing to rescind that authorization despite compelling evidence that DES was *not* in fact effective for its newly approved prenatal uses.

(Dutton 1988: 54)

In 1971 Dr Herbst and colleagues published their research linking DES to a rare form of vaginal cancer in the daughters of women who had taken DES during pregnancy (Finley 1996: 68). DES was eventually shown to cause other gynecological disorders in women, leading to significantly higher rates of miscarriage, ectopic pregnancy, stillbirths and premature delivery, along with higher infertility rates, male reproductive system abnormalities in DES sons, and an increased risk of breast cancer in the mothers (Dutton 1988: 87). In late 1971, a full eight months after receiving the Herbst study, the FDA announced that DES was contraindicated during pregnancy (Finley 1996: 69). It continued to be used in the morning-after pill and in US livestock production for about another decade (Dutton 1988: 32). The DES story provides an example of the trust in wonder drugs that characterised the post-war period, trust by doctors in their unsubstantiated clinical views, inadequate testing by manufacturers and disregard for the risks of drugs during pregnancy, even after thalidomide (National Film Board of Canada 1985). Women were not warned of the product risks even after the product was taken off the market (Dutton 1988: 73–7).

Lawsuits against the primary producers of DES were based on a number of theories, including the duty to test the product for safety and the duty to warn doctors of the product risks, along with breach of warranty of effectiveness in preventing miscarriage and misrepresentation of safety data (Finley 1996: 73). Joyce Bichler, a DES daughter, sued and won a major victory. She claimed that, based on the tests that should have been done, a prudent manufacturer would not have put it on the market (*Bichler v Eli Lilly Corp* [1982]). This argument amounted to a failure of the company to test the product sufficiently. Her action against the industry succeeded on the basis of the concert of action theory, which attributed responsibility to industry members based on the evidentiary basis being sufficient to sustain the jury verdict of concerted action both on conscious parallel conduct and on substantial assistance, a finding that the failure to test on pregnant mice aided or encouraged other manufacturers to follow suit (188).

In addition to the hindrance posed by the lapse of time, other factors prevented women from knowing whether their mothers had taken the drug, including the impediment created by the lack of a legal entitlement to access one's own medical records. Proof of causation was particularly difficult because DES had not been patented and numerous companies produced the product. For this reason, plaintiffs were often unable to determine which manufacturer had produced the specific drug taken by their mothers, to fulfil the tort requirement that causation link a specific defendant to the harm suffered by a particular plaintiff (Weinrib 1989). In *Sindell v Abbott Laboratories* [1980], the California Supreme Court decided that each of the major companies sued, producing 90 per cent of the product in the market, knew or should have known that it was unsafe and ineffective, and held them all liable, attributing responsibility to the manufacturers before the court according to their market share at the time of the injury, unless they could exculpate themselves. The market share liability solution provided some justice, by protecting plaintiffs from losing entirely where all the defendants were negligent and all caused harm to some plaintiffs but where the causal line could not be drawn from the particular manufacturer to the plaintiff although complete compensation was not provided under this theory (Bernstein 2003). Compensation for injury to reproductive capacity in the DES cases was generally low, however, because of the limited value given to the loss of the ability to give birth (Finley 1996: 75). This must have added immeasurably to the tragedy for women who suffered this harm.

Dalkon Shield intra-uterine device

The Dalkon Shield intra-uterine device was a contraceptive product developed by Dr John Davis at Johns Hopkins University along with engineer Irwin Lerner. Dr Davis tested the product on patients over a one-year period and published the very successful low pregnancy rate results of 1.1 per cent, without indicating that he had advised the women to continue using contraceptive foam for the first two to three months after insertion or that the average length of time on the IUD was six months; he did not correct the erroneously reported pregnancy rate when he discovered the correct higher rate of 5.3 per cent (Finley 1996: 79–80). After only hasty testing by its new corporate owner, A.H. Robins Co, the company propelled the product to market. The IUD design created a significant risk. Entwined twin filaments hung from the device down into the vagina and these uncapped threads acted like a wick for bacteria that resulted in pelvic inflammatory disease, potentially fatal infections, and sterility. The company was aware of the wicking problem: Lerner had warned senior executives of a potential problem prior to marketing and the quality control supervisor who investigated advised of the problem soon after (Sobol 1991: 7). The company avoided FDA scrutiny because devices were not required to go through a premarketing approval process comparable to that for drugs, and because they did not reveal that copper had been added to the product. In spite of reports of septic abortions and fatalities when women became pregnant with the Dalkon Shield in place, the company continued to resist investigating and aggressively marketed the product's safety. They promoted it as one that could stay in the body for five years, as a way of increasing doctors' acceptance, in spite of their awareness that the risks increased as the tail string deteriorated (Sobol 1991: 7–8). The company resisted providing warnings, removing the product from the market or paying for removal of the product from women's bodies. The kind of devastating harm created by this device is captured in this reprimand of corporate officers and defence counsel by Chief Judge Miles Lord, issued after the litigation was settled, subsequently set aside as a due process violation by the appellate court:

. . . your company, without warning to women, invaded their bodies by the millions and caused them injuries by the thousands. And when the time came for these women to make their claims against your company, you attacked their characters, you inquired into their sexual practices and into the identity of their sex partners . . . You introduced issues that had no relationship whatsoever to the fact that you planted in the bodies of these women instruments of death, mutilation, and of disease.

(Lord, 1986: 9)

These three cases illustrate the severe forms of harm to women's bodies, and those of their children, when companies disregarded risks to patients, conducted insufficient testing before marketing, failed to conduct tests even when faced with mounting evidence of serious adverse effects, and heavily promoted the product in spite of their own knowledge. Products liability actions had a virtually non-existent deterrent effect. To secure compensation, plaintiffs had to face aggressive litigation tactics, problems of proof of scientific causation in the absence of testing, and significant difficulties meeting the doctrinal demands of causation.

Drug testing and knowledge gaps

Thalidomide, DES and the Dalkon Shield all involved hidden risks. These risks – hidden because of inadequate research, mistaken beliefs and unwillingness to acknowledge known problems – created vast harm among unknowing patients and their children. Lessons of these tragedies were drawn by politicians who saw the need for research to be assessed through a public regulatory process. As noted above, the US and Canadian regulatory systems incorporated an efficacy requirement following the thalidomide tragedy. Medical device regulations were tightened following the Dalkon Shield litigation.

One legal outcome of the thalidomide disaster was the US regulation preventing research on pregnant women. The legal change focused on the prior period of clinical trial exposure, as the period when government had jurisdiction over drug development and could prevent harm. The well-intentioned regulation precluding inclusion of pregnant women was applied widely to women of childbearing age, and as a result, research on women was stifled (Merton 1993; Dresser 1992). The requirement had an advantage for manufacturers in helping them to avoid liability claims through outright exclusion of women. The exclusion was counter-productive for women, ironically leading to less research on women as a result of the very lack of research on women that had caused the initial problem.

Women's health research lagged during this period for other reasons as well. As the literature indicates, men were considered to be adequate substitutes for women and so all-male samples were thought to be scientifically appropriate (Rosser 1989; Scott 1993). At the same time, the differences in women's bodies arising from hormonal fluctuations made women less attractive for drug research since these variations confounded the data. Even today, laboratory research is conducted largely on male mice and rats, for the same reasons, even for conditions such as dementia and pain that occur predominantly in women (Pigg 2011).

Without thorough research on women, knowledge about the safety and efficacy of drugs is missing. Such a knowledge deficit has an impact on prescribing, since doctors have inadequate information on which to base their treatment proposals. Further, the patient's right to make informed decisions is undermined because complete information cannot be provided. As I discuss below, the knowledge deficit is particularly serious for elderly women and pregnant women. Only in the past two decades has this absence of research been identified as problematic (Merkatz 1993). Without research, our beliefs about the efficacy and safety of treatments may be mistaken. For example, Premarin and Prempro, the hormone replacement therapy prescribed exclusively to women for the effects of menopause, had not had their long-term effects studied until research was conducted under the Women's Health Initiative (WHI), a programme established under the US National Institutes of Health to remedy the deficit in knowledge about women's health. In 2002, after five years, this research was stopped on ethical grounds because the risks to the participants outweighed the benefits (Writing Group for Women's Health Initiative Investigators 2002). These data indicated that although the HRT group did show benefits in reducing colorectal cancer (37 per cent fewer among the HRT group than the placebo group) and fracture risks, more women in the HRT group experienced breast cancer (26 per cent), strokes (41 per cent) and coronary heart disease events (29 per cent) (Writing Group for WHI Investigators 2002: 326–7; Millrood 2003: 43–4; Miller 2005–06: 242). In absolute terms, the coronary heart disease event increase of 29 per cent reflected 37 women versus 30 per 10,000 person-years, and the stroke and breast cancer increases 29 versus 21 and 38 versus 30, respectively; the breast cancer increase in relative risk meant eight more cases for each 10,000 women using the product (Twombly 2007: 1829–30). As a result, the researchers concluded that the hormone replacement regime risk-benefit indications were inconsistent with its use to prevent chronic diseases and that HRT should not be used for primary prevention of coronary heart disease (Writing Group for WHI Investigators 2002: 321, 332).

To avoid such deficiencies in drug awareness, drugs need to be tested on the entire population who will use the drug. If the product is to be used by adolescents and girls, elderly women and women of all races, the study samples should be inclusive and include enough people in the sub-samples to permit valid analysis. The data for these groups should be analysed and disclosed. Since increasing sample sizes increases the cost of studies, drug manufacturers have an incentive to avoid doing so, but exclusion on the basis of cost would be considered ethically unacceptable (Lyerly et al 2008: 17; Simon 2005: 1517). Susan Dodds has noted that both men and women experience a range of medical conditions but that women are affected or treated differently. Such known differences provide a basis for determining in a careful way what kind of testing should be done (Dodds 2008: 66–7).

Inclusion should be the starting point, with exclusion justified by the manufacturer or researcher as part of the research protocol for clinical trials. After the inclusion issue emerged through academic studies and women's organisations in the early 1990s, governments took some action in the US, where legislative changes were made, and in Canada, where a clinical trials guideline was created. The Canadian government has made commitments to gender-based analysis in health but the Auditor-General's analysis of Health Canada's implementation of gender-based analysis found limited success (Auditor-General of Canada 2008: ch 8). In 1997, they adopted the Guideline on Inclusion of Women in Clinical Trials, which required inclusion in clinical trials unless reasonable grounds for exclusion could be demonstrated (Health Canada 1997). A similar standard is set out in the ethical standards applying to clinical trials and research funded through federal granting councils (Canadian Institutes of Health Research 2010: Articles 4.1, 4.2). It is clear, however, that stronger measures are necessary to produce research that fills this knowledge gap (Lippman 2006). The fact that the inclusion requirement has been found only in a guideline and a policy statement and not in statutory, or even regulatory, form demonstrates under-commitment to the goal.

Elderly women's health needs should be made a priority. Complex health needs may require multiple medications, leading to the possibility of interaction effects, and these are often unstudied. The drugs are likely to have a different pharmacokinetic impact in older bodies because of low weight and decreased metabolic rates, and dosages need to be calculated and adjusted. These data are unlikely to be available. Abby Lippman has noted that arbitrary upper age limits commonly established for clinical trials exclude these patients and diminish the safety and efficacy information available for them (Lippman 2010: 101). Because of the existence of other medical conditions that are common in elderly patients, adverse drug effects may be attributed to those conditions instead of to the drug (Lippman 2010: 101).

The manufacturer's common law duty with respect to product safety exists when the product is developed and continues with the emergence of data indicating further risks, including those of life-threatening consequences. The drug Vioxx was heavily prescribed as a painkiller, among elderly women with arthritis, for example, a target group for their marketing. In March 2000 the VIGOR (Vioxx Gastrointestinal Outcomes Research) study found a five-fold increased risk of coronary artery blockage in the Vioxx group over the naproxen (Aleve) group in the patients with the highest risk of myocardial infarction (Waxman 2005a). Aggressive marketing of the product followed, including downplaying of the VIGOR data by their sales representatives through characterising naproxen as providing a cardio-protective effect, as the company's internal instructions to detailers indicated they should do (Waxman 2005b). While this cardio-protective effect was one possible interpretation of the data, research was not done to investigate which interpretation was valid. Merck argued that it would have been unethical, and prohibited under FDA rules, to carry out a clinical trial to test the hypothesis (Green 2006–07: 754–5). At the same time, their untested hypothesis was treated as factually based and their marketing campaign was built around this interpretation. The FDA sent Merck a strongly worded warning about their promotional campaign which 'minimizes the serious cardiovascular findings' of the

VIGOR study 'and then, misrepresents the safety profile for Vioxx', selectively presenting their explanation:

> That is a possible explanation, but you fail to disclose that your explanation is hypothetical, has not been demonstrated by substantial evidence, and that there is another reasonable explanation, that Vioxx may have pro-thrombotic properties.
>
> (US Food and Drug Administration 2001)

When their study of colorectal polyps showed in 2004 that the Vioxx arm of the study had a significantly higher relative risk for cardiovascular events such as heart attack and stroke, Merck removed the product from the market.

In the Federal Court of Australia trial decision in *Peterson v Merck Sharpe & Dohme* [2010], Jessup J extensively canvassed the issue of whether the manufacturer carried out adequate testing of the product's safety and found no breach of the duty to test. On the issue of warning, he found that the company had breached its duty to warn by failing to warn the particular doctor. On appeal, the Full Federal Court of Australia allowed the appeal of Merck Sharp Dohme (Australia) [MSDA] of the decision awarding compensation to Mr. Peterson under the trade practices legislation with respect to fitness for purpose and merchantability, finding that no causation existed. Recovery under the defective products section was also rejected on the ground of causation. In the negligence action, the Full Court found that the company had taken reasonable steps to inform doctors about the Vigor signal and potential risks and that Dr. Dickman himself was informed [2011,154,158], and there was no breach of the duty to warn, overruling the Primary Judge's conclusion. The Full Court agreed with the Primary Judge that Mr. Peterson would probably have followed his doctor's advice and the doctor would have continued prescribing Vioxx. The Full Court further found that scientific causation had not been proved since proof of an increased risk – the doubling of cardiovascular risk – failed to meet the material contribution test in Australia under which it must be a necessary condition [102, 104]. Particular causation with respect to Mr. Peterson was not proved either since it was not demonstrated that Vioxx was a necessary condition for his heart attack. The Court noted that the decision was made specifically in relation to the individual respondent, and the company could be found liable to some other class members where the facts differ.

The uncertainty about drug effects during pregnancy places women at risk. Lyerly, Little and Faden have noted that only a dozen medications have been approved by the FDA for use during pregnancy and these have been approved only for gestation, while no drug has been approved for treatment of illnesses (Lyerly et al 2008: 7). Women with continuing health problems such as asthma, multiple sclerosis or cancer need to take drugs during pregnancy. Similarly, women who become ill during pregnancy have a medical need. These authors have suggested that pregnancy often serves as a 'significant wild card in clinical management' (Lyerly et al 2008: 8), giving as one example chemotherapy that was metabolised and excreted before reaching a therapeutic threshold, while still exposing the pregnant women to the toxic effects. The safety for fetuses of more than 91 per cent of drugs introduced into the market over the previous 20 years had not been determined, according to a 2002 study of fetal risk (Lo and Friedman 2002; Lyerly et al 2008: 10). The Lyerly analysis demonstrates that attention needs to be paid to the risks of not intervening and not only to risks of intervening. Similarly, manufacturers should consider the legal risks of not intervening and not only those of intervening.

Another deficit in information is created by the short-term nature of clinical trials testing. Those effects that will show up only in longer-term studies are not usually made part of the application process for drug approval. Premarin's adverse effects, discussed above, are one such example. The breast implant litigation was based on allegations about risks that were actually known to the manufacturer, such as the risk of rupture and the creation of capsular contracture, along with those longer-term hypothesised risks such as the connective tissue disorders and auto-immune disorders. Dow Corning Corporation and other manufacturers had not been required to report adverse effects of the silicone gel breast implant when it was first approved but the company had not revealed to the regulator the existence of certain risks of which they became aware later. It was this revelation that led to the FDA's withdrawal of the product from the market in 1992. The plaintiffs' attempts to secure information from the manufacturers and their parent companies were not successful in producing evidence of knowledge about a causal link to these longer-term effects. As noted above, when research was eventually carried out, the evidence did not support such a causal link to the auto-immune disorders (Angell 1997: 19). In the meantime, Dow Corning Corporation had entered into a settlement as part of its bankruptcy proceedings. Lucinda Finley pointed out that the focus on the scientific causation issue ended in significant down-playing of the known effects of breast implants which caused real pain and harm to women's physical and emotional well-being (Finley 1996).

This section has illustrated the significant knowledge deficit that exists and its impact on women's health. The common law requirement that sufficient infor-mation be available in the manufacturing process provides only some protection for plaintiffs injured by products. Although the assessment of the duty to test when a manufacturer is alerted to a danger was unsuccessfully litigated on the facts in *Peterson*, the case is an important acknowledgement of the duty to test. When products are marketed without information about the risks for the full range of patients who will use them, the duty of care has not been met.

The duty to warn action and knowledge construction through promotion

The duty to warn of product risks arises out of the same principles and concerns as the duty of care applying to manufacturing set out in *Donoghue v Stevenson* [1932]. The Supreme Court of Canada in the case of *Lambert v Lastoplex* [1972] established the duty to warn the consumer of product risks of which the manufacturer has or ought to have knowledge. The manufacturer knows these risks to an extent unmatched by the consumer. The more dangerous the product, the more extensive the warning must be. The duty to warn is continuous, including risks about which the manufacturer has learned after marketing (*Rivtow Marine Ltd v Washington Iron Works* [1974]).

The duty to warn is owed by the manufacturer to the consumer. For products prescribed by a professional, such as a doctor, a direct warning by the manufacturer to the consumer is not required. The manufacturer may discharge the duty by warning the doctor, who is a learned intermediary between the manufacturer and the patient. The doctor has an independent duty to disclose to the patient the material risks, and other matters, in relation to any proposed treatment.

The 'learned intermediary rule' was adopted in the Ontario Court of Appeal decision in *Buchan v Ortho Pharmaceutical (Canada) Ltd* [1986], a case involving the birth control pill's risk of stroke, and subsequently by the Supreme Court of Canada in the leading case of *Hollis v Dow Corning Corp* [1995], a breast implant rupture case. The analyses of Justice Robins in *Buchan* and Justice La Forest in *Hollis* for the unanimous Courts are characterised by an understanding of the hierarchical structure of power between the manufacturer and the patient, based on the superior knowledge of the manufacturer. The patient is at the bottom of the hierarchy, without power in the relationship or knowledge. The doctor has power in relation to the patient but relies on the manufacturer for information about the product. The intermediary becomes 'learned' only when 'fully apprised of the risks associated with the use of the product', and the manufacturer's duty is discharged only when the intermediary's knowledge approximates the manufacturer's (*Hollis*: [31]). As Justice Robins commented, the warning 'should not be neutralized or negated by collateral efforts on the part of the manufacturer' (*Buchan* [101]). The recognition of knowledge's importance in creating power – or in failing to do so – is the foundation for their analyses of the duty to warn action.

In *Hollis*, the Supreme Court of Canada found that Dow Corning Corporation had breached its duty to warn of the risk of breast implant rupture, a risk of which it had received notice. Justice La Forest noted (*Hollis* [55]) that the duty is a continuous one and adopted Justice Robins' comment in *Buchan* that the manufacturer's obligation is to not ignore data but to tell the entire story. Companies also have an obligation under basic duty principles to investigate such reports to determine their product's safety, a position elaborated in the *Peterson* decision (*Peterson v Merck Sharpe and Dohme (Australia) Pty Ltd* [2010]).

Plaintiffs must prove that the breach of the duty to warn has caused their harm. Causation is determined in three ways in such cases. First, causation in drug cases requires proof of the general scientific link: the evidence must demonstrate on the balance of probabilities that the drug causes that harm, such as the stroke in *Buchan*, both in general and in particular. Such proof may be very difficult for a plaintiff, as we saw in the breast implant litigation, where the lack of long-term studies made proof of the alleged causal link to auto-immune disorders virtually impossible (Angell 1997: 216). In contrast, ruptures and capsular contracture (the creation of skin-covered nuggets of silicone) were demonstrably caused by the implants. Secondly, the breached duty to warn must be causally connected to the loss of autonomy of the plaintiff. This element of decision causation is measured subjectively under *Hollis*, where the Court found the test to be subjective, what the plaintiff would have done if she had been informed of the rupture risk. As in *Peterson* [2011] a failure to warn action may fail on the subjective test of causation because the plaintiff would have taken the drug even if the risks had been disclosed. Finally, the Supreme Court of Canada found in *Hollis* that it would be unjust to force a plaintiff to prove a hypothetical, that the doctor would have disclosed the information if the manufacturer had warned the doctor, and created an effective presumption that prevents a manufacturer from relying on the difficulty of proof. The *Peterson* [2011] court did not use this doctrine.

Structuring knowledge through promotion

Product information is structured through the process of drug development, as we have seen in the discussion of knowledge deficits. Product information is further structured through promotional activities as the product is marketed. Drug promotion is important to an understanding of the impact of products liability law because marketing constructs knowledge about the drug.

The duty to warn action requires the manufacturer to warn the patient by disclosing the product's risks to the learned intermediary. As Justice Robins said in *Buchan*, the promotional activities must not undermine the warning, and he commented on the extensive and long-term promotional activities playing a role, along with the inadequate warnings, in creating doctors' views that the birth control pill was safe ([116]). An awareness of how drug advertising is structured will enable us to examine how promotion might undermine warnings. Litigators need to ensure that courts are aware of the structuring of information that underlies disclosure.

Information about drug products is conveyed through a variety of means and promotional activities may take place at the same time. It is provided to doctors by manufacturers through doctor-directed advertising, visits by drug sales representatives known as detailers, drug handbooks, distribution of literature and samples and sponsored activities such as conferences and trips. In addition, information and advertising is directed to consumers in some jurisdictions through direct-to-consumer ads, patient consumer groups and sponsored activities such as sports. In most jurisdictions, direct-to-consumer advertising (DTCA) is prohibited and only in the US and New Zealand is it explicitly permitted. In Canada, DTCA is illegal, but the exception for 'name, price and quantity' advertising has permitted companies to publish 'reminder ads' (drug brand name but no details) and 'help-seeking ads' (ask your doctor about a condition), and these have permitted broad advertising without any form of risk information. These types of ads, along with permissively defined educational activities and the widespread penetration on cable networks of US broadcasts without Canadian broadcast regulation of ad content result in significant amounts of DTCA reaching the Canadian public.

Pharmaceutical advertising is a powerful mechanism that has been shown to have significant effects on health care. It medicalises health, minimises the social determinants of health, promotes interventionist medicine, creates demand for lifestyles through drugs, and uses stereotypes of social relations to promote the product (Peppin and Carty 2001).[1] In this section, I will consider how advertising exercises this power and the nature of its particular impact on women's health.

Advertising creates perceptions and desires for products. These desires, for products such as Coke or Nike, are created through images and text designed to persuade. As media-literate consumers, we understand the seductive power of advertising, even though we remain largely unconscious of the ways it operates to achieve this power, as we are intended to be. Part of this power derives from the engagement of the viewer in creating the meaning of the product. As the semiotic theorists have described it, viewers are 'invited' into the ad to provide meaning to the image, to provide the value or meaning of the material object, person or thing that is being viewed. The meaning or value that the viewer attributes to the object constitutes part of the sign. In other words, a sign is made up of a material object plus meaning.

Drug advertising uses the same techniques to achieve its power. The value attributed by the viewer to the sign is transferred to the product and then over to the viewer. The polar bears drinking Coke are 'cool' and Coke is cool and we will be too if we drink it. An ad for the cardiovascular drug Norvasc which depicted a man salmon fishing alone in an isolated stream emphasised the man's activity, achieving mastery over nature in the form of the salmon and his cardiac problem through the activity of the drug. Drug advertisements promote the activity of intervention as innately beneficial. They convey the idea that drugs are magic (Williamson 1978: 47), able to cure conditions such as depression without accounting for the complexity of mental illness or addressing either social problems that may have triggered it or the social determinants of health such as poverty, aboriginal status or gender. We might conclude that risk information intrudes on the advertisement's magic and appears as an intrusion. It has to be powerful to counteract the spell.

Drug advertising creates a diagnostic image of the population that will be assisted by the drug (Stimson 1975; Peppin and Carty 2001: 356). For example, women have historically been over-represented in psychiatric drug advertisements directed to physicians, even in relation to higher levels of diagnosis. The advertisements suggest that women are the typical patients for the psychiatric conditions, who should receive the drug. Since the diagnostic image is a woman, women may be considered for this diagnosis more quickly than men. Similarly, cardiovascular drug advertisements of the 1990s such as the Norvasc ad typically portrayed men as the persons with the cardiovascular conditions, excluding women except in supportive passive roles, and drawing on traditional stereotypes about women's social roles and physical conditions in spite of the high incidence of cardiovascular disease in women. Multi-racial portrayals were virtually non-existent until the mid-1990s. The unrepresentative portrayals carry the dual risks of promoting over and under-prescription.

Feminist scholars have written extensively about the medicalisation of processes such as pregnancy, menopause and childbirth (for example, Martin 1987; Sherwin 1992). Concern that drug promotion is resulting in medicalising human processes or conditions has developed in the medical literature, particularly as the amount of DTCA in the US has risen precipitously. Moynihan and Cassels brought attention to these concerns in their work on 'Selling Sickness', as they described how everyday circumstances such as baldness and irritable bowel syndrome had been made into diseases requiring treatment (Moynihan and Cassels 2005). Barbara Mintzes asked about a whole class of drugs whose benefits seemed questionable whether the condition of incontinence was a matter of 'Overactive Bladder or Overactive Marketing?' (Mintzes 2010: 24).

The meaning for the ad comes from the viewer. Drug advertisements are constructed to take account of the values of the group from which the viewer comes. The first Prozac advertisement, directed to Canadian physicians in 1990, depicted a blue brain with channels of biochemical activity – the seeming impact of fluoxetine on serotonin levels – that made the science argument for physicians without the need to verbalise it. Physician-directed ads of the 1990s and early 2000s used gendered stereotypes such as the helpless and dependent patient or the overly independent feminist patient who would be led astray by reading the popular press – both stereotypes used in ads for Premarin (Peppin & Carty 2001). The DTCA campaign for Vioxx presented the 1976 Olympic figure skating gold medalist Dorothy Hamill, who would be particularly recognisable to older female viewers, the drug's target audience. The participation of the viewer but lack of conscious construction of meaning, identified by Williamson (1978: 45), helps us to understand how advertising works to create diagnostic conclusions and the feeling of empowerment without true understanding. The promotional efforts of the manufacturer are often strong enough to undermine any educational effect because of the imagery's power.

Information is vital to informed decision-making but the information must be valid, reliable and comprehensible. Drug promotion contributes to medicalisation of normal processes and to intervention without consideration of the patient's context. Creation of diagnostic images can contribute to over-prescription and under-prescription, and fail to take account of particular features of members of those groups. Stereotypes may demean patients while a promotional deluge masks information about real benefits and risks of treatments, and possible alternatives. The skeins of information and promotion entwined in drug advertising are difficult to separate. Because the advertising component achieves its effect without the viewer's consciousness, it appears invisible. Marketing of this sort can undermine the warnings that tort law requires a manufacturer to provide. Autonomy and product honesty fall by the wayside when advertising prevails over disclosure.

Conclusion

Women's health has been affected in significant ways by drugs and the products liability actions designed to provide remedies for harm. Improved knowledge about women's health will enhance the potential for effective treatments and patient choice based on full information. Otherwise, women remain at risk of inadequate treatment and diminished choice. Particular groups are affected including adolescents and children, pregnant women, elderly women and understudied racial groups.

The products liability doctrine needs to be robust, demanding of manufacturers that they investigate and report when adverse effects come to their notice. Litigators as well as regulators should ask whether manufacturers have taken the steps necessary to determine the product's safety and whether their conclusions about effectiveness are sustainable. If the litigation focus shifts to the need for more and better testing – inclusive research, improved risk assessment prior to approval, and long-term testing in the post-marketing period – and if a strong jurisprudence develops around inclusive testing and full reporting, the law may contribute significantly to better health and access to compensation.

Promotional excesses can be targeted by failure to warn actions that identify the undermining effect of the ads on product warnings. Such litigation can focus on misrepresentations in advertising and may include stereotypes, medicalisation and the creation of diagnostic images. Lawsuits based on deficiencies in advertising can be brought on a freestanding basis in actions in fraud, misrepresentation and breach of consumer statutes. Liability for deceptive advertising can be incorporated into the duty to warn action by finding whether the advertising has undermined the role of the doctor as the gatekeeper between the manufacturer and the patient. Enhanced understanding by litigators and judges of the advertisers' means of constructing knowledge can lead to greater success in this area.

Successful litigation brings underlying problems to the attention of legislators and may precipitate legislative changes. Widespread legal actions enhance our understanding of corporate behaviour and discovery processes further enhance understanding among the public. By raising awareness of knowledge deficits and the impact of drug promotion, and applying this awareness in products liability actions, feminist activists may drive the agenda for social change.

Notes

*   I am grateful for the research assistance of Brittany Sargent, Sharon Ford, Candice Lee, and Gillian Bookman, and the financial assistance of the Law Foundation of Ontario and Queen's University Faculty of Law.
1   In studies examining physician-directed ads from the 1990s to the mid-2000s, Elaine Carty and I applied these theories to drug ads to examine the meanings that underlie them and their impact on patient health. The theory and some of the ads are taken from those studies.

Cases

Anns v Merton London Borough Council [1977] 2 All ER 492
Bichler v Eli Lilly Corp [1982] 436 NE 2d 182 (NYCA)
Bolton v Stone [1951] AC 850
Buchan v Ortho Pharmaceuticals (Canada) Ltd [1986] 54 OR (2d) 92
Caparo Industries plc v Dickman [1990] 2 AC 605
Childs v Desormeaux [2006] 1 SCR 642
Cooper v Hobart [2001] SCR 537
Distillers Co (Bio-Chemicals) Ltd v Thompson [1971] AC 458
Donoghue v Stevenson [1932] 1 AC 562
Hollis v Dow Corning Corp [1995] 4 SCR 634
Kamloops (City of) v Nielsen [1984] 10 DLR (4th) 641
Lambert v Lastoplex [1972] SCR 569
Liebeck v McDonald's Restaurants, PTS Inc No. D-202 CV-93-02419, [1995] WL 360309
    Bernalillo County, NM Dist Ct [1994]
Merck Sharp & Dohme (Australia) Pty Ltd v Peterson [2011] FCAFC 128
Murphy v Brentwood District Council [1991] 1 AC 398
Peterson v Merck Sharpe & Dohme (Australia) Pty Ltd [2010] FCA 180
Rivtow Marine Ltd v Washington Iron Works [1974] SCR 1189
Sindell v Abbott Laboratories [1980] 607 P.2d 924
Sullivan v Moody [2001] 183 ALR 404
Sutherland Shire Council v Heyman [1985] 157 CLR 424

Bibliography

Angell, M. (1997) The Truth About the Drug Companies: Science on Trial: The Clash of Medical Evidence and the Law in the Breast Implant Case, New York, NY: W.W. Norton & Co

Auditor-General of Canada (2008) Report of the Auditor General of Canada to the House of Commons, Office of the Auditor General of Canada

Bernstein, A. (2003) 'Hymowitz v Eli Lilly and Co.: Markets of Mothers', in R. Rabin and S. Sugarman (eds) Torts Stories, New York, NY: Foundation Press, 151–78

Canadian Institutes of Health Research, Natural Sciences and Engineering Research Council of Canada, and Social Sciences and Humanities Research Council of Canada, (2010) Tri-Council Policy Statement: Ethical Conduct for Research Involving Humans (TCPS 2), December 2010

Dodds, S. (2008) 'Inclusion and Exclusion in Women's Access to Health and Medicine', International Journal of Feminist Approaches to Bioethics, 1: 58–79

Dresser, R. (1992) 'Wanted: Single, White Male for Medical Research', Hastings Center Report, 22(1): 24–9

Dutton, D. (1988) Worse than the Disease: Pitfalls of Medical Progress, Cambridge, UK: Cambridge University Press

Finley, L. (1996) 'The Pharmaceutical Industry and Women's Reproductive Health', in E. Szockyj and J. Fox (eds) Corporate Victimization of Women, Boston US: Northeastern University Press, 59–110

Flintoff, J-P. (2008) 'Thalidomide: The Battle For Compensation Goes On', Sunday Times, 23 March 2008

Florence, A. (1960) 'Is Thalidomide to Blame?', *British Medical Journal*, 2(5217): 1954

Gerlin, A. (1994) 'A Matter of Degree: How a Jury Decided McDonald's Should Pay a Woman Millions for a Hot-Coffee Spill', *Wall Street Journal*, 1 Sept 1994, A1

Green, R. (2006–07) 'Direct-to-Consumer Advertising and Pharmaceutical Ethics: The Case of Vioxx', *Hofstra Law Review*, 35: 749–59

Haltom, W. and McCann, M. (2004) *Distorting the Law: Politics, Media and the Litigation Crisis*, Chicago IL: University of Chicago Press

Health Canada (1997) 'Therapeutic Products Programme Guidelines: Inclusion of Women in Clinical Trials', Ottawa, Canada: Minister of Health

Heuston, R.H.V. (1957) '*Donoghue v. Stevenson* in Retrospect', *Modern Law Review*, 20: 1–24

Law, S. (1997) 'Tort Liability and the Availability of Contraceptive Drugs and Devices in the United States' *Review of Law & Social Change*, 23: 339–401

Lippman, A. (2006) 'The Inclusion of Women in Clinical Trials: Are We Asking the Right Questions?', Winnipeg, Canada: Women and Health Protection March 2006

—— (2010) 'Trials on Trial: Women and the Testing of Drugs', in A. Rochon Ford and D. Saibil (eds) *The Push to Prescribe*, Toronto: Women's Press, 93–114

Lo, W. and Friedman, J. (2002) 'Teratogenicity of Recently Introduced Medications in Human Pregnancy', *Obstetrics and Gynecology*, 100(3): 465–73

Lord, M. Chief Judge (1986) 'The Dalkon Shield Litigation, Revised Annotated Reprimand by Chief Judge Miles Lord', *Hamline Law Review*, 9: 7–51

Lyerly, A., Little, M. and Faden, R. (2008) 'The Second Wave: Toward Responsible Inclusion of Pregnant Women in Research', *International Journal of Feminist Approaches to Bioethics*, 1: 5–22

Martin, E. (1987) *The Woman in the Body: A Cultural Analysis of Reproduction*, Boston, MA: Beacon Press

Merkatz, R. (1993) 'Women in Clinical Trials: An Introduction', *Food & Drug Law Journal*, 48: 161–6

Merton, V. (1993) 'The Exclusion of Pregnant, Pregnable, and Once-Pregnant People (a.k.a. Women) from Biomedical Research', *American Journal of Law & Medicine*, 19: 369–451

Miller, K. (2005–06) 'Hormone Replacement Therapy in the Wake of the Women's Health Initiative Study: An Opportunity to Reexamine the Learned Intermediary Rule', *William & Mary Journal of Women & the Law*, 12: 239–66

Millrood, T. (2003) 'The Rise and Fall of Hormone Therapy', *Trial*, 39(8): 42–7

Mintzes, B. (2010) '"Ask Your Doctor": Women and Direct-to-Consumer Advertising', in A. Rochon Ford and D. Saibil (eds) *The Push to Prescribe*, Toronto: Women's Press

Moynihan, R. and Cassells, A. (2005) *Selling Sickness: How the World's Biggest Pharmaceutical Companies Are Turning Us All Into Patients*, New York, NY: Nation Books

National Film Board of Canada (1985) video, B. Andrukaitis, and S. Kerr, directors, 'DES: An Uncertain Legacy'

Peppin, P. and Carty, E. (2001) 'Semiotics, Stereotypes, and Women's Health: Signifying Inequality in Drug Advertising', *Canadian Journal of Women & the Law*, 13: 326–60

Pigg, S. (2011) 'Minnie Mouse Left Out of Laboratory Research', *Toronto Star*, 29 March 2011, A1, 12

Rosser, S. (1989) 'Re-visioning Clinical Research: Gender and the Ethics of Experimental Design', *Hypatia*, 4: 125–39

Sanders, J. (1992) 'The Bendectin Litigation: A Case Study in the Life Cycle of Mass Torts', *Hastings Law Journal*, 43: 301–418

Scott, J. (1993) 'How Did the Male Become the Normative Standard for Clinical Drug Trials?', *Food & Drug Law Journal*, 48: 187–93

Sherwin, S. (1992) *No Longer Patient: Feminist Ethics and Health Care*, Philadelphia, PA: Temple University Press

Silverman, W. (2002) 'The Schizophrenic Career of a "Monster Drug"', *Pediatrics*, 110(2): 404–6

Simon, V. (2005) Editorial, 'Wanted: Women in Clinical Trials', *Science*, 308(5728): 1517

Sobol, R. (1991) *Bending the Law: The Story of the Dalkon Shield Bankruptcy*, Chicago, IL: University of Chicago Press

Stimson, G. (1975) 'The Message of Psychotropic Drug Ads', *Journal of Communication*, 25: 153–60

Sunday Times Insight Team (1979) *Suffer the Children: The Story of Thalidomide*, London: Andre Deutsch

Twombly, R. (2007) 'So Far, Victories are Few as Breast Cancer Patients Sue Wyeth Over Hormone Therapy', *Journal of the National Cancer Institute*, 99(24): 1828–35

US Food, Drug and Cosmetic Act [2010] 21 U.S.C. s. 355(a) and (b).

US Food and Drug Administration (FDA) (2001) Warning Letter from Thomas Abrams, Director, Division of Drug Marketing, Advertising & Communications, Dept of Health and Human Services to Merck CEO Raymond Gilmartin, 17 Sept 2001.

War Amputations of Canada (1989) *Report of the Thalidomide Task Force*, Ottawa: War Amputations of Canada

Waxman, H. (2003) 'A History of Adverse Drug Experiences: Congress Had Ample Evidence to Support Restrictions on the Promotion of Prescription Drugs', *Food & Drug Law Journal*, 58: 299–312

—— (2005a) 'The Lessons of Vioxx – Drug Safety and Sales', *New England Journal of Medicine*, 352: 2576–8

—— (2005b) 'The Marketing of Vioxx to Physicians', Committee on Government Reform, Minority Office, US House of Representatives, Memorandum, 5 May 2005

Weinrib, E. (1989) 'The Special Morality of Tort Law', *McGill Law Journal*, 34: 403–13

Williamson, J. (1978) *Decoding Advertisements: Ideology and Meaning in Advertising*, London: Boyars

Writing Group for the Women's Health Initiative Investigators, (2002) 'Risks and Benefits of Estrogen Plus Progestin in Healthy Postmenopausal Women: Principal Results from the Women's Health Initiative Randomized Controlled Trial', *Journal of the American Medical Association*, 288: 321–33

Chapter 7

The Standard of Care in Medical Negligence – Still Reasonably Troublesome?

José Miola

Introduction

Once it has been established that a duty of care is owed by one person to another, the legal obligation is eponymous in nature: there is a duty to take care. The 'standard of care' is the name given to the legal test that determines whether that duty has been discharged in an adequate manner. Some refer to this middle prong in the elements that go to make up negligence as 'breach of duty', since if the defendant's conduct falls below the standard of care required by law then she is said to have breached the duty to take care. The standard of care can thus be said to be the crux of negligence, as it is the part that concerns the actual behaviour of the defendant towards the claimant. Needless to say, how one person acts in relation to another – and indeed how the law *allows* people to act towards each other – has serious policy consequences that can be relevant to feminist discourse (Conaghan 1996b; Peppin 1996). Not least, in the professional setting, it can set the paradigms of the power in the relationship between service provider and the person seeking to access that service. Nowhere can this have more serious ramifications than in the provision of medical treatment, where a relationship that gives power to the professional at the expense of the patient means that the former may have effective control over the body of the latter. Furthermore, women have traditionally been under-represented in the upper echelons of the medical profession, so female doctors may feel that they are at a disadvantage with a legal definition that, as we shall see, defines reasonableness in the actions of a professional's peer group. Thus women may find a lack of empathy from (mostly male) judges and (mostly male) senior doctors in their role as both doctor and patient.

This chapter considers feminist critiques of the law relating to the standard of care. More specifically, it will examine whether the problems identified within the legal system have been addressed by developments in the law, most notably in the case of *Bolitho v City and Hackney Health Authority* [1998], which claim to ensure that it is less paternalistic and less deferential to professionals (Woolf 2000). In 1998, in an early collection in the *Feminist Perspectives* series, Sally Sheldon offered a searing critique of the relationship between the legal and medical professions (Sheldon 1998). Over a decade later, it certainly stands the test of time and remains a sharp diagnosis of what is wrong about the use of the law. Yet her chapter – just – predates the House of Lords' decision in *Bolitho* and with it, if we are to believe the courts, a significant change to both the law *and* judicial philosophy. Post-*Bolitho*, we were told, there would there be excessive deference to doctors, and patients' rights would be protected above medical discretion. Taking Sheldon's and others' arguments as its starting point, this chapter considers how and to what extent this change in attitudes has played out. How, if at all, has the relationship between the two professions changed? And what, if any, have been the benefits to women both within and as users of the medical profession?

It begins by examining the general rules relating to breach of duty, including those that apply to professionals in general and doctors in particular, before going onto focus on the criticisms of the law, and whether they remain valid. Nevertheless, at the outset it is important to note that, just because these issues are pertinent to feminists, it does not mean that they are necessarily limited to women. The power dynamic and the resulting harm applies to everyone regardless of sex. Indeed, the power given to the medical profession by the law should, in theory, provide that male patients will also have been the victims of paternalism by female doctors. However, as Joanne Conaghan notes, women are more at risk from such inter-actions:

> The concept of gendered harm can also embrace those harms which, although not exclusive to women in any biological sense, are risks which women are more likely to incur than men – the risk of rape, incest, sexual harassment, spousal abuse or, more contentiously, the risk of harmful medical intervention.
> (Conaghan 1996a: 407)

Thus, the fact that some of the cases involve male patients and/or female doctors does not detract from the main point. We begin, then, by examining how the law defines the standard of care.

Defining negligence and identifying some conceptual problems – laypersons, professionals and doctors

The test for the standard of care is supposed to be objective (although, as we shall see, such claims are inherently problematic), and rely on the concept of 'reasonable-ness'. In order to achieve the standard of care required by law, it is sufficient to show that the defendant has acted in a 'reasonable' fashion. Thus, the definition of the question of what is reasonable conduct becomes key. It is most clearly explained by McNair J in the case of *Bolam v Friern Hospital Management Committee* [1957]:

> in an ordinary case which does not involve any special skill, negligence in law means this: some failure to do some act which a reasonable man in the circum-

stances would do, or doing some act which in the circumstances a reasonable man would not do . . . How do you test whether this act or failure is negligent? In an ordinary case it is generally said, that you judge that by the action of the man on the street. He is the ordinary man. In one case it has been said that you judge it by the conduct of the man at the top of the Clapham omnibus.

(*Bolam v Friern Hospital Management Committee* [1957]: [586])

There are a number of things to note here. First, it encompasses both acts and omissions – a failure to do something that a reasonable person would do is just as 'unreasonable' as doing something that the reasonable person would not do. Secondly, the conduct is not so much evaluated on its own terms, but instead by reference to what others might have done. This, while perhaps justifiable in an objective test as an expression of socially agreed behavioural norms, inevitably translates into a question of what the judge or members of the jury might have done in the same situation (as they are all, surely, reasonable people). Finally, one cannot help but notice the gender-specific language – however predictable that might have been in 1957. Feminists and others have long noted that the 'ordinary' or 'reasonable' man test is far less objective than it claims to be.[1] It is sufficient for the purposes of this chapter to note that it is not just the fact that the test 'embodies a male point of view, thereby holding women to a standard which was devised without them in mind' (Conaghan and Mansell 1999: 53). Instead:

> [t]his charge of 'maleness' goes well beyond a dislike of the gender-specificity of the standard as traditionally expressed. It is rather a critique of the *approach* which . . . [it] represents . . . which assumes that behaviour can be fairly and objectively evaluated with only limited reference to the context within which it takes place and against a backdrop of abstract and incontrovertible principles which apply in all situations.
>
> (Conaghan and Mansell, 1999: 53)

For this reason, it is an insufficient response to simply substitute the word 'man' for 'person' (Bender 1988: 22; Moran 2003). As Leslie Bender notes, the 'legal world that generated the "reasonable man" was predominantly, if not wholly, male', so even if referred to as the 'reasonable person' it still meant 'person who is reasonable by my standards' and therefore reflected a male perspective, or that of someone trained to think in this way (1988: 22–3). Thus, in a world where judges are still predominantly male (and from a certain social class), any test which invites *him* to assess 'reasonableness' *will inevitably result in his own views and prejudices being applied*. That will be the case whether the test is referred to as relating to the 'reasonable man', 'reasonable person' or even 'reasonable woman'. It is also the reason that claims regarding the objectivity of the test cannot logically be supported.

The failings of the test – or, perhaps more specifically, the way that it is applied – can lead to inequity when the reasonableness or otherwise of the actions of groups other than white, middle-class males are considered. Moreover, the situation when this test is applied to professionals inevitably leads to unfairness. McNair J, continuing his description of the standard of care in *Bolam*, turned his attention towards those with a special skill:

> where you get a situation which involves the use of some special skill or competence, then the test whether there has been negligence or not . . . is the standard of the ordinary skilled man exercising and professing to have that special skill . . . A man need not possess the highest skill at the risk of being found negligent . . . [I]t is sufficient if he exercises the ordinary skill of an ordinary competent man exercising that particular art.
>
> (*Bolam v Friern Hospital Management Committee* [1957]: [586])

Of note here is the way in which the 'reasonable' man metamorphoses into the 'ordinary' professional. This is deeply problematic. As Kenneth Norrie highlights, the distinction between the two words is more than merely semantic. 'Ordinariness' is a descriptive concept – if all architects act in a certain way, then that is enough to satisfy a test of 'ordinariness' as it merely asks what architects *do*. 'Reasonableness', however, is normative. Just because all architects would act in a certain way, it does not *prove* that it is reasonable to do so (although it may be evidence of reasonableness). Rather, '[a] test of "reasonable care" necessarily carries with it a connotation which allows the court to say what *ought to have been done* in the circumstances' (Norrie 1985: 148). Therefore, a test of 'ordinariness' effectively allows a profession to set its own standard of care, whereas a test of 'reasonableness' allows the court to retain ultimate control by reserving the right to classify conduct that it does not like (however ubiquitous) as 'unreasonable'. This distinction is key when it comes to the actual operation of the test, which relies heavily on expert evidence in recognition of the fact that the judge is not, to continue our example, an architect.

The operation of the test therefore involves an expert 'war', with each side lining up its own experts to back their case. The question is whether (and, if so, how) the judge might choose between them if, as is common, both sides find support for their case. *Bolam* itself is somewhat unclear about this. McNair J said that the effect of the test was that:

> [a] doctor is not guilty of negligence if he has acted in accordance with a practice accepted as proper by a responsible body of medical men skilled in that particular art . . . [equally] a doctor is not negligent, if he is acting in accordance with such a practice, merely because there is a body of opinion that takes the contrary view.
>
> (*Bolam v Friern Hospital Management Committee* [1957]: [587])

Thus, what is key is that doctors escape liability by achieving the legal standard if they act in the same way that other doctors would act. The test can therefore be seen to privilege conformity to the professional standard, and obviously the role of expert witnesses cannot be overstated. If the witnesses constitute a 'responsible body' of medical practitioners, then the defendant is held to have acted reasonably.

But how might we determine whether the body is 'reasonable' in practical terms? Is the mere existence of medical evidence on behalf of the defendant sufficient? It is here that the law relating to doctors and other professions diverged for 40 years. Indeed, for all professions *except* the medical profession, the law was that although expert evidence constituted evidence of reasonableness, it was not conclusive proof. Thus, in the case of *Edward Wong Finance Co Ltd v Johnson, Stokes and Master* [1984], the Privy Council held that the universal practice of conveyancers in Hong Kong – of the buyer handing over money to a solicitor in return for an undertaking to hand over the deeds – was unreasonable, as it obviously allowed a dishonest solicitor to abscond with the money. Moreover, this was not limited to the legal profession – the rule that the courts reserved the right to assess and, if necessary, reject the practices of a profession applied to all with one exception.

In the case of doctors, however, the law was applied differently. In the process, *Bolam* was transformed from a minor first instance direction to a jury to the most important case regarding the standard of care. For doctors, the mere existence of expert evidence on behalf of the defendant appeared to prove that the doctor had acted to the requisite standard of care. In *Maynard v West Midlands Regional Health Authority* [1985], for example (decided by the House of Lords only a year after *Edward Wong*), the precise question for their Lordships was whether a judge was even permitted to find for the claimant where the defendant had provided experts to testify in her support. The trial judge had preferred the evidence of the claimant's experts and found the doctor liable, and the appeal was based on whether he was entitled to do so. The House of Lords held, unanimously and categorically, that he should not have done so:

> I have to say that a judge's 'preference' for one body of distinguished professional opinion to another also professionally distinguished is not sufficient to establish negligence in a practitioner whose actions have received the seal of approval of those whose opinions, honestly expressed, honestly held, were not preferred. *If this was the real reason for the judge's finding, he erred in law* . . . For in the realm of diagnosis and treatment, negligence is not established by preferring one respectable body of professional opinion to another. Failure to exercise the ordinary skill of a doctor (in the appropriate specialty, if he be a specialist) is necessary.
>
> (*Maynard v West Midlands Regional Health Authority* [1985]:
> [639], emphasis added)

What can be seen here is the privileging of the medical profession's standards over the law's duty and ability to provide oversight. Doctors, unlike other professionals, were able to set their own standard of care, and judges were *not entitled* to challenge them. Furthermore, the number of experts required to constitute a 'responsible body of medical opinion' was held to be extremely small – in the case of *DeFreitas v O'Brien* [1995], for example, five out of 250 specialists were deemed enough. Essentially, there was a distinction between the medical and other professions based on different interpretations of how 'reasonableness' should be determined. For professions other than medicine, the concept of 'reasonableness' was defined and applied in a normative way – the courts, in Norrie's words, looked at what *ought to have been done*. This involved the judge assessing the expert evidence and, if it made no sense, potentially rejecting it and finding for the claimant. With doctors, as *Maynard* demonstrates, 'reasonableness' was conflated with 'ordinariness' and interpreted descriptively, so the role of the court was little more than a rubber stamp that would merely check whether expert evidence for the defendant existed. If it did, then the doctor was deemed to have acted 'reasonably' whatever the circumstances and it was not open to a judge to find otherwise. Conformity would therefore be rewarded, and a lack of it punished.

And so it continued for 40 years, until the case of *Bolitho*, in 1997. In this case the House of Lords found that this restrictive application of *Bolam* was wrong, and that it *was* open to the courts to declare even the common practice of the medical profession to be unreasonable if it fails to exhibit logical force. The case is discussed in detail below. For present purposes the key point is this. Essentially, doctors were to be treated the same as other professionals, and according to the law as defined in *Edward Wong*.

But why were doctors for so long placed in such an exalted position by judges, and had separate rules to anyone else? In her seminal analysis of *Bolam*, Sheldon argues that the reason is the class, race and *gender* similarities within the legal and medical professions:

> Why is it that judges prioritise one set of policy considerations to the complete occlusion of the others? I would argue that this is best understood within the context of class, race, and gender, where the judges naturally identify with the position of the doctor as a fellow professional. This is not surprising: judges and doctors share the same socio-economic space within society. Judges will probably have similar career aspirations and expectations to doctors and are likely to have family and friends who are doctors and thus should have a clear understanding of their concerns. What becomes clear on a close reading of these cases are the very different reactions to doctor and patient.
>
> (Sheldon, 1998: 21)

The effect of this is an instinctive judicial empathy towards the doctor rather than the patient. The judge can perhaps see himself more as the dedicated professional making difficult decisions in difficult cases more than as a wronged party. Moreover, the medical profession has traditionally been – with the legal profession – amongst the most powerful in society. Thomas Szasz referred to the 'church of medicine' in the last century, arguing that it carried a level of social power analogous to that of the Christian church in the 16th century (Szasz 1979). What is undeniable is that, before *Bolitho*, doctors were treated differently from other professions in English law. That includes other prestigious professionals such as solicitors (see, for example, *Edward Wong*). Sheldon offers no explanation as to why doctors were held in such unique esteem, and it is difficult to divine why. It cannot be the mere scientific nature of medical practice, as this has not stopped the courts from imposing liability on, for example, architects and engineers (Yule 1996).

From a conceptual perspective also, the pre-*Bolitho* law's claim to be an impartial definer of an objective concept of 'reasonableness' is less than convincing. What is 'reasonable' depends on the perspective of the person defining 'reasonableness' – which is of course a subjective calculation. Rather, there is much power at the hands of (predominantly male) judges, and when it is delegated it then resides in a (also predominantly male) medical profession. It is thus unsurprising that 'reasonableness' continues to be criticised by feminists. The inevitability of a 'male' application of the law means that the central tenet of the 'reasonableness' test – that it is an approach which 'assumes that behaviour can be fairly and objectively evaluated with only limited reference to the context within which it takes place' – cannot be supported (Conaghan and Mansell 1999: 53). Moreover, the test also encourages homogenous thinking, with difference punished. The danger is that in so far as female doctors take a different view on the appropriateness of treatments, particularly in the context of obstetrics, they – as well as female patients – will suffer in a male-dominated profession if they do not conform.[2]

Thus, despite the change in the law in *Bolitho*, it does not follow that women will be treated differently by the judiciary. If Sheldon's identification of class, race and gender as factors in judicial deference to the medical profession is correct, then that deference is a reflection of judicial attitudes. Just because judges *can* challenge medical evidence, it does not mean that they *will* do so. Consequently, a change in the law will achieve little without a concurrent change in judicial attitude. The rest of this chapter will investigate whether Sheldon's critique is therefore still valid, or whether *Bolitho* represents something of an empty gesture. It considers Sheldon's critique of the pre-*Bolitho* law, and then continues by examining what effect *Bolitho* has had on her critique.

Sally Sheldon's practical critique

Sheldon began by noting that *Bolam* confused description with prescription – in other words, the courts allowed themselves to become a rubber stamp for common medical practice rather than the ultimate arbiters of conduct. She then asked two specific questions: first, 'why has the law developed in this way and what does locating *Bolam* in the context of gender add to our understanding of its evolution?', and, secondly, 'what particular problems does the . . . conflation of description with prescription – of *accepted* with *acceptable* practice – pose for women?' (Sheldon 1998: 19)

To answer the first she considered cases, in particular from the 1980s, where judges have provided policy arguments in favour of the *Bolam* test. These ranged from the undesirability of allowing medical practitioners to be sued in general to the fact that medicine is 'not easily amenable to being understood, or judged, from the outside' (Sheldon 1998: 20), the 'fact' that the doctor–patient interaction should be characterised by a power imbalance in favour of the doctor, to arguments that negligence claims destroy the doctor–patient relationship (Sheldon 1998: 20). Sheldon argued that the reasons given in favour of *Bolam* all had one thing in common: partiality towards doctors at the expense of patients (Sheldon 1998: 21). Thus, the 'equally compelling' policy arguments in favour of compensating patients (such as victims' need for compensation, and the potential role of tort in driving up standards) were ignored (Sheldon 1998: 21).[3] In other words, the judges had made a *choice* to prioritise one set of policy considerations over another, and were exclusively using them to protect doctors rather than patients. The reason, Sheldon argued, was the shared socio-economic space within society between the medical and legal professions as described above.

Moreover, Sheldon makes clear that the image projected of the doctor was very different to that projected of the patient to make it easier for the courts to reach the policy decisions that they have done. Doctors are portrayed as professionals whose reputations require protection, and with whom there must be an automatic professional empathy. Indeed, as fellow professionals in a position where the making of difficult decisions is both necessary and commonplace, it is perhaps unsurprising that judges will empathise with them. Patients, on the other hand, were seen as being a part of the problem themselves. For example, in *Whitehouse v Jordan* [1981], a child was born brain damaged and the claimant alleged that the doctor had used forceps with too much force. The patient is described as being 'difficult, nervous and at times aggressive' with an 'instinctive revulsion against her vagina being examined' (Lord Denning in Sheldon 1998: 22). The implication was that she was at least partly responsible for the problems that arose. When she finds out about her child being injured, this is then used to paint her as an unreliable witness:

> It is no criticism of Mrs Whitehouse to say that she was so emotionally involved, so bitter, so convinced that Mr Jordan was to blame . . . that it would have been remarkable if she had been an objective and reliable witness on any crucial matter.
>
> (Lord Wilberforce in Sheldon 1998: 22)

Needless to say, the doctor is presented in a different light, being described as 'very able and promising', of the 'highest skill and repute' and 'held in the highest regard' by his peers (Lords Denning and Donaldson in Sheldon 1998: 22). The doctor is, therefore, not just privileged in a professional sense but also in a personal capacity, where integrity and good conscience are assumed – something that is not bestowed on the patient (McLean 1981). Sheldon concludes that the 'policy arguments advanced by the courts are based on a stereotypical, idealised version of the medical relationship', and this serves 'to occlude other visions' (Sheldon 1998: 25). Moreover, the judges' identification with the doctors in cases can be traced back to a shared socio-economic background in which gender plays an important role. Examples are also given from the case of *Sidaway v Board of Governors of Bethlem Royal Hospital* [1985], where Sheldon demonstrates that the claimant is characterised 'precisely by her *difference*' to the judges, and *Maynard* (where the surgeon is again presented as 'careful', 'competent' and 'skilful') (Sheldon 1998: 22–6).

The consequences of this are important for both female patients and female doctors. For the former what Sheldon demonstrates is that pre-*Bolitho*, *Bolam* puts all of the power in the hands of a medical profession that is not able to understand or empathise with the needs of those who are different to them – and this includes women as a class. The standard of care looks at medical conduct not through the eyes of the patient, but instead through a prism of what some other doctors would do. In this sense, any rights that the patient may be given are tangential. As Sheldon highlights, an appeal to the judiciary for help is likely to be fruitless. Indeed, some judges appear to consider an attack on a doctor represented by the patient's complaint to cause as much injury as the physical wounds suffered by the patient. Moreover, this all served to give the medical profession power over patients' bodies, and of course this is of particular significance to women, who have traditionally borne a disproportionate brunt of medical paternalism (Graycar and Morgan 2002). This situation led Sheila McLean to bemoan the fact that *Bolam*'s disregard for patients' rights, coupled with its inexorable expansion into many areas of medical law, had underlined the fact that the law (and doctors) had failed patients:

> No matter the quality of medicine practised, and no matter the doubts of doctors themselves about the appropriateness of their involvement, human life is increasingly medicalised. In part, this is the result of the growing professionalism of medicine, in part our responsibility for asking too much of doctors. In part, however, it is also because the buffer which might be expected to stand between medicalisation and human rights – namely the law – has proved unwilling, unable or inefficient when asked to adjudicate on or control issues which are at best tangentially medical.
>
> (McLean, 1999: 2)

The female *doctor* fares little better. This is perhaps unsurprising given that, just as the patient is an outsider in a test for reasonableness based on what (predominantly male) doctors would do, so is a doctor who is different or has an alternative perspective. It should be made clear here that I am not claiming that female doctors necessarily have a different perspective in all cases nor, of course, that there is a single female doctor 'voice' or that all female doctors think the same. Rather, I suggest that there are some areas – obstetrics and gynaecology being the most obvious example – where a woman's experiences will by definition be markedly different from a male one, and in some cases this may lead to a difference in perspective, as I detail in my example below.

As we have seen, the descriptive interpretation of *Bolam* prioritises what *is* done over what *ought* to have been done, and cases being reduced to a confrontation between expert witnesses means that it is important to conform. As Bender notes, male dominated institutions (and medicine has traditionally been one) 'reflect male values, characteristics, conceptions of reality, and needs', and if women are 'acculturated differently' or have alternative perspectives, they 'will have to relinquish their female training and identity in order to succeed' (Bender 1988: 7). Thus, the female doctor may have to jettison her own female identity in order to conform and satisfy the *Bolam* test. This was certainly the experience for Wendy Savage, a consultant gynaecologist who was suspended from her post in 1985 for, among other charges, allowing a patient to have a trial labour despite the fact that the foetus was in a breech position (Sheldon 1998: 29). Savage's view was that it was psychologically important for the woman to experience for herself that a vaginal delivery was impossible. A factor in the suspension, it would appear, was the fact that Savage was not acting in accordance with normal practice (Sheldon 1998: 29). She was eventually cleared after an enquiry (Savage 1987), but what this shows is that when an alternative, female perspective is utilised it can immediately be questioned, and the law (through *Bolam*) will provide scant protection. Thus female doctors must conform to the male values and characteristics and reflect the profession, rather than the profession reflecting them.

Has the problem of *Bolam* been 'cured' by *Bolitho*?

So far this chapter has outlined Sally Sheldon's critique of the pre-*Bolitho* test for the standard of care for medical professions, and identified the fact that the law has now changed. However, it has also alluded to the fact that it does not necessarily follow that the change in the law will solve the problems with the application of the standard of care to medical professionals. In the following sections, the chapter considers whether *Bolitho* has solved the problems identified with *Bolam*, both on a conceptual level and in the context of Sheldon's critique.

Power is implicit in the question of who gets to define what is reasonable. Something that can be seen from the discussion above is that the test for the standard of care relates to the conduct of the professional rather than the rights of the client. The test in tort considers conduct from the perspective of the actor rather than that of the recipient of the act (Conaghan 1999: 207–8). In the medical interaction, the legal test focuses on the duties of the doctor without reference to the rights of the patient (other than, of course, the right to be treated in a 'reasonable' fashion). Thus, if the profession is given too much power this can translate into a resulting loss of control on the part of the client. In terms of the doctor–patient relationship, this will mean that doctors may have control over the body of the patient, which is why medical practice is such an appropriate and important object of feminist critique. What is undeniable is that this is precisely what has occurred in relation to medical practice, with a resulting loss of autonomy.

One of the reasons for this loss of autonomy on the part of patients is the fact that the test for reasonableness as it was before *Bolitho* made it very difficult for patients to win cases. The small number of doctors required to comprise the 'responsible body of medical opinion' and the lack of opportunity for judges to analyse the evidence, meant that conduct (of the individual practitioner) would effectively have to be universally condemned before a breach of duty would he held to have occurred. As Michael Jones noted pithily, the 'score' in medical negligence cases (up to and including *Bolitho*) in the House of Lords read: claimants – 0; defendants – 6! (Jones 1999: 236).[4] But another factor exacerbated the effect of this interpretation of the *Bolam* test: the fact that *Bolam* grew well outside the boundaries expected by McNair J, and also those appropriate to it. The judicial attitude in the 1980s and well into the 1990s was, in the words of Mike Davies, 'when in doubt, *Bolamise*' (Davies 1996: 120). Thus key issues to do with medical treatment were 'hustled into a *Bolam* straightjacket' (Brazier and Miola 2000: 90). Among them were some of the most important questions relating to the doctor–patient interaction – which were ethical rather than medical in nature (Brazier and Miola 2000: 90).

There have been two House of Lords' decisions relating to medical negligence since Sheldon's piece was published – *Bolitho* and *Chester v Afshar* [2005]. Both are considered to be torch bearers for the 'new', more pro-patient attitude that Lord Woolf has claimed to exist Grubb,1998 (*Bolitho*); Devaney 2005 (*Chester*). Each case shall be examined in turn.

Bolitho v City *and Hackney Health Authority*

It is important to note that *Bolitho*, despite supposedly signifying a change in the law and a retreat from the restrictive interpretation of *Bolam*, still resulted in the claimant losing the case. The medical evidence advanced by the defendant was deemed to be reasonable, that is capable of withstanding logical analysis. For this reason, if no other, the case must be treated with a degree of caution. That said, *Bolitho* does provide a clear change in tone in its interpretation of *Bolam*. Essentially, the case concerns the issue of causation rather than breach of duty, and whether *Bolam* could be applied to that limb of negligence also (Grubb 1998). In the House of Lords, Lord Browne-Wilkinson, with whom all of the other judges agreed, stated that it could. Nevertheless, as we have seen, he reasserted the right of the court – rather than the medical profession – to define the reasonableness of medical conduct. The facts of the case are, in brief, that Patrick Bolitho was two years old, and presented at the hospital suffering from breathing difficulties. He suffered three episodes where his breathing was further compromised, and despite the Senior Paediatric Registrar (Dr Horn) being called on each occasion, she never attended the patient herself. It was found that this constituted a breach of duty, and the appeal was concerned with what would have happened had she attended – a factor that does not concern us here.

Thus, perhaps due to the fact that the defendants admitted the breach of duty, there is virtually no discussion of the actual conduct of the doctor. Rather, the opinion concentrates on the legal points relating to how to determine whether it was reasonable not to intubate, and whether this was relevant to the question of causation in the case. The defendants had argued that, even if they had attended

Patrick, they would not have intubated him. Sheldon's assessment of 'images of doctor and patient' are impossible to replicate in the case because Lord Browne-Wilkinson takes a highly impersonal approach to the case. This is perhaps due to the fact that, as breach of duty had already been admitted by the defendant, his Lordship may have felt that there was no need to examine the conduct of the doctors or their motives. There are only two points of note. The first is that it is only in the final paragraph of his opinion that sympathy is expressed towards the parents of the claimant – who during the events that formed the basis of the litigation suffered catastrophic brain damage: '[t]ragic though this case is for Patrick's mother and much as everyone must sympathise with her, I consider that the judge and the Court of Appeal reached the right conclusions' (Lord Browne-Wilkinson *Bolitho* [1998]: 244).

In contrast, the medical personnel fare much better in the brief mentions that are made of them – perhaps surprisingly given that breach of duty had been admitted. The statements are also brief, and it is important not to oversell what are essentially throwaway comments. That said, the description of Dr Horn's response is intriguing:

> Dr. Horn seemed *alarmed* that Patrick was in such distress when he had appeared perfectly well a short time before during the consultant's round. Sister Sallabank told Dr. Horn that there had been a notable change in Patrick's colour and that he sounded as though something was stuck in his throat. *Dr. Horn said that she would attend as soon as possible. In the event, neither she nor Dr. Rodger [a Senior House Officer working with Dr. Horn] came to see Patrick.*
> (Lord Browne-Wilkinson *Bolitho* [1998]: [236], emphasis added)

The doctor is thus described as being 'alarmed' at the condition of the patient, and promises to attend as soon as possible, which suggests concern and a caring, beneficent attitude. But she neither goes to see the patient nor asks anyone else to do so, which would appear at first glance to be at odds with the implication of being described as being 'alarmed'. Again, it is important not to oversell a possible interpretation of a single word, and there may be a good reason why Dr Horn was not able to attend the patient's bedside (although this is not explored in the opinion, and again we must remember that the defendant admitted that she should have done so), but it is, at least *prima facie*, perplexing that her behaviour and attitude are described without qualification in this way.

The overall message in *Bolitho* is, therefore, somewhat mixed. It did change the law as it was – modifying the previously used restrictive interpretation of *Bolam* – yet the claimant still lost the case. In terms of the 'image' presented of doctor and patient, this was a sober legal reflection that does not lend itself well to such analysis. Sheldon's findings relating to the images of doctor and patient presented by the courts are neither strengthened nor weakened by the case.

Chester v Afshar

Chester v Afshar is a case that should not be *under*sold. The case concerned the issue of informed consent, which is normally litigated through negligence. Essentially, this governs how much information about risks inherent in the suggested treatment a doctor needs to give a patient before the patient's consent to medical treatment is legally valid. In terms of breach of duty, the doctor must disclose to the patient all 'material risks', and to satisfy the causation element the patient must show that, had she been informed of the risk, she would not have consented to the treatment offered. The decision of the House of Lords related to causation. Mrs Chester had admitted that, had she been informed of the risk, she would probably have thought about it more but would eventually have consented. Under the normal rules, she should have lost. However, in a 3–2 decision the House of Lords found for Mrs Chester on the grounds that the function of the law was to protect patients' autonomy, and that if the law did not do so then the law was faulty and must be changed.[5] The case is of huge significance as it demonstrates the House of Lords' willingness not just to consider patient autonomy, but to *prioritise* it, even if that meant changing the law. It is, in attitude, a vindication of Lord Woolf's view that the courts would cease to defer to the medical profession. It is also as far from the 'old' *Bolam* judicial behaviour as it is possible to imagine. In terms of the power imbalance between doctor and patient, the case – particularly given the level of court making the decision – represents a discernible and significant shift.

The standard of care was not an issue for the House of Lords, as it had been found, as a question of fact at first instance, that the risk (a 1 to 2 per cent chance of nerve damage leading to partial paralysis in a pain relieving back operation) was material, and the defendant, Mr Afshar, was refused permission to appeal on this point. This is, in large part, due to the fact that Mr Afshar had claimed that he had attempted to inform Mrs Chester of the risk, a fact that she contested. He could not, therefore, argue that he did not feel that it was significant or material. In any event, the court believed the claimant's account of events, which is again at odds with the attitude towards the parties exhibited in the cases reviewed by Sheldon. For that reason, it is worth considering in a little more detail here. Moreover, their reasons for doing so are instructive. Although they come from the first instance judgment in the case, they are quoted with approval by Lord Hope in the House of Lords:

> [I]t is often a difficult and delicate matter for a consultant to advise a patient about what he regards as comparatively minor risks, particularly when that patient is already suffering from stress, pain and anxiety. He will naturally be anxious to avoid alarming or confusing the patient unnecessarily. In the present case, as the defendant indicated during his evidence, he clearly thought that the risk of damage to the claimant was extremely small. Furthermore he knew that he personally had never caused any nerve damages in the many hundreds of operations he had carried out over 20 to 25 years. It may well be that he considered the claimant over-anxious or over-preoccupied with 'horror stories'

and the possibility of being crippled. In these circumstances I do not find it improbable that, in an attempt to reassure, he deflected her enquiries by answering them in the light-hearted terms which she has described.

(*Chester* [2005]: [151])

While finding that both claimant and defendant were 'honourable people' (*Chester* [2000]: [63]), whose evidence was an honest recollection of the events, the first instance judge believed Mrs Chester on the basis that the event was, for her, a one-off, in contrast to Mr Afshar for whom it was just one interaction out of many (*Chester* [2000]: [64]). What is interesting here is the effective imputation of hubris onto the character of Mr Afshar. He is found to be honest yet 'understandably' overly sure of himself and imbued with a patrician concern not to panic the patient into not accepting the treatment offered. The portrayal of the doctor is not a flattering one. When this is combined with the finding in favour of the claimant (and the rejection of the established legal rules on causation in order to achieve this end), it is easy to see why the case is of such importance. In terms of updating Sheldon's analysis, it must be said that the attitude displayed by the majority of the House of Lords in *Chester* is a total departure from that displayed towards Mrs Whitehouse. It should also be noted, however, that the lack of criticism of this approach, which was seen as understandable by the judge, demonstrates a further assumption: that Mrs Chester *required* a paternalistic approach towards her.

The standard of care – where are we now?

That is not to say that any latent deference to the medical profession has been quashed by cases such as *Bolitho* and *Chester*, or that with a click of the fingers judges have realised that they were acting too deferentially, and simply decided to stop doing so. Rather, we can only identify trends in the law and accept that some cases will not conform to that trend. One such case is that of *Al Hamwi v Johnston and Another* [2005], a first instance decision that nevertheless contains the elements that constitute a recipe for the previous paternalism: a pregnant woman and a doctor potentially opposed to her choice. The precise facts were disputed by the parties, but what is known is that Mrs Al Hamwi, whose family had a history of what she thought was Down's Syndrome (but was actually a chromosomal abnormality), sought amniocentesis. The purpose was to see if the foetus would be born disabled and, if so, her intention was to have a termination. Before the test was performed, she was required to attend a counselling session with a consultant, Ms Kerslake.

The dispute surrounds what was said in this session, but what is known is that Mrs Al Hamwi left the meeting believing (erroneously) that the test carried a 75 per cent risk of harming the foetus. Somewhere along the way there was mis-communication between the parties. Mrs Al Hamwi had, according to her evidence, wanted amniocentesis when she entered the consultation – by the end she had changed her mind. Ms Kerslake stated that she had provided the true figure (a 1 per cent risk of miscarriage), while Mrs Al Hamwi disputed this. Two further factors complicated their interaction. First, Mrs Al Hamwi spoke little English (although she was provided with an interpreter). Secondly, Ms Kerslake was a fervent Christian who had published work that stated that amniocentesis should be discouraged as it was a precursor to abortion.

The court decided as a matter of fact that the explanation had been adequate, and that it would be too onerous a duty on doctors for them to be required to *ensure* understanding (Miola 2006). The judge, quite simply, did not believe that Mrs Al Hamwi was not told of the 1 per cent risk of miscarriage, nor that she believed the true figure to be 75 per cent (*Al Hamwi* [2005: [60]). She was accused of acting with the benefit of hindsight and, in a passage that is reminiscent of Sheldon's findings, that she was simply looking for someone other than herself to blame when addressing why she changed her mind following the session:

> It may have been that, having had one healthy child following a negative blood test, the claimant did not wish to run the risk of jeopardising the life of her child with a procedure that involved a real, albeit statistically slight, risk. It may be that she was influenced by the possibility that, if the test was positive, she would be faced with a decision about termination which would be difficult in view of the stage of her pregnancy and her religious beliefs [she was a Muslim]. She may have been particularly affected by having felt the child move. She may have felt under some form of familial pressure. Despite what I find to have been appropriate counselling, she may have been confused. Her decision may have involved all of these considerations. As Miss Kerslake said, 'people do change their minds'.
>
> (*Al Hamwi* [2005]: [75])

It is important not to take a case such as *Al Hamwi* and blow it out of proportion – it is a first instance decision and it flies in the face of the philosophy behind *Chester*. Nevertheless, the case does also highlight the danger in accepting *Bolitho* and *Chester* as incontrovertible proof of a total change in attitude on the part of the judiciary. Indeed, they are themselves mere snapshots of the thinking of the House of Lords at a particular time, and we would do well to remember that the claimant lost in *Bolitho* (Lord Browne-Wilkinson's opinion was agreed with by the other four judges), and in *Chester* two of the five judges dissented. So, it is clear that the judiciary is as divided as ever.

The effect of the concept of 'reasonableness'

Indeed, post-*Bolitho* case analyses have found it inconsistently applied by the courts, and this inconsistency is only matched by the views taken by academics! Thus Alasdair Maclean has declared *Bolam* 'far from dead' given the inconsistent application of *Bolitho* (Maclean 2002: 211). Rob Heywood is of the same opinion (Heywood 2006). Rachael Mulheron, in the most recent analysis, disagrees, arguing that *Bolitho* is applied more than would make it appropriate to label its use 'rare'

(Mulheron 2010: 610). Yet there is consensus on one point, which is that *Bolitho* does give courts a modicum of control, and what is important is the way in which courts use it. Mulheron identifies factors leading to 'red flags' (Mulheron 2010: 638), while Maclean and Heywood argue that *Bolitho* is being wrongly applied in many cases. Yet another explanation is possible: that *Bolitho* may be inconsistently applied because the 'objective' test is actually subjective. Indeed, *Bolitho* constitutes an opening through which, in some cases, the judge's subjective opinion may be used to overrule that of the expert witnesses. If writers such as Bender and Conaghan are correct, then *Bolitho* does nothing to remove the subjective element of the test – it merely allows another person's subjective opinion to have effect. So *Bolitho* constitutes a change that does not affect the conceptual criticisms of *Bolam*. A similar phenomenon can be seen to apply in *Chester*, where not only is the doctor imagined in a less flattering light than might be expected, but the House of Lords consciously ignores the law to arrive at its preferred conclusion. Any shift in attitude must come from judges as individuals, and cases such as *Bolitho* and *Chester* provide evidence that *sometimes* this has occurred.

In terms of trends, the reasoning behind the two House of Lords decisions is indisputably different to that employed by the courts when Sheldon was writing in the late 1990s. There have always been differences amongst the judiciary, and it is at least progress that the higher courts appear to have changed approach. This can also be seen in terms of the images presented of doctor and patient in the two cases, which are far more positive than in *Whitehouse* and *Maynard*. Moreover, the policy considerations being prioritised are different to what they were, and it is once again *judges* rather than the medical profession that are in control of the legal standard. Yet, as mentioned above, the conceptual problems persist.

For patients, the objectivity of the concept of reasonableness must still be called into question. The law still considers the practice of the medical profession rather than the patient's 'rights'. The changes made by *Bolitho* in allowing the courts to have the final say merely allows for decisions to occasionally be made by a different male-dominated body (the judiciary instead of the medical profession).[6] Indeed, Bender's criticisms are still more than valid. In other words, *Bolitho* does nothing to introduce context or objectivity into the concept of reasonableness. While recent cases show an increased willingness on the part of senior judges to challenge deference to the medical profession in practical terms, it cannot be said that the conceptual problems have disappeared. Rather, it may be argued that they will never do so as any claim to objectivity is fundamentally flawed. This is inevitable – indeed, the law cannot be perfect – but it can at least be mitigated by promoting a more diverse judiciary, and this would certainly involve having more women on the bench.

The story is similar for female doctors.[7] We know from previous feminist analysis that both the judiciary and the medical profession have been criticised as being 'male' institutions (Sheldon 1998: 32). However, with 60 per cent of new doctors being women, there is an expectation that female doctors will outnumber their male counterparts in the next decade, (Tapsfield 2004; Boseley 2009). It might be hoped that a feminisation of the profession – particularly in the field of gender specific harms and treatments as discussed above – might help to foster empathy towards patients. However, the risk is that, despite the gender rebalancing in numerical terms, the (socially constructed) male *way of thinking* might remain, not least because fewer women occupy senior positions. This argument is supported by Carol Black, the first female president of the Royal College of Physicians. Speaking in 2004, she warned that what she termed the 'feminisation' of medicine would lead to a lessening of influence over society: 'Years ago, teaching was a male-dominated profession – and look what happened to teaching. I don't think they feel they are a powerful profession any more. Look at nursing, too.' (Boseley 2009).[8] Her argument was that female doctors were less likely to take on the more influential specialisms in medicine, or serve on government committees, and that they needed support to help to rectify that (such as more flexible working practices and better child care provision). Nevertheless, the message that the more high status specialisms are closed to women unless they act 'like men', and that 'feminisation' would result in a loss of influence on the part of the profession is not encouraging. Whether this changes can only be ascertained in time, in terms of whether there is any palpable feminisation of the medical profession.

What can therefore be seen is that the change in the law introduced by *Bolitho* makes little difference to the theoretical criticisms of 'reasonableness'. Claims of the possibility of objectivity ignore the fact that decisions regarding reasonableness are bound by the decision-maker's own perspectives. Whether it be other doctors or judges does not matter, and the danger is that despite more women in these professions, a 'male' culture will remain.

Conclusion

The situation has certainly improved in the past two decades. What Sheldon identified in practice appears to be less prevalent. As the previous deference to medical professionals has lessened, the image of the doctor, particularly when contrasted with that of the patient, has changed. Patients' interests are now considered more often by judges, as evidenced in cases such as *Chester*. Notwithstanding the fact that the lower courts are perhaps less predictable, it is undeniable that the law is moving in the right direction. However, it is noticeable that the theoretical problems persist. This is because, put simply, the objective nature of the concept of 'reasonableness' has always been a fallacy. Bender's argument that the test for reasonableness encompasses a male view remains valid as long as male perspectives dominate, and there is as yet little to suggest that this is not the case. Moreover, the standard of care test itself (in both pre- and post-*Bolitho* forms) necessarily privileges those who conform, and it will always do so. As Wendy Savage found, dissenting or 'other' voices will struggle to be heard. For this reason, the conceptual shortcomings of the test are as potentially discriminatory for female doctors as they are for female patients. Nevertheless, it must be reiterated that the situation *has* improved. It is noticeable that this has been achieved by the judiciary on its own, despite the theoretical problems. Patients' voices are heard more, and their interests given more weight. The courts are less deferential to the medical profession than they were, and they have changed approach of their own volition, without the need for legislation. Perhaps the message is slowly getting through. *Bolitho* may not be a panacea, but it is evidence that things are moving in the right direction.

Notes

1   For an excellent account, see Conaghan and Mansell (1999: chapter 3), which includes references for further reading; Moran (2003).
2   Indeed this was the experience of consultant gynaecologist Wendy Savage.
3   To give an example of such a factor: the existence of liability insurance had been used in other areas of negligence (such as motor vehicle accidents) as a policy reason to allow claims.
4   This has since changed, and the score now reads 6–1 (since *Chester v Afshar*), which is still far from respectable. Whether this change constitutes a change in direction will be demonstrated in time but, as the analysis of *Chester* in this chapter argues, that case is certainly significant.
5   For an excellent analysis of *Chester*, see Devaney (2005).
6   The judiciary's figures are stark, with only one woman Justice of the Supreme Court (out of 10). Only 8 per cent of Appeal Court judges are women, and the figure is still less than 15 per cent in the High Court ('Judicial Diversity statistics – Gender, Ethnicity and Profession' Judiciary of England and Wales, 1 April 2011).
7   A report from 2009 found that only 28 per cent of consultants are female and only 7 per cent of consultant surgeons are women. See Royal College of Physicians, *Women and Medicine: The Future*, Royal College of Physicians, 2009.
8   Ironically, such a feminisation of the profession might also encourage judges to be less deferential, as their social similarity, as identified by Sheldon, is dissipated.

Cases

Al Hamwi v Johnston and Another [2005] EWHC 206
Bolam v Friern Hospital Management Committee [1957] 1 WLR 582
Bolitho v City and Hackney Health Authority [1998] AC 232
Chester v Afshar [2000] WL 33201379
Chester v Afshar [2005] AC 134
DeFreitas v O'Brien [1995] EWCA Civ 28
Edward Wong Finance Co Ltd v Johnson Stokes and Master [1984] 1 AC 296
Maynard v West Midlands Regional Health Authority [1985] 1 All ER 635
Sidaway v Board of Governors of Bethlem Royal Hospital [1985] 1 All ER 643
Whitehouse v Jordan [1981] 1 All ER 267

Bibliography

Bender, L. (1988) 'A Lawyer's Primer on Feminist Theory and Tort', *Journal of Legal Education*, 38: 3–38
Boseley, S. (2009) 'The Future is Female – How Women are the Transforming Face of the Health Service', *The Guardian*, 3 June
Brazier, M. and Miola, J. (2000) 'Bye Bye *Bolam*: A Medical Litigation Revolution', *Medical Law Review*, 8: 85–114

Conaghan, J. (1996a) 'Gendered Harms and the Law of Tort: Remedying (Sexual) Harassment', *Oxford Journal of Legal Studies*, 16: 407–31

—— (1996b) 'Tort Law and the Feminist Critique of Reason', in A. Bottomley (ed) (1996) *Feminist Perspectives on the Foundational Subjects of Law*, London: Cavendish, 47–68

—— (1999) 'Enhancing Civil Remedies for (Sexual) Harassment: s.3 of the Protection from Harassment Act 1997', *Feminist Legal Studies*, 7: 203–14

Conaghan, J. and Mansell, W. (1999) *The Wrongs of Tort*, London: Pluto Press

Davies, M. (1996) 'The "New *Bolam*": Another False Dawn for Medical Negligence?', *Professional Negligence*, 12: 120–4

Devaney, S. (2005) 'Autonomy Rules OK', *Medical Law Review*, 13: 102–7

Graycar, R. and Morgan, J. (2002) *The Hidden Gender of Law*, 2nd edn: Leichhardt: Federation Press

Grubb, A. (1998) 'Negligence: Causation and *Bolam*', *Medical Law Review*, 6: 378–86

Heywood, R. (2006) 'The Logic of *Bolitho*', *Professional Negligence*, 22: 225–35

High Court (2011) 'Judicial Diversity Statistics – Gender, Ethnicity and Profession', Judiciary of England and Wales, 1 April 2011

Jones, M. (1999) 'The *Bolam* Test and the Responsible Expert', *Tort Law Review*, 7: 226–50

Maclean, A. (2002) 'Beyond *Bolam* and *Bolitho*', *Medical Law International*, 5: 205–30

McLean, S. (1981) 'Negligence – a Dagger in the Doctor's Back?', in P. Robson and P. Watchman (eds) *Justice, Lord Denning and the Constitution*, London: Gower, 34–57

—— (1999) *Old Law, New Medicine: Medical Ethics and Human Rights*, London: Pandora Publishing

Miola, J. (2006) 'Autonomy Rued OK?', *Medical Law Review*, 14: 108–14

Moran, M. (2003) *Rethinking the Reasonable Person*, Oxford: Oxford University Press

Mulheron, R. (2010) 'Trumping *Bolam*: A Critical Legal Analysis of *Bolitho*'s "Gloss"', *Cambridge Law Journal*, 69: 609–38

Norrie, K. (1985) 'Common Practice and the Standard of Care in Medical Negligence', *Juridical Review*, 97: 145–65

Peppin, P. (1996) 'A Feminist Challenge to Tort Law', in A. Bottomley (ed) *Feminist Perspectives on the Foundational Subjects of Law*, London: Cavendish, 69–86

Royal College of Physicians (2009) *Women and Medicine: The future*, Royal College of Physicians

Savage, W. (1987) *A Savage Inquiry: Who Controls Childbirth*, London: Virago Press

Sheldon, S. (1998) 'Rethinking the *Bolam* Test', in S. Sheldon and M. Thomson (eds) *Feminist Perspectives on Health Care Law*, London: Cavendish, 15–32

Szasz, T. (1979) *The Theology of Medicine*, New York: Oxford University Press

Tapsfield, J. (2004) 'Women Weakening Medical Profession', *Daily Telegraph*, 2 August

Woolf, Lord (2000) 'Are the Courts Excessively Deferential to the Medical Profession?', *Medical Law Review*, 9: 1–16

Yule, I. (1996) 'Architects and Engineers', in R. Hodgin (ed) *Professional Liability: Law and Insurance*, London: Lloyds Press, 97–180

Chapter 8

If I Cannot Have Her Everybody Can: Sexual Disclosure and Privacy Law

Janice Richardson

Introduction

It is clear from its widely publicised content that the developing area of tort law aimed at protecting against invasions of privacy raises feminist issues. In this chapter, I will examine a particular example of an invasion of privacy: the cases of ex-lovers, of both sexes, who reveal details of their sexual relationships – their existence and, often, graphic sexual material about the other party. In the case examples this disclosure has different motivations, including the desire to seek revenge (so-called 'revenge porn' (Levmore 2010)), financial gain or more complex motives associated with, what appears to be, kudos and macho male group bonding. As I will illustrate, an examination of these cases of sexual disclosure reverses the stereotype that heterosexual men have a straightforward and easily understood sexuality compared with heterosexual women, who are portrayed as more complex in their desires.

Most cases before the courts involve heterosexuals and I will focus upon these. The motivation for the UK case of homosexual sexual disclosure (*Lord Browne of Madingley v Associated Newspapers Limited* [2007]) appeared, like the cases involving women defendants, motivated by financial gain, although there could be other motivations at play. Sexual disclosure about a sexual partner is an area in which *some* men have tried to employ shame as a weapon against women, based upon historical sexual double standards (along with different, more complex, motives to be discussed) and *some* women have been motivated by financial gain.[1]

The meaning of privacy has been much debated. Writing within the area of information theory, Tavani (2007) usefully categorises theories of privacy into four types and associates them with other values. These are: non-intrusion (the right to be let alone, akin to negative liberty and associated with the paradigmatic legal arguments of Warren and Brandeis (1890)); seclusion (the right to be inaccessible to others, akin to solitude); limitation (the right to restrict areas of knowledge about oneself, akin to secrecy); and control (the right to be able to control the dissemination of information about oneself, akin to autonomy). I have argued elsewhere that the meaning of 'privacy' itself is currently altering, in the West at least, as a result of a number of contingent factors. In particular, these changes are mainly associated with improvements in women's status as a result of continuing feminist struggles and also with the development of computer-mediated communication (Richardson, 2011).

I will briefly explain these two reasons for change in this introduction before considering the development of common law privacy cases. These cases will be discussed not only to outline the current common law position with respect to, what I am describing as, 'sexual disclosure cases', but also to think about how to characterise the harm that arises from such invasions of privacy. The harm in different cases is intimately linked to the claimant's understanding of the situation. Importantly, this includes his/her assessment of the defendant's motivations and these will be considered. It is my view that the courts have often demonstrated a more subtle appreciation of the diverse ways in which invasions of privacy affect the claimants (and hence how to characterise the right to privacy) than the more abstract analysis carried out in legal theory. I outline an example of legal theory in the area, illustrate how it is problematic and then conclude by assessing the current developments of case law.

The term 'privacy' raises important conceptual issues that are central to feminism, such as the way in which it has traditionally been associated with 'women's place' within the home; the Ancient Greek *oikos* as separate from the *polis*. As Pateman (1989) has argued, the 'public/private divide', in which the domestic sphere was defined *against* public issues meant that the *political* analysis of women's traditional subordinate status could be marginalised. Hence, in Western early modern political thought, with the exception of Hobbes, women's subordinate status was viewed as natural and not as political (Richardson 2009). The term 'political' was reserved for an analysis of the relationship between the individual and the state, with power being conceived of as operating in a top-down manner from the state through law. Injustice towards women, including domestic violence, was therefore treated as a 'private' matter, separate from the political. This mechanism by which women's struggles were marginalised as non-political, and even ridiculous, was challenged in the 1960s by the feminist expression, 'the personal is political'.

Changes in women's position, as a result of feminist struggles against subordination, have interacted with other developments that have altered our (Western) experience of the meaning of privacy today, particularly as a result of information technology. There is useful recent work in information theory in which theorists consider the impact of such change. For example, in making a point that information technology has radically altered privacy issues, Floridi (2006a; 2006b) argues convincingly that it is no longer simply the case that technological progress produces greater threats to privacy. In other words, developments in technology do not simply undermine privacy by providing faster and easier means of communication. Instead, the position is more complex with changes in, what he calls, the 'infosphere' (the environment in which information is exchanged) altering the extent of control that individuals can exert over information in unforeseen ways. He gives an example of men visiting the seedy area of Macau, near Hong Kong.

Previously, the mobile phone dialling tone was distinct for Macau and so visitors would turn off their phones to avoid giving away their location to callers. Mobile phone companies recognised why they were losing revenue and promptly altered the dialling tone for Macau to sound like that of Hong Kong. Technological innovation (and commercial interests) thereby increased the privacy of these men. In addition, computer-mediated communication can increase our ability to have access to, and to alter, data held on us, for example in bank accounts. This may increase the risk of data being removed but also gives us some input. We are able to check the data and to seek to have it corrected. Hence, as with the mobile phone example above, new technology brings with it the potential for greater control over our data, along with privacy risks.

I will now turn to the development of the common law cases of sexual disclosure in the UK and Australia and highlight the view of harm in these cases before turning to critique the way in which harm has been theorised in liberal legal theory.

Legal development of privacy law and sexual disclosure cases

The development of the UK common law to protect the right to privacy has occurred as a result of the Human Rights Act 1998 (HRA) coming into force in October 2000. This includes the courts within the definition of public authorities (under section 6 of the HRA) and as such they must act in accordance with the European Convention on Human Rights (ECHR). Hence, the HRA has had the effect of bringing the ECHR into the common law, as it develops on a case-by-case basis. In practice, this has meant that the UK courts have extended the law of breach of confidence in such a way as to give effect to human rights issues. The breach of confidence cases initially covered only a narrow range of facts because the claimant needed to prove that a confidential relationship existed between her (or him) and the defendant. The focus used to be upon the quality of the relationship itself (and not only on the content of the information), the most obvious example being the protection of confidences in business relationships.

In *Argyll v Argyll* [1967] Thomas-Ungoed J held that marriage also constituted a relationship of confidence. He was at pains to point out that, by awarding Lady Argyll an injunction to prevent her ex-husband from giving details of her pre-marital sex life to the press, he did not intend that the law should interfere with marriage as an institution. This is an early case of what has now been termed 'revenge porn', employing the term to include the use of words (which were likely to be sexually graphic) as well as photographic or video images. Lady Argyll had confided the details of her earlier sex life to her husband during the marriage and Thomas-Ungoed J therefore viewed his proposal to publish the information as a breach of confidence.

After the HRA, this traditional equitable remedy of breach of confidence has been interpreted so as to give effect to Article 8 ('the right to respect for his private and family life, his home and his correspondence', subject to Article 8(2) exceptions in the interests of national security, public safety etc) which is balanced against Article 10 (the right to free speech). Neither is given added weight. Hence, the legal test for breaches of privacy in the UK is that of *Campbell v MGN* [2004] and involves two stages. First, the court asks itself: would someone in the position of the claimant have a reasonable expectation of privacy? Secondly, if the first test is affirmative, the claimant's privacy right is balanced against the public interest in free speech. As Eady J has made clear, this balance is not to be understood as the balance between an *individual* right against a public interest because there is also a *public* interest in the protection of the right to privacy (*Max Mosley v News Group Newspapers* [2008]: [715]). Whereas liberalism is historically concerned with protecting the rights of individuals against the state, in recent cases rights are being claimed against the harm that the media or other individuals can exert on an individual by their disclosure of private information, as a result of both old and new technology.

Initially, the cases of sexual disclosure involved famous married men, one of whom had sex with a sex worker in a brothel (*Theakston v MGN* [2002]) and another who had sexual relationships with two women (*A v B Plc* [2003]). They were both refused injunctions to prevent the women, who appeared to be motivated by either financial gain or revenge or both, from publicising their stories. Applying the law in relation to breach of confidence, the courts distinguished these relationships from marriage (and hence from *Argyll v Argyll* [1967]) in that they were described as 'transitory'. Transitory sexual relationships were not viewed as giving rise to a relationship of confidence on which a claim needed to be based. In addition, it was held that the experience could be described as 'belonging' to the women who wanted to disclose the information as much as it 'belonged' to the man who wanted to stop the publicity. As I will discuss below, this way of viewing information in terms of property fits within the way Charles Fried (1984) analyses privacy and, in my view, is problematic for feminists (or at least socialist feminists, the position with which I would identify) even if it does favour women who want to sell their stories in these particular cases. I will return to this issue in the section on Fried below.

The subsequent law has moved away from this position to one of greater protection of privacy. Elizabeth Jagger was allowed an injunction to prevent the publication of CCTV footage of her engaging in sexual activity in the doorway of a nightclub, for example (*Jagger v Darling* [2005]). Unlike the other cases to be discussed, this case did not involve disclosure by her partner but by a worker at the club who (allegedly) accessed the CCTV footage and sought to sell it to the media. Here, the straightforward division between public and private spaces, which has been the subject of much feminist critique, clearly breaks down. The courts rightly recognise that there is a difference between the experience of being seen by a few passersby and being publicised more broadly.[2]

By 2008 Eady J, applying the *Campbell* test, viewed Max Mosley's sexual activity with four sex workers as a case in which there was a reasonable expectation of privacy, with no public interest in disclosure to outweigh it (*Max Mosley v News Group Newspapers* [2008]). This finding was not ruled out by the illegality of the situation. Eady J argued that considerations of illegality were to be weighed proportionally with the right to privacy. He explained this with the use of an analogy: 'Would it justify installing a camera in someone's home, in order to catch him or her smoking a spliff? Surely not' (*Max Mosley v News Group Newspapers* [2008]: [110]). Hence, all information pertaining to sexual relationships now give rise to a reasonable expectation of privacy, satisfying the first part of the test in *Campbell v MGN* [2004]. The court then considers the second part of the test: whether there is a public interest in publication. This is not the same question as to whether the public is actually interested in the disclosure but whether the public *should* be interested because of nepotism, for example. As mentioned above, Eady J also pointed out that this is a rights-based action, in which there is a public interest in the non-disclosure of private information:

> In deciding whether a right has been infringed, and in assessing the relative worth of competing rights, it is not for judges to make individual moral judgements or to be swayed by personal distaste. It is not simply a matter of personal privacy versus the public interest. The modern perception is that there is a public interest in respecting personal privacy. It is thus a question of taking account of conflicting public interest considerations and evaluating them according to increasingly well-recognised criteria.
> (*Max Mosley v News Group Newspapers* [2008]: [715])

The cases sometimes lend themselves to issues of blackmail. As a specialist in media law, Eady J was astute in his criticism of Neville Thurlbeck, chief reporter for the News of the World for his attempted blackmail.[3] In an attempt to persuade the three women who were loyal to Mosley to sell their stories (after they had refused payment) Thurlbeck had threatened to print their names to uncover them as sex workers. They still refused and viewed the fourth sex worker, who sold the story and secret video recording of the sexual activity, as having betrayed both them and Mosley. The impact of betrayal upon the claimant is mentioned in a number of cases (including the lead case of *Campbell v MGN* [2004], whose treatment for drug addiction was detailed to the press by someone at the clinic where she was receiving treatment).

In the next major case, *Terry (previously 'LNS') v Persons Unknown* [2010], Tugendhat J refused to order an injunction. However, this finding focuses upon Terry's failure to attend court and the fact he had instructed his sponsors and not lawyers, which Tugendhat J took as evidence that Terry viewed the situation merely as a business matter. Terry's sponsors had approached the woman with whom he had the affair and persuaded her to sign a document stating that she did not want publicity. She did not attend court to support her own Article 8 privacy claim and the implication was that they had bought her silence. Tugendhat J commented that the sexual relationship appeared to be one of equals and yet such a conclusion sat uncomfortably with the signing of the document. He concluded that Terry was only concerned about publicity because he would lose business sponsorship, associated with him being awarded 'Father of the Year', and therefore Terry's interest was really only with regard to his reputation, for which the relevant tort was defamation and not privacy rights. By employing the term 'reputation', he was stressing that Terry's main concern was that he would lose sponsorship deals and not that his privacy had been intruded upon.

More recently *CTB v NGN Ltd (1) and Imogen Thomas (2)* [2011] confirms the application of the test in *Campbell* that was applied in *Mosley*. Again, it concerned a famous married man and the reporting of a sexual affair. Therefore, the sexual relationship was deemed to raise a reasonable expectation of privacy on behalf of the claimant. This meant that any Article 10 free speech interests had to be weighed against the Article 8 privacy claim. There was no public interest in this sexual activity alone and therefore the injunction was granted. The case raised further legal issues when the man's name was repeatedly reported on Twitter, after the injunction, and then by John Hemming, an MP in Parliament, under the protection of parliamentary privilege. The Prime Minister, David Cameron, commented that privacy injunctions were 'unsustainable' and promised a review (BBC News, 2011).[4]

As a result, NGN Ltd applied to vary the injunction twice on 16 May 2011, returning after the MP had named the claimant, and were rejected by Eady J and then by Tugendhat J. Eady J, rejecting the first application of the day, pointed out that the press would not have bothered applying to dismiss the injunction unless they wanted to continue to run the story. He also felt that a continuation of the injunction could prevent further press harassment of the family. Here, he was clear that the harm of privacy invasion differed from the disclosure of commercial secrets or confidences, which would be lost once they became widely known. Each new disclosure in this case involved greater intrusion and harassment by the press (*CTB v NGN Ltd (1) and Imogen Thomas (2)* [2011]: [23]).

Curiously, NGN Ltd asked that they be given permission to tell the man's wife of the affair, pleading Article 8, ie her right to private and family life! In his judgment, Eady J described such an argument as 'humbug' (at [27]), given that the press were not 'social workers' nor were they motivated by a desire to protect her interests. Whilst Eady J does not state as much, it is clear that the media are 'repeat players' in this area and their application appears to be an attempt to undermine law that threatens their interests. If successful it would have had the effect of further harassing the family, who were unlikely to be the last people in England not to know of the affair.

As mentioned above, there have been arguments that the (younger and poorer) women who have had affairs with celebrities should be able to make money from it (Beckford 2011). This favours the women in the conflict but it is not necessarily a position feminists would (or should) support. It is true that historically the norms of secrecy about what occurred in the privacy of the home allowed men's violence (and other abuse) against women to be normalised. However, this does not mean that women have no interest (as part of a public interest) in safeguarding against invasions of privacy. There are areas of privacy invasion that can themselves be viewed as sexualised abuses of power. As a matter of historical chance, these can be illustrated by examining women's position in the Australian cases.

Australian common law

In Australia, without the imperative of jurisprudence stemming from the ECHR, there has been less development of the common law in this area. None of the sexual disclosure cases have reached the High Court. The only privacy case that the High Court has considered was a bad example of privacy invasion as the claimant was a company (*ABC v Lenah Game Meats Property Ltd* [2001]). However, Gleeson CJ was prepared to hold that information or conduct should be regarded as private if disclosure 'would be highly offensive to a reasonable person of ordinary sensibilities' (*ABC v Lenah Game Meats Property Ltd* [2001]: [13]).

There have, however, been cases of sexual disclosure that did not reach the High Court. In *Giller v Procopets* [2008] the Victorian Court of Appeal awarded damages of $40,000 for breach of confidence after a former *de facto* husband distributed a video-tape of himself and his *de facto* wife having sex. The motivation to humiliate his ex-partner through the use of 'revenge porn' plays upon an odd sexual double standard. The defendant does not seem to have been troubled by circulating sexually explicit material in which he was also involved. However, he did not make the images freely available, only giving the tapes to his ex-partner's relatives (who refused to view them) and her employer.

The motivation for sexual disclosure appears to be different in a case that could be heard in torts law but is currently a criminal case. In April 2011, there was much public debate regarding an 18-year-old female cadet, attending the Australian Defence Force Academy (ADFA), who had consensual sex with another cadet. Without her knowledge, he broadcast them having sex in real time, using Skype, to six other male cadets in the next room. Here, the sense of betrayal, which was mentioned in the UK cases, appears sharper because it took place during the sex act itself and therefore constituted part of his sexual experience. An examination of the young men's motivations may shed light onto the construction of hetero-sexuality in institutionalised male groups, which include sports groups, such as rugby and football. Women appear to be used as objects of exchange for men's relationships, thereby forming a triangular relationship (Levi-Strauss 1974: 47; Irigaray and Porter 1985: 170–91). This can take the form of callous disregard for the woman, who is viewed as irrelevant to the relations between men, or an even darker desire to humiliate her. Those watching obviously wanted to view porn together but there is also the 'Peeping Tom' element, which needs to be understood. Did they get additional pleasure from the fact that they knew that she did not consent to the disclosure or was she entirely irrelevant to the male relationships? This may differ in different cases. What about the additional fact that her sexual partner was part of their group? He was demonstrating loyalty to the male group of fellow cadets, whilst also betraying his sexual partner (another cadet) in the act of having sex. The male sexual partner may be interpreted as taking the hegemonic masculine cliché about sexual boasting to a new level by actually demonstrating his heterosexuality to his friends (in the context of a homophobic culture).[5] Conversely, as noted in another cliché about the homosexual element of macho cultures, he could also be described as showing off his sexual body to his friends who are watching sexually arousing material together, thereby rendering this an odd way of affirming heterosexuality. It is important not to be too quick to categorise this as homosexual activity per se given that they were watching a heterosexual act. A better approach may be to eschew easily available essentialist categories of sexuality.

The female cadet was not a passive victim of either the invasion of privacy or the worrying attempts to minimise the matter by the ADFA. She went public, with the result that the Australian Defence Minister spoke publicly of the failure of the ADFA to take the matter seriously and of the harm of such a betrayal by a sexual partner (Smith 2011). Whilst new media allowed this intrusion upon the female cadet's privacy, greater publicity of the injustice regarding her treatment by the ADFA has resulted in the setting up of a review of sexism within the ADFA. The publicity has resulted in other women coming forward, one of whom said that when she reported being raped within the academy that she was told to 'suck it up' (Nicholson et al 2011). It has also revealed more about the ADFA's dysfunctional culture that puts the misogyny in the context of reports of male rape and violence (News.com.au and Ian McPhedran 2011). As such, the case demonstrates that there is a vital need for publicity to clean up those institutions that could tend to become 'total institutions'[6] in which such abuse and dehumanisation gradually becomes normalised. It is an interesting empirical question as to whether computer-mediated communication will allow people to withstand the sort of pressure that a total institution can exert by keeping them in touch with other friends who can bring an outside perspective to a pack mentality. It is also important to consider not only the motivation of the individual group of men but also the corporate culture that is encouraged within the institution itself by those at the top. Military and sports groups may systematically encourage male bonding through misogyny thereby helping to construct male sexuality for their own purposes.

Before leaving the Australian cases, it is worth considering one case that was only a first instance judgment but that raises important issues about how the Australian law could develop: the Victorian case of *Jane Doe v ABC* [2007]. Jane Doe was a rape survivor whose name had been publicised after the successful prosecution of her ex-husband for raping her. When discussing the harm in this case, Hampel J relied upon psychological evidence that, where there is a conviction, most survivors of rape start to recover from post traumatic shock disorder (PTSD) after the trial. Instead, as a result of the publicity, Jane Doe was faced with having to deal with more people suddenly becoming aware that she had been raped by her ex-husband. She was therefore forced to re-negotiate these relationships, involving her in discussions about the rape rather than leaving it behind after the trial. Fortunately, she was able to travel in Europe, where there had been no publicity, to recover, an option that would not have been available if her details had been disseminated more widely.

ABC had relied upon the legal argument that, because the claimant had confided in a few people, the information about the rape was no longer 'private'.

Hampel J dismissed this argument, making a clear distinction between a confidence given to a few close friends or family and public knowledge. Given that *Jane Doe v ABC* [2007] raises both this issue and the question of sudden disclosure, it is useful, before leaving the case analysis, to consider this aspect of Australian common law alongside the judgment of ECtHR in *Peck v UK* [2003]. This is not a sexual disclosure case but I will discuss it because it illustrates important shifts in the way that privacy is understood, which affects such cases. In particular, there is a change in the way in which the court thinks about the self/other relationship that I view as important and that will discuss further in the next section.

To explain this change it is necessary to outline the facts of the case. Peck tried to commit suicide with a knife whilst on a public street in England. Inevitably, given their ubiquity in the UK, he was caught on CCTV camera. The police intervened and he survived. A television programme obtained and showed the CCTV footage on national television. In the programme his face was pixellated but, in the trailer advertising the programme, his face was not sufficiently disguised and those who knew him recognised him. The question arose as to whether an act that took place on a public street could give rise to privacy rights. The case occurred prior to the enactment of HRA so there was no direct redress in the UK. The ECtHR held that his Article 8 rights had been violated. Like the Victorian court in *Jane Doe*, the ECtHR distinguished between information that is available to the world at large from that which is transmitted to a few people, despite the fact that the act took place on a public street. As mentioned above, this approach was followed in *Jagger v Darling* [2005].

Further, in *Peck v UK* [2003], the harm involved in the breach of privacy was characterised as affecting Peck's ability to make and maintain relationships with others. Importantly, the ECtHR moved beyond the traditional image of an atomistic individual. Instead, it was willing to think in terms of relationships as illustrated by the following comment that Article 8:

> protects a right to identity and personal development, and the right to establish and develop relationships with other human beings and the outside world . . . There is therefore a zone of interaction of a person with others, even in a public context, which may fall within the scope of 'private life'.
>
> (*Peck v UK* [2003]: [289])

There is a link between the willingness of the court to refuse to treat information as public when some others have been told and this characterisation of the harm of privacy invasion as something that could undermine relationships. With regard to both points, the ECtHR are willing to shift from viewing us as isolated individuals and to considering us as embedded in relationships, which can themselves be harmed. To claim to be protecting 'the right to establish and develop relationships with other human beings' would be inconsistent with the view that information immediately loses its private status if it is confided to another. To draw out the novelty of this approach and how it disrupts some elements of the liberal imaginary of the isolated individual, I want to compare it with Charles Fried's analysis of privacy. This will allow me to explain why I think that this approach by the ECtHR and the Victorian Court in *Jane Doe* is to be welcomed.

Charles Fried and property in the person

Charles Fried's (1984) argument is interesting because, although he purports to say something universal about human dignity in order to find an underlying foundation for privacy torts, his presumptions about individual psychology can be situated within a particular historical perspective. Fried's conceptual framework fits neatly within one strand of the liberal tradition. As I will illustrate, this is a framework that has been subject to much feminist critique by Carole Pateman (2002) in her work on property in the person.[7]

Fried's argument is basically that we need to safeguard private information because it 'creates moral capital which we spend in friendship and love' (Fried 1984: 211). In other words, Fried's claim is that without the ability to keep some aspects of our lives secret from the majority of the people we meet, we would not be able to use it to confide in those close to us. Our private information works as a sort of capital that forms the basis of intimate relationships. As I will discuss below, whilst Fried attributes his analysis of privacy to Kant, his view of privacy fits more easily within the analysis of property in the person that is attributed to Locke by Nozick (1974).

I suspect that reading Fried's description may prompt many to ask: what must it be like to have such beliefs and to live like that? He is not 'wrong' (epistemologically) in describing how he feels about privacy. However, he is wrong to assume that his experience can be universalised as an aspect of human nature. In fact, the genealogy of this approach to privacy can account for his view by situating it within a particular historical context, in which human abilities, feelings and experiences are all treated as if they were a special type of property. For this reason, his arguments are in keeping with those who would argue that it is a 'right' to make money from disclosure of information about others, provided it is also your story, a view that formed the basis of the reasoning of the courts in *Theakston v MGN* [2002] and *A v B Plc* [2003], that has now been effectively overruled. For Fried, our own knowledge of ourselves and what we think and feel is viewed as something that we own. We relate to the world as atomistic individuals who have the right not to share anything with others. However, when we are intimate with friends or lovers then we are willing to give up some of this right. The intimate relationship is then reciprocal in the sense that each party is willing to give up this right not to share any aspect of ourselves.

Fried describes his argument as Kantian. In doing so he appears to be claiming that he is concerned with the protection of human dignity and respect for persons (Fried 1984: 206). However, in Fried's framework, we respect others only by treating them as self-owning individuals, who hold rights over different aspects of themselves, as if they were masters in a slave owning society (Cohen 1995). Hence, persons are characterised as having the right to control what happens to their bodies, their ability to work and over their private information, all to be treated as their property. Pateman (2002) has shown how, in modernity, such a view of ourselves has been used in order to manage subordination in both employment contracts, as illustrated by Marx (2004: 270–80), and marriage contracts. She details how historically we come to regard parts of our 'property in the person', such as our ability to work and our ability to give 'consortium' (sex and housework) in marriage as commodities that can be exchanged in contract. As property in the person is a fiction it cannot be exchanged in the same way as we could give blood. Such contracts that involve the exchange of property in the person (those for employment and, traditionally, marriage) represent a way of both creating and regulating subordinate relationships because property in the person cannot be removed from the body. Such contracts require personal service.

I want to explore Fried's claim to be Kantian and how this highlights a tension within Kant's work itself. Fried does not acknowledge this philosophical parallel but it seems to me that Fried's description of the way in which each party, in an intimate relationship, gives up some privacy rights to the other echoes the argumentative structure of Kant's description of sex within the marriage contract in *The Metaphysics of Morals* (1996: 61–4). Fried illustrates his use of the fiction of property in the person when he says that:

> The entitlements of privacy are not just one kind of entitlement among many that a lover can surrender to show his love. Love or friendship can be partially expressed by the gift of other rights – gifts of property or of service. But these gifts without the intimacy of shared private information, cannot alone constitute love or friendship.
>
> (Fried 1984: 211)

For Fried, these human attributes are all to be treated as 'property in the person' with some property valued more than others. The reciprocity is important but each individual stands in relation to an important part of him/herself as if he or she is an owner who is giving away part of him or herself as a gift of property. I want to illustrate a parallel with Kant's discussion of marriage in his section on 'Rights to Persons akin to Rights to Things' in *The Metaphysics of Morals*, save that, importantly, Kant is aware of (and rejects) the fiction of property in the person.

Kant is concerned to show how both a man and woman can give away sexual access to their bodies in marriage, and have access to the other's body, whilst still being treated as 'persons'. Kant views personhood as an important legal and moral category. Persons should be treated as ends in themselves rather than merely as a means to an end, in this case of sexual gratification. Kant's answer is that in marriage alone – which he describes as a contract for 'lifelong possession of each other's sexual attributes' – there is a mutual giving and receiving, which allows a continuation of respect for personhood (Kant 1996: 62). There is a parallel between the structure of Fried's argument that intimacy occurs as a result of the reciprocal exchange of private information and Kant's discussion of marriage being the reciprocal access to each other's sexual organs and capacities.[8]

Unlike Fried, Kant recognises the problem that property in the person cannot be taken from a human being and states this explicitly: '[A]cquiring a member of a human being is at the same time acquiring the whole person, since a person is an absolute unity' (Kant 1996: 62). So Kant's argument is that even though it appears to be treating someone as a means to an end (ie as a 'thing' that is used for sexual gratification) whenever one has sex, this is not so in the case of sex in marriage. Referring to marriage he states:

> There is only one condition under which this is possible: that while a person is acquired by another *as if it were a thing*, the one who is acquired acquires the other in turn; for in this way each reclaims itself and restores its personality.
> (Kant, 1996: 62, italics in the original)

Men and women sound as if they are equally situated here and yet it is clear that they are not. The view that this is a right against persons and is also a right against a thing is demonstrated by the fact that, if one spouse leaves the matrimonial home, the other is able to bring the partner back, 'just as it [sic] is justified in retrieving a thing' (Kant 1996: 62). The odd reference to 'it' rather than 'he' does not succeed in obscuring the gender difference in the ability to implement such a right. Kant is clear that 'a *man* acquires a *wife*, a *couple* acquires *children*; and a *family* acquires *servants*' (Kant 1996: 61, italics in the original).

In some of the privacy literature, including that of Fried, the term 'Kantian' is employed, without further analysis of Kant. It simply appears to be a short-hand way of saying that the writer is concerned that we treat each other as persons; with respect as an end in him/herself rather than as a means to an end. This is what Benn, for example, references when he says that in the George Bernard Shaw's play *Pygmalion*, Eliza Doolittle accuses Higgins of failing to show proper respect for her when he treats her as an object to be observed: 'He is treating people as objects or specimens, like "dirt" – and not subjects with sensibilities, ends and aspirations of their own' (Benn 1984: 227). However, Pateman has demonstrated that the employment of the conceptual framework of 'property in the person' has been used in employment and marriage in order to do the opposite of respect, that is, in order to treat areas of someone's life, their abilities and (in this example) their innermost thoughts and feelings as if they were commodities. In workplaces and homes this has produced relationships (the roles of employer/employee, husband and wife) that have been hierarchical rather than characterised by respect for equal personhood (Richardson 2009).

To summarise, my argument is that the oddness of Fried's claim to be Kantian, irrespective of how it was meant, can be used to illustrate a tension in Kant's work itself. The structure of Fried's argument mimics Kant's analysis of the swapping of access to sexual organs (rather than secret information) within the marriage contract. When this approach is extended by Fried (and paradigmatically by

Nozick's (1974) reading of Locke) respect for persons means treating others as if they were owners of their human abilities. They are respected by virtue of having the right to treat aspects of themselves as if it were their own property. The position therefore mimics the move from being a feudal self, without rights in oneself, to being a worker in a capitalist society, who owns himself (and later herself), thereby standing in relation to aspects of himself or herself as if to a commodity.

Kant has a more complex view of selfhood than that of Fried, whose individualism is closer to Nozick (1974). This is demonstrated by Fried's comments regarding relationships in which we trust someone else but are not necessarily friends with them. He states that '[i]t is one of those relations, less inspiring than love or friendship, but also less tiring, through which to express our humanity' (Fried 1984: 212). Whilst he is being deliberately wry, it does seem true that from this position it is costly to us to maintain relations with others. We start out alone and then reveal parts of ourselves as gifts or property to others. (As mentioned, this is consistent with the idea that if something is revealed that could be commodified then it is another's 'right' to do so.) Fried explores his argument with an example of a prisoner whose release depends upon the condition that there is complete surveillance of him at all times. Fried explains why this constant surveillance would undermine the prisoner's ability to be intimate in terms of his failure to be able to give exclusive knowledge of himself to another. The surveillance deprives him of this 'private property'. Fried's imagery is of an individual and his/her thoughts and feelings at the centre of a circle, in which some are not shared with anyone and others are shared (like the property of the home) with intimates and then (in outer circles) with friends. For Fried, we are to have exclusive control over our private information just as we are to have control over our private property. It is central to our ability to be intimate that we can bestow such gifts.

It is possible to apply a Kantian analysis to the question of sexual disclosure. Kant would surely have moved the focus of attention onto the moral duty of the defendant (and not the consequential harm to the claimant in losing his/her secrets) to view privacy invasions as immoral because the defendant fails to treat the subject of disclosure as a person, who should be treated as an end in his or her self. From this perspective, the actual consequences of the immoral act are irrelevant.[9]

Conclusion

The cases that involve sexual disclosure as an invasion of privacy raise different issues about the construction of heterosexuality at this point in time. It is possible to characterise the harm in broadly Kantian terms (as an immoral act by the defendant in treating his/her ex-lover as a means to an end). Whilst I think this is right as far as it goes, it does not give a nuanced view of the situations with which the courts grapple. The cases reveal harm that is intimately linked to the claimant's perception of the situation, which includes the claimant's assessment of the defendant's motivation. Sportsmen may not be unduly concerned by the women with whom they have sex attempting to make money from the encounter, which in some instances may have been a clear motivation from the start – although this did not preclude a sense of betrayal being expressed by some of the sex workers in *Max Mosley v News Group Newspapers* [2008]. In *CTB v NGN Ltd (1) and Imogen Thomas (2)* [2011], Eady J also recognised the harm of press harassment as well as the potential embarrassment of revelations. Conversely, in *Terry (previously 'LNS') v Persons Unknown* [2010] Tugendhat J felt that the claimant did not experience embarrassment but only worried about the sponsorship deals, which did not demonstrate a breach of privacy per se but damage to reputation. In practice, most privacy disclosures will also involve concerns about reputation, amongst other issues, and the harm that ensues may depend upon the reaction of both intimates and the public regarding the revelation itself.

While there may be cases of men attempting to make money from disclosure and women motivated by revenge or more complex desires, it is the men in the case law who demonstrate these potentially darker desires. In the cases of 'revenge porn' they have attempted to employ and reinforce sexual double standards in order to humiliate a sexual partner who has rejected them. There may be many more cases of 'revenge porn', whose victims do not have the resources of footballers that would enable them to use the courts. There has been much public concern around adolescent girls, texting revealing pictures of themselves to their boyfriends, who then, accidently or purposely, betray their confidence by disseminating the pictures. This commonly reported 'sexting' needs to be regulated in ways that do not criminalise many adolescents as themselves child pornographers.[10] Whilst footballers can look after themselves in the courts there needs to be fast and cheap ways of having 'revenge porn' removed from web sites.

The case of the ADFA cadets also raises issues about the hegemonic masculinity of men in close groups formed by institutions such as the military, football and rugby teams in which new technology (and its abuse) may shine light into a culture in which the emergence of sexual (and other) abuse may serve an institutional purpose. There is already much work in this area (for example, Connell 2005; Collier 1995) but it is important to consider the genealogy of this development and not to assume that male heterosexuality is innately oppressive of women nor that they are passive victims.

A further harm that can now result from new technology is that the publication may last indefinitely because it is difficult to delete fully. The psychological evidence in the case of *Jane Doe v ABC* [2007] was that it was important for rape survivors to feel that the matter was closed after the trial. In this case the harm was the extended PTSD that occurred as a result of the disclosure of her name and that of her rapist who was her ex-husband. Applying his argument to those who do not have psychiatric harm, Mayer-Schonberger (2009) argues that the inability to delete information can have unfortunate psychological consequences for us generally, as it then becomes difficult to move beyond past mistakes. We feel branded by something on the Internet that may be seen by later acquaintances and future employers. This is particularly clear when the material is private sexual material that was the content of a privacy invasion, particularly when the motives were based upon revenge or associated with abuse (for a relevant analysis from her discussion of pornography, see Cornell 1995: 95–166).

Turning to the question of remedies, the law has viewed psychiatric harm (as in *Jane Doe v ABC* [2007]) as a head of damage. The other aspects of harm already discussed tend to involve other emotions, which are not usually viewed as a head of damage.[11] As privacy is now viewed as a right in the UK, compensation arises as a result of the breach of such a right. The issue of compensation is not the central question in such cases, however, because the better remedy is that of a super-injunction. This is an injunction to stop the publication of material that also prevents the publication of the existence of the injunction itself. The aim is to avoid undermining the injunction itself by alerting the media of a potential secret. The use of super-injunctions has prompted concern in the UK that their use will result in the suppression of information that is actually in the public interest. Historically, feminists have been successful in pointing out that abuse within the home, which was characterised as 'private', was political and should be publicised. It is also the case that publicity is required to shine light on the practices within corporate cultures and institutional practices, such as the ADFA. However, there is a clear distinction between this sort of abuse (wrongly labelled as 'private') and the content of the sexual disclosure cases, the publicising of which does not raise public interest issues. It is easy to think of instances in which the two could conflict. For example, the unnamed woman who revealed the way in which she had been treated by the cadets and the ADFA may have been discouraged from such an important public disclosure if she had no safeguard against being named in public.

Whilst I have described abuse within the home as 'wrongly labelled' as private, I do not want to give the impression that there is one clear meaning of privacy that pertains in all cultures (see Geuss 2003). On the contrary, I have argued elsewhere (Richardson 2011) that our understanding of privacy is changing, in part because of feminism as well as developments in computer-mediated communication. This change can be detected in the courts' analysis of privacy. One element that I find encouraging is the move away from Fried's view of the isolated individual, who is characterised as owning his/her private information to be 'spent' on others. It is progressive to recognise that invasions of privacy are better understood as disrupting relationships with others rather than as stealing a piece of our property in ourselves.

Notes

1   For an analysis of sexual double standards and shame, see Purdom (2000).
2   This is recognised in other cases, such as *Peck v UK* [2003] in the European Court of Human Rights (ECtHR), and in Australia in *Jane Doe v ABC* [2007], to be discussed below.
3   Eady J was also alive to potential blackmail in the case of *CTB v NGN Ltd (1) and Imogen Thomas (2)* [2011]. It is also of note that Eady J's criticism of NGN's methods of reporting occurred in advance of the later phone hacking scandal, which resulted in the News of the World being closed. Eady J's criticism of Thurlbeck's methods was referred to in

the Culture, Media and Sport Select Committee's (2011) questioning of Rupert and James Murdoch, owners of the paper (House of Commons Select Committee 2011: Q173).

4 Whilst Cameron talked in terms of strengthening the Press Complaints Commission, this now appears less tenable, given its failures to regulate News International.

5 Hyde et al (2009) conducted an empirical study on hegemonic masculinity in young men in Ireland. They concluded that these adolescents were worried that negative evaluations of their sexual performance would be reported back to their (all male) peer group. This rather mean group of young men seemed to dominate each other's lives because the more rational concern (for heterosexuals who wanted sex) would be to focus upon women's evaluation given to other women, which ironically would be more likely to focus upon whether the young men treated them as badly as they treated each other. The men had an additional worry that they may be perceived as gay within what was still a homophobic institution. Cross-cultural comparisons are difficult, however, especially as Australian men are not a demographic noted for being unduly burdened by angst.

6 Goffman defines 'total institutions' as 'social arrangements which regulate, under one roof and according to one rational plan, all spheres of individual lives – sleeping, eating, playing and working' (Goffman 1991: 5–6). He produces a paradigmatic analysis of their dehumanising effects.

7 Fried's presumption about humanity can also be described in terms of self-ownership, analysed by Cohen (1995) or 'possessive individualism', MacPherson (1962), both of whom provide similar critiques.

8 The two 'exchanges' coincide in the cases of sexual disclosure save that the disclosure necessarily involves a third party and so is characterised by Fried as a gift or sale of property.

9 Thanks to Patrick Emerton for this point.

10 There has been much publicity about the fact that, in most common law countries, if the girl is under age, then the sender, receiver and any intermediary can be charged with child pornography. See, for example, Forbes (2011).

11 This can act to women's detriment as illustrated by Graycar's analysis in this collection.

Cases

A v B Plc [2003] QB 195

ABC v Lenah Game Meats Property Ltd [2001] 185 ALR 1

Argyll v Argyll [1967] Ch 302

Campbell v MGN [2004] UKHL 22

Lord Browne of Madingley v Associated Newspapers Ltd [2007] EWCA Civ 295

CTB v NGN Ltd [1] and Imogen Thomas [2] [2011] EWHC 1326 (QB), [2011] EWHC 1334 (QB).

Giller v Procopets [2008] VSCA 236

Jagger v Darling, unreported, UKHC, Bell J, 9 March 2005

Jane Doe v ABC [2007] VCC 281

Max Mosley v News Group Newspapers [2008] EWHC 1777

Peck v UK [2003] EMLR 289

Terry [previously 'LNS'] v Persons Unknown [2010] EWHC 119 (QB)

Theakston v MGN [2002] EMLR 78.

Bibliography

BBC News (2011) 'Privacy Injunctions Unsustainable, says Cameron', 23 May

Beckford, M. (2011) 'Louise Bagshawe: Rich Men Using Injunctions To "Gag" Women', *The Daily Telegraph*, 24 April

Benn, S.I. (1984) 'Privacy, Freedom and Respect for Persons', in F.D. Schoeman (ed) *Philosophical Dimensions of Privacy: An Anthology*, Cambridge: Cambridge University Press, 223–4

Cohen, G.A. (1995) *Self-ownership, Freedom, and Equality*, Cambridge: Cambridge University Press

Collier, R. (1995) *Masculinity, Law and Family*, 1st edn, London: Routledge

Connell, R.W. (2005) *Masculinities*, 2nd edn, Cambridge: Polity Press

Cornell, D. (1995) *The Imaginary Domain: Abortion, Pornography and Sexual Harassment*, London: Routledge

Floridi, L. (2006a) 'Four Challenges for a Theory of Informational Privacy', *Ethics and Information Technology*, 8: 109–19

Floridi, L. (2006b) 'The Ontological Interpretation of Informational Privacy', *Ethics and Information Technology*, 7: 185–200

Fried, C. (1984) 'Privacy (A Moral Analysis)', in F.D. Schoeman (ed) *Philosophical Dimensions of Privacy: An Anthology*, Cambridge: Cambridge University Press, 203–22

Forbes, S.G. (2011) 'Note: Sex, Cells and SORNA: Applying Sex Offender Registration Laws to Sexting Cases', *William and Mary Law Review*, 52: 1717–46

Geuss, R. (2003) *Public Goods, Private Goods*, Oxford: Princeton University Press

Goffman, E. (1991) *Asylums: Essays on the Social Situation of Mental Patients and Other Inmates*, London: Penguin

House of Commons Select Committee (2011) Uncorrected Transcript of Oral Evidence: Phone Hacking, 19 July 2011 (HC 903ii).

Hyde et al (2009) 'Young Men's Vulnerability in Constituting Hegemonic Masculinity in Sexual Relations', *American Journal of Men's Health*, 3(3): 238–51

Irigaray, L. and Porter, B. (1985) *This Sex Which is Not One*, Ithaca NY: Cornell University Press

Kant, I. (1996) *The Metaphysics of Morals*, Mary J. Gregor and R.J. Sullivan (eds), 2nd edn, Cambridge: Cambridge University Press

Levi-Strauss, C. (1974) *Structural Anthropology*, New York: Basic Books

Levmore, S. (2010) 'The Internet's Anonymity Problem', in S. Levmore and M.C. Nussbaum (eds) *The Offensive Internet: Speech, Privacy and* Reputation, Harvard: Harvard University Press, 50–67

MacPherson, C.B. (1962) *The Political Theory of Possessive Individualism: Hobbes to Locke*, Oxford: Clarendon Press

Marx, K. (2004) *Capital: Critique of Political Economy v. 1*, London: Penguin Classics

Mayer-Schonberger, V. (2009) *Delete: The Virtue of Forgetting in the Digital Age*, Princeton: Princeton University Press

News.com.au and McPhedran, Ian (2011) 'Live Updates: Defence Force Cadet Sex Scandal' *News.com*.au, 12 April 2011

Nicholson, B., Dodd, M. and Rout, M. (2011) 'Defence Cadet 'Raped and Told to Suck it Up', *The Australian*, 8 April.

Nozick, R. (1974) *Anarchy, State and Utopia*, New York: Basic Books

Pateman, C. (1989) 'Feminist Critiques of the Public/Private Dichotomy', in *The Disorder of Women*, Oxford: Polity Press, 118–40

—— (2002) 'Self-Ownership and Property in the Person: Democratization and a Tale of Two Concepts', *The Journal of Political Philosophy*, 10(1): 20–53

Purdom, J. (2000) 'Judging Women: Rethinking Shame through Corporeality', in J. Richardson and R. Sandland (eds) *Feminist Perspectives on Law and Theory*, London: Routledge Cavendish, 209–28

Richardson, J. (2009) *The Classic Social Contractarians*, London: Ashgate Publishing

—— (2011) 'Privacy, Online Identity and Contemporary Feminist Philosophy', *Minds and Machines*. DOI 10.1007/s11023-011-9257-8

Smith, S. (2011) 'Interview with Fran Kelly – ABC Breakfast', Transcript, 12 April

Tavani, H.T. (2007) 'Philosophical Theories of Privacy: Implications for an Adequate Online Privacy Policy', *Metaphilosophy*, 38(1): 1–22

Warren, S.D. and Brandeis, L.D. (1890) 'The Right to Privacy', *Harvard Law Review*, 4(5): 193–220

Chapter 9

Tort Claims for Rape: More Trials, Fewer Tribulations?

Nikki Godden

Introduction

In a well-known civil claim for rape, *A v Hoare and other appeals* [2008], Hoare won £7 million in a national lottery and was sued by his victim, Mrs A, 16 years after the offence. While it may be this case that springs to mind when rape and tort law are mentioned, it only somewhat tangentially involved rape. The central legal issue in the case was limitation periods, and the House of Lords' decision is significant primarily in relation to claims for the harms of child sex abuse brought by adult survivors. However, there are a number of cases where tort law does tell a story about rape specifically, drawing on and informing ideas as to the wrong and harms of rape, and what constitutes consent and when sex is (non)consensual. Take *Lawson v Executor of the Estate of Dawes (Deceased)* [2006] for example, a case in which a woman was awarded £259,000 in damages after being falsely imprisoned for three days, during which she was sexually assaulted and raped a number of times. The trial centred on the question of whether or not she consented to all that went on in the defendant's hotels on the island of Alderney.

Nevertheless, civil cases of rape remain relatively rare, notwithstanding that there is a clear cause of action: it has long been recognised that the trespass to the person torts – battery, assault and false imprisonment – encompass the act of rape, other sexual assaults and domestic violence (eg Lord Denning, *R v Chief Constable of Devon and Cornwall, ex parte CEGB* [1982]: [471], referring to Heuston 1977: 120). One significant reason for this, Martha Chamallas and Jennifer Wriggins explain, is that tort law has been developed largely without women and the particular harms they suffer in mind (2010). Feminists have created a good picture of this skewed history, illustrating the gender disparate effects of tortious rules and principles, as well as exposing its gendered (and gendering) form and content (for an overview, see Conaghan 2003). In short, the gender bias of tort is well known. And yet perhaps the point for many, Joanne Conaghan considers, is to question whether tort law can be used strategically to 'good egalitarian ends' in spite of this (2003).

To what extent, if at all, encouraging civil claims for rape is a worthwhile strategy is a question that has gained some attention, although the majority of the scholarly literature is located in the US and Canada where cases of this kind are more common (Feldthusen 1993; West 1992; LeGrand and Leonard 1978). One detectable concern is that framing rape as a civil as opposed to a criminal wrong, and placing the responsibility of pursuing a case on the survivor, could trivialise and privatise the wrong and harm of rape. But the argument is not that tort law should replace the criminal law in this respect, and indeed it cannot be emphasised strongly enough that efforts to improve the criminal justice system must continue. Rather, tort law can offer an additional response to rape by compensating for the harms and consequential losses. Nevertheless, the point that it can also provide legal recognition that a wrong has been done may be particularly significant in England and Wales where report after report has exposed the flaws and failings in the criminal justice system's response to rape, and the consequently low conviction rate (Baroness Stern 2010). In this respect, the use of tort law could serve to underline the problems that pervade the criminal law and criminal justice system (Godden 2011). There are, of course, other practical issues which may limit claims in tort, such as the potentially high costs of civil litigation, the likelihood of a lengthy and stressful process, combined with the risk of losing the case or that the defendant will be unable to pay damages if awarded. However, if and when rape survivors wish to pursue such claims then they should be supported and encouraged as far as is possible.

Instead of taking an approach which primarily aims to assess the value of bringing civil claims for rape, the emphasis will be on exploring changing interpretations and applications of tortious principles – some due to its increasing deployment in cases of sexual violence and abuse – and the implications for tort cases involving rape. This chapter will focus on three civil cases of rape and consider to what extent, if at all, the potential to utilise tort law as a means by which to offer rape survivors redress is increasing. It will focus on the common issues raised in these cases, explore changes and developments in the courts' approaches and assess the implications for future civil claims for rape. *Parrington v Marriott* [1999], *Griffiths v Williams* [1995] and *Lawson* have been chosen because they are three of the most recent reported cases of this kind, and therefore are the most up to date in relation to legal principles. Also, the legal focal points that are discussed in the higher courts are likely to be significant for most civil suits brought for rape. Included are elements of substantive law, notably consent, of procedure, mainly the standard of proof, and finally in relation to remedies, the level of damages awarded. It will be argued that the judicial development of tortious rules and principles has made some improvements in tort law – at least on its own terms – so that it may offer a better response to rape.

Three tort tales of rape

Parrington v Marriott [1999]

On 13 May 1985, Ms Parrington began working as a lab technician at Hi-Tech Yarns Ltd in Leicester, where Mr Marriott was employed as the production manager. Following the breakdown of her marriage, Ms Parrington claimed that

Mr Marriott sexually harassed her over a period of 18 months and raped her twice in 1992. Towards the end of that year she terminated her employment at Hi-Tech Yarns and began receiving counselling from the Rape Crisis Centre; she suffered from depression and post-traumatic stress disorder, and had a breakdown at the beginning of 1994. After this crisis point, she turned to the law for redress. She did this in three ways over the course of the year: first, she brought a case against Hi-Tech Yarns for unfair constructive dismissal and sex discrimination; secondly, she made a criminal complaint; and finally, she made a tortious claim for damages. The Crown Prosecution Service decided not to proceed with a prosecution, and the application to the Employment Tribunal was stayed pending the outcome of the tort litigation, although it is unknown whether these proceedings continued or if so what the outcome was. This leaves only the tort case which conclusively provided the claimant with a remedy. An action to hold the company vicariously liable was struck out, but the trial judge found Mr Marriott liable for rape and sexual harassment and Ms Parrington was awarded £73,778.06 in damages. The Court of Appeal upheld this decision, rejecting the defendant's arguments that the trial judge's findings were against the weight of the evidence, and that the level of damages was excessive.

Griffiths v Williams [1995]

In *Griffiths v Williams*, Ms Griffiths was raped by her landlord when he approached her at her flat, claiming that she owed him rent money. Following this, he harassed and stalked her. At trial he claimed that she was a sex worker and consented to sex with him in lieu of rent. The case was first tried – rather unusually for a civil case – before a jury at Truro County Court[1] which found in favour of the claimant and awarded her £50,000 in damages for rape and sexual harassment. The defendant appealed on the grounds that the judge had been wrong in relation to allowing two sources of evidence to be admitted, that the direction as to the standard of proof was inadequate, and that the level of damages was too high. The Court of Appeal dismissed the appeal; the claimant was successful.

Lawson v Executor of the Estate for Dawes (Deceased) [2006]

Ms Lawson was falsely imprisoned for three days by Mr Dawes in his hotels on the island of Alderney, during which she was raped on multiple occasions, sexually assaulted and forced to consume intoxicating substances. A mutual friend had informed Ms Lawson that she was invited to attend a job interview with Mr Dawes and it was for this purpose that she had flown to Alderney. However, upon her arrival it became clear that Mr Dawes had other intentions. He did not mention an employment vacancy, but transported Ms Lawson between his hotels on the island, telling her that they were haunted by Hitler's ghost, they were under constant surveillance and that the telephones were 'bugged'. He forced her to consume intoxicants and raped and sexually assaulted her a number of times. It was three days before she managed to raise the alarm and contact the police. A criminal investigation was initiated but it came to an end when Mr Dawes died. Consequently, Ms Lawson brought a civil suit seeking general and aggravated damages for the rapes, assaults and false imprisonment, and special damages in respect of past and future lost earnings on account of the post-traumatic stress disorder she suffered as a result. Eady J awarded Ms Lawson damages amounting to nearly £259,000.

The basis of liability

While claims in tort for rape are relatively unusual, to some extent they are straightforward. It is well established that liability for rape can be grounded in the torts comprising trespass to the person which protect against intentional conduct which interferes with a person's right to bodily and mental integrity, and liberty. It is perhaps because this is clear that it was not explained by the court in either *Parrington v Marriott* or *Lawson*, and in *Griffiths v Williams* notice was limited to a parenthetical reference (Rose LJ: p n/a). However, specifically, acts of rape or other non-consensual physical sexual engagements typically fall squarely within the tort of battery which is defined as intentional, direct and unlawful – in this context usually meaning non-consensual – physical contact with another person (see eg Lord Denning, *R v Chief Constable of Devon and Cornwall, ex parte CEGB* [1982]: [471]; referring to Heuston 1977: 120).

However, in *Parrington v Marriott* it was not just two rapes that Hall J found Mr Marriott liable for at first instance but also sexual harassment over an 18-month period (upheld in the Court of Appeal). When Ms Parrington initiated her civil claim in 1994 there was no legal definition of harassment, and pinning it down to a tortious basis for liability was challenging (eg see *Waters v Metropolitan Police Commissioner* [2000]; and discussion in Conaghan 2002). Yet while the courts were grappling with the possibility of developing a common law tort of harassment (*Khorasandjian v Bush* [1993]; *Burnett v George* [1992]), Hall J's finding of liability for harassment was upheld by the Court of Appeal, with no reference or explanation as to the legal grounds.

Similarly, in another civil claim for rape, *Moores v Green* [1991], Mrs Moores' case was successful at first instance, and Griffiths J awarded her £7,500 in damages for 'rape and the surrounding circumstances', described as 'other less serious matters of harassment' (Balcombe LJ, p n/a). Also, in *Griffiths v Williams* the fact that the claimant was subject to sexual harassment for three years after the rape was a factor that went to justifying the level of damages awarded (Rose LJ, p n/a). At a time where there was, strictly speaking, no 'tort of harassment' (*Patel v Patel* [1988]), this is interesting. However, without the legal arguments being readily available this leaves only speculation, and the possibility that perhaps the claimants' successes (at least at first instance – the Court of Appeal ordered a retrial in *Moores v Green* as new evidence had come to light) were more down to their own tenacity, clever barrister tactics and luck. Nevertheless, it is significant that the courts recognised '*sexual* harassment' as a compensable harm, indicating that gender was a relevant dimension to the abuse of power which can be seen to tie sexual harassment to (inter alia) rape (Kelly 1988). Moreover, since these cases, there has, of course, been the enactment of the Protection from Harassment Act 1997 which offers a civil remedy (section 3). This welcome addition to tort law may be important in relation to future civil claims for rape given that these three cases – a significant number of those litigated in the higher courts – also involved sexual harassment.[2]

Rape myths and consent

Consent is a significant issue in *Parrington v Marriott*, *Griffiths v Williams* and *Lawson*. Similarly to distinguishing between lawful sex and rape (Sexual Offences Act 2003, section 1), the absence or presence of consent can draw the line between lawful and unlawful intentional interferences with a person's physical and or mental integrity, as consent is a defence to each of the trespass to the person torts.[3] Feminist critiques of consent are well known in the context of rape law, and much attention has been paid to the gendered underpinnings of the concept (Naffine 1994) and rape myths which influence ideas as to when, where and with whom women consent to sex (eg Estrich 1987 through to Temkin and Krahé 2008). With these myths far from women's lived experiences of rape, those within and outwith the criminal justice system are often doubtful of and hostile towards complaints of rape, which contributes to maintaining the high attrition rate and low conviction rate (Kelly et al 2005; Temkin and Krahé 2008). Given the gender-based assumptions and stereotypes feminists have found harboured in the history of tort law, scepticism towards the way in which consent may be conceptualised and applied in the context of tort law is not unwarranted. Yet, perhaps surprisingly, almost all the reported civil claims brought for rape have been successful. This raises questions as to the courts' interpretation and application of the consent defence in relation to the trespass to the person torts, and if – or to what extent – this differs from the legal tests regarding consent in relation to the crime of rape.

Similar to the position in the Sexual Offences Act 2003 (section 74), in tort law the claimant must have the freedom and capacity to consent or refuse consent (Scott LJ, *Bowater v Rowley Regis Corporation* [1944]: [479]). Traditionally, only fraud or (threats of) physical violence would vitiate consent (*Latter v Braddell* [1881]); however, in *Freeman v Home Office (No. 2)* [1984] the Court of Appeal recognised that the hierarchical context was a necessary component to consider when determining whether a prisoner freely consented to medical treatment. Nevertheless, the court concluded that the claimant had validly consented, reflecting, Joanne Conaghan argues, a tendency in the practice of the courts to rely on more limited conventional understandings (1998: 149). This seems to be borne out in the small body of case law regarding civil claims for rape. There are no traces of references to even formally recognised positions of trust and power. For instance, in *Parrington v Marriott* there is no evidence that the courts took account of the fact that the defendant was the claimant's manager in determining whether or not the claimant freely consented. This exemplifies a failure of the courts to consider, at least to some extent, the ways in which power imbalances can influence, limit and shape individuals' choices, and when this may render appeals to 'free' choice meaningless.

Better though is the courts' approach as to the scope of the defence. They seem to have adopted the widespread view that only the claimant's actual or 'apparent' consent – that is, where the claimant's actions or behaviour gave the objective appearance of consent[4] – will negate liability in trespass to the person, and that a defendant's belief in consent, however reasonable it is deemed to be, will not suffice (Sedley J, *Hepburn v Chief Constable of Thames Valley Police* [2002]: [24]; Sir John Donaldson MR, *Freeman v Home Office (No.2)* [1984]: [557]).[5] As Rose LJ said in *Griffiths v Williams*, the trial judge explained that the claimant need only prove that the defendant had sex with her without her consent, whereas in the criminal law it must also be proved that the defendant held no belief in consent (p n/a). This difference between the crime of rape and consent in relation to the trespass to the person torts may be one reason why claimants may have a greater chance of a civil claim succeeding, even after a criminal case has ended either before trial or without a conviction.

Tort law does not, of course, offer a means by which to challenge problematic ideas as to when it is 'reasonable' to believe in consent – instead, it provides a way to simply side-step the issue. Nevertheless, it is significant that it can provide legal recognition that sexual contact was non-consensual. The focus on actual consent emphasises that each individual has the right to be free from interferences with her or his bodily and mental integrity and freedom of movement, which is the starting point and basis of the trespass to the person torts (Lord Scott, *Ashley v Chief Constable of South Sussex Police* [2008]: [20]–[22]; Lord Donaldson, *Re T (Adult: Refusal of Treatment)* [1992]: [102]). As such, it can be argued, where a person violates these rights and takes a liberty they did not have, even if they 'reasonably' believed that they did, should not outweigh the claimant's right to be free from such interferences (Lord Scott, *Ashley*: [18]; Stevens 2007: [101]–[2]). This, therefore, can be seen to strike the right balance in the civil law where the defendant is to compensate the claimant for harm caused by their wrongful conduct, in contrast to the criminal law where it would be unjustifiable to punish a defendant for a reasonable mistake as to the claimant's consent to sex (Lord Scott, *Ashley*: [18]).

However, there is a possibility that the balance is tipping in tort law. In *Ashley v Chief Constable of South Sussex Police*, the House of Lords held that an honest and reasonable belief in the need for self-defence would be enough to raise the defence to trespass to the person. Three of the Law Lords debated whether this would extend to other defences, such as consent, but this point was left open (Lord Bingham: [75]; Lord Carswell: [3]; Lord Scott: [22]). If a defendant's 'reasonable' belief in consent will negate liability, then this may weaken the position of claimants bringing civil actions for rape and reduce tort law's potential to protect women's sexual autonomy and integrity.[6]

This is not to say that in these few civil claims for rape the claimants' sexual autonomy and integrity has been properly respected. While the operation of consent in tort law offers an advantage over the criminal law (or at least has until *Ashley*), rape myths and gendered stereotypes have nevertheless played a prominent role in relation to proving (lack of) consent. The admissibility and use of the claimant's sexual history as evidence in civil trials makes this most apparent.

Sexual history evidence

The use of sexual history as evidence at trial has been a prominent problem that feminists have attacked in their efforts to improve the treatment of survivors in the criminal justice system (Adler 1987; McColgan 1996; Temkin 2003). This problem is also evident in civil trials. In *Griffiths v Williams*, the defence called two witnesses who had attended a staff party at the hotel in January 1991 who gave evidence in support of the allegation that the claimant 'picked up blokes for cash'. The purpose of this, Thompson J assumed, was primarily to blacken the claimant's character (as mentioned by Rose LJ, p n/a). However, it is also likely that it was intended to support the defendant's claim that she consented to sex with him to cover the rent payments she (allegedly) owed him. Underpinning this evidence and its supposed relevance to the case are ideas that 'promiscuous' women are unreliable and untrustworthy, and therefore are not credible witnesses; and that a woman who has consented to sex in a particular set of circumstances is likely to do so again in another similar set of circumstances. Similarly, in *Lawson v Dawes* evidence was submitted to show that the claimant was sexually adventurous, went to fetish clubs and took cocaine, which Eady J presumed was to invoke the idea that the claimant was likely to have consented to taking drugs and having sex with the defendant because she had similar experiences in the past [94]. In *Parrington v Marriott* the defendant claimed that the claimant had consensual sex with a number of men following her divorce, because, the underlying assumption implies, if she had consensual sex with other men she was likely to have had consensual sex with him.

These myths relating to credibility and consent operate to undermine unfairly the claimant's case and deny respect for women's sexual autonomy. They are a significant reason why there is a *prima facie* ban on admitting sexual history as evidence in criminal trials, and why there is a specific prohibition of any such evidence which is primarily adduced to discredit the claimant's character (Youth Justice and Criminal Evidence Act 1999, section 41; Home Office 1998). And yet, notwithstanding the distorting presence of rape myths, ultimately the jury in *Griffiths v Williams* and judges in *Lawson* and *Parrington v Marriott* found in favour of the claimants. While it is undoubtedly good that such myths appear not to have had a significant impact on the outcome of these cases, it is nevertheless problematic that such evidence is seen as relevant (McColgan 1996). In addition, allowing sexual history evidence and questioning rape and sexual assault survivors as to the intimacies of their sexual life in a public trial can be distressing and traumatic, and can cause further harm. Indeed, this may have been Ms Griffiths experience as Thorpe LJ commented that the 'defendant's attack on the claimant's character' and 'the manner in which the defendant conducted the litigation [was] extreme' (p n/a; see also similar comments by Rose LJ).

So, while the scope of the defence of consent is more limited than the role consent has to play in the criminal law, which is an advantage to claimants, they nevertheless face considerable challenges in proving consent, and a potentially distressing and traumatic trial. The claimant's credibility and case is likely to be attacked by the use of – for the most part irrelevant – evidence relating to their sexual history, and is an issue which should be addressed by challenges to the relevance, and admissibility, of sexual history evidence.

The standard of proof

A possible reason – and perhaps the most significant reason – as to the success of each claimant in *Parrington v Marriott*, *Griffiths v Williams* and *Lawson* is the lower standard of proof in the civil law. The claimant has to prove the case on the balance of probabilities rather than the prosecution having to prove the defendant was guilty beyond reasonable doubt. This also highlights the point that a successful civil claim can be made even after an unsuccessful criminal case.

However, until relatively recently there was a judicial acceptance that where a civil case involved matters of a criminal nature the case has to be proved to a greater degree (Lord Denning, *Bater v Bater* [1950]: [37]; *Re W (Minors) (Sexual Abuse: Standard of Proof)* [1994]). Or, as put by Rose LJ in *Griffiths v Williams*, one has to be 'much more careful before [one is] satisfied that the allegation was proved' (p n/a). While it is clear that this is not an application of the standard of proof required in the criminal law, the courts were essentially applying a standard of proof higher than the ordinary balance of probabilities – an 'intermediate' standard.[7] In all the reported civil claims for rape which discuss the standard of proof, this is the way in which it has been applied, which may have lessened the claimants' chances of success. It appears the reason for this is purely because the allegation is 'serious'; as Rose LJ justifies, it is not simply a 'run-of-the-mill case' (*Griffiths v Williams*: p n/a). But this itself does not have any particular implications for a finding of civil liability. The level of damages is determined in relation to the harm the claimant suffered, and there is not the same risk of punishment – paradigmatically by imprisonment – as in the criminal law, nor is there the same stigma and censure which attaches to a criminal offence and its particular label – here, 'rape'. Consequently, one of the advantages of bringing a civil claim in comparison to a criminal case has been improperly limited because of the connotations that flow from rape being seen as a particular crime.

Since then, fortunately, the position has changed. It has been clarified that there are only two legal standards of proof: the balance of probabilities and proof beyond reasonable doubt, and that in civil cases where there is no possibility that criminal-like sanctions will be imposed it is the former which is to apply, even where the case involves matters of a criminal nature (*Re H and others (Minors) (Sexual Abuse: Standard of Proof)* [1996]; *Re B (Children) (Sexual Abuse: Standard of Proof)* [2008]).

However, Lord Nicholls explained in *Re H* that serious criminal acts are usually, by their nature, less probable and thus more evidence is required to prove them on balance, satisfying 'one's instinctive feeling that even in civil proceedings a court should be more sure before finding serious allegations proved than when deciding less serious or trivial matters' [586]. In subsequent cases this has been read as meaning that the claimant must prove their case to a high degree (eg *(R) McCann v Crown Court at Manchester* [2003] which Baroness Hale and Lord Hoffmann explain in *Re B* is a misinterpretation and misapplication of *Re H*: [12] and [62] respectively). This was the way in which Lord Nicholls' statement was interpreted in *Parrington v Marriott* where the Court of Appeal confirmed that Hall J had applied the correct standard of proof, having found that the claimant's case was 'proved to the necessary high standard' (Mummery LJ, quoting Hall J at first instance: p n/a).

But there is also a second misreading of Lord Nicholls' statement and that is 'the more serious the allegation, the more cogent the evidence needed to prove it'. However, as Baroness Hale explained in *Re B*, how probable an event is will depend on the facts and not necessarily upon its severity; for example, she says, murder is highly probable if there is a dead body with the throat cut and no nearby weapon [72]. This is an accurate statement of the way in which the standard of proof should apply in the civil law. Nevertheless, exactly how the standard of proof will be applied in future tort cases involving rape is unclear, and there is the possibility that the courts could assume that 'serious' events require either a higher standard of proof or more evidence to prove they occurred (*Re D* [2008]). Either way, the effect is the same: the claimant bears a greater burden to prove their case.

On the whole, however, the judicial approach to the standard of proof in civil claims which have involved matters that could also constitute a crime has improved over the last decade. Yet despite the fact that in many (if not all) such cases involving rape up until now the courts have required the claimant to prove her case to a high degree, the claimant has been successful. Hopefully, though, the balance of probabilities test will be applied in the correct way, which would make civil cases for rape fairer to claimants, and which could mean claimants have an increased chance of winning their case.

The level of damages and payment of compensation

The level and categorisation of damage awards in tort law have been shown to typically privilege men's interests over women's and offer compensation more readily for the losses they suffer (see eg Graycar, this volume). Not only is this evident in looking at, for instance, gendered assessments of loss of earning capacity and the courts' evaluation of ways in which financial losses flow from personal injuries, but also in relation to the characterisation of the nature and extent of harm suffered (Feldthusen 1994; Adjin-Tettey, this volume). So in *W v Meah; D v Meah* [1986] where two women were subject to serious physical and sexual violence, the level of damages was set at £6,750 to Ms W and £10,250 to Ms D. Woolf LJ explained that such experiences must have been 'distressing' and 'sensational', however, efforts should be made to keep damages in line with 'more conventional' personal injury cases: 'Although these ladies underwent terrible experiences . . . unfortunately, very often the physical injuries that the victims of traffic accidents sustain are much more serious than the physical injuries that these two ladies suffered' [942].

But assessing the level of damages in relation to the physical injuries and their consequences fails to capture the pain of these sexual assaults in the violation of a person's physical and mental integrity, and any ensuing psychological, emotional and other intangible harms (see further Adjin-Tettey, this volume). Bruce Feldthusen sees similarities in the Canadian case law on this topic, arguing that the alignment of sexual assaults and rape with other forms of personal injury represents a judicial failure to recognise the gender-specific harms of 'sexual batteries' (1993). At the same time, he points out, ordinary principles relating to damage quantification are rarely employed, particularly non-pecuniary damages for lost earning capacity, resulting in systematic under-compensation in sexual battery cases (1994).

However, with so few civil claims for rape in the UK, and of those even fewer where a detailed description of the calculation of damages is available, a strong conclusion cannot be reached in this context. Nevertheless, it is clear that the level of damages awarded in such cases has risen significantly, notwithstanding inflation. In line with *Meah*, £8,000 was awarded to a woman raped by a police officer in *Makanjuola v Commissioner of Police for the Metropolis and Another* [1989], and in 1990, the claimant in *Moores v Green* was initially awarded £12,500. In comparison, in *Griffiths v Williams* the claimant was awarded £50,000, with Rose LJ and Millett LJ recognising that rape was, by then, treated more seriously and 'is in quite a different category to personal injury cases in general' (p n/a). Subsequently, in *Parrington v Marriott* damages amounted to just under £75,000, and more recently, in *Lawson* Eady J awarded Ms Lawson damages amounting to nearly £259,000, which is thought to be the highest payout granted in the civil courts for rape (Herman 2006; and see the press release from the claimant's solicitor's firm, Field Fisher Waterhouse 2006). Of this, £78,000 was calculated for general and aggravated damages and the rest was assessed as special damages for lost past and future earnings on account of the post-traumatic stress disorder she suffered as a result of her experience at Alderney.

A significant factor, however, was that Ms Lawson owned and ran a business – a hairdressing salon – which was apparently thriving before the rapes, but which dwindled afterwards, eventually being sold as she found the work too stressful. The high payout, then, could be interpreted as a representation of tort law's gendered assessment of lost earning capacity. Nevertheless, the point can still be made that the psychological harms and consequential losses which can result from rape have, to a much greater extent, been recognised by the courts; perhaps, as Elizabeth Sheehy suggests, highlighting the social costs which flow from rape (1994: 206). Furthermore, on the whole, the increasing level of damages awarded may be a reflection of improvement in relation to judicial understandings of the harm of rape. So viewed, the potential of tort law to offer redress for the harms of rape may be increasing.

But there is a problem tied to this climbing level of damages, and the recognition of the psychological consequences rape can have. Bruce Feldthusen explains, 'to win "big", the lawyer is encouraged to portray [the claimant] as . . . a person needing therapy for a long time and . . . whose potential will never be fully realized', which may reinforce and reify such effects, and thus could be damaging strategically (Feldthusen et al 1998: 449). Indeed, it seems that this picture was painted of the claimant in *Lawson*; Eady J explained the point as put to him: before the rapes the claimant had built up her business over 10 years which was 'apparently flourishing' from her 'flair and experience', but afterwards she underwent a 'personality change', going from being 'bubbly, energetic and forthcoming' to a person who was 'withdrawn and lacked confidence' [28], and that, suffering from post-traumatic stress disorder, she was incapable of working for the rest of her life [3]. This may be seen as an almost unavoidable consequence of turning to tort law, even if, as Bruce Feldthusen et al suggest, punitive damages were awarded more liberally to recognise the severity of the wrong of rape without potentially reifying the harms (1998: 449), or, alternatively, Joanne Conaghan argues, high levels of aggravated damages were awarded to achieve this (1998: 146).

However, Feldthusen highlights that rape and sexual assault survivors may not be bringing a claim primarily for compensation but for retribution and punishment, or for a sense of therapeutic justice, through bringing a legal action themselves against the defendant (1993).[8] Further, Nora West argues, rape survivors could be empowered in playing an active role in a system of formal equality – in contrast to being a witness to the state's action in the criminal justice system with 'victim' status – which may reflect a reversal of the gender inequalities expressed and experienced through rape (1992; and see Perry 2008–09 more generally). Overall, what might be most significant for rape survivors is that they receive legal validation of the wrong and harm (Feldthusen 1993: 211–12), finding 'closure' so that they can then move on with their lives (Eady J, *Lawson*: [129]).

Although survivors may be viewing the case as being about 'a just result', it is likely that in many cases the challenges of bringing a civil suit – the potentially high costs, the stress, time, effort and risk of not being believed (Conaghan 1998: 160) – may not be outweighed unless there is also the chance of some form of financial recompense. It can be no coincidence that three of the civil cases involving rape – and the most well-known ones – were brought against particularly wealthy defendants. In *Lawson*, the tortfeasor was an extremely well-off business tycoon; in the much reported case of *A v Hoare*, a civil claim for rape was brought after the defendant won £7 million in a lottery; and in *W; D v Meah* the claimants initiated the case after the defendant was awarded damages in a tort claim of his own (*Meah v McCreamer (No. 1)* [1985]). It may be that the majority of rape survivors are unlikely to bring a case with little prospect of receiving damages, if awarded, from an impecunious defendant.[9] Nevertheless, civil claims for rape continue to be brought; in the last five years there has been, at least reported, *Lawson, N v Chief Constable of*

Merseyside Police [2006] and *A v Hoare*, and it has been reported that civil actions are being instigated by a number of the sexual assault survivors of the headline cases of John Worboys and Stephen Mitchell (Fresco 2009; BBC News 2010). If rape survivors wish to turn to the civil law – as it seems they sometimes do – they should be fully supported, and incremental improvements should be pushed for, following the beneficial changes already witnessed in tort law's response to rape.

Conclusion

Feminists are well aware of the gendered limitations of tort law. Martha Chamallas and Jennifer Wriggins have collated their research and illustrate this by exposing the race and gender bias of tort law's allegedly 'neutral', 'individual' and 'universal' rules, and its disparate distributional effects (2010; see also Conaghan 2003). Nevertheless, they remain optimistic that improvements can be – and have been – made to recognise that social identities and the context to injuries are relevant and should be accounted for to make for a more equal tort system (2010). The stories of the rape survivors who have brought civil claims for rape that are presented here hopefully add to the reasons for Chamallas and Wriggins' optimism. This is particularly important in a context where the criminal justice system all too often fails to provide justice for rape survivors, and tort law can offer an alternative way in which to provide legal recognition that a wrong has been done and harm has been caused, even if imperfectly (Godden 2011).

In the earliest instance of a woman initiating a civil suit against her abuser, *W v Meah; D v Meah*, the gender dimension to the sexual assaults and rape was largely lost, and it was compared to and aligned with 'more conventional' personal injury cases. However, by the time of *Parrington v Marriott* the court seemed to acknowledge – at least to some extent – the gendered nature of the wrong and the way in which the harm is experienced, recognising the *sexual* harassment to which the defendant subject the claimant, and its connection to two instances of rape. Moreover, Hall J and the Court of Appeal clearly viewed sexual harassment as an injury worthy of redress, holding Mr Marriott liable with apparently little comment or difficulty, even though contemporary cases showed signs of a struggle to find a tortious basis for liability for harassment. Of course, section 3 of the Protection from Harassment Act 1997 now provides for this, which could be significant given that three – a significant proportion – of the reported civil claims for rape also involved harassment.

Given the relatively secure basis for liability for rape, it may be that the challenges in these cases lie primarily with proving consent or lack of consent. As shown by *Griffiths v Williams* – to give just one example – rape myths, gendered assumptions and sex stereotypes play a prominent role in civil trials, facilitated by the lack of limitations on the admissibility of sexual history evidence. Further, the standard of proof that has been applied has placed a higher burden on the claimant than the ordinary balance of probabilities, as the criminal law and its conceptions of rape have influenced judicial responses to civil cases of rape. Yet, notwithstanding these troubles, in the majority of cases the claimant has been successful, the court accepting her version of events and evidence over the defendant's. However, the courts have adapted their approach to the standard of proof over the past decade or so in relation to civil cases involving matters which can also constitute crimes, reiterating the point that in such cases it should be the ordinary balance of probabilities test. This may make it fairer for claimants bringing civil claims for rape in the future.

Further, as *Lawson v Dawes* demonstrates, the level of damages awarded has been increasing as the courts have been more sensitive to the nature and extent of the harms of rape. While this can be seen as providing a better measure of the injury, there is the possibility that this could be strategically damaging by encouraging a representation of rape survivors as inevitably and forever shattered by their experience. However, as far as this point goes towards an argument against bringing claims in tort for rape, it must be balanced with a background in which the majority of rapes go without legal recognition or condemnation due to the high level of non-reporting, high attrition rate and low conviction rate. As such, it is significant that improvements have been made in tort law's response to claims of rape, and important that, where survivors wish, they have the opportunity to seek legal recognition of, and redress for, the harms they suffer.

Notes

1   This may have been because the court accepted that the rape amounted to or involved false imprisonment as such cases have a qualified right to a jury trial (Supreme Court Act 1981, section 69(1)), or it could have been argued that this case was 'unusual' and particularly serious (Lord Denning, *Ward v James* [1966] at [295]) so as to be appropriate to be heard by a jury (under section 69(3) of the Supreme Court Act 1981).

2   There are, nevertheless, limitations to the Act; for a discussion with reference to the gender dimension and sexual harassment in particular, see Conaghan (1999).

3   Consent is traditionally conceptualised as a defence (*Ashley v Chief Constable of South Sussex Police* [2008]), however, the absence of consent can also be seen as a constituent of the tort as rendering the conduct unlawful, with the burden of proof on the claimant (*Freeman v Home Office (No. 2)* [1984]).

4   The difference between apparent consent and reasonable belief in consent is that the former is deduced only from the claimant's actions and behaviour, whereas 'all the circumstances' can be taken into account in relation to the latter, which could extend to what was reasonable for the *particular defendant* to have believed (at least, this is the position in the criminal law; section 1(2) of the Sexual Offences Act 2003; for a discussion of the issues with this subjective element, see Finch and Munro 2006: 317).

5   There is, however, some inconsistent authority on this point; for a discussion, see Keren-Paz and Levenkron (2009: 454–6).

6   Precisely because of this Elizabeth Adjin-Tettey argues for a defence only of actual and voluntary consent in Canada where constructive consent will exonerate a defendant (2006). For the view that constructive consent should not exonerate a defendant in England and Wales, and *Ashley* should not be applied to the defence of consent which can be distinguished from self-defence, see Godden (2011).

7   Although it was often said that it was the balance of probabilities test, one just had to be 'more sure' this was met, or prove this to a greater degree; this is a contradiction in

terms: one cannot be more sure that it is proved on balance or not, it either is or is not, or else it is a greater degree of probability that is required (Lord Nicholls, *Re H*: [587]; Mirfield 2009: 31–32).

8   As a further illustration, Frances Wright (2011), a member of the Climate Camp Legal Team, was 'disappointed' that a *Guardian* article (Dodd 2011) put an emphasis on compensation in a report of their high court victory in which the police were held to have unlawfully detained protesters at a central London G20 protest on climate change (using 'kettling' tactics). The motivation for bringing the case, she explained, was to 'stop the police thinking they have carte blanche to deprive people of their liberty'.

9   Notably, in three different cases a claim was brought against the tortfeasor's employer in an attempt to hold them vicariously liable and presumably pay the damages the tortfeasor could not (*Parrington v Marriott; Makanjuola; N v Chief Constable of Merseyside Police* [2006]). In each case the employer escaped liability on the basis that the tort was not committed 'in the course of employment' but the tortfeasor was held responsible either or both in civil and criminal law.

Cases

A v Hoare and other appeals [2008] UKHL 6
Ashley v Chief Constable of South Sussex Police [2008] UKHL 25
Bater v Bater [1950] 2 All ER 458
Bowater v Rowley Regis Corporation [1944] KB 476
Burnett v George [1992] 1 FLR 525
Freeman v Home Office (No. 2) [1984] QB 524
Griffiths v Williams [1995] *The Times*, 24 November
Hepburn v Chief Constable of Thames Valley Police [2002] EWCA Civ 1841
Khorasandjian v Bush [1993] 3 All ER 669
Latter v Braddell [1881] 50 LJQB 166
Lawson v Executor of the Estate of Dawes (Deceased) [2006] EWHC 2865
Makanjuola v Commissioner of Police for the Metropolis and Another [1989] *The Times*, 8 August
Meah v McCreamer (No. 1) [1985] 1 All ER 367
Moores v Green [1991] *The Guardian*, 13 September
N v Chief Constable of Merseyside Police [2006] EWHC 3041
Parrington v Marriott [1999] All ER (D) 168
Patel v Patel [1988] 2 FLR 179
R v Chief Constable of Devon and Cornwall, ex parte CEGB [1982] QB 458
Re B (Children)(Sexual Abuse: Standard of Proof) [2008] UKHL 35
Re D [2008] 1 WLR 1499
Re H and others (Minors)(Sexual Abuse: Standard of Proof) [1996] 2 WLR 8
Re T (Adult: Refusal of Treatment) [1992] 3 WLR 782
Re W (Minors)(Sexual Abuse: Standard of Proof) [1994] 1 FLR 419
(R) McCann v Crown Court at Manchester [2003] 1 AC 787
W v Meah; D v Meah [1986] 1 All ER 935
Ward v James [1966] 1 QB 273
Waters v Metropolitan Police Commissioner [2000] 1 WLR 607

Bibliography

Adjin-Tettey, E. (2006) 'Protecting the Dignity and Autonomy of Women: Rethinking the Place of Constructive Consent in the Tort of Sexual Battery', *University of British Columbia Law Review*, 39: 3–61

Adler, Z. (1987) *Rape on Trial*, London: Routledge and Kegan Paul

Baroness Stern (2010) *The Stern Review – An Independent Review Into How Rape Complaints Are Handled by Public Authorities in England and Wales*, London: Home Office

BBC News (2010) 'Northumbria Police Face Stephen Mitchell Damages Claim', 28 November, Online

Chamallas, M. and Wriggins, J. (2010) *The Measure of Injury: Race, Gender and Tort Law*, New York: New York University Press

Conaghan, J. (1998) 'Tort Litigation in the Context of Intra-familial Abuse', *Modern Law Review*, 61(2): 132–61

—— (1999) 'Enhancing Civil Remedies for (Sexual) Harassment: s. 3 of the Protection from Harassment Act 1997', *Feminist Legal Studies*, 7: 203–14

—— (2002) 'Law, Harm and Redress: A Feminist Perspective', *Legal Studies*, 22(3): 319–39

—— (2003) 'Tort Law and Feminist Critique', *Current Legal Problems*, 56: 175–209

Dodd, V. (2011) 'Thousands May Sue Over Police Kettling at G20 Protests', *The Guardian*, 14 April, Online

Estrich, S. (1987) *Real Rape*, Cambridge MA: Harvard University Press

Feldthusen, B. (1993) 'The Civil Action for Sexual Battery: Therapeutic Jurisprudence', *Ottawa Law Review*, 25: 203–34

—— (1994) 'Discriminatory Damage Quantification in Civil Actions for Sexual Battery', *University of Toronto Law Journal*, 44: 133–68

Feldthusen, B., Des Rosiers, N. and Hankivsky O.A.R. (1998) 'Legal Compensation for Sexual Violence: Therapeutic Consequences and Consequences for the Legal System', *Psychology, Public Policy and Law*, 4: 433–51

Field Fisher Waterhouse (2006) 'High Court Awards One of the Highest Ever Damages in a Rape Case to Victim', press release, 14 November, Online

Finch, E. and Munro, V.E. (2006) 'Breaking the Boundaries: Sexual Consent in the Jury Room', *Legal Studies*, 26(3): 303–20

Fresco, A. (2009) 'Victims of Taxi Driver Rapist John Worboys to Claim Compensation', *The Times*, 20 May, Online

Godden, N. (2011) 'Civil Claims for Rape: A Valuable Remedy or Damaging Strategy?', *King's Law Journal*, 22: 157–82

Herman, M. (and PA) (2006) 'Rape Victim Wins £259,000 From Tycoon's Estate', *The Times*, 14 November, Online

Heuston, R.F.V. (1977) *Salmond on Torts*, 17th edn, London: Sweet & Maxwell

Home Office (1998) *Speaking up for Justice*, London: Home Office

Kelly, L. (1988) *Surviving Sexual Violence*, Oxford: Oxford University Press

Kelly, L, Lovett, J. and Regan, L. (2005) *A Gap or a Chasm? Attrition in Reported Rape Cases, Home Office Research Study 293*, London: Home Office

Keren-Paz, T. and Levenkron, N. (2009) 'Clients' Strict Liability Towards Victims of Sex Trafficking', *Legal Studies*, 29(3): 438–63

LeGrand, C. and Leonard, F. (1978) 'Civil Suits for Sexual Assaults: Compensating Rape Victims', *Golden Gate University Law Review*, 8: 479–514

McColgan, A. (1996) 'Common Law and the Relevance of Sexual History Evidence', *Oxford Journal of Legal Studies*, 16: 275–308

Mirfield, P. (2009) 'How Many Standards of Proof are There?', *Law Quarterly Review*, 125: 31–8

Naffine, N. (1994) 'Possession: Erotic Love in the Law of Rape', *Modern Law Review*, 57: 10–37

Perry, R. (2008–09) 'Empowerment and Tort Law', *Tennessee Law Review*, 76: 959–92

Sheehy, E. (1994) 'Compensation for Women Who Have Been Raped', in J.V. Roberts and R.M. Mohr (eds) *Confronting Sexual Assault: a Decade of Legal and Social Change*, Toronto: Toronto University Press

Stevens, R. (2007) *Torts and Rights*, Oxford: Oxford University Press

Temkin, J. (2003) 'Sexual History Evidence – Beware the Backlash', *Criminal Law Review*, 217–43

Temkin, J. and Krahé, B. (2008) *Sexual Assault and the Justice Gap: a question of attitude*, Oxford: Hart Publishing

West, N. (1992) 'Rape in the Criminal Law and the Victim's Tort Alternative: a Feminist Analysis', *University of Toronto Faculty Law Review*, 50: 96–130

Wright, F. (2011) 'Our victory over the Metropolitan Police Was Not About Compensation', *The Guardian*, 22 April, Online

Chapter 10

Sexual Wrongdoing: Do the Remedies Reflect the Wrong?

Elizabeth Adjin-Tettey*

Introduction

Feminist theorising has helped to unpack the relationship between law and society and the ways in which they influence and draw on each other in the legal and social imagination. Examples include the marginalisation of women's experiences, construction of gender roles, and the perception and valuation of injuries that predominantly affect women (Conaghan 2003: 181; Wishik 1985; Chamallas 1997). It is also important to be attentive to intersecting factors that determine one's experiences in law and society in addition to gender, such as race, (dis)ability, sexual orientation, religion, etc, that enhance vulnerability for sexual victimisation.

Sexual victimisation may be experienced irrespective of gender and socio-economic status. However, perpetrators often target society's most vulnerable; persons lacking social, economic and political power. Victims are overwhelmingly female and/or vulnerable on other grounds, such as childhood, disability, racialisation, socio-economic location and institutionalisation (Brennan and Taylor-Butts 2008: 12–23; British Columbia Law Institute 2001; Adjin-Tettey 2006; Feldthusen 1994; Martin 1994; Statistics Canada 2006: 8, 13, 36; *R v Osolin* [1993]: [165]–[166]). Commenting on the nature and effect of sexual assault on victims, Cory J noted:

> It cannot be forgotten that a sexual assault is very different from other assaults. It is true that it, like all the other forms of assault, is an act of violence. Yet it is something more than a simple act of violence . . . It is an assault upon human dignity and constitutes a denial of any concept of equality for women.
>
> (Cory J in *Osolin*: [165])[1]

It is therefore important that the process of seeking redress and remedies provided for sexual interference should not exacerbate survivors' experiences of marginalisation. Rather, their interests should be valued and protected in ways that promote therapeutic outcomes for survivors (Seidman and Vickers 2005: 471–3). This may require a re-conceptualisation of the purpose of tort remedy beyond the current focus on *restitutio in integrum*, which is grounded in corrective justice. Harms from sexual wrongdoing tend to be intangible and do not always map onto traditional notions of tortious injury. Hence, a broader view of the goal of tort remedy that is attentive to survivors' experiences of victimisation is required to ensure remedies are meaningful (Watson 2010: 211, 212; Pryor 2003).

The goal of this chapter is to explore whether the tort system is sufficiently attentive to the unique circumstances of survivors of sexual wrongdoing. While there has been greater receptivity to claims of sexual wrongdoing, remedies are not equally attentive to the nature and consequences of sexual interference for survivors. This is in part due to the characterisation of harms commonly experienced by survivors as intangible, which are generally devalued in the tort system compared to tangible harms.

Importance of tort claims for sexual victimisation

The tort system is an inefficient mechanism for compensating personal injury victims; access is limited to those injured by the fault of others, who can afford the financial and emotional cost of initiating and maintaining civil suits, and are able to prove their case on a balance of probabilities. This huge expenditure of resources often does not directly benefit victims (Cane 2006: 22–5), and may not be the most appropriate avenue for remedying sexual victimisation.[2]

Notwithstanding these concerns, a tort claim may be the most realistic avenue for redress (Godden, this volume). Although criminal prosecution constitutes public recognition of survivors' victimisation and is important in responding to sexual wrongdoing, it may not be an adequate or effective response to sexual violation and may leave survivors feeling re-victimised (Katz 2010; Roberts 2009; Doe 2003: 70–2; Adjin-Tettey 2006: 26–7; Comack and Peter 2005: 297–8). Furthermore, criminal prosecution may not be an option, for example where the perpetrator is deceased.[3] Meanwhile, tort damages can be enforced against the perpetrator's estate, assuming solvency,[4] employers by way of vicarious liability, and third parties, such as employers, parents and partners through negligence claims where there has been direct wrongdoing enabling the victimisation, such as inadequate safeguards (*Hockley v Riley* [2007]: [14]; *Blackwater v Plint* [2005]: [20]; *J(LA) v J(H)* [1993]; *KK v KWG* [2006]; *KM v Canada (Attorney General)* [2004]).

Feminist scholars and activists continue to draw attention to the nature and consequences of sexual victimisation, including its gendered nature and its tendency to occur in unequal power relationships, constituting abuse of vulnerable parties. Additionally, the vulnerable party is often marked by intersecting grounds of marginalisation such as gender, class, racialisation, disability, childhood/youth, etc. There is increasing awareness and sensitivity to survivors, and recognition of the need for improved access to justice and effective compensation (Adjin-Tettey and Kodar 2011; *Bazley v Curry* [1999]: [30]). For example, the potential of power differential to vitiate apparent consent has been recognised in many cases (*Norberg v Wynrib* [1992]; *TO v JHO* [2006]). Also, obstacles to initiating claims in a timely manner have been acknowledged, resulting in generous constructions or elimination of limitation periods for sexual wrongdoing. Further, the expanded scope of vicarious liability based on enterprise risk allows plaintiffs to sue third parties who did not authorise the abuse (*Bazley*: [22], [37]–[38], [41]).[5]

Attitude towards compensation for non-pecuniary losses/hedonic damages

In this section, I ask whether improved access to the tort system and broader scope of liability for sexual victimisation has resulted in effective remedies for survivors. This inquiry requires a broader look at the nature of harms arising from sexual wrongdoing, attitudes towards compensation for those injuries and whether there is a risk of inadequate compensation for victims.

Sexual victimisation may result in physical and/or emotional or psychological injuries, which may be mostly intangible. Sexual wrongdoing can have serious short- and long-term consequences for survivors, and are a source of distress, unhappiness and loss of enjoyment of life. In addition to physical injuries sustained during the assault, survivors are more likely to experience long-term numerous physical ailments, compared to those who have not been similarly victimised (Campbell et al 2003; Golding 1999; *Norberg*: [56]; *Evans v Sproule* [2008]: [122]). Long-term harm may also be psychological, affecting self-esteem, feelings of safety, ability to focus and obtain education, difficulties maintaining employment and interpersonal relationships, mistrust of people and authority figures where the abuse was perpetrated by persons in such positions, etc. Survivors of childhood sexual abuse often suffer from sexual dysfunction and other sex-related issues later in life (Walser and Kern 1996; Luster and Small 1997; Stock et al 1997), as well as from other general psychological problems (Briere and Elliott 1994; Cheasty et al 1998; Luster and Small 1997; Trickett and Putnam 1993; Banyard and Williams 1996). These types of harms often give rise to damages for non-pecuniary losses (general and aggravated) and non-compensatory damages (punitive damages) in addition to medical expenses (BCLI 2001: 15–16, 38; Daylen et al 2006: 389–90; *Norberg*: [56]–[58]; *CM v Canada (Attorney General)* [2004]; *EDG v Hammer* [1998]: [12], [57], affirmed [2003] 2 SCR 459).

Critics have questioned both the basis and quantum of compensation for intangible losses, which are perceived to defy objective proof and quantification. Intangible losses are viewed as being suspect, prone to exaggeration and dependent on variables unconnected to the defendant's wrongdoing (King 2004: 177; *Ipp Report* 2002: 13.20, 13.21), resulting in their devaluation.[6] This gives rise to a potential for under-compensating survivors of sexual wrongdoing as compensation depends on the effect of victimisation on the survivor, which may often be intangible (*MA v Canada (Attorney General)* [2001]: [86]–[93], varied on other grounds: 2003 SKCA 2, 227 Sask R 260). There is support for compensation for intangible losses where plaintiffs also suffer tangible/physical injuries, and they may recover relatively higher damages for such losses (Atiyah 1997: 18).

Compensation for intangible losses must be 'fair' but not provide 'full' compensation as damages for pecuniary losses (Daylen et al 2006: 390–1; *Andrews* v

Grand and Toy Alberto Ltd [1978]: [87]–[90]; *Lindal v Lindal (No 2)* [1981]: [12]–[26]; *Ipp Report* 2002: 13.3). This understanding of the goal of compensation for intangible losses underlies the functional approach that determines availability and quantum of non-pecuniary damages in Canada. Awards are limited to what is necessary to provide solace to the plaintiff (Berryman 2010: 167). Compensation is considered futile, an unnecessary burden on the defendant, and ultimately society, unless the amount can assist the plaintiff in dealing with the effects of the injury (Ogus 1972: 17). These views devalue intangible injuries and privilege tangible injuries, resulting in disproportionate effects for plaintiffs whose injuries are mostly intangible (Finley 2004: 1279).

Incommensurability of non-pecuniary losses

The goal of fair as opposed to full compensation for intangible harms is justified because these losses are perceived as being incapable of monetary quantification and qualitatively different from tangible harms. As Dickson J stated in *Andrews*:

> There is no medium of exchange for happiness: There is no market for expectation of life. The monetary evaluation of non-pecuniary losses is a philosophical and policy exercise more than a legal or logical one. The award must be fair and reasonable, fairness being gauged by earlier decisions; but the award must also of necessity be arbitrary or conventional. No money can provide true restitution.
>
> (Dickson J *Andrews*: [87])

Damages for tangible losses are intended to provide *equivalent* compensation for the plaintiff's loss whereas awards for non-pecuniary losses provide *substitute* compensation because it is impossible to give the plaintiff exactly what has been lost. Consequently, greater justification is required for such awards (Cane 2006: 412–14; McGregor 2003: 35–210; Hammond 2010: 179). Concerns about compensation for non-pecuniary losses include incommensurability; that they are incapable of monetary quantification, and hence not subject to market exchange. Therefore, it makes no sense for the law to quantify in monetary terms something that cannot be translated into money (Jaffe 1953: 222). Cane states:

> The calculation of damages for non-pecuniary damages has an air of unreality about it. Something that cannot be measured in money is 'lost', and the compensation principle requires some monetary value to be placed on it. There appears to be no objective way of working out any relationship between the value of money – what it will buy – and [non-pecuniary] damages awarded . . . All such damages awards could be multiplied or divided by two overnight . . .[7].
>
> (Cane 2006: 162)

Incommensurability presents several challenges to compensation for intangible losses. If non-pecuniary damages are antithetical to the legal and economic theories that justify tort law, why do courts continue to award compensation for such losses? According to Berryman:

> . . . most people understand why money cannot substitute for suffering. But the argument is out of sympathy with our emotional response. We feel pain; we empathise with others in their suffering. We are motivated by compassion at the sight of others loss; we wish to do something.
>
> (Berryman 2010: 181)

The incommensurability argument against compensation for intangible losses stems from the corrective justice underpinning of tort damages that seeks to restore plaintiffs to their *status quo ante*. As Radin (1993: 68) notes, '[i]f corrective justice requires rectification, and if injury cannot be translated into money, how can payment of money ever amount to rectification so as to satisfy the demands of corrective justice?' Also, Berryman (2010: 180) suggests that while damages for intangible losses have utility by allowing the plaintiff to purchase things that can provide solace for their losses, this form of compensation reflects distributive and not corrective justice. It follows that compensation for intangible losses do not easily fit within the corrective justice justification of tort liability. According to King (2004), the incommensurability of these losses results in unpredictable outcomes, disparity in awards and undermines optimum deterrence. As well, King (2004: 180–5) argues that the potential for large awards for intangible losses threatens the loss distribution function of the tort system.[8]

While incommensurability could justify not providing compensation for intangible losses, the opposite is equally sustainable. Arguably, since no amount of money can provide true substitutes for intangible losses, it follows 'that only very substantial awards could properly recognize the reality of the loss' (*BMG v Nova Scotia* [2007]: [122]). There is nothing self-evident in choosing the former position to limit or exclude compensation for non-pecuniary losses. In fact, such a position masks the ideological bias of traditional tort law that favours tangible injuries and/or those that affect a person's public image such as defamation, as the legitimate consequence of tortious conduct.[9] The traditional view is premised on an assumption of a normative understanding of what it means to restore plaintiffs to their *status quo ante*. While the lack of common understanding does not justify rejecting the restorative principle, it does undermine the incommensurability argument against the availability of compensation for intangible losses and the privileging of tangible harms (Pryor 2003: 662, 664).

An extension of the futility argument against compensation for intangible losses is that such compensation should only be forward looking because money is of no use for intangible harms the plaintiff has already endured (Chapman 1995: 421). However, as Ogus notes, this would give defendants incentives to delay resolution of claims and is unfair for plaintiffs. Hence, compensation must necessarily include past and future losses, even if this is inconsistent with the conceptual basis of the award (Ogus 1972: 16). This is reflected in practice, as courts do not separate compensation for past and future intangible losses. This is particularly important in historical abuse claims where plaintiffs' losses may have largely occurred in the past.

The perception that non-pecuniary damages defy meaningful compensation because of lack of market equivalence may be a gendered characterisation of harms that further marginalises women's experiences based on, for example, ideological assumptions about women's nature and responses to harm. Specifically, that women are emotional beings and more susceptible to psychological harms. The valuation of pecuniary losses in cases of sexual victimisation is equally problematic, especially in relation to future losses, in light of the common law position of lump sum damages (Rabin 2006: 361–2). Further, the restorative goal of compensation for tangible losses is not objectively ascertainable. In *Andrews* ([48]), Dickson J referred to the process of assessing future losses as crystal ball gazing and yet the exercise must be undertaken, yet courts have not shied away from that exercise, however imprecise it might be. Rather, courts have noted that difficulties of assessment should not preclude compensation for future losses. In fact, courts have adopted a lower threshold for establishing such losses based on substantial possibility rather than balance of probabilities to avoid the all-or-nothing approach (*Conklin v Smith* [1978]; *Schrump v Koot* [1977]; *BMG*: [172]; *Morris v Rose Estate* [1996]: [24]). The gendered problem in awarding future damages is made even more visible by some courts characterising harms that mostly affect women, such as involuntary parenthood, as non-pecuniary for policy reasons when in fact those losses are tangible, such as the costs of raising an unplanned child (Adjin-Tettey 2007a).

Admittedly, monetary damages, whether for tangible or intangible losses, are limited in their ability to restore victims to their *status quo ante*. This is inherent in the restorative principle that seeks only to return plaintiffs to their pre-tort state as far as money can do. Attempts to undervalue intangible harms exacerbate the systemic under-compensation of tortious injuries. In the context of sexual wrongdoing, this also constitutes discrimination against already marginalised victims and should be avoided.

Time heals wounds

Arguments have also been raised about the ephemeral nature of intangible losses and whether they should be compensable. Relying on the robustness of human nature and the tendency to adjust or 'rebound' after adversity, some psychologists and legal scholars question the enduring nature of non-pecuniary losses, and hence the need for compensation, especially in relation to future losses. Pain and suffering, loss of enjoyment of life and loss of amenities that do not impact the plaintiff's financial losses, such as working capacity and care costs,[10] are perceived to diminish over time and eventually be eliminated. It is expected plaintiffs will adjust to their victimisation with time, thereby eliminating or diminishing the need for long-term compensation for such losses.

Arguments about intangible losses tapering off over time are often based on evidence of psychologists who testify the plaintiff's injuries should be short-lived. Also, judges sometimes substitute their own opinions that the victim's injuries should be short-lived in place of opposing expert evidence (Feldthusen 1994: note 111; *SMAB v JNH* [1991]; *Gray v Reeves* [1991]: [118]; *CCB (Litigation Guardian of) v IB*, [2009]: [36]). There tends to be a general mistrust of survivors' (mostly women) descriptions of their subjective experiences of the consequences of victimisation, especially when uncorroborated by experts. This may be due in part to the perception that women tend to exaggerate the consequences of their victimisation.[11] Even where there is evidence the plaintiff's injuries have persisted longer than 'usual', plaintiffs are sometimes blamed for failure to seek treatment or deal with the effects of their victimisation in a timely manner (*Glendale v Drozdzik* [1990]: [16], [19], varied on other grounds: [2008] 1 SCR 27; Adjin-Tettey 2006: 52).

Perceiving intangible losses as short-lived means at most, compensation for such losses should be modest. To do otherwise may provide compensation for a period when the plaintiff no longer experiences those losses, or at least not to the same extent as at the time of judgment, and would constitute a windfall contrary to the compensatory goal of tort damages.[12] Meanwhile, expert accounts often come from a place of power and privilege. In addition to the experiential gap, these kinds of expert testimonies tend to be dispassionate perceptions of the effects of the plaintiff's victimisation.

Even assuming merits of the resilience rationale for denying or limiting compensation for intangible losses, it may not be justifiable in situations of conduct known to frequently result in long-term intangible injuries, such as sexual victimisation. This is not intended to pathologise survivors of sexual wrongdoing. Rather, it acknowledges the reality of their victimisation and the need for a contextualised response to survivors' claims for compensation while also bearing in mind the potential for exaggeration and malingering intended to attract higher damages (Godden, this volume).

Compensation argument

It has also been argued that emphasis should be on compensation for tangible harms rather than intangible harms. Consequently, there is a need to expand the bases and/or scope of compensation for tangible losses, and in return, limit or eliminate compensation for non-pecuniary losses (Abel 2006: 315–20; Ogus 1972: 17; *Hartling v Novia Scolta (Attorney General* [2009]: [88]–[94]). This is the model used in many no-fault systems, such as workers' compensation and no-fault automobile insurance regimes, and is sometimes seen as a better and more efficient way to spend society's limited resources (Cane 2006: 166). The compensation argument is implicitly premised on the hierarchy of harms and the alleged superiority of tangible compared to intangible harms, the incommensurability of intangible losses as well as the view that such harms are easily feigned and often not susceptible to scientific proof.

Further, the compensation argument is rooted in the idea of paramountcy of care – that it is better for plaintiffs to be adequately compensated for their pecuniary losses, especially care costs. There is no justification for additional compensation for intangible losses when that money would serve no useful purpose. At best, compensation for intangible losses must be modest (*Iwanik v Hayes* [2011]: [136]). Adoption of the functional approach by the Supreme Court of Canada in the 1978 personal injury trilogy was partly justified on the basis of the paramountcy of care and the desirability of not burdening society with compensation for intangible losses (*Andrews*: [87]–[90]).[13] Given the need for 'moderation' in the award of damages, generally because the public ultimately pays for these damages, modest non-pecuniary damages may be justifiable where the plaintiff has received substantial compensation for their tangible losses. However, the paramountcy of care argument is not justifiable in cases involving little or no tangible losses where the plaintiff has not otherwise received substantial damages.

Ex ante insurance argument

Critics have also invoked economic rationality as a reason for not awarding full compensation for non-pecuniary losses. Insurance is not something the plaintiff would have rationally purchased in advance as evidenced by the fact that there is no market for intangible losses. Rather, most rational people will insure against tangible losses such as lost income, which justifies compensation for such losses (Chapman 1995: 410; Atiyah 1997: 16). The insurance justification for modest or no compensation for intangible losses entails a privileging of tangible harms over intangible losses and presupposes that people will choose only to protect themselves against the former.

Meanwhile, how much a person would be prepared to spend to avoid intangible harms depends on their own financial status, which will vary from person to person. Thus, the *ex ante* insurance argument cannot be used to justify eliminating or diminishing compensation for intangible losses. Perhaps a better comparator might be how much an individual would be willing to accept in return for incurring the harm in question. However, this is still inadequate for determining availability and quantum of compensation for intangible losses because the individual's socio-economic location is likely to influence that decision, with wealthy people demanding a higher price compared to poorer people, thereby resulting in the perception of unequal moral worth. Ultimately, a regime that privileges tangible losses over intangible harms disadvantages those who suffer mostly non-pecuniary losses as is the case for survivors of sexual wrongdoing (Finley 2004: 1263). Further, the absence of insurance for intangible losses may in fact be a reason for compensation for such losses through the tort system and not its abolition.[14]

Functional approach argument

Similar to the incommensurability argument, the argument here is that monetary compensation for intangible losses cannot realistically restore a plaintiff to her *status quo ante* and is therefore not a good use of money, and also raises the problem of quantification (King 2004: 172–4, 180; Atiyah 1997: 15–16; Dobbs 1993: 398–9; Fischer 1999: 383; O'Connell 1981: 341–2; Radin 1993: 70). The Supreme Court of Canada acknowledged the impossibility of money to restore intangible losses in the 1978 personal injury trilogy, which also served as the basis for adopting the functional approach by which the purpose of the award is to give the plaintiff solace by providing substitutes for what has been lost rather than attempting to compensate the loss (*Andrews*: [87]–[90]; *Lindal*; *Abbott v Sharpe*, [2007].[15] The functional approach calls for an individualised assessment of the effect of the defendant's wrongdoing on the plaintiff and, more importantly, the amount necessary to provide her solace subject to the rough upper limit for non-pecuniary damages set in the trilogy. This requires evidence that non-pecuniary damages can make a difference in the plaintiff's situation through the purchase of some amenities.[16]

The functional approach for assessing non-pecuniary damages was adopted in the context of personal injury cases arising from motor vehicle-related accidents or, more generally, negligence claims. It has now been accepted that the functional approach is equally applicable in assessing non-pecuniary damages in sexual wrongdoing (battery) cases. However, the assessment requires a contextual approach that remains attentive to the nature of the injury and the purpose of the award in relation to that injury in particular circumstances (*BMG*: [124]–[126]). In claims for sexual battery, the purpose of the award is to provide solace for the victim's pain and suffering and loss of enjoyment of life, to vindicate the victim's dignity and personal autonomy, and to recognise the humiliating and degrading nature of the wrongful acts (*BMG*: [127]–[132]; *Evans*: [124]). Factors relevant to the assessment of non-pecuniary damages include the plaintiff's age at the time of the sexual interference and her vulnerability, the nature of the relationship between the plaintiff and the perpetrator, that is, any power imbalance or trust relationship, the nature and frequency of the abuse, consequences for the plaintiff, etc (*Plint*: [89]; *BMG*: [133]–[135]; *Evans*: [126]).

Commodification anxiety

Another argument against the availability of damages for intangible harms is that it commodifies such interests by trying to put a monetary value on aspects of human life that are priceless and treats these interests as alienable commodities that can be exchanged in the capitalist market contrary to the sacredness of human life, entailing a risk of normalising commodification and extending it to other aspects of life (Abel 2006, referring to Radin). A variant of the commodification anxiety is the issue of moral panic about the corruptibility of intangible interests when such interests are brought into the commercial sphere or subject to market analysis (O'Byrne 2009; Bandes 2000).

Arguments about commodification, inalienability and pricing the priceless tend to be made mostly in relation to issues that predominantly affect women, such as reproductive harms, surrogacy, egg donation, etc. Similarly, distributive justice has been evoked to justify non-compensation for some harms that women disproportionately suffer, such as the cost of raising a child conceived and/or born due to the negligence of health care professionals (*McFarlane v Tayside Health Board* [1999]; *MY v Boutros* [2002]; *Bevilacqua v Altenkirk* [2004]; *Mummery v Olsson* [2001]), and equality justice claims by women (*Newfoundland (Treasury Board) v NAPE* [2004]).

Further, the desire to justify compensation only where there is a monetary equivalence of the loss in question is grounded in an instrumentalist view of tort damages that treats such interests as fungible commodities with a consequent dehumanisation of intangible aspects of human life. Also, limited or no compensation for intangible losses means damages awards do not reflect the true social costs of the injurer's conduct; compensation is determined not by corrective justice or the plaintiff's entitlement to have the defendant set things right. Rather, the innocent plaintiff is made to bear part of the costs resulting from the defendant's wrongdoing. This, coupled with the often depressed damages for marginalised plaintiffs, the prime targets for sexual victimisation, exacerbates the vulnerability of such persons to sexual abuse, devalues their bodily integrity and security, and undermines efforts to address a serious social problem.[17] At the very least, compensation for intangible losses reaffirms the societal interest in and respect for values such as bodily security and autonomy even if the defendant's wrongdoing does not result in tangible injuries and no monetary equivalent is possible (Goldberg 2003: 525, 527; Radin 1993: 61).[18] It also recognises the need for restoring normative equilibrium (assuming an egalitarian *status quo*) where one person has wrongfully interfered with another's protected interests as mandated by corrective justice (Zipursky 2003: 695). A strictly economic analysis for the justification of monetary damages ignores the disruption in the plaintiff's life caused by the defendant's wrongful conduct regardless of the form of the loss and whether it has currency in the market. Such an approach also offends a law and economic analysis of tort law because the wrongdoer does not fully bear the consequences of their wrongdoing and there is no indication that such a position maximises the overall societal welfare. In fact, externalisation of some of the consequences of sexual victimisation makes not just the victim, but society as a whole, worse off.[19] Further, an approach that undervalues intangible harms and perpetuates systemic discrimination can hardly be considered just from a distributive justice perspective.

There is no reason why plaintiffs' losses should be valued only in instrumentalist terms, specifically reductive instrumentalism (Zipursky 2003: 697). Accepting the incommensurability of such interests, Radin suggests a non-commodified approach to valuation of the plaintiff's losses. She notes that the difficulties posed by incommensurability of intangible losses may be avoided by thinking of tort damages not as rectification but rather as redress and public acknowledgement of the interference with the plaintiff's rights, for example the right to bodily inviolability. Compensation is justified within a redress paradigm as a symbol of respect for the right in issue, the necessity to restore moral balance between the parties, and disapproval of the defendant's wrongful conduct without the need to resort to an economic analysis of the loss as demanded by the rectification theory (Radin 1993: 61, 69).[20] This non-instrumentalist and non-commodified approach to personhood demands respect for personal inviolability and engenders a sense of diminishment in victims regardless of the nature of interest interfered with, consistent with the Kantian notion of equal respect for all persons (Richardson 2007: 41). In Jean Hampton's model of Feminist Contractarianism, she recognises this Kantian notion and the idea that all people have an intrinsic, non-instrumental value, and to recognise that persons are deserving of reciprocity – for her argument, reciprocity in terms of morality and relationships – does not commodify them, or make them commodities in society. Conceiving of relationship and morality in terms of a 'contract' does not mean the persons involved are mere commodities, nor does it detract from the person's intrinsic self worth (Hampton 2002). A non-commodified approach to compensation for intangible injuries can result in an optimal and efficient regime of tort law:

> one that is both just and moral . . . It advises those behaving under its regimen of what is expected, of what is discouraged, and of the consequences of departure from the desirable. It does not compensate excessively, but rather, in proportion to the harm. Neither does it under-compensate, as only through justifiable compensation is the rule's deterrent value most effective.
>
> (Madden 2005: 47)

Intangible injuries are generally considered suspect and susceptible to exaggeration by victims. Arguments against intangible losses marginalise non-pecuniary interests and perpetuate the privatisation of such injuries, which in turn has detrimental consequences for plaintiffs who suffer predominantly intangible losses such as survivors of sexual victimisation.

Misconception about the nature of non-pecuniary losses

Notwithstanding concerns about intangible losses, financial compensation for these harms is considered a legitimate aim of tort damages (Cane 2006: 4). Arguments against compensation for non-pecuniary losses are partly premised on a conflation of adjusting to the effects of one's victimisation with the elimination of the psychological consequences of the defendant's wrongdoing. It also takes the focus away from the basis of the claim – violation of the plaintiff's fundamental right to bodily inviolability. The misconception about non-pecuniary losses is compounded for survivors of sexual wrongdoing given there is often an experiential gap by those who have not been similarly victimised, and who lack appreciation of the magnitude and effects of the victimisation (West 1991: 117; Feldthusen 1994: 133; Omatsu 1999: 181). It must be noted that while the experiential gap does not preclude the possibility of empathy and appreciation of the experiences of victim-isation, the possibility or likelihood of patronising attitudes is likely to influence perceptions not just about the sexual wrongdoing but also the nature, magnitude and duration of the effects of that victimisation.[21] Also, the expectation of diminishment and eventual elimination of non-pecuniary losses is inconsistent with evidence that the effects of sexual victimisation often entail short- and long-term consequences. It also diminishes hopes of fair compensation for sexual abuse to truly reflect the nature of that experience and the magnitude of its effects on survivors.

Hierarchy of harms/responses to tortious injury

Harm is socially constructed, such that particular victimisations may be recognised as legal harms only to the extent permitted by the law (Conaghan 1996: 429) and are often divorced from survivors' subjective experiences. The perception of pecuniary losses as commanding greater justification for compensation than non-pecuniary damages entails normative judgments about those interests and privileges the former, inter alia, based on marketability. Devaluation of non-pecuniary damages may reinforce and exacerbate existing inequalities (Abel 2006: 303).

Valuing consequential financial losses more than intangible losses could also be understood as gendered characterisation of harms, marginalising women's vic-timisation and reinforcing the use of men as the normative standard for assessing responses to tortious injuries (Godden, this volume). In *Theobald v Ry Passengers' Assurance Co* [1854], Pollock CJ stated that it was 'an unmanly thing to make such a claim. Such injuries are part of the ills of life, of which every man ought to take his share' (Abel 2006: 315). This shows how decision makers' values and idio-syncrasies, sometimes reflecting majoritarian values, can influence their perception of what constitutes legitimate harms or losses as well as their value (Abel 2006: 313–14).

The tendency is to take serious tangible harms inflicted in public places or that have a public manifestation, directly impacting what occurs in the public sphere such as inability to participate in the capitalist market.[22] On the other hand, intangible harms affect one's inner being and may not be immediately visible. The perception is that such harms tend to be exaggerated and are consequently highly suspicious (Abel 2006: 303–4) and/or something that is simply to be endured, and therefore not the proper domain of tort compensation. This perception of emotional or psychological harms has defined and continues to influence liability for psychological injuries or nervous shock (Ruda 1993: 216–19). Perceiving tangible injuries as the proper domain of tort law underlies not only the limited scope of recovery but also the requirement that the assault on the plaintiff's psyche must be severe, with a physical manifestation of the nervous shock in the form of a recognisable psychiatric injury, and recovery is limited to situations where an objectively reasonable person would have reacted in a similar manner (*Mustapha v Culligan* [2008]). This apparently neutral conceptualisation of tangible and intangible injuries fails to acknowledge the gender bias in such a characterisation that favours harms traditionally associated with the public, male dominated sphere while undervaluing injuries typically associated with women (Conaghan 1996: 75; Spitz 2005: 433).

The privileging of tangible over intangible harms is partly rooted in classical Western thought, specifically the Cartesian reason/emotion dualism and the perception of 'public' and/or tangible harms as the paradigmatic tortious injury. The foundational values of tort law are linked to Cartesian conception of the two worlds which has informed theories about the dualism of the body and mind. For Descartes, the mind and body are separate and distinct entities and they inhabit separate spheres; the public and private respectively (Baker and Morris 1996: 11). Also, the two spheres have an oppositional relationship with one another. Descartes argued that 'in order to attain knowledge or reason, one had to detach one's essential self – or mind – from one's passionate and irrational self – or body' (Spitz 2005: 436). Within this mind and body dualism, Descartes theorised that reason was located in the mind and emotion, while interacting in some respects with the mind, was essentially based in the body. Emotions, or passions as Descartes referred to them, interact with the rational mind through their origins in the body. Since the body 'is baser, it is mundane, it is inferior, and it is natural' (Naffine 1998: 202), this suggests that the reasonable mind is superior to the emotional body. In its basic components, the Cartesian dualism values the reasonable mind over the physical body, which is the originating source of emotions (Baker and Morris 1996: 59; Prokhovnik 2002: 63).

Feminist scholars have argued that gender stereotypes based on socially constructed dichotomies have influenced the development of tort law through the Cartesian dualism and association of women with emotion and irrationality. For instance, Spitz argues that women have historically been associated with emotion whereas men have traditionally been associated with reason. She states:

> Over time, that oppositional association came to simply be: men are rational; women are irrational; men are reasonable; women are emotional. Therefore, men's injuries are reasonable and compensable; women's injuries are unreasonable, if not imaginary.
>
> (Spitz 2005: 436)[23]

This characterisation of compensable injury is reflected in the assessment of damages for tortious injury. Damages in tort law are based on rationality rather than emotions and the privileging of tangible over intangible harms as the proper focus of tort compensation. Among other things, tangible harms are perceived to be 'public', capable of objective verification and hence deserve greater protection compared to intangible harms that tend to be experienced subjectively. Naffine argues that self-ownership or a property right in oneself is 'conceived as mind controlling body'. It is this notion of property rights in oneself that underlies the law's protection of bodily autonomy and integrity (Naffine 1998: 205). Hence, it is desirable to recognise tangible harms as attacks on the property rights of the rational mind. However, the invisible aspects of the consequences of interference with autonomy interests have not received the same attention as legitimate losses compared to tangible harms, partly based on the dichotomous worldview rooted in Cartesian dualism.

'Privatising' sexual wrongdoing

Changing attitudes towards sexual victimisation have enabled survivors to increasingly seek justice through the tort system for victimisation that occurs mostly in private. Notwithstanding the public purpose of actions for sexual abuse and as a response to a social problem, specifically exploitation of unequal power relationships, remediation for sexual victimisation is perceived as a matter of individual rather than societal responsibility. 'Privatisation' of the consequences of sexual victimisation is also evident in the characterisation of such harms as intentional and hence excluded from indemnification under liability insurance and the loss spreading goal of modern tort law (Reaume 2004; Brown and Randall 2004; *Scalera*: [95 ff]; *JAS v Gross* [2002]). Even where plaintiffs successfully establish their claims of sexual victimisation against the perpetrator, there is no guarantee of recovering damages from the perpetrator. It is not uncommon in historical abuse claims for perpetrators to be impecunious, in prison or dead, with no assets to satisfy the plaintiff's losses. Meanwhile, intentional/criminal injury exclusions in insurance contracts prevent indemnification through the insurance system (*Non-Marine Underwriters Lloyd's of London v Scalera* [2000]: [91]–[94]).[24] Emphasis in such cases is on corrective justice, direct responsibility, accountability and deterrence.[25] Within this framework, liability is expected to be borne personally by the perpetrator, not society.[26] While the emphasis on individual responsibility appears appropriate in deliberate and targeted abuse of vulnerable persons, it also raises a potential for re-victimisation given the high likelihood of unsatisfied judgments. In the end, the inability of individual perpetrators to satisfy damage awards undermines the expected deterrent objective of individual responsibility (Arlen and MacLeod 2005: 122–3).[27] Although monetary awards serve a public function by signalling societal disapproval of the defendant's wrongdoing (Hammond 2010: 186), the personal responsibility rationale for the intentional/criminal injury exclusion subordinates victims' interests to allegedly broader societal interests.

In the context of sexual wrongdoing, the admonitory and deterrent rationale supports a view of individual responsibility of perpetrators and creates/reinforces the perception of sexual wrongdoing as stemming from individual perpetrators' moral failures rather than a societal problem deserving collective responses. This belies the prevalence of sexual victimisation as well as the resulting human and social costs. More importantly, the focus on personal responsibility, deterrence and the resulting exclusion of damages for sexual wrongdoing from the liability insurance regime has a disproportionate effect on survivors who are often marginalised on the basis of gender, racialisation, age, disability, etc (Reaume 2004).

Perpetrators are often judgment-proof, making it unlikely survivors will obtain compensation. A plaintiff's losses may be made good through first party insurance. However, given the often marginalised status of victims of sexual wrongdoing, few will have such coverage.[28] Liability of third parties based on, for example, negligence, vicarious liability or breach of fiduciary duty, may provide additional/effective sources of compensation. While compensation may also be obtained from publicly-funded schemes, it is often inadequate as compensation may be capped and/or limited to certain types of losses.[29] The rationales for limited benefits under publicly-funded schemes include limiting financial obligations of taxpayers (Brown and Randall 2004: 331; Ontario 1997). However, if sexual victimisation is a social problem, why should compensation be constrained by the impact on the public purse or a charity-minded approach (Brown and Randall 2004: 339–41)?[30] If harms from sexual wrongdoing are often non-economic, then exclusion of non-pecuniary losses has a particularly gendered effect given that victims continue to be disproportionately female and are also often marginalised on other grounds such as race and disability.

Lack of, or inadequate compensation for, sexual victimisation may undermine the desire to seek redress and exacerbate the effects of victimisation, resulting in anti-therapeutic outcomes for a serious social problem that mostly affects women and other vulnerable groups. The exclusion of intentional torts from the liability insurance regime, and accordingly the opportunity for loss spreading, is premised on the paradigmatic view of tortious injury as arising from accidental conduct associated with industrialisation and interference with physical integrity and security, without recognising the broader range of interests protected by modern tort law such as emotional well being and dignitary interests (Wriggins 2005: 143–4, 154).[31] This failure also devalues such interests as is evident in the tort system's response to intangible harms. Also, it ignores the importance of liability insurance for tort liability and the former being a mechanism for the loss/risk spreading function of modern tort law. The inability to obtain compensation from tortfeasors deprives survivors of material benefits of successful actions and undermines judicial and legislative initiatives that have improved survivors' access to the civil justice system such as generous constructions or elimination of limitation periods.[32]

Punitive damages

Sexual victimisation involves the intentional violation of personal autonomy, bodily integrity and security compared to other forms of bodily interferences (*Scalera*: [37]; Adjin-Tettey 2006: 1, 20). It is often an act of aggression and is oppressive. It can also be dehumanising and robs victims of their human dignity, personhood, and sexual autonomy and exacerbates their vulnerability (*Osolin*: [165]; Adjin-Tettey 2006: 20). It often involves abuse of trust, thereby making it reprehensible, high-handed and in disregard for the physical and emotional integrity/well being of vulnerable persons. These factors make punitive damages readily available for sexual abuse.[33] Although not compensatory, punitive damages increase the overall damages award for survivors, and may be important in remedying sexual victimisation, especially given the increasing resistance to compensation for non-pecuniary losses.

Although punitive damages would often be appropriate in cases of sexual wrongdoing,[34] the purpose of such damages is punishment, deterrence or retribution rather than compensation. The focus of punitive damages is on the enforcement of social norms and has been referred to as 'socially compensatory damages' because the goal of such damages is 'to make society whole' compared to compensatory damages that are designed 'to make the individual victim whole' (*Ciraolo v City of New York* [2000]: [245]). The focus of punitive damages is on broader societal interests and not the plaintiff's harms. This runs the conceptual risk of diminishing harm to the individual and therefore justice between the doer and sufferer.

Availability and quantum of punitive damages in Canada are limited by the rationality test, whereby punitive damages are warranted only if the defendant's conduct is outrageous, reprehensible, high-handed, and compensatory damages, including aggravated damages, do not adequately punish the defendant (*Whiten v Pilot Insurance* [2002]; *Honda Canada Inc v Keays* [2008]; *Performance Industries Ltd v Sylvan Lake Golf and Tennis Club Ltd* [2002]; *Fidler v Sun Life Assurance Co of Canada*, [2006]; *Pawlett v Dominion Protection Services Ltd* [2008]; *MLH v RGR* [2007]).[35] Prior criminal sanctions may be a reason for courts not to award punitive damages because there is no additional need for punishment and deterrence (see *Fleury v Fleury* [2001]; *BO v ET* [1994]: [20]–[22]; *MLH v RGR* [2007], Gillese JA (dissenting); *McIntyre v Grigg* [2006]: [76]; *Sage v Renner* [2007]: [76]). This will often arise in cases of sexual victimisation where the defendant's conduct is usually also criminal. There may still be room for punitive damages, for example where a court finds criminal punishment inadequate (although some courts prefer not to question the adequacy of criminal sanctions in civil suits given the variety of factors a court considers in arriving at an appropriate punishment), or where criminal prosecution was not for exactly the same conduct as the tort action. The effect is that punitive damages may not be awarded (*Hockley*; *KK v KWG*; *AJ v Cairnie Estate* [1999]; *MB v British Columbia* [2000]; *JG v SAG* [1998]; *Loveridge v British Columbia* [2006]; *RBL v British Columbia* [2006]) or the amount may be considerably low.[36]

Even when available, punitive damages may not necessarily increase survivors' damages. The perpetrator may be insolvent or deceased, which is common in historical abuse claims.[37] Further, punitive damages may not be awarded against third parties held liable for plaintiff's victimisation, for example on the basis of negligence.[38] Punitive damages may also be inappropriate against vicariously liable defendants absent reprehensible conduct specifically attributable to the employer (*Plint*; *Hill* v Church of Scientology [1995]: [195]). Additionally, unlike compensatory damages, there is no joint and several liability for punitive damages (*Plint*), further limiting its availability.

Conclusion

Survivors of sexual wrongdoing are increasingly seeking justice through the tort system, with some success in establishing liability. However, remedies for sexual victimisation may not adequately reflect efforts to improve access to the civil justice system for survivors, principally because harms from sexual victimisation tend to be mostly intangible. Tort reformers view intangible injuries as suspect and have criticised compensation for interference with such interests as inconsistent with the make-whole goal of tort damages, and hence should be abolished or be limited to modest amounts. Although tort law continues to recognise intangible injuries, compensation for such losses tend to be modest, especially when unaccompanied by tangible injuries. Inadequate compensation can discourage plaintiffs from initiating actions and may exacerbate the effects of victimisation, resulting in anti-therapeutic outcomes for a serious social problem that mostly affects women and members of other vulnerable groups. As Daylen et al states:

> In the event that the court denies a claim for damages, or the award falls short of that expected, the plaintiff could feel devastated. Such an outcome can exacerbate pre-existing problems (for example, low self-esteem, depression, or mistrust) or can lead to emotional difficulties not previously experienced. In some cases, the plaintiff may feel victimised by the system and cynical about the world in general. Some plaintiffs become preoccupied, ruminating about the litigation or their victimisation. Their thoughts may provoke self-blame, anger, anxiety, or depression and may increase the risk of unhealthy coping. These plaintiffs may have considerable difficulty moving on with their lives or managing these distressing thoughts and feelings.
>
> (Daylen et al 2006: 415–16)

Given the obstacles that survivors continue to face in obtaining compensation in the tort system, Brown and Randall (2004) advocate an improved public compensation scheme that will systematically remedy sexual victimisation similar to other regimes such as workers' compensation and no-fault automobile insurance. The rationale for the proposal is the comparable social and economic consequences of sexual victimisation and these other sources of harm. This will make compensation for sexual victimisation a social responsibility comparable to industrial and automobile-related injuries. In proposing this scheme, Brown and Randall do not advocate abandoning tort law as an avenue for sexual and domestic violence. Rather, they note that given the limits and complexities of the tort system and its inability to provide adequate compensation for survivors, there needs to be a publicly-funded system to provide effective compensation.

An effective publicly-funded system would be an ideal solution, among other things, because all survivors will benefit from such a scheme, but it remains utopian at least for the moment, especially in light of current financial constraints and the increasing privatisation of care and responsibility characteristic of the neo-liberal state (Cane 2006: 16–19). Although the tort system is a forensic lottery that benefits only a few tort victims generally and survivors of sexual victimisation in particular, it is important that we pay attention to gendered issues regarding compensation within that system. The focus of compensation, whether for tangible or intangible losses, should be on what is necessary to adequately compensate plaintiffs for their losses and not fairness to defendants or society generally (Luntz 2002: 1.1.7; Goldberg 2006: 437).

Notes

*   Thanks to Freya Kodar for helpful discussions about this chapter. Thanks also to Rose Keates, Lianne Kramchynski, Lindsay Rodenburg and Natalie Smith for their research assistance.

1   See also *R v McCraw* [1991]: [28] where Cory J notes the serious consequences of sexual assaults on victims compared to non-sexual assaults.

2   Complainants may obtain remedies under no-fault schemes such as crime victims' compensation schemes. Benefits may be limited to economic losses and/or capped. See Crime Victim Assistance Act, SBC 2001, c 38 and Crime Victim Assistance (General) Regulation, BC Reg 161/2002, Crime Victim Assistance (Income and Vocational Services or Expenses Benefits) Regulation, BC Reg 162/2002; Victims of Crime Act, RSA 2000, c V-3 and Victims of Crime Regulation, Alta Reg 63/2004; Victims of Crime Act, SS 1995, c V-6.011 and Victims of Crime Regulations, 1997, RRS c V-6.011 Reg 1; Victims' Bill of Rights, CCSM, c V55 and Designated Offences Regulation, Man Reg 138/2001, Victims' Rights Regulation, Man Reg 214/98; Compensation for Victims of Crime Act, RSO 1990, c C.24; Crime Victims Compensation Act, RSQ, c I-6; Victims Services Act, SNB 1987, c V-2.1 and Compensation for Victims of Crime Regulation, NB Reg 96-81; Compensation for Victims of Crime Act, RSNS 1989, c 83; Victims of Crime Act, RSPEI 1988, c V-3.1 and General Regulations, PEI Reg EC566/89; Victims of Crime Act, RSNWT (Nu) 1988, c 9.

3   One reason charges may not be laid in sexual assault cases is because the perpetrator is deceased (Brennan 2008: 11, (Table 1)).

4   See Estate Administration Act, 1996 RSBC, c 122, ss 59–61; Estate Administration Act, RSY 2002, c 77, ss 59–61; Trustee Act, 1990 RSO, c T.23, s 38(2).

5   Strict constructions of enterprise liability, especially in relation to sexual wrongdoing, can undermine its potential as a progressive development in tort law: *Bazley* [42]; *Jacobi v Griffiths* [1999]; *EB v Order of the Oblates of Mary Immaculate in the Province of British Columbia* [2005]; *H (SG) v Gorsline* [2004] ABCA 186; 354 AR 46; Feldthusen (2007); Adjin-Tettey (2007); Dickinson (2001–02).

6   Mechanisms for limiting compensation for intangible losses include judicial and legislative caps: *Andrews v Grand and Toy Alberta Ltd* [1978]: [87]–[98]; *Injury Regulation – Insurance Act*, NB Reg 2003-20, s 4; *Automobile Insurance Tort Recovery Limitation Regulations*, NS Reg 182/2003, s 3; *Minor Injury Regulation*, Alta Reg 123/2004, s 6. Courts have affirmed the constitutionality of these regulations. See *Hartling v Nova Scotia (Attorney General)*, [2009], affd: [2009] NSCA 130, application for leave to appeal to SCC dismissed: *Gionet v Nova Scotia (Attorney General)* [2010]; *Morrow v Zhang*, [2009], leave to appeal to SCC dismissed, [2009] SCCA. Similar limits on non-economic losses exist in other jurisdictions. See Civil Liability Act, 2002 (NSW), s 16. The characterisation of predominantly gendered interests and hence their devaluation in the tort system is also evident in the perception of impaired capacity to perform housework following tortious injury as intangible losses where the plaintiff did not obtain replacement services and the devaluation of care work for the benefit of accident victims. See Graycar, this volume.

7 See also Atiyah (1997: 14–15).
8 See also Jaffe (1953: 224–5, 231). It must be noted that given the cap on non-pecuniary damages and the functional approach, higher damages is unlikely to be an issue in the Canadian system and specifically in the context of claims for sexual wrongdoing. Awards for sexual wrongdoing can range from $25,000 to $300,000; see *MA*: [86]–[93].
9 Attitudes towards compensation for intangible injuries generally may be contrasted with compensation for defamation, which tends to be higher. General damages are presumed and the award is to intended to compensate the plaintiff for damage to their reputation and mental distress caused by the defamation. See *Cragg v Stephens* [2010]: [29]–[30]; *Hill v Church of Scientology* [1995]. Compensation is not dependent on evidence that the award of money can remedy the damage to the plaintiff's reputation. Given the historical exclusion of women from the public domain, it becomes clear that actions in defamation protects men's public persona without regard to incommensurability concerns.
10 Based on the utility argument, it has been suggested that compensation for the cost of services such as therapy is only justifiable in relation to present and future non-pecuniary losses but not for past losses since the plaintiff cannot purchase reasonable substitutes for past loss (Chapman 1995: 420, 421).
11 Sutherland (1993) has argued that the experiential gap will be rectified if courts were to give greater weight to victim's own stories about their victimisation rather than through the lens of power and privilege that often characterise expert testimonies. See also Streseman (1995: note 208).
12 Criticisms of damages for intangible losses seem to be stronger in relation to future losses because of the uncertainty of whether the plaintiff will continue to experience those losses, and the extent and duration of those losses. This is a general critique of the lump sum system and not peculiar to damages for non-pecuniary losses. For example, see Jaffe (1953: 253), who notwithstanding his objection to compensation for intangible losses notes that compensation for past intangible losses may be justifiable in cases of intentional wrongdoing.
13 The other cases in the trilogy are *Teno v Arnold* [1978]; *Thornton v Prince George School District No 57* [1978]. These cases involved catastrophically injured plaintiffs who received significant amounts for their tangible losses (although the female plaintiff in *Teno* received a depressed award for her impaired working capacity based on her gender and parental background). There appears to be some uneasiness where others, usually the general public, have to pay for a plaintiff's intangible injuries in addition to paying for their tangible losses. It appears that compensation for intangible losses may seem justifiable where they are paid for by tortfeasors similar to punitive damages (Cane 2006: 410, 415). This view of compensation for intangible losses supports a personal responsibility model for such losses and is consistent with the attitude towards sexual victimisation as a private matter.
14 For a critique of the insurance argument, see Croley and Hanson (1995).
15 King (2004: 174–6) critiques the solace rationale as substituting one form of incommensurability for another and, in any event, does not avoid the difficulties of valuation and disparity in awards.
16 Hence, the plaintiff's cognitive awareness and ability to appreciate the expenditure of money are supposed to be an important indicator of the availability and quantum of non-pecuniary damages. This partly explains why unconscious plaintiffs receive limited or no compensation for non-pecuniary losses. See *Knutson v Farr* [1984]; *Wipfli v Britten* [1984]. Although the functional approach continues to provide the philosophical underpinning for non-pecuniary damages, the spirit of that approach may be weakening as some courts are awarding significant amounts, sometimes close to the rough upper limit, for plaintiffs with severe cognitive deficiencies who may not appreciate the expenditure of money. See *Strachan (Guardian ad litem of) v Winder* [2005]; *Chow v Hiscock* [2005]; *Brimacombe v Mathews* [2001], leave to appeal refused: [2001] SCCA No 325.

17 In addition to low compensation for tangible losses such as impaired working capacity based on factors such as gender, race, class, disability, etc (Adjin-Tettey (2007b); Adjin-Tettey (2010)), there is also empirical evidence that marginalisation status, especially race, influences valuation of tortious injuries and settlements offered by insurance companies (Galligan, et al 2007: 16).

18 This rationale has been used, among others, to justify recognition of tort claims to protect purely intangible interests such as assault and false imprisonment. Also, the same rationale underlies the position that actions for trespass to the person should be actionable without proof of damage and the reversal of onus in such actions under Canadian law. See *Non-Marine Underwriters Lloyd's of London v Scalera* [2000].

19 Law and economics and corrective justice approaches to tort law tend to be at odds, with the former focusing on economic efficiency and deterrence, and the latter primarily concerned with compensation and justice between the parties (Zipursky 2003: 669–706). However, under- or no compensation for intangible harms is one area where these two otherwise opposing theories of tort law could both support better recognition and compensation for such harms.

20 Economic theorists like Chapman (1995: 425) will respond to the redress argument that given the fact of incommensurablity and the futility of money damages in relation to non-pecuniary losses, the plaintiff will likely spend the money to improve their welfare in other areas of her life unrelated to the consequences of the defendant's wrongful conduct. Chapman finds this possibility inconsistent with a corrective justice rationale and a reason for nominal damages for non-pecuniary losses.

21 Sutherland (1993) notes that it is likely many members of the judiciary are increasingly appreciating the nature and consequences of sexual victimisation and hence may be in a better position to assess the damages in such cases. However, this awareness and sensitivity is not reflected in the quantum of awards for such injuries.

22 Wriggins (2005: 143–4, 153) notes that tort law's preoccupation with tangible harms and/or those that occur in public places stem from the fact that tort law and, in particular, negligence liability, evolved in response to industrialisation, specifically harm in public places (work) resulting from the process of industrialisation. Thus, tortious injury is often conceptualised as physical injury.

23 See also, for example, Prokhovnik (2002: 1, 4, 7, 75).

24 In Canada, battery may be committed either intentionally or negligently – *Cook v Lewis* [1951], affirmed in *Scalera*: [4], [5]. However, the Court held in *Scalera* that sexual battery can only be committed intentionally.

25 This ties to the idea of outcome responsibility; see Honoré (1995: 81–3); Wriggins (2001: 165).

26 In *Y(S) v C (FG)* [1996], the BCCA justified the inapplicability of the cap on non-pecuniary damages in cases of sexual wrongdoing, among other things, because it will not detrimentally affect the public purse or be a drain on insurance funds principally because the defendant will be personally responsible for paying damages.

27 Although these comments were made in the context of vicarious liability and arguments against agent liability in thinking about optimum tort rules, it is equally applicable in thinking more generally about the deterrent goals of tort liability and the overall effectiveness of the tort regime.

28 First party insurance tends to be an employment benefit and hence available to those with standard employment with benefits. Protection may also be purchased through professional associations or by individuals with disposable income. The purchase of optional insurance is often perceived as a prudent thing to do and also a matter of choice for individuals. This neo-liberal argument ignores the fact that true choice must be predicated on a prior just distribution of resources, which is not the case in the liberal state.

29 See range of compensation available under crime victim legislation in some Canadian jurisdictions. Compensation may be capped for as low as $10,000; see Compensation for Victims of Crime Regulation, NB Reg 96-81, s 6(1). For example, there is currently no compensation for non-pecuniary losses in British Columbia (see Criminal Injury Compensation Act, RSBC 1996, c 85, s 2(4.1)) and benefits under the scheme may be capped at $50,000 (Criminal Injury Compensation Act, ibid, s 13(1)). There are similar limitations on compensation under such schemes in other jurisdictions; see also, Cane (2006: 319–24).

30 Most provinces compensate victims based on surcharges collected on provincial and federal offences. Compensation in Nova Scotia is provided through a Consolidated Revenue Fund; see Nova Scotia, Department of Justice Victims' Services Division Activity Report: 1 April 1998 – 31 March 1999, online: 22. In Saskatchewan, the Victims of Crime Act, 1995 allows for funds from the general revenue fund to be advanced to the victims' fund; see Victims of Crime Act, 1995, SS 1995, c V-6.011, s 6(2)(d).

31 Similarly, the common law has not shown enthusiasm about recognising and compensating for intangible personal losses usually due to invasions of a person's privacy. It is particularly telling that the movement to recognise the importance of privacy interests started with providing remedies for misappropriation of a person's name or likeness for financial purposes, something that transcends the private nature of the wrong and brings it into the public sphere of the market as well as a medium for evaluating the wrong, that is, in economic terms (Osbourne 2007: 253–4).

32 Reasons for liberal limitation regimes include recognition of the devastating nature of sexual victimisation and the need to ensure access to justice. Also, the effects of sexual wrongdoing may not become apparent until later in the future and, even then, the victim may not immediately associate these effects with the sexual wrongdoing – see discussion in the context of incest in M(K) v M(H) [1992]: [25]–[26].

33 Finley (2004: 1307) suggests that, in the United States, punitive damages awards are more frequent in sexual wrongdoing actions than other tort actions as they are more likely to involve egregious behaviour.

34 See McLachlin's description of sexual battery as a deliberate and targeted conduct against the victim in Scalera: [21]; Norberg: [26], [58]–[59], La Forest J. See generally Aoláin (2009: note 2).

35 Relevant factors, in addition to the amount of compensatory damages, include the defendant's conduct, such as admission of liability and goodwill gestures towards the plaintiff, for example an apology and not raising defences that could otherwise defeat the plaintiff's claim such as the limitation defence. See Muir v Alberta [1996], 179 AR 321 (QB).

36 See WRB v Plint [2001] (punitive damages for multiple plaintiffs of $40,000, $20,000, $5,000, $20,000, $2,000, $3,000); Plouffe v Roy [2007] ($10,000); MK (total award, including punitive damages: $50,000); Norberg ($10,000); P(V) v Canada (Attorney General) [2000] ($25,000).

37 Generally, punitive damages may not be awarded where the perpetrator is deceased. Although an award of punitive damages may serve the goal of general deterrence, there will be no specific deterrence in such cases. See JES v Estate of PDM (Official Administrator of) [1998]: [22]; KLM v RJP. Estate [2001]: [103]; in both cases the Court refused to grant punitive damages because the defendant was deceased and such damages would have no deterrent effect. However, see also SAD v EEP Estate [2003]: [159]–[160], where the court awarded punitive damages against the perpetrator's estate.

38 Punitive damages are rarely awarded for negligent conduct, among other things, because liability is based on objective fault and not subjective blameworthiness, thereby not warranting the need for punishment in many cases.

Cases

AJ v Cairnie Estate [1999] MJ No 176
Abbott v Sharpe [2007] NSCA 6
Andrews v Grand and Toy Alberta Ltd [1978] 2 SCR 229
Bazley v Curry [1999] 2 SCR 534
Blackwater v Plint [2005] SCC 58
BMG v Nova Scotia [2007] NSCA 120
BO v ET [1994] YJ No 14
Bevilacqua v Altenkirk [2004] BCSC 945
Brimacombe v Mathews [2001] BCCA 206
CCB (Litigation Guardian of) v IB [2009] BCSC 1425
CM v Canada (Attorney General) [2004] SKQB 174, 248 Sask. R.1
Chow v Hiscock [2005], 41 CCLT (3d) 155 (BCSC)
Ciraolo v City of New York [2000] 216 F3d 236, CA 2
Conklin v Smith [1978] 2 SCR 1107
Cook v Lewis [1951] SCR 830
Cragg v Stephens [2010] BCSC 1177
EB v Order of the Oblates of Mary Immaculate in the Province of British Columbia [2005] 3 SCR 45; 2005 SCC 60
EDG v Hammer [1998] 53 B.C.L.R. (3d) 89 (BCSC)
Evans v Sproule [2008] OJ No 4518 (SCJ)
Fleury v Fleury [2001] OJ No 1720 (CA)
Fidler v Sun Life Assurance Co of Canada [2006] SCC 30
Gionet v Nova Scotia (Attorney General) [2010] SCCA No 63
Glendale v Drozdzik [1990] BCJ No 1489 (SC)
Gray v Reeves [1991] 89 DLR (4th) 315
H (SG) v Gorsline [2004] ABCA 186; 354 AR 46
Hartling v Nova Scotia (Attorney General) [2009] NSSC 2
Hill v Church of Scientology [1995] 2 SCR 1130
Hockley v Riley [2007] ONCA 804, 880.R. (3d) 1
Honda Canada Inc v Keays [2008] SCC 39
Iwanik v Hayes [2011] BCSC 812
JAS v Gross [2002] ABCA 36, 299 AR 111
JES v Estate of PDM (Official Administrator of) [1998] BCJ No 1461 (SC)
JG v SAG [1998] NSJ No 234
J(LA) v J(H) [1993] 13 OR (3d) 306 (Gen Div)
Jacobi v Griffiths [1999] 2 SCR 570
KIM v RJP Estate [2001] OJ No 1691 (Sup Ct J)
KK v KWG [2006] OJ No 2672 varied on other grounds: 2008 ONCA 489, 90 OR (3d) 481
KM v Canada (Attorney General) [2004] SKQB 287, 251 Sask R 12
Knutson v Farr [1984] 55 BCLR 145 (BCCA)
Lindal v Lindal (No 2) [1981] 2 SCR 629
Loveridge v British Columbia [2006] BCSC 966
MA v Canada (Attorney General) [2001] SKQB 504; 212 Sask R 241
MB v British Columbia [2000] BCJ No 909
M(K) v M(H) [1992] 3 SCR 6
MLH v RGR [2007] 88 OR (3d) 1 (CA)
MY v Boutros [2002] ABQB 362
McFarlane v Tayside Health Board [1999] 4 All ER 961 (HL)
McIntyre v Grigg [2006] 83 OR (3d) 161 (CA)
Morris v Rose Estate [1996] BCCA 263
Morrow v Zhang [2009] ABCA 215
MLH v RGR [2007] ONCA 804

Muir v Alberta (1996) 179 AR 321 (QB)
Mummery v Olsson [2001] OJ No 226 (Sup Ct J)
Mustafa v Culligan [2008] SCC 27
Newfoundland (Treasury Board) v NAPE [2004] SCC 66
Non-Marine Underwriters Lloyd's of London v Scalera [2000] 1 SCR 551
Norberg v Wynrib [1992] 2 SCR 226
P(V) v Canada (Attorney General) [2000] 1 WWR 541
Pawlett v Dominion Protection Services Ltd [2008] ABCA 369
Performance Industries Ltd v Sylvan Lake Golf and Tennis Club Ltd [2002] SCC 19
Plouffe v Roy [2007] OJ No 3453
R v McCraw [1991] 3 SCR 72
R v Osolin [1993] 4 SCR 595
RBL v British Columbia [2006] BCJ No 1455
SAD v EEP Estate [2003] BCSC 1535
SMAB v JNH [1991] BCJ No 3940 (SC)
Sage v Renner [2007] BCSC 1357
Schrump v Koot [1977] 18 OR (2d) 337 (CA)
Strachan (Guardian ad litem of) v Winder [2005] BCSC 59
Teno v Arnold [1978] 2 SCR 287
Theobald v Ry Passengers' Assurance Co [1854] 26 Eng L & Eq R 43
Thornton v Prince George School District No 57 [1978] 2 SCR 267
TO v JHO [2006] BCSC 560
Whiten v Pilot Insurance [2002] SCC 18
Wipfli v Britten [1984] 56 BCLR 273 (CA)
WRB v Plint [2001] BCJ No 1446
Y(S) v C (FG) [1996] 26 BCLR (3d) 155 (CA)

Bibliography

Abel, R. (2006) 'General Damages are Incoherent, Incalculable, Incommensurable and Inegalitarian (But Otherwise a Great Idea)', *De Paul Law Review*, 55: 253
Adjin-Tettey, E. (2006) 'Protecting the Dignity and Autonomy of Women: Rethinking the Place of Constructive Consent in the Tort of Sexual Battery', *University of British Columbia Law Review*, 39: 3
—— (2007) 'Accountability of Public Authorities through Contextualized Determinations of Vicarious Liability and Non-Delegable Duties', *University of New Brunswick Law Journal*, 57: 46
—— (2007a) 'Claims of Involuntary Parenthood: Why the Resistance?', in J. Neyers, E. Chamberlain and S. Pitel (eds) *Emerging Issues in Tort Law*, Oxford and Portland, Oregon: Hart Publishing
—— (2007b) 'Righting Past Wrongs through Contextualization: Assessing Claims of Aboriginal Survivors of Historical and Institutional Abuse', *Windsor Yearbook of Access to Justice*, 25(1): 95
—— (2010) 'Discriminatory Impact of Application of *Restitutio in Integrum* in Personal Injury Claims', in Justice R. Sharpe and K. Roach (eds) *Taking Remedies Seriously*, Montreal: Canadian Institute for the Administration of Justice
Adjin-Tettey, E. and Kodar, F. (2011) 'Improving the Potential of Tort Law for Redressing Historical Abuse Claims: The Need for a Contextualized Approach to the Limitation Defence', *Ottawa Law Review*, 42: 95–122.
Aoláin, F.N. (2009) 'Emerging Paradigms of Reality: Exploring a Feminist Theory of Harm in the Context of Conflicted and Post-Conflict Societies', *Queen's Law Journal*, 35: 219

Arlen, J.H. and MacLeod, W.B. (2005) 'Beyond Master-Servant: A Critique of Vicarious Liability', in M.S. Madden (ed) *Exploring Tort Law*, Cambridge: Cambridge University Press

Atiyah, P.S. (1997) *The Damages Lottery*, Oxford: Hart Publishing

Baker G. and Morris, K.J. (1996) *Descartes' Dualism*, New York: Routledge

Bandes, S.A. (2000) (ed) *The Passions of Law*, New York: New York University Press

Banyard V.L. and Williams, L.M. (1996) 'Characteristics of Child Sexual Abuse as Correlates of Women's Adjustment: A Prospective Study', *Journal of Marriage and Family*, 58: 853

Berryman, J. (2010) 'Rethinking Damages for Personal Injury: Is It Too Late To Take The Facts Seriously?', in R.J. Sharpe and K. Roach (eds) *Taking Remedies Seriously*, Montreal: Canadian Institute for the Administration of Justice

Brennan, S. and Taylor-Butts, A. (2008) *Sexual Assault in Canada 2004 and 2007*, Statistics Canada, Canadian Centre for Justice Statistics Profile, Ottawa: Minister of Industry, available online at: http://www.statcan.gc.ca/pub/85f0833m/85f0033m2008019-eng.pdf

Briere J.M. and Elliott, D.M. (1994) 'Immediate and Long-Term Impacts of Child Sexual Abuse', *Future of Children*, 4: 54

British Columbia Law Institute (BCLI) (2001) *Civil Remedies for Sexual Assault*, Vancouver: British Columbia Law Institute

Brown, C. and Randall M. (2004) 'Compensating the Harms of Sexual and Domestic Violence: Tort Law, Insurance and the Role of the State', *Queen's Law Journal*, 30: 311

Campbell, R., Sefl, T. and Ahrens, C. (2003) 'The Physical Health Consequences of Rape: Assessing Survivor's Somatic Symptoms in a Racially Diverse Population', *Women's Studies Quarterly*, 31: 90

Cane, P. (2006) *Atiyah's Accidents, Compensation and the Law*, 7th edn, Oxford: Cambridge University Press

Chamallas, M. (1997) 'Importing Feminist Theories to Change Tort Law', *Wisconsin Women's Law Journal*, 11: 389

Chapman, B. (1995) 'Wrongdoing, Welfare and Damages: Corrective Justice and the Right to Recover for Non-Pecuniary Loss', in D. Owen (ed) *Philosophical Foundations of Tort Law*, Oxford: Oxford University Press

Cheasty M., Clare, A.W. and Collins, C. (1998) 'Relation Between Sexual Abuse in Childhood and Adult Depression: Case-Control Study', *British Medical Journal*, 316: 198

Comack, E. and Peter, T. (2005) 'How the Criminal Justice System Responds to Sexual Assault Survivors: The Slippage between "Responsibilization" and "Blaming the Victim"', *Canadian Journal of Women and Law*, 17: 283

Conaghan, J. (1996) 'Gendered Harms and the Law of Tort: Remedying (Sexual) Harassment', *Oxford Journal of Legal Studies*, 16: 407

—— (2003) 'Tort Law and Feminist Critique', *Current Legal Problems*, 56: 175

Croley, S.P. and Hanson, J. (1995) 'The Nonpecuniary Costs of Accidents: Pain and Suffering in Tort Law', *Harvard Law Review*, 108: 1785

Daylen J., van Tongeren Harvey, W. and O'Toole, D. (2006) *Trauma, Trials, and the Transformation: Guiding Sexual Assault Victims Through the Legal System and Beyond*, Toronto: Irwin Law

Dickinson, G.M. (2001–02) 'School Board Liability for Sexual Misconduct of Employees: A Losing Cause?', *Education & Law Journal*, 11: 367

Dobbs, D.B. (1993) *Law of Remedies*, 2nd edn, St. Paul, Minn: West Pub Co

Doe, J. (2003) *The Story of Jane Doe: A Book About Rape*, Toronto: Random House Canada

Feldthusen, B. (1994) 'Discriminatory Damage Quantification in Civil Actions for Sexual Battery', *University of Toronto Law Journal*, 44: 133

—— (2007) 'Civil Liability for Sexual Assault in Aboriginal Residential Schools: The Baker Did It', *Canadian Journal of Law & Society*, 22: 61

Finley, L. (2004) 'The Hidden Victims of Tort Reform: Children, Women and the Elderly', *Emory Law Journal*, 53: 1263

Fischer, J.M. (1991) *Understanding Remedies*, New York: M. Bender

Galligan, T.C. Jr, Haddon, P.A., Maraist, F.L., McClellan, F., Rustad, M., Terry, N.P. and Wildman, S. (2007) *Tort Law: Cases, Perspectives, and Problems*, 4th edn, Bender: LexisNexis

Goldberg, J.C.P. (2003) 'Twentieth-Century Tort Theory', *Georgetown Law Journal*, 91: 513

——— (2006) 'Two Conceptions of Tort Damages: Fair and Full Compensation', *De Paul Law Review*, 55: 435

Golding, J.M. (1999) 'Sexual-Assault History and Long-Term Physical Health Problems: Evidence from Clinical and Population Epidemiology', *Current Directions in Psychological Science*, 8: 191

Hammond, G. (2010) 'Beyond Dignity', in J. Berryman and R. Bigwood *The Law of Remedies: New Directions in the Common Law*, Toronto: Irwin Law

Hampton, J. (2002) 'Feminist Contractarianism' in Antony, L.M. and Witt, C. (eds), *A Mind of One's Own: Feminist Essays on Reason and Objectivity*, 2nd Edition, Boulder, Colorado: Westview Press

Honoré, T. (1995) 'The Morality of Tort Law – Questions and Answers', in D. Owen (ed) *Philosophical Foundations of Tort Law*, Oxford: Clarendon Press

Jaffe, L.L. (1953) 'Damages for Personal Injury: The Impact of Insurance', *Law and Contemporary Problems*, 18: 219

Katz, K.M. (2010) 'Opposing Scales of Justice: Victims' Voices in the Sentencing Process', *Canadian Criminal Law Review*, 14: 181

King, J.H. Jr (2004) 'Pain and Suffering, Noneconomic Damages, and the Goals of Tort Law', *Southern Methodist University Law Review*, 57: 163

Luntz, H. (2002) *Assessment of Damages for Personal Injury and Death*, 4th edn, Sydney: Butterworths

Luster T. and Small, S.A. (1997) 'Sexual Abuse History and Number of Sexual Partners Among Female Adolescents', *Family Planning Perspectives*, 29: 204

Madden, M.S. (2005) 'Tort Law Through Time and Culture: Themes of Economic Efficiency', in M.S. Madden (ed) *Exploring Tort Law*, New York: Cambridge University Press

Martin, S. (1994) 'Some Constitutional Considerations on Sexual Violence Against Women', *Alberta Law Review*, 32: 535

McGregor, H. (2003) *McGregor on Damages*, 17th edn, London: Sweet & Maxwell

Naffine, N. (1998) 'The Legal Structure of Self-Ownership: Or the Self-Possessed Man and the Woman Possessed', 25 *Journal of Law and Society*, 193

Negligence Review Panel (2002) *Review of the Law of Negligence – Final Report*, Canberra: Commonwealth of Australia (*Ipp Report*)

O'Byrne, S.K. (2009) 'Giving Emotions their Due: Justice Bertha Wilson's Response to Intangible Loss in Contract', in K. Brooks *Justice Bertha Wilson: One Woman's Difference*, Vancouver: UBC Press

O'Connell, J. (1981) 'A Proposal to Abolish Defendants' Payment for Pain and Suffering in Return for Payment of Claimants' Attorney Fees', *University of Illinois Law Review*, 333

Ogus, A.I. (1972) 'Damages for Lost Amenities: For a Foot, A Feeling or a Function', *Modern Law Review* 35: 1

Ontario (1997) *Criminal Injuries Compensation Board: 25th Annual Report*, Toronto: Ministry of the Attorney General

Osborne, P.H. (2007) *The Law of Torts*, 3rd edn, Toronto: Irwin Law

Omatsu, M. (1999) 'On Judicial Appointments: Does Gender Make a Difference?', in

J.F. Fletcher (ed) *Ideas in Action: Essays on Politics and Law in Honour of Peter Russell*, Toronto: University of Toronto Press

Prokhovnik, R. (2002) *Rational Women: A Feminist Critique of Dichotomy*, 2nd edn, Manchester: Manchester University Press

Pryor, E.S. (2003) 'Rehabilitating Tort Compensation', *Georgetown Law Journal*, 91: 659

Rabin, R., (2006) 'Pain and Suffering and Beyond: Some Thoughts on Recovery for Intangible Loss', *De Paul Law Review*, 55: 359

Radin, M.J. (1993) 'Compensation and Commensurability', *Duke Law Journal*, 43: 56

Reaume, D.G. (2004) 'Insurance and Intentional Torts: The Case of Sexual Battery', *Torts Law Journal*, 12: 76

Richardson, J. (2007) 'On Not Making Ourselves the Prey of Others: Jean Hampton's Feminist Contractarianism', *Feminist Legal Studies*, 15: 33

Roberts, J.V. (2009) 'Listening to the Crime Victim: Evaluating Victim Input at Sentencing and Parole', *Crime and Justice: A Review of Research*, 38: 347

Ruda, L.M. (1993) 'Caps on Noneconomic Damages and the Female Plaintiff: Heeding the Warning Signs', *Case Western Reserve Law Review*, 44: 197

Seidman I. and Vickers, S. (2005) 'The Second Wave: An Agenda for the Next Thirty Years of Rape Reform', *Suffolk University Law Review*, 38: 467

Spitz, L. (2005) 'I Think, Therefore I Am; I Feel, Therefore I Am Taxed: Descartes, Tort Reform, and the Civil Rights Tax Relief Act', *New Mexico Law Review*, 35: 429

Statistics Canada (2006) *Measuring Violence Against Women: Statistical Trends 2006*, Commissioned by Federal/Provincial/Territorial Ministries responsible for the Status of Women, Ottawa: Minister of Industry

Statistics Canada (2008) *Canadian Centre for Justice Statistics Profile: Sexual Assault in Canada 2004 and 2007*, Ottawa: Minister of Industry

Stock, J.L., Bell, M.A., Boyer, D.K. and Connell, F.A. (1997) 'Adolescent Pregnancy and Sexual Risk-Taking Among Sexually Abused Girls', *Family Planning Perspectives*, 29: 200

Streseman, K.D. (1995) 'Headshrinkers, Manmunchers, Moneygrubbers, Nuts & Sluts: Reexamining Compelled Mental Examinations in Sexual Harassment Actions Under the Civil Rights Act of 1991', *Cornell Law Review*, 80: 1268

Sutherland, K. (1993) 'Measuring Pain: Quantifying Damages in Civil Suits for Sexual Assault', in K. Cooper-Stephenson and E. Gibson (eds) *Tort Theory*, North York, Ont: Captus University Publications

Trickett P.K. and Putnam, F.W. (1993) 'Impact of Child Sexual Abuse on Females: Toward a Developmental, Psychobiological Integration', *Psychological Science*, 4: 81

Walser R.D. and Kern, J.M. (1996) 'Relationships Among Childhood Sexual Abuse, Sex Guilt, and Sexual Behavior in Adult Clinical Samples', *Journal of Sex Research*, 33: 321

Watson, P. (2010) 'Redressing Dignitary Injuries and Non-Economic Loss in Novel Torts: Challenges for the Law of Remedies', in J. Berryman and R. Bigwood (eds) *The Law of Remedies: New Directions in the Common Law*, Toronto: Irwin Law

West, R. (1991) 'The Difference in Women's Hedonic Lives: A Phenomenological Critique of Feminist Legal Theory', in M. Fineman and T. Thomadsen (eds) *At the Boundaries of Law: Feminism and Legal Theory*, New York: Routledge

Wishik, H.R. (1985) 'To Question Everything: The Inquiries of Feminist Jurisprudence', *Berkeley Women's Law Journal*, 1: 64

Wriggins, J.B. (2005) 'Toward a Feminist Revision of Torts', *American University Journal of Gender, Social Policy & the Law*, 13: 139

Wriggins, Jennifer (2001) 'Domestic Violence Torts', *Southern California Law Review*, 75: 121

Zipursky, B.C. (2003) 'Civil Recourse, Not Corrective Justice', *Georgetown Law Journal*, 91: 695

Chapter 11

Damaging Stereotypes: the Return of 'Hoovering as a Hobby'

*Reg Graycar**

Introduction

More than a quarter of a century ago, I first discovered that cases about personal injury damages assessment, a seemingly gender neutral area of law, graphically illustrate how what appear to be neutral or 'black letter' rules and legal principles can in fact operate in ways that significantly disadvantage women (Graycar 1985a; 1985b). Throughout the late 1980s and 1990s and into this century, I have explored the gendered nature of damages assessment in some detail (see Graycar 1992; 1993; 1995; 1997; 2002; 2003). Examining how those damages are calculated, and the many ways in which they tend to be reduced in cases involving women, casts light on some of the ways that unstated assumptions about gender, and about the differing roles of women and men, affect legal decision making more broadly.

This chapter looks back at that work and asks whether some of that critique has had the effect of ameliorating any of that identified gendered disadvantage. However, before that question can be addressed, it is necessary to explain the gendered nature of damages assessment in somewhat more detail.

There are three main ways in which women can be disadvantaged in the context of damages assessments, and I consider each of these in this chapter. First, where women are injured in accidents, their damages for loss of earning capacity (the loss of capacity to do paid work that is brought about by the accident) tend to be artificially depressed by gendered assumptions about women's lack of attachment to the paid labour market and the assumption that women's paid work is secondary to their role as mothers and carers. Secondly, a woman's loss of capacity to work in the home, doing non-market or caring work, has historically been treated by the law as a loss to someone else, through the action for loss of consortium. Some jurisdictions have either abolished the action for loss of consortium, or extended it to women for loss of their husband's consortium, but for reasons explained below, neither approach effectively addresses the gendered assumptions about the nature of the loss. Even in those cases where such a loss is treated as a woman's own loss, rather than a loss to someone else, as the discussion below will show, it tends to be treated as a loss of amenity – a non-economic loss. This characterisation is significant because damages for non-economic loss have increasingly been targeted by legislatures for either reduction or abolition altogether.

Finally, assumptions about gender also affect the assessment of damages for the costs of caring for accident victims. Many accident victims need considerable amounts of post accident care, care that is often provided by close family members. But that formulation of the issue is, like many such propositions, deceptively gender-neutral: most of the carers of accident victims are women. Care for children, the aged, the sick, people with disabilities, and people otherwise unable to look after themselves, is considered quintessentially women's work – even where, as will be illustrated, it is done by men – and valued (or perhaps, more accurately, devalued) accordingly.

The examples given in this chapter are mostly, though not exclusively, from Australia. Many of them are not particularly recent. But their continued relevance lies in the fact that an area of law generally seen as somewhat prosaic and certainly not usually seen as raising gender issues (in the manner of, say, sexual assault law, or family law) is, when closely examined, replete with unstated gendered assumptions. The purpose, therefore, of unmasking the 'hidden gender' of damages assessment is to remind us that any area of law is equally susceptible to a gendered analysis (compare Graycar and Morgan 2002).

Damages for loss of earning capacity: loss of capacity to do paid work

When women are injured in an accident, assessment of their damages can be negatively affected by stereotypes and assumptions. Sometimes this happens explicitly, for example by the use of depressed 'female' wage figures or 'female' work life tables for women.[1] Equally importantly, though less overtly, sometimes this happens implicitly through the use of stereotypes and gendered assumptions about women's lack of attachment to the paid labour market. Each of these will be considered in turn.

The use of gendered (or racialised) actuarial data to calculate loss of future earning capacity

There is a considerable literature in North America dealing with the use of explicitly gendered and sometimes race-specific actuarial tables in the context of damages assessment.[2] This trend of using gendered wage tables does not seem to have captured widespread currency in Australia, although it is certainly not wholly absent from damages assessments. For example, in one case in NSW, the plaintiff was a young woman and the Court of Appeal had to choose between using average female earnings to estimate her loss of future earning capacity, or using median female earnings (*Rosniak v Government Insurance Office* [1997]). Notably, no question was raised about whether it was appropriate to use female wage rates, which have been and continue to be consistently lower than men's.[3]

By contrast, the use of such data has been commented upon critically by courts in both the United States and Canada. One of the earliest such discussions was in a 1991 decision from British Columbia called *Tucker v Asleson* [1991]. There the female plaintiff[‡] argued that her loss of future earning capacity should be assessed on the basis of tables of average earnings for a university educated man (an amount of $947,000) while the defendant argued that female tables should be used (because of the history of sex discrimination in employment, this would have amounted to a mere $302,000). The trial judge accepted the plaintiff's argument about the use of male wage figures, a decision that was not disturbed by the majority of the British Columbia Court of Appeal (*Tucker v Asleson* [1993]).

In 2005, the Ontario Court of Appeal affirmed a decision of the Ontario Superior Court of Justice which had decided to reject the use of female wage data in assessing damages for a 17-year-old girl catastrophically injured in an accident, who, at the time of her injury, had not yet completed high school (*Walker v Ritchie* [2005]).[5] Both the trial court and the Court of Appeal reviewed the Canadian case law on this issue, starting with *Tucker v Asleson*. The trial judge had concluded:

> In my view, the use of statistical figures which reflect the entire population, without division as to gender . . . avoids the problem of having two separate tables and then having to choose between them and apply what seem like appropriate adjustments. The choice of the general average figures for university graduates seems especially appropriate here where the court is attempting to make a forecast stretching many years into the future, and where a couple of the suggested future professions, barring the accident, are teaching in which pay equity has been achieved, and human kinetics, where a good deal of the employment is with government or government supported institutions, where pay equity is mandated.
>
> (*Walker v Ritchie* [2004]: [135])

The Ontario Court of Appeal endorsed this approach, noting that while damages assessments must be based on the particular evidence in the individual case, a 'court must be equally cognizant of the fact that gender-based earnings statistics are grounded in retrospective historical data that may no longer accurately project the income a person would achieve in the future' (*Walker v Ritchie* [2004]: [45]).

In their recently published treatise, *The Measure of Injury: Race, Gender, and Tort Law*, Martha Chamallas and Jennifer Wriggins provide an overview of the status of gendered and racialised wage tables in assessing personal injury damages in the United States (Chamallas and Wriggins 2010: 158–70). They refer to a 2008 judgment where it was held that the use of raced life expectancy data to calculate personal injury damages in tort cases violates the equal protection and due process guarantees enshrined by the US Constitution (Chamallas and Wriggins 2010: 156; see also Wriggins 2008: 53–7). The court was hearing a case involving an African American victim of the 2003 Staten Island Ferry crash, and held that 'by allowing the use of "race"-based life expectancy tables, which are based on historical data, courts are essentially reinforcing the underlying social inequalities of our society rather than describing a significant biological difference' (*McMillan v City of New York* [2008]).

While the focus of this decision was raced life expectancy figures, Weinstein J also commented that 'Courts are increasingly troubled by "race"- and gender-based figures for calculating loss of future income' (253) before going on to review some of the cases that had applied raced earnings related data, to the detriment of plaintiffs. Those he considered included *Wheeler Tarpeh-Doe v United States* [1991].[6] Although it would perhaps be premature to see the decision in *McMillan* as having the effect of reversing the trend of using raced or gendered wage tables, the focus on the dubious constitutionality of that practice, at least in relation to life expectancy, does suggest that it might soon come to be viewed as inappropriate (Chamallas and Wriggins 2010: 166).[7]

Chamallas and Wriggins also refer to the approach taken by Kenneth Feinberg, the Special Master of the federal September 11 Victim Compensation Fund, who 'made a choice to ignore race and to reject the use of gender-based statistics that would have lowered awards for families of female victims' on the basis of considerations of public policy and equity (Final Rule 2002; Chamallas 2003). They claim (perhaps optimistically) that what is most significant about these two recent US examples is:

> that, after years of neglecting the issue, some courts are finally expressing doubts about the legality and fairness of gender- and raced-based assessments and are reaching to reform damage calculations in a manner consistent with constitutional principles and civil rights norms.
>
> (Chamallas and Wriggins 2010: 166)

But while it is important, at least symbolically, to confront the inherent bias that flows from using gendered or raced wage tables, the decision as to which table to use may not in fact be anywhere near as important to the final outcome of a case as a trial judge's choice of what figure to use as the appropriate reduction for vicissitudes (the issue of 'vicissitudes' is discussed below, in the context of 'implicit' rather than explicit ways in which damages are reduced). In *Tucker v Asleson* [1991] while the judge used male rather than female figures, he then applied a 60 to 65 per cent reduction for vicissitudes, leading to a much smaller award. So the result is a somewhat hollow victory for the plaintiff. What this demonstrates clearly is that these explicitly gendered rationales for reduction of damages are perhaps not so separate as they may superficially appear from the less explicit uses of gender stereotypes. The same factors that lead to women's average earnings being significantly less than those of men (such as the unequal distribution of work in the home and discriminatory assumptions about women's lack of attachment to paid work) are relied on by courts to reduce damages for vicissitudes. Moreover, the use of gendered wage tables *and* a reduction for vicissitudes would constitute double discounting. On this basis, I would endorse the cautionary view of Supreme Court of Canada Justice Dickson in *Andrews v Grand and Toy Alberta* [1978]:

> The apparent reliability of assessments provided by modern actuarial practice is largely illusionary for actuarial science deals with probabilities, not

actualities. . . . [A]ctuarial evidence speaks in terms of group experience. It cannot, and does not purport to, speak as to the individual sufferer.

[236]

Assumptions about women's lack of attachment to the paid labour market

While gendered wage data may not have generated the same debates in Australia as in North America, the case law in this country is replete with examples of the implicit rationales – the 'damaging stereotypes' – that are used to reduce awards for loss of earning capacity to women accident victims (compare Graycar 1995). A case that reached Australia's High Court provides a clear example (*Wynn v NSW Insurance Ministerial Corporation* [1995a]). Maree Wynn was injured in a motor vehicle accident when she was 30 and a senior employee of American Express. She had been promoted several times, had a number of staff responsible to her, and worked long hours, often working at home until 1 or 2 am. The extensive computer work aggravated her whiplash injury, and she was forced to resign at age 32. The work she undertook subsequently was far less remunerative and only part time. By the time her damages claim came to trial, she had married her long-term partner (with whom she lived while employed by American Express) and had a child.

The main basis of the respondent's challenge to the trial judge's award was, as put by Handley JA in the NSW Court of Appeal, that the judge 'had failed to make proper allowance for vicissitudes. He held that it was not probable that but for injury, the plaintiff would simply have retired to the laudable but limited role of housewife and mother and abandoned her business career' (*Wynn v NSW Insurance Ministerial Corp* [1994]: 61,740). The trial judge had assessed damages on the basis that Ms Wynn would have worked for American Express until age 60 and, after considering all the factors raised (such as possible maternity leave etc), reduced her assessed damages by 5 per cent for vicissitudes.

In the NSW Court of Appeal, much was made of the stressful nature of her job and the onerous responsibility it carried, along with the very long working hours. With regard to child care, the Court said: 'If the plaintiff . . . continued her demanding business career after marriage, and after the birth of her child or children, she and her husband would necessarily have been faced with the necessity of engaging a full time nanny for the children and substantial household help during the week' (*Wynn v NSW Insurance Ministerial Corporation* [1994]: 61,741), and her damages were reduced to take this cost into account.

The Court also expressed a number of reservations about the trial judge's finding that she was likely to continue working at a senior executive level. First, they did not accept that she would be further promoted because that would have required another overseas posting:

It would have involved separation from her fiancé or husband, whose business interests would have kept him in Sydney, except during holidays, and likewise either separation from any children or a decision not to have any. The plaintiff was thirty-two when she resigned and her childbearing years were already limited . . .

(*Wynn v NSW Insurance Ministerial Corporation* [1994]: 61,741)

The Court held that the trial judge had erred in allowing only 5 per cent for vicissitudes. Not only was the possibility of 'burn out' not taken into account, but the Court did not agree with the trial judge that it was 'quite probable' that she would have been further promoted (though there is no mention of any evidence to the contrary that was before the court). After adding 'a fair allowance' for domestic help, a figure the Court expressly acknowledged was based on no direct evidence ('the Court must do the best it can'), the Court of Appeal summed up as follows:

> The allowance for vicissitudes . . . should include two years' absence from work to have two children (8 per cent of the 23.75 years [*the estimated period of working life*]) together with an allowance for the prospect that the plaintiff would be unable or unwilling to remain in her job which placed such heavy demands on her time, energy and health and the love and patience of her husband. The plaintiff, of course, could have worked until sixty or later in a less demanding job but would then have earned substantially reduced salary and benefits. . . . A fair allowance for such vicissitudes in my opinion would be 20 per cent and this with the 8 per cent allowance for having two children gives a total deduction for vicissitudes of 28 per cent which I would adopt.
>
> (*Wynn v NSW Insurance Ministerial Corporation* [1994]: 61,742)

Applying this reasoning, Ms Wynn's damages for loss of future earning capacity were reduced from over $700,000 to $411,350. She appealed and during the special leave application (the hearing in which the High Court considers whether to hear the case) one member of the High Court, McHugh J asked: 'Well, supposing the applicant had been a male, could you imagine a judge making a finding like this'? (*Wynn v NSW Insurance Ministerial Corporation* [1995b]).[8] Or is it more likely that in that event, the court might instead have described the plaintiff as another court described a similar, though not chromosomally challenged, plaintiff, as 'a young man with bright prospects, who has been deprived of the ability to choose to continue his career'? (*Tucker v Westfield Design and Construction Pty Ltd* [1993]: [28]).[9]

Wynn's case resonates with many of the cases I came across when researching damages cases in the 1990s:[10] what they have in common is a tendency to treat women's paid work as marginal, as worthy of comment, as requiring an explanation, rather than as something that adult gender neutral people just do. The judgments often provide an explanation for why a woman works, coupled with an underlying assumption that should the particular reason given for her employment disappear she would no longer engage in paid work (see Graycar 1995). For example, a woman works because her husband left her and she's a single parent (*Harper v Bangalow Motors Pty Ltd* [1990]: 9); or she might become one (*Wallen v Hird* [1993]). One woman works to escape her husband who is violent (*Stekovic v City Group Pty Ltd* [1994]: [84]). Another works because her husband is unemployed and therefore cannot support her and the children (*Angelopolous v Rubenhold*, [1991]: 8), while yet another wants to help her daughter to attend university (*Randall v Dul* [1994]). One woman's religious beliefs were said by a judge to lie behind her view that 'her role was to provide financial support to her maximum capacity for her husband and children' (*Kelson v Transport Accident Commission* [1994]). A young South Australian woman had her damages reduced on appeal because it was held that she was unlikely to take over her mother's role in the management of a family business as she had three brothers and the business may have to support their families.[11] Perhaps the best explanation comes from Lord Denning in 1974:

> Many a married woman seeks work. She does so when the children grow up and leave the house. She does it, not solely to earn money, helpful as it is, but to fill her time with useful occupation, rather than sit idly at home waiting for her husband to return. The devil tempts those who have nothing to do.
>
> (*Langston v AEUW* [1974]: [987])

A common assumption in the Australian case law is that sole parents are more likely than women in two parent households to be in paid work: in fact, the opposite is true, both in Canada and in Australia, according to data from both the Australian Bureau of Statistics and Statistics Canada.[12] I mention this to draw attention to a phenomenon that seems common in these cases: that is, basing fact-finding and judicial decision making on completely erroneous assumptions, a theme considered more fully below.

Paid work for women, particularly married women, is often seen to be in direct competition with other aspects of their lives – with other roles they fulfil or are expected to fulfil. In one Australian case, the court decided that a woman would not be successful running her own business because 'she may have succumbed to competing family demands' (*Becin v GEC Australia and Ors*, [1993]). Women's capacity to bear children is also used, in a number of different (and often contrasting) ways, to disadvantage women. For young women, damages are discounted because they may in the future have time out of the workforce to have children, irrespective of whether they indicate that they did not want to do so, or planned to have no more children (compare Handley JA in *Bondin v Lamaro* [1994]: [5]; Dunford J in *Partridge v GIO* [1993]: [8]). In 1996, the British Columbia Court of Appeal reduced a trial judge's award, deciding that the plaintiff would not have spent her working life at her pre-accident employment: 'She hopes to raise a family when her spouse is suitably employed' (*Lee v Swan* [1996]: [55]). But an older woman might have her damages reduced when she no longer has children to care for (*Reece v Reece* [1994]: [3]) or because she is considered unemployable after a history of time out of the paid workforce for family responsibilities (Kirby P in *NSW Insurance Ministerial Corporation v Rayner* [1993]: [6]), or because, in the words of one judge, she 'may well have taken breaks from her employment, for example, when her children married and had families to visit and to assist them with their children . . .' (*Tully v G J Coles* [1993]).

Just like in Wynn's case, a court may consider that the workplace might prove too demanding for a woman who could not be expected to keep up such a pace (see Priestley JA in *Rasmus v GIO* [1992]: [4]) or, that a woman's husband might not want her to undertake full-time paid work because, as she and he 'aged and became financially secure, her husband's attitude might have induced [her] to retire early or to reduce her working hours' (*Park v Hobart Public Hospitals* [1991]: [12]). And, while the New South Wales Court of Appeal treated the difficulties that would confront Ms Wynn in travelling overseas to secure her promotion as almost insurmountable, another female plaintiff's award was reduced since she 'may well have taken breaks from her employment . . . during any transfers in his work by her husband' (*Tully v G J Coles* [1993]). For yet another woman, damages for future economic loss were reduced because of her husband's peripatetic employment since, according to the court, 'there must also be taken into account . . . the consequences of being married to a serviceman' (*Isabella Smith v Michael Smith* [1991]: [69]).

When the High Court reviewed the decision in *Wynn*, they allowed the appeal in part. The Court decided that a more appropriate reduction for vicissitudes was 12.5 per cent and refused to discount the award to allow for the costs of child care pointing out that such costs may be incurred by men or women whether or not the child's mother is in the paid workforce. The Court also said that there was 'nothing in the evidence to suggest that the appellant was any less able than any other career oriented person, whether male or female, to successfully combine a demanding career and family responsibilities' (*Wynn v NSW Ministerial Corporation* [1995a]: [494]).

Gendered assumptions about the economic consequences of marriage for women have also historically informed awards of damages to surviving female spouses in wrongful death actions. In *De Sales v Ingrilli* [2002b], the High Court reconsidered the issue of taking into account the prospects of a widow's remarriage as a factor in reducing such an award. The case received some media attention as it involved assessing the widow's prospects of remarriage by reference to her likely 'attractiveness' to a new partner. During the special leave hearing, the following exchange ensued between Hayne J and Gaudron J (the latter was at that time the only woman on the High Court):

> HAYNE J: But here, the leading judgment in the Full Court, seems to deal with the subject entirely after some introductory remarks by saying, 'Only for my part, I would think that a woman of the appellant's age and credentials, a 20 per cent deduction would be appropriate'. What does his Honour mean?
> GAUDRON J: What his Honour means is she is relatively good looking.
> (*De Sales v Ingrilli* [2002a])

By a majority of 4:3, the High Court overturned what had been a long-established practice of making deductions on account of the assumed economic benefits of a woman's remarriage. In their joint judgment, Gaudron, Gummow and Hayne JJ explained their rationale for deciding that the prospect of remarriage should no longer form the basis of a separate award or be used to increase the discount for general vicissitudes as follows:

> Even if these difficulties of predicting that a surviving spouse will form some new continuing relationship were to be surmounted, the financial consequences of its occurrence are even less predictable. Who is to say that the new relationship will endure, and that, if it endures, it will provide financial advantage to the person who is now the surviving spouse? And if it is a financially beneficial relationship at its outset, who is to say what events will intervene thereafter? Will the new spouse or partner suffer some catastrophe and the person who is now the surviving spouse then have to care and provide for the new partner, the children of the first union, any children brought by the new partner to the new union, and any children born of the new union? Who can say?
>
> (*De Sales v Ingrilli* [2002b]: [74])

The valuation of a woman's loss of capacity to work in the home

Because the law of torts values some losses of working capacity over others, injuries to women have often been characterised as causing non-economic loss, a characterisation that has significant consequences in damages assessments. The failure to recognise the economic nature of women's work in the home is closely related to the common law's historical treatment of a woman's loss of domestic working capacity as a loss not to herself but to her husband through his action for loss of 'consortium' and 'servitium'.

At common law, a loss of capacity to provide household services, although historically characterised as an economic loss, was actionable only by the woman's husband in an action for loss of consortium (the action included damages not only for loss of services, but also for loss of society and companionship, including sexual services). After it was held by the House of Lords in 1952 that at common law, women did not have a corresponding right of action for loss of their husband's consortium (*Best v Samuel Fox and Co Ltd* [1952]), the action was extended to women in some jurisdictions (eg the Australian states of South Australia and Queensland) while in others (eg NSW) it was abolished.[13]

Neither approach addressed the real problem, as was so clearly shown in a 1981 article called 'Sex, Housework and the Law' (Riseley 1981). The extension to women of the ability to sue for loss of their husband's consortium is a graphic illustration of how empty the formal equality or sameness model of equality can be for women (compare Graycar and Morgan 2002: 28–48). If the major element in a loss of consortium award is the loss of services, the 'reform' is pyrrhic only: most women do not lose their husbands' household services when the latter are injured since they never had them in the first place. And, as for abolishing the action, while that approach has clear rhetorical appeal,[14] in practice there is a real loss which is then left to lie where it falls.

The only satisfactory approach is to replace the secondary action for loss of consortium with a primary cause of action for loss of capacity to work in the home. This has been done by statute in Australia only in the ACT.[15] Some Canadian provinces have effectively achieved this by common law development (notably in *Fobel v Dean* [1991] (Saskatchewan)[16] and *McLaren v Schwalbe* [1994] (Alberta)[17]).

The old approach (that the loss was a loss to someone else and compensable via a secondary action) allowed some tortious conceptualisations of a woman's injury as partly hers and partly someone else's (and remember that only a *de jure* husband ever had a right to claim damages for that loss). In one case, which was recently approved by the High Court of Australia in *CSR v Eddy* [2005]: [16], [71], a NSW court described a woman's loss of capacity to work in the home as 'a partial loss of capacity to carry out housework resulting in (a) a loss to the family of part of her services . . .; (b) a loss to herself by inability to fully satisfy her personal needs in daily life . . .; and (c) a personal loss of the capacity to perform services for others voluntarily' (*Burnicle v Cutelli* [1982]: [27]).

The personal loss, the part claimed by the woman herself, has tended to be characterised as non-economic, rather than economic, as a loss of amenity or loss of enjoyment of life. This characterisation mirrors what is effectively a false dichotomy between work (something done outside the home for wages), and other non-remunerated activity (compare Graycar 2002). So, for example, the court in *Burnicle v Cutelli* said: 'the injured plaintiff has in such a case as this lost part of a capacity, the exercise of which can give to her pride and satisfaction and the receipt of gratitude, and the loss of which can lead to frustration and feelings of inadequacy' [28]. This approach, of characterising a loss of capacity to work in the home as a loss of enjoyment of life and therefore non-economic, is the approach that I have characterised as 'Hoovering as a Hobby' (Graycar 1985b; 1997).

A number of consequences flow from characterising women's work in the home as non-economic: first, non-economic losses tend to be much lower than economic losses and, secondly, non-economic losses are increasingly being abolished or limited by statutory modifications to common law damages (Graycar 2003: 153–4; Finley 1997). In all the jurisdictions (such as NZ) that made changes to accident compensation in the 1970s and 1980s, little if any account was taken of the impact of those changes on the ways in which women's work was treated in damages assessment (Graycar 2003: 140–3).

Another related trend is to assume that since women increasingly work outside the home, housework is shared. This assumption is, of course, unfounded as a large body of recent empirical evidence clearly tells us that women's increased participation in the paid labour market has had little or no effect on the distribution of housework,[18] yet remarkably, for some reason, courts state this erroneous conclusion as if it were a matter of which judicial notice could be taken.

This assumption is not confined to damages law as a well-known Australian custody case illustrates:

[T]here has come a radical change in the division of responsibilities between parents and in the ability of the mother to devote the whole of her time and attention to the household and the family. As frequently as not, the mother works, thereby reducing the time which she can devote to her children. A corresponding development has been that the father gives more of his time to the household and to the family.

(*Gronow v Gronow* [1979]: [528])

The High Court did not cite any evidence for this: indeed, it would have been nigh on impossible to find any.[19] This misperception would not be of any particular significance were it not for the fact that it is used to reduce a woman's damages for loss of capacity to do housework. In a number of cases this same assumption – that housework is shared – has been used to reduce the damages either where this loss is recognised as a primary loss, or in the older cases, where the loss is treated as a loss of consortium. In one of the latter cases, a NSW court decided that the loss to the husband of his wife's services was not so great since, as the judge put it, 'we must take account of public mores . . . and where a husband and wife are both working, the sharing of domestic burdens with the wife is expected of the husband, even where his wife is perfectly healthy' (*Kealley v Jones* [1979]: [741]). In another case in British Columbia, a trial judge noted:

This is a family of two spouses both of whom work outside the home. The plaintiff plans to continue her career. In that type of family as opposed to a traditional family where one spouse remains at home, it is reasonable to expect both spouses to contribute fairly equally to the domestic work.

(*Kroeker v Jansen* [1995]: [20])

While this may be reasonable, it is not empirically sound, in either Australia or in Canada. Although we all might share the hope that housework will be more fairly shared in households, particularly those where both members of a couple are in paid work, my concern is that reducing damages on the basis of assumptions that bear no relationship either to the individual case or to the national statistical data, is not likely to lead the way to more equal sharing of work in the home.[20]

Damages for the costs of caring for accident victims: *Griffiths v Kerkemeyer* damages

The third and final issue concerns damages for the costs of care (known in Australia as *Griffiths v Kerkemeyer* [1977] damages). Accident victims often need considerable amounts of care, care that is often provided by close family members most of whom (though of course not all) are women.[21] Care for children, the aged, people suffering from illness, people with disabilities, and those generally unable to look after themselves is considered quintessentially women's work – even where it is done by men[22] – and valued accordingly.[23]

In *Griffiths v Kerkemeyer* [1977], the High Court decided that an injured plaintiff can recover damages for the costs of care even where the care is provided 'gratuitously', thereby recognising that for an accident victim there is often a person or group of people whose lives are significantly affected by taking on the onerous task of caring for the injured person. The *Griffiths v Kerkemeyer* doctrine, which recognises damages for the costs of care as an economic head of damages, is quite clearly distinct from the more usual characterisation of women's work in the home as non-economic in the context of women's claims for compensation for their own injuries. However, while *Griffiths v Kerkemeyer* damages relate to work done by carers (usually women), they are not paid to the care provider but instead are awarded to the accident victim in recognition of the injured person's need for the services (Graycar 1992: 104–5).

In a series of cases starting almost immediately after the High Court's 1977 judgment, courts started reducing the damages payable by reference to a quaint notion that, since caring work is part of the 'ordinary currency of family life and obligation', it is excessive to pay damages to injured accident victims for those services (*Kovac v Kovac* [1982]: [668]; Graycar 1992: 95–7).

The devaluation of caring work by the courts was reinforced by a number of statutory modifications (including in some cases abolition) of *Griffiths v Kerkemeyer* damages (*CSR v Eddy* [2005]: [9]–[10]). In *Van Gervan v Fenton*, a case that brought the issue to the High Court again in 1992, the damages paid to the accident victim for the costs of his care had been calculated by reference, not to what the caring services would cost if they had to be purchased on the market, but by reference to the wages the accident victim's wife had forgone by leaving her work as an unskilled nurse's aide to look after him. It was this quantification that was the issue on appeal (*Van Gervan v Fenton* [1992]).

When I was asked to write about this case prior to the High Court's review of the decision (Graycar 1992), I thought it important to contextualise the issue by looking at the facts of both the case under appeal, and some other cases where something of the lives of the accident victim (and where possible, the carer) is known. I wanted to illustrate all of the day-to-day ways in which the plaintiff was affected by the accident, in other words, all of the things his wife now had to do in caring for him. I was responding to the rarity with which judgments, especially appellate judgments, provide any real picture of the parties and their lives, or any sense of the factual context in which people's problems come before the courts. I also looked at empirical data on work in the home that showed that women do most of the work in the home, even where they also work outside the home. I noted that women with 'retired husbands' have an even heavier work load than others, and pointed out that the burden of caring for accident victims also falls disproportionately on women.[24] I then suggested that the trend towards abolishing or limiting *Griffiths v Kerkemeyer* damages flows from a series of assumptions, many of which are false, that courts use intuitively (eg that housework is shared), rather than from any available evidence. A primary assumption in these cases is that the relationships people are in remain stable and unaffected by accidents. The reality, of course, is quite different: accidents and injuries are often significant causes of relationship breakdown (see, eg, *O'Brien v O'Brien* [1983]; *Williams v Williams* [1984]). Another related issue I came across was the very real issue of violence by accident victims towards their carers, and a peculiar tendency to discuss this dispassionately, purely as a matter going to the contingency of whether the target of violence (usually the wife or mother) would remain available to continue to undertake the caring work.[25] Sometimes it is not discussed at all, or expressly declared irrelevant.

The Tasmanian Full Court had decided (and the High Court dissenters agreed) that Mrs Van Gervan's work caring for her husband in their home was easier than her work at the nursing home, even though she had to look after him all the time (not just for 40 hours a week): after all, he could be left 'alone for periods of the order of an hour or more' (*Van Gervan v Fenton* [1991]: [68], [923]; *Van Gervan v Fenton* [1992]: [345]). I concluded that while it may be fair to describe some of her work as a labour of love, it was hard labour, and far more onerous than bringing someone cups of tea from time to time (Graycar 1993).

On the issue of the valuation method (opportunity or replacement cost), I suggested that using the opportunity cost, ie what the carer/wife lost by giving up her paid work, must seem attractive to courts in a world where women earn around two-thirds of what men earn, but would not be considered apposite if the carer gave up her job as a brain surgeon or High Court judge to care for him (an unlikely event in our real world, given occupational and industrial segmentation of the workforce). Realistically, the only option is market or replacement cost for a number of reasons I outlined (and with which the High Court majority agreed).

But while the High Court majority in *Van Gervan v Fenton* upheld the doctrinal basis of *Griffiths v Kerkemeyer* damages, a number of other developments have limited the utility of the decision. First, it has been the subject, almost since the original *Griffiths v Kerkemeyer* decision, of statutory modifications that limit recovery in a number of ways: there is currently no state or territory in which the full market cost is actually recoverable for this head of damages. Moreover, what had appeared to be a logical extension to this head of damages by the NSW Court of Appeal in 1999 (*Sullivan v Gordon* [1999]) was firmly wound back by the High Court in its 2005 decision in *CSR v Eddy* [2005]. In their majority judgment, Gleeson CJ, Gummow and Heydon JJ summarised the development of this type of damages:

> [S]ome jurisdictions, whether by purported application of the rules in *Griffiths v Kerkemeyer*, or by extension of them, or otherwise, permit recovery of damages reflecting the impaired capacity of plaintiffs to provide domestic services to their families. This claim was rejected in New South Wales by Reynolds and Mahoney JJA (Glass JA dissenting) in *Burnicle v Cutelli*. That case was followed by a majority (Kennedy and Olney JJ, Wickham J dissenting) of the Full Court of the Supreme Court of Western Australia in *Maiward v Doyle*. To those jurisdictions can be added Scotland. However, the Queensland Court of Appeal (Macrossan CJ, Davies JA and Fryberg J) accepted the claim in *Sturch v Willmott*. So did the English Court of Appeal in *Daly v General Steam Navigation*

Co Ltd and the Full Court of the Federal Court of Australia sitting on appeal from the Supreme Court of the Australian Capital Territory. A bench of five members of the New South Wales Court of Appeal in *Sullivan v Gordon* then adopted a concession by counsel that *Sturch v Willmott* was correct and *Burnicle v Cutelli* was incorrect. Since then, *Sullivan v Gordon* has been followed in Western Australia and the Australian Capital Territory. The opposite view has been taken by a majority of the Full Court of the Supreme Court of South Australia. Principles similar to those stated in *Sullivan v Gordon* are applied in Canada, although there have been dissenting judgments. In the United States there is an avenue of recovery for 'a homemaker who is not a wage earner but whose earning capacity is devoted to providing household services'. This was done by extension of principles relating to loss of earning capacity.

Finally, the *Sullivan v Gordon* principle has been assumed, subject to various limitations to be examined later, by the legislatures in Queensland and Victoria, and enacted in the Australian Capital Territory.

(*CSR v Eddy* [2005]: [9]–[10])

In *Sullivan v Gordon* [1999], a five member bench of the NSW Court of Appeal expressly overruled its earlier decision in *Burnicle v Cutelli* (discussed above). The Court of Appeal held that when a woman loses her capacity to care for others (in that case, her children), as a consequence of tortious injury, damages are available for that loss of capacity via the *Griffiths v Kerkemeyer* head of damages. As Mason P (with whom Spigelman CJ, Stein JA and Powell JA agreed) put it: 'Acknowledgment that a mother's interrupted capacity to make her usual contributions to a household is compensable involves the law's belated recognition of the economic value of such work' (*Sullivan v Gordon* [1999]: [331]–[332]). But that development was firmly set aside by the High Court in *CSR v Eddy* [2005] when that Court took the opportunity, in effect, to rebuke the NSW Court of Appeal, declaring that there was no such category as '*Sullivan v Gordon*' damages. The Court reinstated the orthodoxy of *Burnicle v Cutelli* and overruled all the cases that had purported to award '*Sullivan v Gordon*' damages.

In *CSR v Eddy*, the plaintiff had developed mesothelioma as a consequence of exposure to asbestos in the workplace. While the company did not contest liability, it took the matter to the High Court after the trial and intermediate appellate courts had awarded the plaintiff '*Sullivan v Gordon*' damages in relation to the care he had previously provided for his wife who suffered from arthritis (two hours per week).

In the High Court, the plaintiff (there the respondent) argued that *Sullivan v Gordon* damages are a natural extension of *Griffiths v Kerkemeyer* damages. The majority of the High Court did not agree: while they did not abolish *Griffith v Kerkemeyer* damages altogether, they held that they were both 'controversial' (as evidenced by the numerous statutory modifications) (*CSR v Eddy* [2005]: [26]) and 'anomalous' as they depart from the 'usual rule that damages other than damages payable for a loss not measurable in money are not recoverable for an injury unless the injury produces actual financial loss' (*CSR v Eddy* [2005]: [26]). The majority characterised *Sullivan v Gordon* damages as purporting to compensate for 'loss to the family', and held that this was not the usual domain of damages in tort law, which 'concentrates on compensating injured plaintiffs' (*CSR v Eddy* [2005]: [42]).

The High Court decided that while loss of the capacity to provide 'gratuitous' personal or domestic services was compensable, compensation was available only as part of general damages (that is, as non-economic loss) rather than as a separate head of damages, the amount of which would otherwise be separately assessed according to the commercial cost of providing the services that the plaintiff can no longer provide. In taking this view, the High Court rejected the existence of this category of damages as a common law doctrine (*CSR v Eddy* [2005]: [54]), though it acknowledged that it had been assumed by legislatures in Queensland and Victoria, legislated for in the Australian Capital Territory and was accepted doctrine in Canada (*CSR v Eddy* [2005]: [9]–[10]).[26]

The majority of the Court treated the provision of care for family members as, in effect, just one of the many voluntary pastimes that an injured plaintiff might engage in, and therefore too remote to address via a head of damages. This approach emerges perhaps most clearly in the following extract from the joint judgment of Gleeson CJ, Gummow and Heydon JJ (footnotes omitted):

> *Where is the line to be drawn?* . . . How far, then, does the *Sullivan v Gordon* principle go? To loss of capacity to care for close family members (de jure or de facto), or any family members (de jure or de facto), or foster children, or members of the plaintiff's household, whether 'immediate' or 'extended'; and if to any of these classes, only to dependent members of them, or all members of them? If only to close family members, what is 'closeness'? If only to dependent members, what is 'dependency'? If the test turns on damage to capacity, why should recovery not extend beyond domestic services? Should it apply beyond domestic services to the wide range of educative services healthy parents supply their children of an academic, sporting or cultural kind? And if the incapacity to give gratuitous services is a loss to the giver, ought one not to pay the pious spinster whose charitable works are inhibited by injury? Or should it extend to services provided to friends, or to neighbours? Should it extend to plaintiffs who customarily visited or helped many hospital patients, or old people, or destitute people; or provided volunteer emergency services to others even though they were complete strangers to that plaintiff?
>
> (*CSR v Eddy* [2005]: [61])[27]

And in a separate concurring judgment, McHugh J commented:

> As a matter of principle, *Griffiths v Kerkemeyer* damages are an anomaly. There is no reason in principle why the inability of an injured person to meet his or her needs should be regarded as a special case, no reason why that inability should be distinguished from incapacities such as restriction of use or movement or the pursuit of social, sporting or business activities. Incapacities falling

into the latter categories are compensated under the head of general damages. They are compensated in the same way as pain and suffering under the general head of the loss of enjoyment of life. They are not given a special award of damages. In principle, neither should incapacity resulting in the need for services, except in respect of liabilities incurred up to the date of verdict.

(CSR v Eddy [2005]: [91])

Conclusion

The reversal of *Sullivan v Gordon* by the High Court in *CSR v Eddy* was a disappointing setback to what had appeared to be an increasing recognition of the economic value of work in the home.[28] Over the 25 years that I have worked in this field there did appear (at least until 2005) to have been some element of a progress narrative in Australian case law developments and a sense that some of the academic work of feminist scholars in this field had had some impact on judicial decision making.[29] But the High Court has firmly rejected this characterisation and has returned work in the home to its 'proper place' in tort law, general damages for non economic loss.

A loss of capacity to work in the home is not the same as providing the charitable work undertaken by the 'pious spinster'; it is the day-to-day work that facilitates the economic activity that takes place outside the home. It is simply not appropriate to characterise this work as a loss of amenity, a loss analogous to the loss of ability to play golf (compare Graycar 2002).

As long ago as 1977, the late High Court Justice Lionel Murphy clearly recognised the economic nature of work in the home when in *Sharman v Evans* (1977) he said:

> A woman who loses her capacity to make the usual contributions of a wife and mother in a household suffers great economic deprivation. Actions for loss of services correctly treat this as economic injury, but as a loss to the husband on the archaic view of the husband as master or owner of his wife. The economic loss is one to the wife or mother. It is her capacity to work, either in the household or outside, which is affected.

(Sharman v Evans [1977]:[598])

It was precisely this characterisation of the nature of that work that was adopted by the NSW Court of Appeal in *Sullivan v Gordon* ([1999]: [322]), only to be rejected by the High Court in *CSR v Eddy* where the Court has once again relegated that work to the field of non-economic loss (and therefore made it susceptible to statutory caps or abolition).[30]

While this chapter has divided the issues examined into separate topics, at least the second and third are clearly related, focusing as they do on work in the home. And of course women's capacity to participate effectively in paid work is necessarily dependent on their being able either to combine that work with work in the home, or to afford to outsource those services (for those not lucky enough to live in those households where, if we believe the case law, housework is shared). Each of the three aspects of damages assessment discussed in this chapter fundamentally involves attitudes to and understandings of women's work and, in particular, its economic contribution to the community. With this emphatic restatement of the non-economic nature of that work, we can only wonder where the next 30 years of judicial decision making on damages assessment will take us.

Notes

* Thank you to Margie Cronin, who worked with me on damages in the 1990s, and to Anthea Vogl, who assisted me in bringing this work into the current century.

1 See the actuarial tables in the appendices to Harold Luntz's *Assessment of Damages for Personal Injury and Death* (2002), which are divided into those for female earnings and those for male earnings (and see 5.3.4); see also *Lewis v Shimokawa* [2008].

2 See eg Chamallas and Wriggins (2010); Chamallas (1994); Cassels (1995); Adjin-Tettey (2000); Adjin-Tetty (2004); Chamallas (1998); Chamallas (1995); Wriggins (2008); Finley [1997]; and Koenig and Rustad (1995).

3 See also *Lewis v Shimokawa* [2008] a NSW District Court decision where the trial judge rejected the use of average female earnings as the plaintiff in that case had no children and therefore would not be likely to need to work part time or intermittently, 'to the detriment of [her] earning capacity' ([280]).

4 Note that the use of adjectives, such as 'female' is itself a marker of 'otherness': see for an analogous discussion Graycar (2008: 79–80).

5 See also the discussion of this case in Adjin-Tetty (2004: 319).

6 This was a case involving a plaintiff with one white and one black parent (discussed in detail by Chamallas and Wriggins (2010: 161–2)).

7 Chamallas and Wriggins (2010: 163) refer there to another case, also referred to by Weinstein J of his decision, *US v Bedonie* ([2004]: 253–4), where a federal judge refused to use raced or gendered tables to determine the compensation award for the families of two native American homicide victims, one of whom was female. The judge in *Bedonie* held that as a matter of public policy, blended tables should be used to determine lost earnings.

8 McHugh J commented in response to the 28 per cent deduction for vicissitudes: 'I cannot ever remember a case that got anywhere near that figure' (*Wynn v NSW Insurance Ministerial Corporation* [1995b]: [3]). Deane J also suggested that the amount of discount for her child care responsibilities 'seems to assume retarded children', since 'the child minding seems to go on for a long time' (*Wynn v NSW Insurance Ministerial Corporation* ([1995b]): 2–3).

9 For further discussion of *Wynn*, see Cooper-Stephenson (1995); Graycar (1995).

10 This research was funded by a grant from the Australian Research Council for the project 'A Labour of Love: Women's Work and Accident Compensation'. For some of the results of that work, see Graycar (1992; 1993; 1995, 1997; 2002; and 2003).

11 See 'Compo Cut Raises Gender Issue', *Sydney Morning Herald* (9 August 1993), reporting *Doherty v Footner* (1993).

12 See *Australian Social Trends* 2008 (ABS, Cat No 4102.0: 121). For Canada, see *Statistics Canada*, 'Women in Canada: A Gender-based Statistical Report', Catalogue 89-503-XWE (2011: Chapter 1).

13 In South Australia and Queensland consortium is available to a wife where her husband is injured, and in New South Wales, Western Australian, Tasmania and the ACT, the action has been abolished completely: for details see *CSR v Eddy* [2005]: [44]). The action remains available to a husband in the Northern Territory and Victoria, except in

circumstances where the claimant's wife has been injured in a road or industrial accident: see discussion below and Motor Accidents (Compensation) Act 1979 (NT) s 5; and Transport Accident Act 1986 (Vic), s 93. The action has also been abolished in the UK: see Administration of Justice Act 1982, s 2.

14 Note that when debated in Parliament in NSW, politicians referred to equality as one of the rationales for reform: 'I would support an amendment . . . that would make marital consortium responsibility a two-way operation applicable to both husband and wife – a situation in which either party could seek redress if he or she wishes. The constant attacks, either directly or by implication, on the traditional family, or what some of the women's groups call the patriarchal family, almost as if it were a swear word, are to be regretted' (NSW Legislative Council, Hansard (10 May 1984: 549) (Sen Fred Nile)).

15 Nearly 20 years ago, the ACT abolished the action for loss of consortium and replaced it with a statutory cause of action for the primary accident victim: see for the current version, Civil Law (Wrongs) Act 2002 (ACT), s 100. In assessing damages under that section, it is immaterial whether the plaintiff performed the domestic services for the benefit of other members of the household or solely for her or his own benefit; nor is account to be taken of the fact that the plaintiff neither paid, nor will s/he have to pay someone else to perform those services, or that they have been or are likely to be performed gratuitously by others (s 100 (2)(a)–(d)). For background to this legislation, see Australian Law Reform Commission, *Loss of Consortium: Compensation for Loss of Capacity to Do Housework* (1986) and Community Law Reform Committee of the Australian Capital Territory, *Loss of Consortium; Loss of Capacity to do Housework* (1991). See *CSR v Eddy* [2005]: [53]).

16 The court in *Fobel v Dean* relied upon the English Court of Appeal decision in *Daly v General Steam Navigation* [1980].

17 Adjin-Tetty (2000: 530) notes that consortium has been abolished in most jurisdictions in Canada. See eg Law and Equity Act, RSBC 1996, c. 253, s 63 (British Columbia); The Equality of Status of Married Persons Act, SS 1984-85-86, c.E-10.3 (Saskatchewan), s 6; and The Equality of Status Act, RSM 1987, c. E130 (Manitoba), s 1(1)(c).

18 In 2006, the Australian Bureau of Statistics reported that women still do two-thirds of all household work in Australia: Australian Bureau of Statistics, *How Australians Use their Time*, 2006 (ABS, Catalogue No 4153.0), Table 1. The results of data from three national surveys in Australia showed that females in dual-earner families still spend significantly more time doing housework, and males in dual earner families spend more time doing paid work: see Jenny Chesters et al (2008); and Baxter et al (1990).·

19 A recent study undertaken by the Australian Institute of Family Studies confirmed that it is still overwhelmingly mothers who are the primary caregivers of children: see Ruth Weston et al (2011). For men in 2006, the average time per day spent doing housework in 2006 was 43 minutes. For women, the average time spent on housework was over triple this amount, at 2 hours 11 minutes a day in 2006. In 2006 men spent, on average, 22 minutes a day on child care activities and women spent 59 minutes a day on child care activities: *How Australians Use Their Time*, 2006 (ABS, Cat No 4153.0).

20 See also a study of male and female judges in the US, where, among other things, it emerged, not surprisingly, that women judges took far more responsibility for housework than their male counterparts: Martin (1990).

21 'Care at home necessarily entails devoted care on someone else's part, often a wife or woman relative who may have to abandon her ordinary employment to nurse the plaintiff and who will in any event find the task a demanding one' (Stephen J, *Griffiths v Kerkemeyer* [1977]: [170]–[171]).

22 In *Veselinovic v Thorley* [1988], the plaintiff was a man who, as part of his claim, sought damages for his loss of ability to provide care for his wife. The Court described this

husband carer as 'a grown man who deliberately takes himself outside the workforce to provide this type of service' [195].

23 See for some data on these types of work: Australian Bureau of Statistics, *How Australians Use their Time*, 2006 (ABS, Catalogue No 4153.0), Table 1 and Table 7; Australian Bureau of Statistics, *Managing Care and Work New South Wales*, 2005 (ABS, Catalogue No 4912.1), Summary of Findings; and Australian Bureau of Statistics, *Disability, Ageing and Carers Australia*, 2009 (ABS, Catalogue No 4430.0), Summary of Findings.

24 Ibid. While these studies did not specifically consider unpaid work done by women in caring for family members who are the victims of accidents, injuries or disease, it seems reasonable to extrapolate from its findings to conclude that women carers would perform particularly large amounts of unpaid household work.

25 See the cases discussed in Graycar (1996: 86–7).

26 At [27], the majority referred to a decision of the Court of Appeal of Nova Scotia, *Carter v Anderson* ([1998]: [473]), where, they noted, Roscoe J summarised that court's reasons for following intermediate appellate courts in Saskatchewan, British Columbia, Alberta, Prince Edward Island and Newfoundland in adopting *Sullivan v Gordon* principles.

27 It seems the 'pious spinster' has a life of her own in the law: compare Graycar and Millbank (2007).

28 Note, however, that at least in NSW, the effect of the decision was reversed by legislation: see now Civil Liability Act 2002, s 15B(2) (introduced in 2006). The amending legislation and its history are discussed by Campbell JA in *Amaca v Novek* ([2009]: [27]–[29]), with whom Giles and Tobias JJA agreed.

29 At the risk of some degree of immodesty, it is perhaps worth noting that the decision in *Sullivan v Gordon* referred to some of this author's work on these issues.

30 For examples of statutory caps on non-economic loss awards see Civil Liability Act 2002 (NSW), s 16.

Cases

Amaca v Novek [2009] NSWCA 50

Andrews v Grand and Toy Alberta [1978] 2 SCR 229

Angelopolous v Rubenhold [1991] SA Sup Ct, 3 April 1991, Full Court (unreported)

Becin v GEC Australia and Ors [1993] Qld Sup Ct, 13 May 1993 (unreported)

Becker v Queensland Investment Corporation [2009] ACTSC 134

Best v Samuel Fox and Co Ltd [1952] 1 AC 716

Bondin v Lamaro [1994] NSWCA 29

Burnicle v Cutelli [1982] 2 NSWLR 26

Carter v Anderson [1998] 160 DLR (4th) 464

CSR v Eddy [2005] 226 CLR 1

Daly v General Steam Navigation [1980] 3 All ER 696

De Sales v Ingrilli [2002a] P57/2001 (17 April 2002) High Court of Australia transcript. Online available: <http://www.austlii.edu.au/au/other/HCATrans/2001/541.html>

De Sales v Ingrilli [2002b] (2002) 212 CLR 338

Doherty v Footner [1993] SA Supreme Court, Full Court 29 April 1993 (unreported)

Fobel v Dean [1991] 83 DLR (4th) 385 (Saskatchewan Court of Appeal)

Griffiths v Kerkemeyer [1977] 139 CLR 161

Gronow v Gronow [1979] 144 CLR 513

Harper v Bangalow Motors Pty Ltd [1990] NSWCA 85

Kealley v Jones [1979] 1 NSWLR 723

Kelson v Transport Accident Commission [1994] Vic Sup Ct, 5 May 1994 (unreported)

Kovac v Kovac [1982] 1 NSWLR 656
Kroeker v Jansen [1995] 123 DLR (4th) 652
Langston v AEUW [1974] 1 All ER 980
Lee v Swan [1996] BCJ No 259 (BCCA); [1996] 19 BCLR (3d) 21
Lewis v Shimokawa [2008] NSWDC 244
McLaren v Schwalbe [1994] 16 Alta LR (3d) 108
McMillan v City of New York [2008] 253 FRD 247 at 250 (EDNY 2008)
NSW Insurance Ministerial Corporation v Rayner [1993] NSWCA 197
O'Brien v O'Brien [1983] FLC 91-316
Park v Hobart Public Hospitals [1991] Tas Sup Ct, 12 December 1991 (unreported)
Partridge v GIO [1993] NSW Sup Ct, 5 May 1993 (unreported)
Randall v Dul [1994] Aust Torts Reports 81-307
Rasmus v GIO [1992] NSWCA 201
Reece v Reece [1994] NSWCA 259
Rosniak v Government Insurance Office (NSW) [1997] 41 NSWLR 608 (NSWCA)
Sharman v Evans [1977] 138 CLR 563 (HCA)
Smith v Smith [1991] ACTSC 40
Stekovic v City Group Pty Ltd [1994] ACT Sup Ct, 2 November 1994 (unreported)
Sullivan v Gordon [1999] 47 NSWLR 319 (NSWCA)
Tucker (Guardian Ad Litem) v Asleson [1991] 86 DLR (4th) 73 (BCSC)
Tucker (Guardian Ad Litem) v Asleson [1993] 102 DLR (4th) 518 (BCCA)
Tucker v Westfield Design and Construction Pty Ltd [1993] 46 FCR 20 (Federal Court)
Tully v G J Coles [1993] Qld Sup Ct, 13 Oct 1993 (unreported)
U.S. v Bedonie [2004] 317 F.Supp.2d 1285 (D. Utah 2004)
Van Gervan v Fenton [1991] Aust Torts Reports 81-103 (Tas Full Court)
Van Gervan v Fenton [1992] 175 CLR 327 (High Court of Australia)
Veselinovich v Thorley [1988] 1 Qd R 191 (Queensland Court of Appeal)
Walker v Ritchie [2004] 2 CPC (6th) 163; [2004] OJ No 787 (QL) (Ontario Superior Court
     of Justice)
Walker v Ritchie [2005] 197 OAC 81; [2005] OJ No 1600 (QL) (Ontario Court of Appeal)
     * set aside by the Supreme Court of Canada on unrelated grounds: [2006] scc 45
Wallen v Hird [1993] S Ct Q, 4 Oct 1993 (unreported)
Wheeler Tarpeh-Doe v United States [1991] 771 F Supp 427 (DDC 1991)
Williams v Williams [1984] FLC 91-541 (Full Fam Ct)
Wynn v NSW Insurance Ministerial Corp [1994] Aust Torts Rep 81-304 (NSW Court of Appeal)
Wynn v NSW Insurance Ministerial Corp [1995a] (1995) 184 CLR 485 (High Court of Australia)
Wynn v NSW Insurance Ministerial Corp S135/1994 [1995b] [1995] HCATrans 105 (18 April
     1995). Online available: <http://www.austlii.edu.au/au/other/HCATrans/1995/
     105.html>

Bibliography

Adjin-Tettey, E. (2000) 'Contemporary Approaches to Compensating Female Tort Victims
     for Incapacity to Work', *Alberta Law Review*, 38: 504
—— (2004) 'Replicating and Perpetuating Inequalities in Personal Injury Claims Through
     Female-Specific Contingencies', *McGill Law Journal*, 49: 309
Australian Law Reform Commission (1986) *Loss of Consortium: Compensation for Loss of Capacity
     to Do Housework*, Report No 32, Australian Government Publishing Service

Baxter, J., Gibson, D. with Lynch-Blosse, M. (1990) 'Double Take: The Links Between Paid and Unpaid Work', Australian Government Publishing Service

Cassels, J. (1995) '(In)Equality and the Law of Tort: Gender, Race and the Assessment of Damages', *Advocates' Quarterly*, 17: 158

Chamallas, M. (1994) 'Questioning the Use of Race Specific and Gender Specific Economic Data in Tort Litigation: A Constitutional Argument', *Fordham Law Review*, 63: 73

—— (1995) 'A Woman's Worth: Gender Bias in Damage Awards', *Trial*, 31: 38

—— (1998) 'The Architecture of Bias: Deep Structures in Tort Law', *University of Pennsylvania Law Review*, 146: 463

—— (2003) 'The September 11th Victim Compensation Fund: Rethinking the Damages Element in Injury Law', *Tennessee Law Review* 71: 51

Chamallas, M. and Wriggins, J. (2010) *The Measure of Injury: Race, Gender, and Tort Law*, New York: New York University Press

Chesters, J., Baxter, J. and Western, M. 'Paid and Unpaid Work in Australian Households: Towards an Understanding of the New Gender Division of Labour', paper presented at the 10th Australian Institute of Families Studies Conference, Melbourne, July 2008, Online

Community Law Reform Committee of the Australian Capital Territory (1991) *Loss of Consortium; Loss of Capacity to do Housework*, Report No 4, Canberra: Community Law Reform Committee

Cooper-Stephenson, K. (1995) 'Women's Earnings and Personal Injury: A Canadian Perspective: *Wynn v NSW Insurance Ministerial Corporation*', *High Court Review*, 1: 14

Final Rule (2002), September 11th Victim Compensation Fund of 2001, 67 Fed Reg No 49 11233-01, 13 March 2002, Online

Finley, L. (1997) 'Female Trouble: The Implications of Tort Reform for Women', *Tennessee Law Review*, 64: 847

Graycar, R. (1985a) 'Compensation for Loss of Capacity to Work in the Home' *Sydney Law Review*, 10: 528

—— (1985b) 'Hoovering as a Hobby: The Common Law's Approach to Work in the Home', *Refractory Girl*, 28: 22

—— (1992) 'Women's Work: Who Cares?' *Sydney Law Review*, 14: 86

—— (1993) 'Love's Labour's Cost: The High Court Decision in *Van Gervan v Fenton*', *Torts Law Journal*, 1: 122

—— (1995) 'Damaged Awards: The Vicissitudes of Life as a Woman', *Torts Law Journal*, 3: 160

—— (1996) 'Telling Tales: Legal Stories about Violence Against Women', *Australian Feminist Law Journal*, 7: 79 (also published in *Cardozo Studies in Law and Literature* 8: 297)

—— (1997) 'Hoovering as a Hobby and Other Stories: Gendered Assessments of Personal Injury Damages', *University of British Columbia Law Review*, 31: 17

—— (2002) 'Sex, Golf and Stereotypes: Measuring, Valuing and Imagining the Body in Court', *Torts Law Journal*, 10: 205

—— (2003) 'Putting Gender on the Damages Agenda: Michael Chesterman's Contribution to Accident Compensation', in Kam Fan Sin (ed), *Legal Explorations: Essays in Honour of Professor Michael Chesterman*, Sydney: Lawbook Co, 139–54

—— (2008) 'Gender, Race, Bias and Perspective: OR, How Otherness Colours your Judgment', *International Journal of the Legal Profession*, 15: 73

Graycar, R. and Millbank, J. (2007) 'From Functional Family to Spinster Sisters: Australia's Distinctive Path to Relationship Recognition', *Washington University Journal of Law and Policy*, 24: 121

Graycar, R. and Morgan, J. (2002) *The Hidden Gender of Law*, 2nd edn, Sydney: Federation Press

Koenig, T. and Rustad, M. (1995) 'His and Her Tort Reform: Gender Injustice in Disguise', *Washington Law Review*, 70: 1

Luntz, H. (2002) *Assessment of Damages for Personal Injury and Death*, 4th Edition, Butterworths

Martin, E. (1990) 'Men and Women on the Bench: Vive la Difference?', *Judicature*, 73: 204

Riseley, A.C. (1981) 'Sex, Housework and the Law', *Adelaide Law Review*, 7: 421

Weston, R., Qu, L., Gray, M., Kaspiew, R., Moloney, L. and Hand, K. (2011) 'Care-Time Arrangements After the 2006 Reforms: Implications for Children and Their Parents', *Family Matters*, 86: 19

Wriggins, J. (2008) 'Damages in Tort Litigation: Thoughts on Race and Remedies, 1865–2007', *Review of Litigation*, 27: 37

Index